AS/400 Primer

Ernie Malaga

Fifth Edition, October 1995

DISCLAIMER

We have made every effort to ensure the accuracy of all material presented in this book as of OS/400 Version 3, Release 1, Modification 0. It is the reader's responsibility to determine if the commands, programs and other information are suitable for the user's installation.
No warranty is implied or expressed.

© 1994, 1995 by Midrange Computing
ISBN: 1-883884-25-X
Reproduction in any manner, in whole or in part, is prohibited.
All rights reserved.

Midrange Computing
5650 El Camino Real, Suite 225
Carlsbad, CA 92008
(619) 931-8615
Fax (619) 931-9935

TABLE OF CONTENTS

Introduction 1
    Installation 2
    Operations 2
    Administration 2
    System Architecture 2
    Programming 3
    System/36 Environment 3
    Troubleshooting 3
    Appendix 3
    A Couple of Conventions 4

Part I: Installation

Chapter 1: Getting Up and Running 5

Section 1: Planning Physical Space 5
    The Computer Room 5
    Computer Room Requirements 6
    Flooring 7

AS/400 Primer

    Leave It to The Specialist 7
    Laying Out the Computer Room 8

  Section 2: IBM's Part of the Deal 9
    Call IBM 9
    Hardware Installation 9
    Software Installation 9
    Peripheral Installation 10

  Section 3: You Take Over 10
    Do Not Connect Other Devices 10
    Setting Up Security 10
    Setting Up Device Descriptions 11
    Setting Up User Profiles 12
    Setting Up Subsystem Descriptions 13

  Section 4: Make The System Available 13
    Allowing Sign-On 14

Part II: Operations

Chapter 2: Powering Up and Down 15

  Section 1: Unattended IPL 15

  Section 2: Attended IPL 16

  Section 3: The Start-Up Program 16
    Marking a Program as The Start-Up Program 16
    Changing IBM's Start-Up Program 18

  Section 4: Ending Subsystems 19
    Announcing Power Down 20
    The ENDSBS Command 21

  Section 5: Power Down the System 21
    The PWRDWNSYS Command 22

  Section 6: Automatic Power Schedule 22
    Setting Up The Schedule 22

TABLE OF CONTENTS

Chapter 3: Controlling The System 25

Section 1: The System Console 25
Alternative Consoles 26

Section 2: QSYSOPR 26
The User Profile 26
The Message Queue 26
Displaying QSYSOPR Messages 26
Answering QSYSOPR Messages 28
Getting Help 29

Section 3: Checking System Activity 30
Commands to Work With Jobs 30
Display Jobs 32
Job Logs 34
The System Log, QHST 36

Chapter 4: Subsystems 39

Section 1: Running QBASE 39
Advantages 40
Disadvantages 40
Changing to Multiple Subsystems 40

Section 2: Running Multiple Subsystems 41
QCTL 41
QINTER 41
QBATCH 42

Section 3: Maintaining Your Own Subsystems 42
Creating a Subsystem 43
Workstation Entries 44
Job Queue Entries 45
Changing the Start-Up Program 45

Chapter 5: Working With Printed Output 47

Section 1: Output Queues 47
What Is an Output Queue? 47

iii

AS/400 Primer

　　　What Is in Your Output Queues? 48
　　　Holding and Releasing 49

　　Section 2: Commands to Control Printed Output **50**
　　　Redirecting to a Specific Printer 50
　　　Displaying a Report 51
　　　Changing a Report 53
　　　Deleting a Report 55
　　　Holding and Releasing 56
　　　Restarting a Report 56

　　Section 3: Controlling Printer Writers **56**
　　　Starting and Ending Writers 57
　　　Holding and Releasing Writers 58
　　　Changing Writers 58
　　　Replying to Printer Messages 58
　　　Displaying Messages Automatically 60

Chapter 6: Backup and Recovery 61

　　Section 1: Initializing **62**
　　　Initializing Tapes 62
　　　Initializing Diskettes 63

　　Section 2: Backing Up **64**
　　　Saving Libraries 65
　　　Saving Individual Objects 66
　　　Saving Changed Objects 67
　　　Saving The System 67
　　　Saving Documents and Folders 68
　　　Saving Configuration and System Values 69

　　Section 3: Restoring **69**
　　　Restoring Libraries 70
　　　Restoring Individual Objects 71
　　　Restoring Documents and Folders 71
　　　Restoring Configuration Objects 72
　　　Restoring System Values 72

TABLE OF CONTENTS

Section 4: Disaster Recovery Planning 72

Section 5: Using Save Files 73
What Are Save Files? 73
Using Save Files 73

Section 6: AS/400 & S/36 Media Exchange 74
From S/36 to AS/400 74
From AS/400 to S/36 75

Chapter 7: Operational Assistant 77

Section 1: Accessing OA 78
Organization of OA 78
Starting Up OA 78

Section 2: OA Menus 78
ASSIST: The Main Menu 79
BACKUP: Backup Tasks 80
CLEANUP: Cleanup Tasks 81
CMNCFG: Communications Configuration Tasks 82
DEVICESTS: Device Status Menu 83
DISKTASKS: Disk Space Tasks 84
INFO: Information Assistant Options 85
MANAGESYS: The System Management Menu 86
POWER: Power On/Off Tasks 87
RUNBCKUP: Run Backup 88
SETUP: Customize Your System, Users, and Devices 89
SETUPBCKUP: Set Up Backup 91
TECHHELP: Technical Support Tasks 92
USERHELP: Documentation & Problem Handling 93

Chapter 8: User Messages 95

Section 1: Sending Messages 95
The SNDMSG Command 96
Sending to Multiple Users 96
Sending Messages to Special Users 97
Sending Inquiry Messages 97

v

Section 2: Displaying Messages 98
The DSPMSG Command 98
Function Keys in DSPMSG Panel 99

Section 3: Sending Break Messages 99
The SNDBRKMSG Command 100
Handling Break Messages 101

Chapter 9: Commands and System Help 103

Section 1: Command Names 103
OS/400 Command Name Structure 103
Some Abbreviations 104
A Few Examples 104

Section 2: Finding a Command 105
The SLTCMD Command 106
Command Menus 107

Section 3: Customizing IBM Commands 111
The Simple Approach 112
The Learned Approach 112
Document Your Changes 113

Section 4: The Command Prompter 113
Invoking the Command Prompter 114
Command Parameters 114
Changing Parameter Values 115
Requesting Help 116
Function Keys 116

Section 5: System Help 117
The Support Menu 118
The Search Index 119

TABLE OF CONTENTS

Part III: Administration

Chapter 10: System Values 123

Section 1: Overview 123
What Are System Values? 123
System Value References 123

Section 2: Managing System Values 124
Listing System Values 124
Displaying System Values 125
Changing System Values 125

Section 3: Date, Time And Edit System Values 126
System Date 126
System Time 126
Editing System Values 127

Section 4: Security System Values 127
Security Level 127
Default Public Authority Upon Creation 128
Idle Display Stations 129
Password Management 130
Sign-On Control 131

Section 5: Library List System Values 132
System Portion 132
User Portion 133

Section 6: System Control System Values 133
Some Unchangeable System Values 133
Device-Related System Values 133
Power Up and Down System Values 135
Interactive Job System Values 135

Chapter 11: Elements Of Security and Configuration 137

Section 1: Introduction 137
Authorities 137
Private Authorities 139

AS/400 Primer

Public Authorities 140
Special Authorities 140
Security Levels 142
Changing Security Levels 143

Section 2: User Profiles **143**
Naming User Profiles 144
Maintaining User Profiles 144

Section 3: Group Profiles And Authorization Lists **146**
Group Profiles 146
Authorization Lists 147

Section 4: Device Descriptions **148**
Naming Device Descriptions 149
Maintaining Device Descriptions 150
Listing Device Descriptions 152

Section 5: Job Descriptions **153**
What Is a Job Description? 153
Benefits of Job Descriptions 154
Naming Job Descriptions 154
Maintaining Job Descriptions 155

Section 6: Output Queues **155**
Naming Output Queues 156
Maintaining Output Queues 156
Assigning Output Queues to Users 156

Chapter 12: Printing 159

Section 1: Output Queues **159**
Output Queues You Can Use 159
Where to Keep These Output Queues 160
Output Queue Security 161
Securing Output Queues 161

Section 2: Printers **162**
Automatic On-Line (ONLINE) 162
Message Queue (MSGQ) 163

Printer Error Messages (PRTERRMSG) 164
Assigning a Printer to a User 164

Section 3: Workstations **164**
Output Queue (OUTQ) and Printer Device (PRTDEV) 165
Printer File (PRTFILE) 165

Section 4: Where Output Goes **166**
The Path for Settings 166

Chapter 13: Maintenance **169**

Section 1: Mechanical **169**
IBM or Third Party? 170
Maintenance Agreements 170

Section 2: IPLing Regularly **171**
Performing an Unattended IPL 171

Section 3: Reclaiming Storage **171**
Reclaim Storage (RCLSTG) 171
Reclaim Documents (RCLDLO) 172

Section 4: DASD Saving Techniques **173**
Monitoring Available Space 173
Recovering Disk Space 174

Chapter 14: Manuals **177**

Section 1: IBM's Manuals **177**
Printed Manuals 177
Computerized Manuals 178

Section 2: Some Important Manuals **178**
Programming Manuals 179
Operations & Administration Manuals 181

AS/400 Primer

Chapter 15: Upgrading To a New Release 183

Section 1: Why Upgrade? 183

Section 2: Preparation 184
Order the New Release 184
Read IBM's Documentation 185
Take Inventory of Tapes Received 185
Get Cume PTF Tapes for New Release 185
Estimate Downtime 186
Schedule Downtime 186
Get SE's Home Phone Number 186
Initialize Lots of Tapes 186

Section 3: Execution 187
Backing Up 187
Saving Configuration and System Values 187
Print Subsystem Descriptions 188
Have IBM's Documentation Ready 188
Get a Dedicated System 188
Apply PTFs Permanently 189
Start Upgrade 189
Load Any Cume PTF Tapes 189
Apply PTFs Temporarily 189
Verify Configuration, System Values and Subsystems 190
Reapply Changes to System Objects 190
Make System Available 190

Part IV: System Architecture

Chapter 16: Libraries, Objects and Library List 191

Section 1: Review of Concepts 191
The System Architecture 191
Single-Level Storage 191
Libraries 192
Objects 192
Other System Storage 193

TABLE OF CONTENTS

Section 2: IBM Libraries **193**
   QSYS 194
   QUSRSYS 194
   QHLPSYS 195
   QGPL 195
   QSPL 195
   QDOC 196
   Product Libraries 196
   Special Environments 196

Section 3: User Libraries **197**
   Working with Libraries 197
   Creating Libraries 197
   Displaying Libraries 198
   Working with Objects 199
   Deleting Libraries 199

Section 4: QTEMP **201**
   The Privacy Act 202
   Automatic Delete 202
   Using QTEMP 202
   QTEMP and SBMJOB 202

Section 5: Objects **203**
   Authorization List (*AUTL) 203
   Command (*CMD) 203
   Controller Description (*CTLD) 203
   Device Description (*DEVD) 204
   Document (*DOC) 204
   Data Area (*DTAARA) 204
   Data Queue (*DTAQ) 204
   File (*FILE) 204
   Folder (*FLR) 205
   Job Description (*JOBD) 205
   Job Queue (*JOBQ) 205
   Journal and Journal Receiver (*JRN & *JRNRCV) 206
   Library (*LIB) 206
   Line Description (*LIND) 206
   Menu (*MENU) 206
   Message File (*MSGF) 206
   Message Queue (*MSGQ) 207

Module (*Module)*MODULE 207
Output Queue (*OUTQ) 207
Program (*PGM) 207
Panel Group (*PNLGRP) 207
Subsystem Description (*SBSD) 207
Service Program (*SRVPGM) 208
S/36 Machine Description (*S36) 208
User Profile (*USRPRF) 208

Section 6: Library List **208**
Definition 208
Structure 209
The System Portion 210
The User Portion 210
Changing the Library List 210
Using the Library List 211

Chapter 17: Everything About Files 213

Section 1: Classification of Files 213

Section 2: Physical Files 214
Record Formats 214
File Members 215
Database Files 215
Source Files 217

Section 3: Simple Logical Files 217
Creating a Simple Logical File 218
Adding and Removing Members 218
Using Simple Logical Files 218

Section 4: Join Logical Files 219
Record Structure in Join Logicals 219
Updating Data 220

Section 5: Display and Printer Files 221
Common Features 221
Display Files 221
Printer Files 222

Section 6: Sharing Files 223
Open Data Paths 223
Coding Files For Sharing 223
Disadvantages of Sharing 224

Section 7: Overriding Files 224
The Concept 224
Override File Commands (OVRxxxF) 225
Scope of the Override 225
Accumulating Overrides 225
A Few Gotchas to Watch Out For 226
Some OVRDBF Uses 226

Part V: Programming

Chapter 18: DDS 229

Section 1: General Overview 229
What Is DDS? 229
Coding DDS 230
The A-Specs 230
Complexity of DDS 232

Section 2: Physical Files 232
A Simple Example 232
Defining by Reference 234

Section 3: Simple Logical Files 235
Defining Another Key 236
Selecting And Omitting Records 237

Section 4: Join Logical Files 238
What Is a Join File? 238
An Example of Join File 239
Joining Three Files 240

Section 5: Multi-Format Logical Files 241
General Overview 241
A Simple Example 241
Using the Multi-Format Logical 242

Using a Format Selector Program 243

Section 6: Display Files **244**
Record Formats 245
Function Keys 245
Do Not Forget PRINT and BLINK 246
Displaying Variables and Constants 246
Input Validation Basics 246
Using the Display File 247
Displaying Error Messages 248
CUA Standards 249

Section 7: Printer Files **250**
General Overview 250
Sample Report 251
Using the Printer File 253

Chapter 19: CL 255

Section 1: General Overview **255**
Commands and Parameters 255
When to Use CL 256
Parts of a CL Program 256
CL Variables 257
Giving Values to Variables 258

Section 2: Control Commands **259**
IF and ELSE Commands 259
GOTO Command 261
CALL Command 261
ENDPGM and RETURN 262

Section 3: Dealing With Errors **262**
*ESCAPE Messages 262
The MONMSG Command 263
Global MONMSG Command 264

Section 4: Retrieving Data **264**
Data Areas 264

TABLE OF CONTENTS

    System Values 265
    Other Information 265

   Section 5: Using Files **266**
    The DCLF Command 266
    Other Commands 267

Chapter 20: RPG/400 269

   Section 1: General Overview **270**
    RPG Specifications 270
    Fixed Format 271
    RPG Names 272
    Indicators 272
    The RPG Cycle 273

   Section 2: The C-Specs **274**
    Anatomy of a C-Spec 274
    File I/O Operations 275
    Structured Operations 276
    Unstructured Operations to Avoid 279

Chapter 21: Sorting Data 281

   Section 1: Using a Logical File **282**
    Logical Files 282
    Specifying Sequence 282
    Including and Omitting Records 283
    CRTLF Options and Performance 283
    Using the Logical File 283

   Section 2: Using OPNQRYF **284**
    The OPNQRYF Command 284
    Sorting Records 284
    Selecting and Omitting Records 285
    QRYSLT in CL Programs 286
    Using OPNQRYF 287

AS/400 Primer

Section 3: Using FMTDTA 287
Drawbacks of FMTDTA 288
An Example of Use 288

Chapter 22: IBM Utilities 293

Section 1: PDM 293
PDM's Main Menu 294
Working with Libraries 295
Working with Objects 297
Working with File Members 300
Changing Defaults 302

Section 2: SEU 303
A Sample SEU Session 303
Coding RPG/400 Source in SEU 308
SEU Line Commands 311
Top-Line Commands 313
Function Keys 314

Section 3: SDA 316
Starting Up SDA 317
Working with Fields 333
Finishing Up 334

Chapter 23: Journaling and Commitment Control 337

Section 1: Journaling 337
Journals And Journal Receivers 337
Journaling Files 338
Journaling with SNDJRNE 339
Maintaining Journal Receivers 340
Journaling for Recovery 340

Section 2: Commitment Control 343
The Concept 343
Prerequisites for Commitment Control 344
The COMMIT and ROLLBACK Operations . . . 345

Part VI: System/36 Environment

Chapter 24: Understanding the S/36 Environment 347

Section 1: AS/400 Versus S/36 347
Libraries and Objects 348
Source Code 348
Names 349
Jobs 349
S/36E Structure 349

Section 2: Entering the Environment 350
The STRS36 Command 350
The STRS36PRC Command 351
S/36E at Sign-On 351

Section 3: Leaving the Environment 352

Section 4: Maintaining the Environment 353
The CHGS36 Command 353
Changing Devices 354
Changing Environment Values 356

Section 5: Operations 357
Unsupported Commands 357

Chapter 25: Programming in the S/36 Environment 359

Section 1: OCL 359
SSP Procedures 359
#STRTUP1 and #STRTUP2 360
Unsupported and Ignored Procedures 360
New Procedure (FLIB) 361
Non-Supported and Ignored OCL Statements 362
New OCL Statements 362
Mixing OCL and CL in Procedures 363
New Substitution Expressions 364
Unsupported IF Expressions 364

Section 2: RPG II 364
Compiling Programs 365
Files With Several Record Types 365
Fields 366
Unsupported Features 366
New Operation Codes 367
Differences in Old Operations 367
Differences in Limitations 368

Part VII: Troubleshooting

Chapter 26: Basic Troubleshooting 371

Section 1: Severe Trouble 371
Power Failure 371
The System Freezes Up 372
Other Severe Trouble 373

Section 2: Mild Trouble 373
A Display Station Does Not Work 373
A Printer Does Not Work 374
A Tape Drive Does Not Work 375

Chapter 27: Using ECS 377

Section 1: Managing ECS 377
Changing Your Own Identification 378
Voice Phone Numbers for IBMLink 381
Voice Phone Numbers for Reporting Problems 385
Changing IBMLink Connection Number 388
Changing Problem Reporting Connection Number 391

Section 2: Uses of ECS 392
To Call IBM 392
Other Uses 393

TABLE OF CONTENTS

Chapter 28: Reporting Problems 395

Section 1: The ANZPRB Command 395

Section 2: Working with Problem Logs 415
The WRKPRB Command 415
Deleting Old Problem Logs 416

Chapter 29: PTF Management 419

Section 1: Overview 419
What Is a PTF? 419
Reporting a Problem 419
Individual and Cume PTFs 420
HIPER PTFs 420
Cover Letters 421

Section 2: Requesting PTFs 421
The SNDPTFORD Command 421
Determine the PTF Number 422

Section 3: Installing PTFs 422
Cumulative PTF Packages 423
Individual PTFs 423

Section 4: Managing PTFs 424
Displaying PTFs 424
Applying PTFs Permanently 425
Removing PTFs 426

Part VIII: Appendix

ILE Concepts 429
What is ILE? 430
Calling Programs and Modules 430
Service Programs 431
ILE Languages 431
Business as Usual 431

Glossary 433

Index 439

Introduction

The Application System/400 (AS/400) is IBM's newest member of the "classical" line of midrange computers. This line started with the System/3, a computer that, except for the model 15D, only supported batch processing in the form of punched cards. Later, IBM introduced first the System/32 and then, in 1978, the System/34. The System/34 was IBM's first popular, multi-user midrange computer to offer interactive processing using display stations. Shortly thereafter, IBM announced the System/38.

The S/38 was the AS/400's predecessor. You could even say that the AS/400 got most of its architecture and operating system from the S/38. The AS/400 architecture lacks the simplicity of the S/34 (or the S/36, which replaced the S/34 a few years later). Indeed, the AS/400 architecture is complex and the operating system (named OS/400) is therefore complicated. To the uninitiated, it can be downright intimidating.

The purpose of this book is to present the basics to the beginner, yet cover as much territory as possible. This book does not attempt to cover any topic in a thorough, exhaustive manner. The purpose of this book is to introduce the AS/400 in a light manner. For your convenience, each chapter ends with a "Further Reading" book list where you can find additional information.

The book is divided in eight parts: Installation, Operations, Administration, System Architecture, Programming, System/36 Environment, Troubleshooting, and the Appendix.

Installation

Part I gives some basic advice about the process of installing an AS/400 in your office. If the computer is already installed, you do not need to read this part.

Operations

Part II teaches you how to turn the computer on and off, how to perform an IPL, how to modify the start-up program, how to control the system through the console, the system operator and how to check on running jobs.

Part II also teaches you how to control subsystems, how to maintain your own subsystems, working with output queues and control printers. This section also describes how to perform backups, restore from backups, and how to use OS/400's Operational Assistant to automate some of the operating chores.

User messages also are covered. There is a whole chapter on OS/400 commands, how to use them and how to find the command you need to run.

Administration

Administering an AS/400 is no small job. Part III shows how you can configure your system through system values and gives you a primer on Security that includes how to set up users and display stations.

Part II includes a chapter on controlling the printer and working with output queues. Part III, Administration, covers the other side of the coin: how to make the system send output to a particular output queue or printer by changing settings in different places.

Finally, Part III shows you how to decide on a hardware maintenance provider and what you can do to keep your AS/400 humming. You get a list of the basic manuals (briefly described) and the process of upgrading your system to a new release of the operating system.

System Architecture

Part IV describes how the AS/400 is organized. It covers the concept of libraries, objects, library list and practically everything you need to know about files.

Programming

A machine as complicated as the AS/400 cannot be programmed with your eyes closed, especially if you are new to this computer. Part V teaches you the basics of DDS, CL, RPG, sorting, and how to use the programmer utilities, plus journaling and commitment control. If all these terms are foreign to you, relax. They will be explained in terms you will find easy to understand.

System/36 Environment

If your background is in the System/36 and you plan to use the S/36 Environment, you will appreciate Part VI of the book. This section describes the main differences between the AS/400 and the S/36 and how to use, maintain and operate the system from within the S/36 Environment. A separate chapter covers programming OCL and RPG II in the S/36 Environment.

Troubleshooting

"If something can go wrong, it will," said the immortal Murphy. This law is especially true of computers. Part VII tells you what to do in case of trouble, how to request help from IBM, how to report problems to IBM and how to manage PTFs.

Appendix

Finally, the last part of the book contains an appendix on ILE concepts. A glossary and an index are also included.

This book does not attempt to replace IBM manuals. IBM manuals contain infinitely more information on all topics, and you should obtain as many of them as you need or can afford. This book presents the information in a simpler, more accessible manner.

You can obtain additional information in trade magazines like *Midrange Computing* and in user groups and organizations like COMMON. The more you know, the better off you will be.

This book is not intended to be read in a single sitting from cover to cover, or even sequentially; you can read the chapters that interest you most, skip some and jump back and forth because the chapters are independent and loosely organized.

A Couple of Conventions

System commands and program code always present typesetting problems because they usually require a font that preserves a fixed spacing between characters. In this book, two different fonts are used for this purpose:

- *Courier*, for system commands that you are directed to type at the command line for immediate execution:

    ```
    PWRDWNSYS OPTION(*IMMED) RESTART(*YES)
    ```

- *OCR-B*, for programming code in any language and for system commands that are to be included in a CL program:

    ```
    PWRDWNSYS OPTION(*IMMED) RESTART(*YES)
    ```

Part I:
Installation

1

Getting Up and Running

Section 1: Planning Physical Space

The AS/400 needs a certain amount of space as well as a special environment. Both must be provided for a successful installation.

The Computer Room

The place where you install the AS/400 is typically known as the computer room, although the machine can, in theory, be installed anywhere.

In most cases, you will have to make do with whatever space has been made available for the computer room in an existing building. However, you should plan the location of the computer room carefully whether the building is in the planning stages, or you can choose among several rooms of an existing building.

The computer room does not have to be located near the computer users because, in theory, the users do not need access to the machinery. The users only need access to their own display stations and printers. However, you should consider placing the computer room somewhere in the Administration area because Information Systems (or Data Processing) is usually considered an administrative department.

AS/400 Primer

Computer Room Requirements

The computer room should have the following minimal attributes:

- Be large enough to contain the AS/400 processing unit, all the racks, tape drives, the system console, the system printer, a desk, chair, bookshelf and filing cabinet or drawer pedestal. Ideally, there should be room for the uninterrupted power supply unit (UPS) that protects the machines from power surges, spikes and power failures, but this is not as important. The computer room should be large enough to provide room for all these units and plenty of walking space around the units. This walking space is required not only for easy access, but for easy maintenance. It is easy to make the mistake of allowing so little space that you have to walk sideways between the machines.

- Have its own power supply. For example, the room can have a different power line from the rest of the building to minimize the risk of power problems. You should insist on this feature even if your system is going to be protected with an uninterruptible power supply (UPS) unit. The UPS unit should be considered mandatory for all AS/400 models that are not equipped with a built-in battery. Even though the built-in battery can keep the system going in the event of a power outage, the more sophisticated UPS units also protect the system from irregularities in the power supply such as spikes and surges.

- Have its own air conditioning unit, with a thermostat that only you can control. This air conditioning unit should have no effect outside of the computer room. This "private" air conditioning unit ensures that the computer room is kept at a temperature suitable for computer equipment. As a general rule, the air conditioning thermostat should be set so that the air is kept around 70°F. This temperature provides comfort for both the people and the machines. Humidity is also a major concern if you work in a place where humidity is high. An air conditioning specialist can recommend a dehumidifier to keep the humidity at a reasonable level in the computer room.

- Have its own telephone. To work well, the computer room must have its own telephone extension. Large companies even provide the computer room with a direct line for incoming or outgoing calls outside the company, so the calls do not have to go through the switchboard. If you think this is a superfluous frill, think about the times when Data Processing has to stay working after regular office hours and needs to receive important phone calls (possibly from IBM).

- All AS/400s have a facility called Electronic Customer Support (ECS), which is described in Chapter 27. ECS lets your system contact IBM electronically through a telephone line. The computer room, therefore, requires an additional telephone line for the use of ECS.

- If your AS/400 is going to communicate with the outside world, you also need several phone lines for communications. Some phone companies are slower than others in installing telephone lines. Order your phone line sufficiently ahead of time.

- Depending on the type of security you need to implement, you may want to consider having a lock on the computer room door so that only authorized personnel can enter. This is not an idle request you make just to feel important. Implementing system security through passwords and object authorities is worthless if the system itself is within reach of unauthorized persons.

Flooring

Although IBM says that carpets do not usually present a problem, you probably will want to remove all carpeting from the computer room because it can generate static electricity. Static electricity accumulates in the bodies of the people who walk on the carpet, and is discharged when the person touches a metallic object, such as the computer. This discharge can damage the equipment and can give you quite a jolt.

☞ The best kind of flooring you can provide for the computer room is a raised floor. Raised floors consist of independent square tiles that sit on metal beams and columns and are usually raised about 1 ft (30 cm) from the real floor.

A raised floor gives you added protection against floods because the water will accumulate under it instead of on top of it. Flooding is not an unlikely event. Think of those fire extinguishing sprinklers hanging from the ceiling, and what would happen if they were activated. Of course, floods due to rain are not uncommon in certain areas.

Leave It to The Specialist

Most details of the building of the computer room can (and should) be left to a specialist in such matters. This book will not attempt to offer guidance beyond the basics.

Three other matters to consider are:

- Cabling. Should you use twinax, twisted pair, or other kinds?

- Fire prevention. Have special extinguishers available, but you probably should not install sprinklers on the ceiling. Halon is a safe and effective fire extinguishing system, but it is not environmentally sound.

- External interference. Are there large machines close to the computer room that might produce magnetic fields? Is there radiofrequency (RF) interference from a nearby radio, television or radar station ?

Laying Out the Computer Room

Unless you are an architect or an engineer on the side, drawing the components to scale on charting paper will not mean much. Instead, consider the following method.

First, draw the walls of the computer room on paper, using a scale that is easy to work with (such as 1 ft = 1 in, or 1:10 in the metric system). The scale should let you include the entire computer room in a single sheet of paper, yet occupy as much of the sheet as possible.

Next, cut rectangular pieces of cardboard, sized to the same scale, which represent the computer room components, such as the computer unit, the racks, printer, desk, and so forth. You can obtain the dimensions of the machines from IBM's *Planning Guide*, or use a tape measure and jot down the machine sizes if they are available to you.

Play with the cardboard pieces by placing, shifting and arranging them in different ways on the drawing of the computer room until you find an arrangement that seems to work out well. (Only you can be the judge of this.)

Now comes the interesting part. Get some masking tape from a hardware store and stick it on the computer room floor, delineating with it the objects as you laid them out with cardboard. No matter how good it looks on your scale model, there is nothing like reality. You should be able to tell now if your model will actually work out as well as you thought it would.

Repeat this process as many times as needed. It is a lot of work, but it saves you from having to shift the actual machines after they arrive to your computer room. Pushing little cardboard pieces is a lot easier than pushing a rack full of DASD units.

Chapter 1 - Getting Up and Running

Section 2: IBM's Part of the Deal

Call IBM

After you have completed all your planning and are ready for the actual installation, you should call IBM (or whatever company sold you your AS/400) to have them perform the actual installation.

While you wait for the technician to arrive, you can help save time and effort by uncrating the machines yourself. Save all the packing lists and the uncrating instuctions, and follow the instructions carefully. If some crates show visible damage, *do not open them!* Let the IBM technician see the damage.

Also, move the uncrated machines to the place you planned for them, with the help of one or more friends or co-workers. You should not attempt to move the machines alone; most of them are extremely heavy and you may injure your back. When IBM's technician arrives, he will be ready to start working on the real installation such as hooking the units together.

Hardware Installation

An IBM technician will arrive at your site and perform the actual hardware installation. The amount of time it takes depends on the size and number of the machines.

☞ The technician has a lot to do. Help him by staying out of his way, but be available in case he needs something from you. Keep all non-essential personnel out of the computer room for as long as the installation is in process.

Software Installation

IBM's part of the deal includes ensuring that OS/400 is loaded on your machine. OS/400 was probably loaded at the factory, which is good because loading OS/400 can take many hours.

The IBM technician is not responsible for the installation of other software (such as your application software) on your system. He cannot help you do it, and it is unfair to ask. You should call the company that sold you the software. If the software is complex (such as MAPICS or BPCS), the software company may send someone to your office to install the software for you or, at the very least, will give you instructions on how to do it.

Peripheral Installation

IBM's technician should not be asked to install and connect the peripherals (displays and printers, for example) to your system. In the first place, it is not his job to do it. More importantly, newly-connected display stations could give someone in your company easy access to the AS/400, which is still unprotected. Keep your AS/400 confined to the computer room until you have had a chance to set up security.

IBM's technician may be able to help you with some large printers, such as the 6262 if they have the IBM logo on them. If they are manufactured by someone else, you should call the company that sold you the peripheral, if you cannot install it yourself.

Section 3: You Take Over

After the AS/400 is installed and ready to go, it is time for you to take over the rest of the installation process. This section gives you some basic advice.

Do Not Connect Other Devices

You should resist the temptation (and pressure from other people in your organization) to connect their display stations and printers at this stage because it is still premature. Before doing that, you must set up security, subsystems, user profiles and device descriptions (at the very least).

Perhaps you will need some analogy to justify your actions when people request to be connected at once. Tell them that it is like moving into a new house that does not yet have water and power, or carpeting, or even finished walls. The house is not ready, and neither is the AS/400. You need time to finish up the "house" before you let the new tenants move in.

Setting Up Security

Security is very important. The AS/400 provides five levels of security: 10, 20, 30, 40 and 50, (in order of increasing security). However, when IBM finishes the installation, your

AS/400 is set to security level 10, which provides no security at all. Anyone can sign on and perform any task. You must ensure that no one touches a display station until you have had time to change the security level to at least 20.

Security level 20 allows you to control who can sign on to the system because a person must enter a user profile name (also called "user ID") and a password, which must have been set up beforehand. Still, once the user signs on, there is no limit as to what the user may do. The only way to control users when your system is at security level 20 is to provide them with a menu that does only what they need to do on the system, and give them limited capabilities so they cannot enter any commands at the command line provided by the menu. Limited capabilities can be assigned with the LMTCPB parameter of the Create User Profile (CRTUSRPRF) or Change User Profile (CHGUSRPRF) commands. These commands are explained in some detail in Chapter 11.

Security levels 30, 40 and 50 are similiar in that they all require not only a user ID and password to sign on, but they cause the system to check authorizations whenever the user attempts to perform tasks on objects or resources. In addition, levels 40 and 50 prevent users from accessing system objects (such as internal programs) or do anything without going through "proper channels." The difference between 40 and 50 is small although level 50 also prevents passing invalid parameter values to system programs.

To change your system from security level 10 to 20 (or 30, 40 or 50), you need to change system value QSECURITY with the Change System Value (CHGSYSVAL) command, then IPL the system. When the IPL is complete, your system will operate under the new security level. Do the following:

```
CHGSYSVAL SYSVAL(QSECURITY) VALUE('20')
ENDSBS SBS(*ALL) OPTION(*IMMED)
PWRDWNSYS RESTART(*YES)
```

The first command changes the security level to 20. If you want to change it to 30, replace '20' for the appropriate value. The second command ends all subsystems and prepares the system for the IPL performed by the last command.

Setting Up Device Descriptions

Device descriptions are objects that describe a device to the system. The word "object" means something different to the system. An object is a section of disk storage that contains information, has a name and is contained in a library. For a better description of libraries and objects, refer to Chapter 16.

AS/400 Primer

To configure peripherals on the AS/400, you need to create a device description for every display station and every printer you plan to connect to the system. This configuration process can be performed at any time, even when users are actively using the system. Older midrange computers such as the S/36 force you to IPL the system before a new device can be used. The AS/400 does not need an IPL; the new device becomes available immediately.

The AS/400 is capable of configuring devices automatically, or it can let you do it manually. If you want to use automatic configuaration, change system value QAUTOCFG to '1.' To disengage automatic configuration (so you must configure devices manually), change that system value to '0.' You change the system value with the CHGSYSVAL command. For example, to activate automatic configuration:

```
CHGSYSVAL SYSVAL(QAUTOCFG) VALUE('1')
```

Automatic configurationsome has some obvious advantages. The most visible advantage is that you do not have to worry about it. All you do is plug in a new display or printer and turn it on, and the AS/400 configures it and makes it available. Before you use automatic configuration please consider the following disadvantages:

1. The device must be connected and powered on before the system configures it. This can reduce your chances to control how the device is configured and who has access to it because the system makes it available to the users immediately.

2. You have no control over the name given to the device. Under automatic configuration, the system uses generic and meaningless names such as DSP02 and PRT03, although you can change the system-generated name with the Rename Object (RNMOBJ) command. Devices can have names of up to 10 characters, which makes it possible for youto come up with names that mean something. Chapter 11 contains information on possible naming conventions. If you decide to turn off automatic configuration, run the following command before you attach any other devices:

```
CHGSYSVAL SYSVAL(QAUTOCFG) VALUE('0')
```

Now go to Chapter 11, where you will find instructions for the creation and maintenance of device descriptions.

Setting Up User Profiles

You must create a user profile for each person you want to have access to the system. The user profile is actually another system object that you can create and maintain.

Chapter 11 has detailed information about creating user profiles, including guidelines about naming and organizing them sensibly.

If you change your system's security level to 20 or higher, no one can sign on to the system before you create a user profile for that person, unless that person knows about the user profiles provided by IBM (such as QSECOFR and QSYSOPR) and their passwords.

☞ Before you give your users access to the system, you must change the passwords of the IBM-supplied user profiles because the passwords they have when your AS/400 is installed are too obvious.

Setting Up Subsystem Descriptions

A subsystem description is another type of object, used to describe a subsystem to the computer. All work in the system is carried out by the different subsystems. When the AS/400 is first installed, almost all work is performed by subsystem QBASE. Although this arrangement has the benefit of simplifying management of the computer (which is a big bonus for beginners), it does not take advantage of the system resource. Your system will not perform as well as it could.

IBM ships the AS/400 with a set of subsystems you can use instead of QBASE. You can read more about them in Chapter 4, or in IBM's *Work Management Guide*, although IBM's manual is not light reading.

Section 4: Make The System Available

When the installation is complete, you then can make the system available to your users. Do so only when you can answer yes to all the following questions:

1. Is IBM finished doing its part of the installation?

2. Have you changed the system security level to at least 20?

3. Have you created user profiles for all your users?

4. If you have decided to use manual configuration, have you turned off automatic device configuration and created device descriptions for all the devices you are connecting?

5. If the application software is required at this stage, have you installed it on your AS/400?

6. Have you physically connected all display stations and printers to the system?

7. Do your users really need access to the AS/400? Are you sure they are not asking for the AS/400 just to play with the "new toy"?

Allowing Sign-On

If all questions receive a yes answer, you need to vary on all display stations if they are not varied on already. To find out, run the Work with Configuration Status (WRKCFGSTS) command, as follows:

```
WRKCFGSTS CFGTYPE(*DEV) CFGD(*DSP)
```

The WRKCFGSTS command presents a panel listing all display stations in name sequence. The status column should read "SIGNON DISPLAY." If some or all devices do not show that status, enter an option 1 to vary on that particular device and press Enter. You can key in multiple 1s on different lines and press Enter. All devices marked in this way are varied on at the same time.

When all display stations show the "SIGNON DISPLAY" status, they will show the sign-on display which allows your users to sign on to the AS/400.

FURTHER READING

IBM's Physical Planning Guide and Reference.

Part II:
Operations

2

Powering Up and Down

Powering up the system consists of two steps: physically switching on the central processing unit (CPU) and performing an Initial Program Load (IPL).

The system needs to be IPLed periodically because IPL is the only time the operating system performs certain essential "housekeeping" tasks. You should plan for a periodic IPL schedule, even if your organization needs to have the system up and running 24 hours a day, 7 days a week. As you will see in Section 6, Operational Assistant can simplify the task of scheduling IPLs.

There are two basic types of IPL: unattended and attended. A third type, remote IPL will not be described in this book.

Section 1: Unattended IPL

Unattended IPLs are the easiest type of IPL to perform because there is nothing to do other than turning on the CPU. Make sure the key lock on the CPU's control panel is in the NORMAL or SECURE position; the AS/400 takes care of the rest.

AS/400 Primer

When you perform an unattended IPL, the AS/400 eventually shows the sign-on display at the system console and, if the start-up program specifies it, at all other display stations as well. Start-up programs are described in Section 3 later in this chapter.

You should perform unattended IPLs unless there is a compelling reason to perform an attended IPL. Keep your CPU's key lock in NORMAL or SECURE.

Section 2: Attended IPL

The attended IPL requires the presence of a system operator. To start an attended IPL, make sure the CPU's key lock is in the MANUAL position when you turn on the CPU. After some time, the system console shows a panel with options. The first option is for performing an IPL. Type "1" and press Enter. The system displays the IPL Options panel where you can set certain important values such as the system date and time. When you are done with the IPL Options panel, press Enter to proceed.

IPL continues and shows a series of informational messages until it presents the sign-on display at the system console. IPL is then complete.

☞ Attended IPLs are not recommended because they are much more complicated than unattended IPLs, and they require the system operator to be present. However, sometimes attended IPLs are required (such as when you upgrade to a new release of OS/400). As mentioned at the end of the previous section, you should keep your CPU's key lock in either NORMAL or SECURE, for unattended IPLs.

Section 3: The Start-Up Program

The system runs a *start-up* program, each time you IPL it. Although this program can be written in any language and can perform any task you want, in practice the program is written in CL because CL is the only practical language to start up subsystems, spool writers, and perform other typical "start up" activities.

Marking a Program as The Start-Up Program

System value QSTRUPPGM contains the qualified name of the start-up program. You can display its name with the Display System Value (DSPSYSVAL) command, as follows:

```
DSPSYSVAL SYSVAL(QSTRUPPGM)
```

Chapter 2 - Powering Up and Down

If you change this system value, the system will execute a different program during IPL. For example, if you create a program called IPLPGM in library MYLIB and you want to make it the start-up program, change system value QSTRUPPGM so it contains the name of the new program:

```
CHGSYSVAL SYSVAL(QSTRUPPGM) VALUE('IPLPGM    MYLIB')
```

☞ Note that there is no slash (/) between the program and library name, and that the name of the program comes first. System values that accept qualified names usually require this format. You must make sure that the first ten characters are the name of the program and that the next ten characters (or less) are the name of the library.

It is easier to make these changes with the Work with System Values (WRKSYSVAL) command. The WRKSYSVAL command shows a list of all system values (or of those system values that belong to a certain type) and lets you select option 2 to change a system value or option 5 to display it. For example, use WRKSYSVAL to change system value QSTRUPPGM:

```
WRKSYSVAL SYSVAL(QSTRUPPGM)
```

The system presents the following panel:

```
                       Work with System Values
                                                         System:   MC PGMR
 Position to  . . . . . .            Starting characters of system value
 Subset by Type . . . . .                 F4 for list

 Type options, press Enter.
   2=Change    5=Display


         System
 Option  Value       Type      Description
   _     QSTRUPPGM   *SYSCTL   Startup program




                                                                    Bottom
 Command
 ===>
 F3=Exit   F4=Prompt   F5=Refresh   F9=Retrieve   F11=Display names only
 F12=Cancel
```

When you select option 2 and press Enter, the system prompts you for the new value in a much friendlier manner than CHGSYSVAL could offer:

```
                       Change System Value

 System value . . . . . :   QSTRUPPGM
 Description  . . . . . :   Startup program


 Type choices, press Enter.

   Startup program  . . . . . .   STARTUP___    Name, *NONE
     Library  . . . . . . . . .   MGTLIB____    Name










 F3=Exit    F5=Refresh    F12=Cancel
```

Now all you need to do is type over the current values and press Enter.

Changing IBM's Start-Up Program

If you do not want to write a new start-up program from scratch, you can just copy IBM's start up file, make slight modifications and give it a different name.

To change IBM's start-up program, perform the following steps:

1. Decide in which library you will place the new program. The program can be placed in any library, but do not place it in any IBM-supplied library (those beginning with the letter Q) because you may lose the program the next time you upgrade to a new release. Choose one of your own libraries. Use a library that you use for normal "housekeeping" tasks that will never be deleted or cleared.

Chapter 2 - Powering Up and Down

2. Make up a name for your start-up program. If inspiration fails you, use the name START_UP. The underscore character is valid.

3. Create source physical file QCLSRC in the library you chose in Step 1, or use a source physical file that already exists in the library. To create the source physical file, use the Create Source Physical File (CRTSRCPF) command:

```
CRTSRCPF FILE(xxx/QCLSRC) TEXT('CL Source')
```

4. Run the DSPSYSVAL command to find out the name of IBM's start-up program and record it on a piece of paper:

```
DSPSYSVAL SYSVAL(QSTRUPPGM)
```

5. Retrieve the source code of IBM's start-up program. Place it into the appropriate source physical file of your library:

```
RTVCLSRC PGM(library/program) SRCFILE(library/file) +
         SRCMBR(new_program_name)
```

6. Edit the source with SEU by running the Start SEU (STRSEU) command. Make any necessary changes:

```
STRSEU SRCFILE(library/file) SRCMBR(new_program_name)
```

7. Compile your program with the Create CL Program command:

```
CRTCLPGM PGM(library/new_program_name) +
         SRCFILE(library/file)
```

8. Change system value QSTRUPPGM. Mention the name of your program. Use either the CHGSYSVAL or the WRKSYSVAL command as explained above.

Section 4: Ending Subsystems

Powering down an advanced computer system like the AS/400 is no simple matter. You cannot simply flip the power switch to the OFF position, or pull the plug.

The AS/400 is so complex when it powers down because at any given time there may be dozens of users signed on performing all sorts of tasks. The system may also be running batch jobs, communicating with another system elsewhere in the world, or printing reports (to name a few possible functions). Before you can shut down your system, you must ensure that all active tasks have ended.

☛ You can check system activity with the Work with Active Jobs (WRKACTJOB) command. This command shows what jobs are currently active (i.e. which jobs are actually running). Some jobs are "system" jobs that you will see all the time, even when you are the only person using the system. This situation is normal.

You must not use the WRKACTJOB command indiscriminately all day long. WRKACTJOB builds a large overhead in order to display statistical information about each job. If you do not need to see all active jobs during your normal daily work, you should consider using the Work with User Jobs (WRKUSRJOB) command which displays jobs by user profile name, or the Work with Subsystem Jobs (WRKSBSJOB) command which displays jobs by subsystem name.

The easiest way to ensure that no new jobs start on the system is to end all subsystems. You can end subsystems in two different ways: by letting jobs already running to continue, or by forcing them to end.

The first thing you should do to power down the system is to announce it to all your users by sending them a message. The message should be friendly yet authoritative. Your users should understand that if you are going to cut them off the system it is because you have a good reason to do so. Keep the users' viewpoint in mind; do not think that the work they are doing is unimportant. Give the users plenty of time to end the tasks they are performing.

Announcing Power Down

The best way to announce the upcoming power down is to send everyone a break message using the Send Break Message (SNDBRKMSG) command. When you send a message with this command, the message is immediately displayed at the user's screen and interrupts whatever the user is doing. The user is forced to read the message and must press Enter to return to whatever he was doing.

Prompt for the SNDBRKMSG. you will have to type the message text and identify who should receive the message. For example:

```
SNDBRKMSG MSG('Shutting down the system in 30 minutes. +
          Please sign off as quickly as possible.') +
          TOWS(*ALLWS)
```

This command sends the same message to all display stations, whether they are signed on or not. Appendix A contains utility command SNDBRKACT to send a break message to only the active display stations.

Chapter 2 - Powering Up and Down

The ENDSBS Command

When you prompt for the End Subsystem (ENDSBS) command, the system asks you for the name of the subsystem you want to end, and whether you want a controlled end (*CNTRLD) or an immediate end (*IMMED).

If you specify OPTION(*CNTRLD), all active jobs are allowed to continue for as long as the DELAY parameter specifies. You can change the value presented by default for a given number of seconds or *NOMAX. *NOMAX literally means "no maximum," so it lets active jobs continue indefinitely.

☞ Because few people enjoy waiting, it is tempting to request *IMMED every time. You must resist that temptation. Ending jobs immediately forces the system to take drastic measures to end jobs. If the jobs were updating files (especially keyed files), the system will have to spend additional time to repair the files the next time you IPL.

If you used the SNDBRKMSG command as indicated above, you can run the ENDSBS command now. Specify *ALL subsystems and a DELAY of 1800 seconds (30 minutes):

```
ENDSBS SBS(*ALL) OPTION(*CNTRLD) DELAY(1800)
```

You must run this command from the system console. When you execute this command, the following will happen:

- All workstations that are presently showing the sign-on display will be varied off. The sign-on display disappears and the cursor moves to the top-left corner. This makes all display stations unusable except the system console.

- All active jobs are given 30 minutes to end of their own accord (such as by signing off).

- Thirty minutes from now, the system forces all jobs to finish, no matter what they are doing.

All subsystems will be ended, including the controlling subsystem. The only display station that remains available is the system console. Do not sign off from the console.

Section 5: Power Down the System

Once all subsystems are ended, you can actually power down the system. This is done with the Power Down System (PWRDWNSYS) command.

The PWRDWNSYS Command

The PWRDWNSYS command actually turns off the system. Like the ENDSBS command, it has an OPTION parameter which accepts either *CNTRLD or *IMMED. This parameter is valuable only if you have not ended the subsystems beforehand. If all subsystems are ended, the value you select in this parameter is irrelevant.

The RESTART parameter is more important. If you specify *NO, the system actually shuts itself down. The system removes electrical power from all of the CPU components (all racks in a rack-mounted system).

If you specify *YES, the system goes through the motions of powering down but, at the last moment, it starts again. This is the way to perform an IPL without shutting down the system entirely.

Remember that shutting down the system with PWRDWNSYS does not cut electrical power from peripheral devices such as display stations and printers. You still have to turn those off with their power switches.

Section 6: Automatic Power Schedule

OS/400 has a facility called Operational Assistant that has a feature to schedule, in advance, when you want to turn the system off and on.

Setting Up The Schedule

From any command line, execute the command

GO CMDPWR

and the following menu appears:

Chapter 2 - Powering Up and Down

```
CMDPWR                        Power Commands

 Select one of the following:

   Commands
       1. Change Power On/Off Schedule                    CHGPWRSCD
       2. Change Power Schedule Entry                     CHGPWRSCDE
       3. Display Power On/Off Schedule                   DSPPWRSCD
       4. Power Down System                               PWRDWNSYS
       5. Retrieve Power Schedule Entry                   RTVPWRSCDE




                                                                Bottom
 Selection or command
 ===> 1_____

 F3=Exit    F4=Prompt   F9=Retrieve   F12=Cancel   F16=Major menu
 (C) COPYRIGHT IBM CORP. 1980, 1991.
```

AS/400 Primer

This is one of the Operational Assistant menus. Select option 1 and press Enter twice:

```
                    Change Power On/Off Schedule              MC PGMR
                                                     07/06/92  07:48:46
Start list at . . . . . . . .  _____  Date

Change times and descriptions below, then press Enter. To change defaults,
  press F10.

                    Power   Power
Date       Day      On      Off      Description
07/06/92   Mon      _____  _____   _____
07/07/92   Tue      _____  _____   _____
07/08/92   Wed      _____  _____   _____
07/09/92   Thu      _____  _____   _____
07/10/92   Fri      _____  _____   _____
07/11/92   Sat      _____  _____   _____

07/12/92   Sun      _____  _____   _____
07/13/92   Mon      _____  _____   _____
07/14/92   Tue      _____  _____   _____
07/15/92   Wed      _____  _____   _____
07/16/92   Thu      _____  _____   _____
                                                                    More...
F1=Help   F3=Exit   F10=Change power on/off defaults    F12=Cancel
```

The system presents a calendar that starts at the current date. You can now type in the times at which you want to power the system on and off. F10 lets you define a default schedule to be repeated every week.

You can let the automatic power scheduler power down and IPL the system for you. With its help, you can schedule a weekly (or monthly) IPL on a Sunday evening or other times your system is idle.

FURTHER READING

IBM's *System Operator's Guide*.

3

Controlling The System

To run your AS/400 computer efficiently, you need to be able to control it. Fortunately, the AS/400 has been designed to be easy to control. This chapter explores the main avenues available to you.

Section 1: The System Console

Most computer systems have one display station designated as the system console, from which you control system activity. In some cases, computer systems cannot be controlled in any way except by the system console.

The AS/400 lacks this specialization. Any display station can control the system, if the user who signs on has been given sufficient authority.

One display station always is the system console. The display station you connect to port 0, address 0, of the first workstation controller is the system console. The system communicates with the system console (exclusively) during attended IPLs, when you use Dedicated Service Tools (DST), and during system shutdown. Therefore, it is important to keep this device near the CPU.

AS/400 Primer

Alternative Consoles

The system can support two other display stations as the system console, but you must be sure to connect them in very specific locations.

The first alternate console is the display station you connect to port 1, address 0 of the first workstation controller. The second alternative console is the display station you connect to port 0, address 0 of the second workstation controller.

Either display station can work as the system console in the event the primary console becomes inoperative.

Section 2: QSYSOPR

QSYSOPR is the name IBM gave to the built-in system operator profile, and it is the name of a user (just like any other) who can sign on to the system.

The User Profile

User profile QSYSOPR was created by IBM. When you install your AS/400, it already has QSYSOPR defined. You can sign on as QSYSOPR whenever you need to perform system operator tasks such as backing up libraries and objects, restoring from tape or powering down the system.

The Message Queue

QSYSOPR has its own message queue that is also named QSYSOPR. This message queue is where the system sends error and informational messages about jobs that are running and need some kind of special intervention. Typically, the system sends messages to QSYSOPR when it finds jobs that you or someone else submitted to batch through a job queue.

Displaying QSYSOPR Messages

The messages contained in QSYSOPR are messages. You can display them with the Display Message (DSPMSG) command. Supply QSYSOPR as the name of the user profile or the message queue:

Chapter 3 - Controlling The System

```
DSPMSG   MSGQ(QSYSOPR)
```

The system presents a panel like this:

```
                            Display Messages
                                              System:    MC PGMR
   Queue . . . . . :   QSYSOPR       Program . . . . :   *DSPMSG
     Library . . . :      QSYS         Library . . . :
   Severity  . . . :   40            Delivery  . . . :   *HOLD

   Type reply (if required), press Enter.
     Cleanup of OfficeVision/400 calendar items started.
     Cleanup of operator and work station messages started.
     User cleanup program started.
     User cleanup program successfully completed.
     Cleanup of system journals and system logs started.
     Cleanup of operator and work station messages successfully completed.
     Cleanup of user messages successfully completed.
     Cleanup of job logs and other system output successfully completed.
     Cleanup of OfficeVision/400 calendar items successfully completed.
     Cleanup of system journals and system logs successfully completed.
     Cleanup has completed.
     Controller MALERN contacted on line QTDL200100.
     All sessions ended for device EDTDSP0500.
                                                                  Bottom
   F3=Exit            F11=Remove a message              F12=Cancel
   F13=Remove all     F16=Remove all except unanswered  F24=More keys
```

This panel offers several function keys to process the messages in different ways. These function keys are explained in detail in Chapter 8. However, you should *never*, under any circumstances, press F13 when you display QSYSOPR messages (you will see why in a moment).

Messages sometimes require a reply; these are called inquiry (*INQ) messages. The system sends inquiry messages when it wants to ask the system operator, for example, whether to ignore a certain error condition, to try again, or to cancel the job that produced the error. These three options are listed after the message, as in (C I R). "C" stands for cancel, "I" stands for ignore and "R" stands for retry.

You can remove (erase) a message from the DSPMSG panel by positioning the cursor at the appropriate message and pressing F11. If the message required a reply (which was not yet given), the system assumes the default reply. This reply may not have been the one you wanted to select.

☞ Therefore it is impractical (and even dangerous) to let the computer choose the reply for you. The F13 key erases all messages at once, and gives the default reply to all inquiry messages that had not been replied to at that time. After F13 is pressed, the DSPMSG panel has no messages. You do not know what inquiry messages were there and what reply was given by the system.

Answering QSYSOPR Messages

Here is a simulated inquiry message that you could see in QSYSOPR:

```
Feed me another diskette (C G I R)
Reply: _____
```

The system is requesting another diskette, probably to continue a save operation. The valid replies (or options) are listed in parentheses. OS/400 message replies have been standardized so that the same letters are used to signify the same action all the time.

```
C:    Cancel
G:    Go (continue)
I:    Ignore
R:    Retry
```

There are other replies, but you will see these four most of the time.

At this point, you can do one of the following:

- Reply with a C (cancel). The task ends. For example, you would select reply if you ran out of diskettes, .

- Insert the next diskette and reply with a G (go). The save operation continues where it left off.

- Reply with an I (ignore) if you want to ignore the present operation but want to continue with the next one within the current program.

- Reply with an R (retry) after you take corrective action to try the task again.

Chapter 3 - Controlling The System

Getting Help

At the beginning you will not understand many of the QSYSOPR messages. If you see a message you do not understand, do not ignore it or enter an option. Get help by moving the cursor to the message in question and pressing the Help key.

When you press Help, the system displays another panel with a more detailed explanation of the message, what caused it (there may be more than one possible explanation), and what you can do to solve the problem. Here is an example:

```
                        Additional Message Information

 Message ID . . . . . . :   CPF2758           Severity . . . . . . :   00
 Message type . . . . . :   INFO
 Job . . :   QSYSARB          User . . :   QSYS          Number . . :   024252
 Date sent . . . . . . :   05/24/92          Time sent  . . . . . :   12:34:54
 From program . . . . . :   QSWLDFR          Instruction  . . . . :   0000

 Message . . . . :   All sessions ended for device EDTDSP0500.
 Cause . . . . . :   All system network architecture (SNA) sessions for the
   device have been ended because of a forced end of the device.
 Recovery  . . . :   Contact the remote operator to determine the corrective
   actions.




                                                                     Bottom
 Press Enter to continue.

 F3=Exit            F12=Cancel
```

The help panel also explains what replies you can give and what the system will do in each case. It will even let you enter your reply directly from the help panel.

Section 3: Checking System Activity

Often you will need to find out what jobs are running in the system, how far they have progressed, or what printed output they are producing. The AS/400 gives you a wealth of information about jobs.

Commands to Work With Jobs

You can look up jobs using several different commands:

Work with Active Jobs (WRKACTJOB): This command shows all jobs that are active. "Active" means the jobs are still running. WRKACTJOB also presents complicated statistics about CPU usage for each job. These statistics require system overhead. You should avoid running the WRKACTJOB command whenever possible. Fortunately, OS/400 has other methods that work just as well. This is what the WRKACTJOB screen looks like:

```
                       Work with Active Jobs
                                                      05/24/92  12:46:25
    CPU %:      .0    Elapsed time:   00:00:00    Active jobs:   25
    Opt  Subsystem/Job  User       Type  CPU %  Function      Status
    __    MCRSC         QSYS       SBS     .0                 DEQW
    __    QBATCH        QSYS       SBS     .0                 DEQW
    __    QCMN          QSYS       SBS     .0                 DEQW
    __     EDTDSP0500   MALERN     EVK     .0   * -PASSTHRU   EVTW
    __     EDTDSP0500   MALERN     EVK     .0   * -PASSTHRU   EVTW
    __     EDTDSP0500   MALERN     EVK     .0   * -PASSTHRU   EVTW
    __    QCTL          QSYS       SBS     .0                 DEQW
    __     QSYSSCD      QPGMR      BCH     .0   PGM-QEZSCNEP  EVTW
    __    QINTER        QSYS       SBS     .0                 DEQW
    __     EDTDSP05S1   MALERN     INT     .0   CMD-WRKACTJOB RUN
    __    QPGMR         QSYS       SBS     .0                 DEQW
    __    QSPL          QSYS       SBS     .0                 DEQW
    __     EDTDSP05P1   QSPLJOB    WTR     .0                 EVTW
    __     SYSPRT01     QSPLJOB    WTR     .0                 MSGW
    __    QXFPCS        QSYS       SBS     .0                 DEQW
    __    QXFAUTO       QSYSOPR    ASJ     .0                 DEQW
                                                              More...
    ===> _____
    F21=Display instructions/keys
```

Chapter 3 - Controlling The System

Work with Subsystem Jobs (WRKSBSJOB): With this command, you can display the jobs running in a particular subsystem. You can display the interactive jobs in QINTER or the batch jobs in QBATCH, for example. WRKSBSJOB is a good substitute for WRKACTJOB because in most cases you are concerned with either batch or interactive jobs, but rarely both at once.

The following is an example of WRKSBSJOB:

```
                         Work with Subsystem Jobs
                                                          10/27/93  22:18:18
  Subsystem . . . . . . . . . . :   QINTER

  Type options, press Enter.
    2=Change   3=Hold   4=End    5=Work with   6=Release   7=Display message
    8=Work with spooled files    13=Disconnect


  Opt  Job          User        Type     - - -Status- - -  Function
  __   RMTPC01S1    MALERN      INTER    ACTIVE            CMD-WRKSBSJOB




                                                                       Bottom
  Parameters or command
  ===> _____
  F3=Exit   F4=Prompt   F5=Refresh   F9=Retrieve   F11=Display schedule data
  F12=Cancel
```

31

AS/400 Primer

Work with User Jobs (WRKUSRJOB): The WRKUSRJOB command lists all jobs from a single user or all users. You also can indicate that you want to see only jobs that are in job queues, jobs that are active, or complete jobs. WRKUSRJOB is versatile and convenient. Use this command whenever you know the name of the user whose job you want to examine.

Here is an example of WRKUSRJOB:

```
                        Work with User Jobs              MC PGMR
                                                  10/27/93  22:18:56
 Type options, press Enter.
   2=Change    3=Hold    4=End    5=Work with   6=Release   7=Display message
   8=Work with spooled files    13=Disconnect


 Opt  Job         User      Type      - - -Status- - -   Function
  __  RMTPC01S1   MALERN    INTER     ACTIVE             CMD-WRKUSRJOB
  __  RMTPC0100   MALERN    CMNEVK    ACTIVE              *  -PASSTHRU
  __  RMTPC0100   MALERN    CMNEVK    ACTIVE              *  -PASSTHRU
  __  RMTPC0100   MALERN    CMNEVK    ACTIVE              *  -PASSTHRU




                                                                  Bottom
 Parameters or command
 ===> _____
 F3=Exit     F4=Prompt     F5=Refresh     F9=Retrieve    F11=Display schedule data
 F12=Cancel   F21=Select assistance level
```

All three commands provide typical "work with" panels from which you can key in option numbers to perform certain job controlling tasks. For example, you can enter an option 5 to display a job, option 2 to change a job, or option 4 to end (cancel) a job. You must have enough authority to perform these tasks. If the Security Administrator has given you *JOBCTL special authority, you can work with someone else's jobs.

Display Jobs

As mentioned above, an option 5 entered at any of the WRKxxxJOB commands will display the job information. Option 5 runs the Display Job (DSPJOB) command. You can

Chapter 3 - Controlling The System

either press Enter or F4. If you press Enter, the system presents a menu with several options for you to choose from, as follows:

```
                            Display Job
                                              System:   MC PGMR
  Job:   EDTDSP05S1    User:   MALERN     Number:   025105

  Select one of the following:

       1. Display job status attributes
       2. Display job definition attributes
       3. Display job run attributes, if active
       4. Display spooled files

      10. Display job log, if active or on job queue
      11. Display program stack, if active
      12. Display locks, if active
      13. Display library list, if active
      14. Display open files, if active
      15. Display file overrides, if active
      16. Display commitment control status, if active
                                                        More...
  Selection
     __


  F3=Exit    F12=Cancel
```

If you press F4, you can select the option directly by entering a code in the OPTION parameter.

The first few options in the menu are for "static" information, such as when the job began, the job's priority and time slice. Other options display valuable information about the job you are working with. For example, you can examine the job's program stack (what programs it is running), object locks (what objects it is using), open files (what files it is reading or updating), and the all-important job log. The job log is described in detail below.

The DSPJOB command shows a lot of information, and there is no danger of harming the job because you only are displaying data. The system will not let you change anything, no matter how much authority you have.

Job Logs

All jobs have a log where the system records what the user is doing (the commands entered) and practically all of the messages the user sees on the screen for whatever reason. This facility is called the job log.

You can display your own job's job log with the Display Job Log (DSPJOBLOG) command. You do not need to supply any parameters. The Display Job Log screen gives you an instant history listing of everything you have done since you signed on. This command lets you go back and examine what you did and reread messages you may have missed:

```
                         Display Job Log
                                                  System:    MC PGMR
   Job . . :   QSYSSCD        User . . :  QPGMR   Number . . . :  024266
  > CALL PGM(QSYS/QEZSCNEP)












                                                                 Bottom
  Press Enter to continue.

  F3=Exit    F5=Refresh   F10=Display detailed messages   F12=Cancel
  F16=Job menu           F24=More keys
```

From this panel, you can press F10 to display all of the messages that have been recorded, not just the requests you have entered:

```
                        Display All Messages
                                              System:    MC PGMR
 Job . . :   QSYSSCD        User . . :   QPGMR    Number . . . :    024266

 > CALL PGM(QSYS/QEZSCNEP)
   Job 024314/QPGMR/QCLNUSRMSG submitted to job queue QCTL in library QSYS.
   Job 024315/QPGMR/QCLNSYSMSG submitted to job queue QCTL in library QSYS.
   Job 024316/QPGMR/QCLNSYSPRT submitted to job queue QCTL in library QSYS.
   Job 024317/QPGMR/QCLNSYSLOG submitted to job queue QCTL in library QSYS.
   Job 024318/QPGMR/QCLNCALITM submitted to job queue QCTL in library QSYS.
   Job 024319/QPGMR/QCLNUSRPGM submitted to job queue QCTL in library QSYS.
   Job 024492/QPGMR/QCLNUSRMSG submitted to job queue QCTL in library QSYS.
   Job 024493/QPGMR/QCLNSYSMSG submitted to job queue QCTL in library QSYS.
   Job 024494/QPGMR/QCLNSYSPRT submitted to job queue QCTL in library QSYS.
   Job 024495/QPGMR/QCLNSYSLOG submitted to job queue QCTL in library QSYS.
   Job 024496/QPGMR/QCLNCALITM submitted to job queue QCTL in library QSYS.
   Job 024497/QPGMR/QCLNUSRPGM submitted to job queue QCTL in library QSYS.
   Job 024663/QPGMR/QCLNUSRMSG submitted to job queue QCTL in library QSYS.
                                                                    More...
 Press Enter to continue.

 F3=Exit   F5=Refresh   F12=Cancel   F17=Top   F18=Bottom
```

You also can display someone else's job log if you have sufficient authority (such as *JOBCTL). All you need to do is access the job you are interested in with any of the WRKxxxJOB commands, enter an option 5 to display the job, press Enter, and select the right option from the menu presented. You can do this for any job in the system, whether it is interactive, batch, communications or spool.

The DSPJOBLOG panel lets you roll back and forth and display a number of messages at a time. These messages cannot be removed. You can display full information by positioning the cursor at the message line and pressing the Help key. You also can press F10 to include all detailed messages, F17 to go directly to the beginning of the job log, and F18 to go to the end. F5 updates the job log panel, which includes new messages and entries that may have occurred after you began displaying the job log.

Although you can force the system to print the job log whenever jobs end (whether normally or in error), you probably will not want to. You would soon have dozens (or hundreds) of printed job logs, some of which can be hundreds of pages long.

☞ Job logs are always printed when a job ends abnormally. For example, if you submit a job that prints a customer master listing to batch, but the program cannot find the customer master file, the job ends abnormally and the system prints a job log. If you sign on to a display station and the system operator cancels your job; the job will end abnormally which causes a printed job log.

To control the printing of the job log, use the Change Job (CHGJOB) command to change the LOG parameter's value. A value such as (4 00 *NOLIST) ensures that job logs are printed only if the job ends abnormally. If you always want a job log, set the value to (4 00 *MSG) or (4 00 *SECLVL). The difference between these two values is that *SECLVL also prints the second-level text for every message. *SECLVL provides text that can mean the difference between understanding and not understanding why the job ran into trouble. However, *SECLVL also causes considerably longer job logs. If you do not need that much information, consider using *MSG instead of *SECLVL.

You can set the LOG parameter at the job description level with the Change Job Description (CHGJOBD) command. Job descriptions are described in detail in Chapter 11.

The System Log, QHST

OS/400 also provides a systemwide log called QHST. QHST records events in this log, which provides a history of system activity.

Contrary to other computer systems like the System/36, which provides a comprehensive history file, the AS/400's system log gives very little information because most of that information is recorded in job logs. Both the system log and the job logs are not adequate means to keep track of how much each user utilizes the system. If you are looking for that application, you should check Job Accounting. Job Accounting is not discussed in this book. If you need more information, you should check the *Work Management Guide*.

The Display Log (DSPLOG) command displays or prints the system log. You can provide some selection through parameters and, as with job logs, display complete information for the messages recorded in the log by positioning the cursor and pressing Help.

The system log looks like the following:

Chapter 3 - Controlling The System

```
                    Display History Log Contents

Controller MALERN contacted on line QTDL200100.
Job 025098/MALERN/EDTDSP0500 started on 05/24/92 at 12:34:51 in subsystem QCM
Unit of work identifier APPN.S1034786-A5BD03C5620A-0001 assigned to job 02509
All sessions ended for device EDTDSP0500.
Job 025098/MALERN/EDTDSP0500 ended on 05/24/92 at 12:34:55; 1 seconds used; e
Job 025099/MALERN/EDTDSP0500 started on 05/24/92 at 12:34:58 in subsystem QCM
Unit of work identifier APPN.S1034786-A5BD03CC620B-0001 assigned to job 02509
Job 025100/MALERN/QXFSERV started on 05/24/92 at 12:35:01 in subsystem QXFPCS
Job 025099/MALERN/EDTDSP0500 ended on 05/24/92 at 12:35:02; 1 seconds used; e
Job 025101/MALERN/EDTDSP0500 started on 05/24/92 at 12:36:35 in subsystem QCM
Unit of work identifier APPN.S1034786-A5BD0429620D-0001 assigned to job 02510
Vary off completed for device EDTDSP05P1.
Description for device EDTDSP05P1 changed.
Vary on completed for device EDTDSP05P1.
Job 025102/MALERN/EDTDSP0500 started on 05/24/92 at 12:36:40 in subsystem QCM
Unit of work identifier APPN.S1034786-A5BD042E620E-0001 assigned to job 02510
Job 025103/MALERN/EDTDSP0500 started on 05/24/92 at 12:36:42 in subsystem QCM
                                                                      More...
Press Enter to continue.

F3=Exit   F10=Display all   F12=Cancel
```

The system log is a message queue object (*MSGQ); you can write to the system log directly with the Send Message (SNDMSG) command and supply TOMSGQ(QHST). For example:

```
SNDMSG MSG('Security violation at display station DSP13.') +
       TOMSGQ(QHST)
```

QHST has a fixed size. When it fills up, the system automatically creates a copy in a database file and then clears QHST of all contents. These old copies have names that begin with "QHST" plus a few digits. They are not message queues but files. These files accumulate in your system's QSYS library, and it is your responsibility to delete them periodically. Operational Assistant (see Chapter 7) can help you keep old system logs under control.

FURTHER READING

IBM's *System Operator's Guide.*

IBM's *New User's Guide.*

IBM's *Work Management Guide.*

4

Subsystems

All work the system performs is actually done in subsystems. Think of a subsystem as a department in your company. Employees belong to one department or another. Each department specializes in some kind of work such as sales, accounting, marketing, production or shipping. By the same token, AS/400 subsystems are also specialized. There is, however, one general-purpose subsystem called QBASE.

You can run your system using QBASE to do all the work, or you can split the work among several subsystems. IBM ships the AS/400 with the QBASE option.

Section 1: Running QBASE

Initially, you will be running your system in QBASE. QBASE is a general-purpose subsystem provided by IBM. Using QBASE has certain advantages and disadvantages that will be explored in this section.

When you use QBASE, all interactive and batch jobs run in QBASE.

Advantages

The main advantage of running your system in QBASE is the simplicity in management because you need to control only one subsystem.

For example, you can work with all jobs with the Work with Subsystem Jobs (WRKSBSJOB) command by supplying QBASE as the subsystem name. Also, you can power down the system by ending subsystem QBASE with the ENDSBS command, instead of specifying *ALL and waiting for all subsystems to end.

You are urged to keep QBASE at first. It will simplify your job enormously. Give yourself some time to learn and understand the concepts behind subsystems and then you can think about using other subsystems.

Disadvantages

Think again of the office analogy. You would not consider grouping all employees in a single department and make them wear several hats, so that every employee had to do some accounting, some receiving, some manufacturing and some sales. Specialization brings efficiency.

In the same way, subsystem QBASE is inefficient because that one subsystem is forced to do everything. You cannot tune your system well in these conditions. It is possible that the AS/400 will not perform well.

Changing to Multiple Subsystems

Before you change your system to work with multiple subsystems, learn about work management. Section 3 of this chapter contains basic information about work management, but you should also consider reading IBM's *Work Management Guide* which contains a full treatment of the topic.

☞ To change from QBASE to multiple subsystems, you only need to change system value QCTLSBSD from "QBASE" to "QCTL." System value QCTLSBSD contains the name of the controlling subsystem. When you change QCTLSBSD to "QCTL," the system will understand that you want to start using multiple subsystems.

To change, run the Work with System Values (WRKSYSVAL) command, as follows:

```
WRKSYSVAL SYSVAL(QCTLSBSD)
```

Chapter 4 - Subsystems

Now key in option 2 (to change) and press Enter. The system will show the current value (QBASE). Type the word QCTL over it and press Enter.

This change will not become effective until you IPL the system. You do not have to IPL the system immediately, but you can if you desire.

Section 2: Running Multiple Subsystems

As mentioned before, running your system with multiple subsystems is a better choice because each subsystem is specialized for a certain kind of work, and you can exert better control of the system. Tuning up the AS/400 for performance also becomes easier.

The three main subsystems will be discussed in this section. QCTL, QINTER and QBATCH are all already provided by IBM.

QCTL

QCTL is the controlling subsystem. It is called QCTL because it controls the system and is also the subsystem to which the system console is attached.

If you end subsystem QCTL, you end all subsystems automatically. If you restart subsystem QCTL, you restart all subsystems automatically. Again, this is because QCTL is the controlling subsystem.

QCTL should not be used for regular application software jobs (either interactive or batch) because doing so would degrade system performance. QCTL should be reserved for the system console only.

QINTER

QINTER is the interactive subsystem. Interactive jobs should run in QINTER. Batch jobs never should run in QINTER. Doing so will degrade performance .

Use QINTER to sign on to all display stations except the system console. Never submit a batch job to job queue QINTER.

Ending subsystem QINTER affects all display stations except the console. If a display station is showing the sign-on display, the display station is made unavailable. The sign-on display disappears and the cursor moves to the top-left corner of the screen. If you use

OPTION(*CNTRLD) in the ENDSBS command when you end QINTER, all interactive jobs are allowed to continue for the amount of time (in seconds) specified by the DELAY parameter.

If you end QINTER with OPTION(*IMMED), however, all interactive jobs are terminated immediately and will produce job logs.

When you run the system in multiple subsystems, ending QINTER is the easiest way to prevent your users from using the system.

When you start QINTER, the system will show the sign-on display on all display stations again.

QBATCH

Use QBATCH to process batch jobs. Batch jobs are jobs you submit to a job queue for processing. QBATCH is specially designed to run batch jobs, and will perform poorly with interactive jobs.

Ending QBATCH is the easiest way to hold all submitted batch jobs. If you specify OPTION(*CNTRLD) DELAY(*NOMAX), all batch jobs currently running are allowed to continue until they end normally. If you specify a value other than *NOMAX in the DELAY parameter, the jobs can continue for the number of seconds indicated. This is not, however, a good option for batch jobs.

☞ Resist the temptation to specify OPTION(*IMMED) because many batch jobs perform mass-updates of some kind. Forcing them to end immediately can result in a mangled database.

Section 3: Maintaining Your Own Subsystems

OS/400 lets you create and maintain your own subsystems. For example, you can create duplicates of QINTER (call them INTER1, INTER2, and so on), so you can subdivide interactive work in groups. For example, you could assign INTER1 to the Accounting department, INTER2 to the Production Control department, and so on.

This subdivision has one benefit: you can quickly control what departments can use the system by ending all interactive subsystems except the one you want to allow. You also can fine tune each subsystem for better performance. For example, the Production Control department usually performs more interactive activity than Accounting. Therefore, you can give more memory resources to the Production Control subsystem to accommodate its heavier work load.

If you do not want to bother with the chore of allocating memory resources among the many interactive subsystems you create, you can assign them all a shared memory pool. Doing this gives you the best of both worlds: it lets you subdivide display stations into subsystems, and yet you do not have to worry about memory allocations or fine-tuning the subsystems.

Programmers are another group of people who deserve a subsystem of their own. There is an IBM-supplied subsystem, QPGMR, that you can use for batch jobs such as compiles. Subsystem QPGMR is not started automatically at IPL because the start-up program supplied by IBM has no specific instruction to start QPGMR. You need to change IBM's program (or create your own) to start QPGMR at each IPL. Changing the start-up program is described later in this chapter.

Creating a Subsystem

You can create a subsystem in two ways. You can run the Create Subsystem Description (CRTSBSD) command, or create a copy of an existing subsystem that more or less fits the bill.

The CRTSBSD command is simple to use, but subsystems are more than just a subsystem description. Subsystems also contain job queue entries, workstation entries, routing entries, and settings such as memory pools that you must get right.

In most cases, you will want to create a subsystem that resembles an existing one because you will put the new subsystem to a similar use. For example, you can create a duplicate of QINTER in order to assign the new subsystem to interactive work for a certain group of users. Because QINTER already contains everything an interactive subsystem needs to work well, duplicating it is easier than creating a new subsystem from scratch. To copy QINTER, run the following command:

```
CRTDUPOBJ OBJ(QINTER) FROMLIB(QSYS) OBJTYPE(*SBSD) +
          TOLIB(MYLIB) NEWOBJ(DUPQINTER)
```

The Create Duplicate Object (CRTDUPOBJ) command makes a replica of QINTER, gives it the name DUPQINTER and places it in library MYLIB. Now that you have the new subsystem, you can adjust it as necessary using the Change Subsystem Description (CHGSBD) command. If you need to delete DUPQINTER at a later date, run the Delete Subsystem Description (DLTSBSD) command.

You also could create a duplicate of QBATCH in order to have a separate batch subsystem where you could run jobs from another division of your company.

Workstation Entries

Interactive subsystems (like QINTER) need workstation entries to determine what display stations are to work in each subsystem. Suppose you have a subsystem named ACGQINTER for your Accounting department. You want all display stations in the Accounting department to work in ACGQINTER and nowhere else.

Suppose the Accounting display stations are named DSP37, DSP42 and DSP68. ACGQINTER must have three workstation entries, which you can add to the subsystem with the Add Workstation Entry (ADDWSE) command, as follows:

```
ADDWSE SBSD(ACGQINTER) WRKSTN(DSP37) AT(*SIGNON)
ADDWSE SBSD(ACGQINTER) WRKSTN(DSP42) AT(*SIGNON)
ADDWSE SBSD(ACGQINTER) WRKSTN(DSP68) AT(*SIGNON)
```

AT(*SIGNON) indicates that subsystem ACGQINTER must acquire the display station at sign-on. As soon as you power on any of these display stations, they will be working in ACGQINTER already.

If you created ACGQINTER by duplicating QINTER, you still have a workstation entry you must get rid of: the one that says WRKSTNTYPE(*ALL) AT(*SIGNON). Because QINTER has the same workstation entry, the two subsystems will compete to grab workstations at sign-on. To remove the workstation entry, do:

```
RMVWSE SBSD(ACGQINTER) WRKSTNTYPE(*ALL)
```

However, subsystem QINTER still has the workstation entry with WRKSTNTYPE(*ALL) AT(*SIGNON), which means that the Accounting display stations may go to QINTER instead of ACGQINTER. To solve this problem, you must add three workstation entries to QINTER:

```
ADDWSE SBSD(QINTER) WRKSTN(DSP37) AT(*ENTER)
ADDWSE SBSD(QINTER) WRKSTN(DSP42) AT(*ENTER)
ADDWSE SBSD(QINTER) WRKSTN(DSP68) AT(*ENTER)
```

AT(*ENTER) means that subsystem QINTER will not attempt to attach these display stations unless the user who signs on to them (in ACGQINTER, of course) runs the Transfer Job (TFRJOB) command and presses the Enter key. The TFRJOB command can be used to transfer a job from one subsystem to another.

Chapter 4 - Subsystems

Job Queue Entries

Just as there are workstation entries to identify the workstations that work with the subsystem, there also are job queue entries. A job queue can receive job requests anytime (a user runs the Submit Job [SBMJOB] command). These jobs accumulate in the job queue and will not execute unless the job queue is attached to a subsystem.

A job queue can be attached to only one subsystem, but a subsystem can have any number of job queues attached. This attachment is performed by the Add Job Queue Entry (ADDJOBQE) command. You can also change job queue entries with the CHGJOBQE command, or remove them with the RMVJOBQE command. When you run RMVJOBQE, the job queue is no longer attached to the subsystem.

Changing the Start-Up Program

Subsystems must be started in order to perform any kind of work. When you IPL the system, only the controlling subsystem is brought up. This controlling subsystem can be either QBASE or QCTL, depending on system value QCTLSBSD. Actually, the subsystem can be any subsystem at all (even one you create).

At IPL, the system runs the start-up program named in system value QSTRUPPGM. This program starts printer writers and subsystems. Unless you change the start-up program to include a new Start Subsystem (STRSBS) command, the subsystems you have created will not start.

For more information about the start-up program, refer to Chapter 2.

FURTHER READING

IBM's *Work Management Guide*.

5

Working With Printed Output

Section 1: Output Queues

What Is an Output Queue?

Output queues tend to confuse people who are just beginning to use the AS/400. Basically, an output queue is nothing but a temporary repository where reports wait to be printed.

When you request a report such as a screen image generated with the Print key or a 2,000-page transaction history, the report is produced within an output queue. In the output queue (an object of type *OUTQ), the report waits for its turn to reach the printer.

The system can have any number of output queues, and you can put them to any use you see fit. The administrative aspect of output queues is described in more detail in Chapter 11. Chapter 11 describes how to create and maintain your own output queues.

AS/400 Primer

What Is in Your Output Queues?

The Work with Output Queue (WRKOUTQ) command lets you see what output queues are available and what reports are in them. This dual function is possible because of the OUTQ parameter; if you specify *ALL, the WRKOUTQ command begins by listing the output queues by name. You can then select one of them for viewing by entering an option 5:

```
                    Work with All Output Queues

 Type options, press Enter.
   2=Change   3=Hold    4=Delete    5=Work with   6=Release   8=Description
   9=Work with Writers              14=Clear

 Opt      Queue         Library       Files    Writer         Status
  __      QEZDEBUG      QUSRSYS         0                     RLS
  __      QEZJOBLOG     QUSRSYS         0                     RLS
  __      QDKT          QGPL            0                     RLS
  __      QPFROUTQ      QGPL            0                     RLS
  __      QPRINT        QGPL            0                     RLS
  __      QPRINTS       QGPL            0                     RLS
  __      QPRINT2       QGPL            0                     RLS

                                                                    Bottom
 Command
 ===> _____
 F3=Exit    F4=Prompt    F5=Refresh    F12=Cancel    F24=More keys
```

If you prefer, you can skip this step (and save time) by entering the name of the output queue you want to see directly into WRKOUTQ's OUTQ parameter, as follows:

WRKOUTQ OUTQ(QPRINT)

In this case, the system goes directly to output queue QPRINT and shows a list of the reports waiting there. The system skips the output selection panel entirely:

Chapter 5 - Working With Printed Output

```
                    Work with Output Queue
Queue:    QPRINT          Library:    QGPL        Status:    RLS

Type options, press Enter.
  1=Send    2=Change   3=Hold   4=Delete   5=Display   6=Release   7=Messages
  8=Attributes         9=Work with printing status

Opt   File       User       User Data     Sts   Pages   Copies   Form Type   Pty
 _    QPJOBLOG   QSPLJOB    SFWPRT01      RDY     2        1      *STD        5
 _    QPJOBLOG   QSPLJOB    EDTDSP04P1    RDY     1        1      *STD        5
 _    QPJOBLOG   QSYS       MCRSC         RDY     1        1      *STD        5
 _    QPJOBLOG   QSYS       QBATCH        RDY     1        1      *STD        5
 _    QPJOBLOG   QSYS       QPGMR         RDY     1        1      *STD        5
 _    QPJOBLOG   QSYS       QCMN          RDY     1        1      *STD        5
 _    QPJOBLOG   QSYS       QSPL          RDY     1        1      *STD        5
 _    QPJOBLOG   QSYS       QINTER        RDY    36        1      *STD        5
 _    QPJOBLOG   QSYSOPR    QXFAUTO       RDY     1        1      *STD        5
 _    QPJOBLOG   HOFSHA     QXFSERV       RDY     1        1      *STD        5
                                                                         More...
Parameters for options 1, 2, 3 or command
===> _____
F3=Exit    F11=View 2    F12=Cancel    F22=Printers    F24=More keys
```

Holding and Releasing

Sometimes you may need to tell the system not to print anything that is in a certain output queue. For example, suppose you have an output queue named SALES which is used by your company's Sales department. If there are several reports in that output queue that you need to put on hold, you can run the Hold Output Queue (HLDOUTQ) command:

`HLDOUTQ OUTQ(SALES)`

Later, when you are ready to resume printing their reports, you can use the Release Output Queue (RLSOUTQ) command:

`RLSOUTQ OUTQ(SALES)`

Section 2: Commands to Control Printed Output

Being able to control printed output is a natural concern. After all, you need to be able to send it to the proper printer, make sure it uses the right type of forms, and so on. OS/400 provides a number of commands that let you do precisely that.

Before getting too far into the different tasks you can perform to control printer output, you should become familiar with at least two commands that present lists of reports as they exist in output queues.

- The Work with Output Queue (WRKOUTQiWRKOUTQ) command. If you run it without specifying any value in the OUTQ parameter, you accept the default value of *ALL. This value presents a list of output queues available in the system. From there you can select one by keying in an option 5. Alternatively, you can display the reports in a specific output queue directly by giving its name in the OUTQ parameter. In this case, the output selection panel is skipped entirely.

- The Work with Spool Files (WRKSPLF) command. This command lets you find reports in output queues by selection criteria other than output queue. The most commonly used criterion is the name of the user who requested the report, but other selection criteria also are available.

Redirecting to a Specific Printer

A report can be redirected to a specific printer at three different times:

- After the job begins, but before the report is generated. Doing this is somewhat tricky, but it can be done.

- After the report is generated, but before it begins printing. This time is the best time to channel a report to a printer.

- After it begins printing. If you discover a little late that the report is printing on the wrong printer, you can redirect it (although it is a little complicated).

To specify a printer at any of these times, you need to execute the Change Spool File Attributes (CHGSPLFA) command to indicate the name of the new printer in the DEV parameter. In order to run the CHGSPLFA command successfully, you need to give it the following information:

- The name of the printer file, in the FILE parameter. This parameter is required.

- The name of the job that generated the report, in the JOB parameter. This parameter defaults to *, which means your own interactive job. If you are changing someone else's report, you need to supply the job name as a qualified name that consists of three parts.

- The number of the spool file within the job, in the SPLNBR parameter. You can give an actual number, or use the special values *FIRST or *LAST.

Running CHGSPLFA manually is quite a challenge because you would not have all the information required to run CHGSPLFA successfully.

Executing CHGSPLFA manually from the command line is too tedious and prone to error. It is far easier to run it as an option 2 from any of the list panels presented by WRKxxx commands, such as the WRKSPLF or WRKOUTQ commands. When you select option 2, as mentioned, the system fills out the FILE, JOB and SPLNBR parameters for you.

If the job has started but the report has not been produced yet, you need to begin by running the Work with User Jobs (WRKUSRJOB) command and supply the name of the user who started the job. This user may have more than one job started so you need to find the job that will produce the report. When you find it, select option 2 to change the job, press Enter, and find the parameter that changes the printer that will print the report. Type the printer name and press Enter.

If the report has been generated but has not started printing, use WRKOUTQ or WRKSPLF to find the report and key in option 2. When you press Enter, you will be able to change the printer name.

It is more difficult to change the printer if the report is already printing. Use WRKOUTQ or WRKSPLF to find the report, then key in option 3 to hold it. Now key in option 2 and change the printer name. Finally, key in option 6 to release the report; that will let it print again, starting from page 1. If you do not want it to start printing on page 1, use option 2 to change the number of the starting page before you release the report.

Displaying a Report

Reports do not always have to be printed. Many times the user who requested it only needs to look at the last page to check some bottom totals, or wants to verify that he has got the report he wants before printing it.

The AS/400 makes it easy to display a report. Use WRKOUTQ or WRKSPLF to find the report, then key in option 5 to run the Display Spool File (DSPSPLF) command, which looks like this:

AS/400 Primer

```
                        Display Spooled File
 File . . . . . :    QPJOBLOG             Page/Line   1/1
 Control . . . . .   _____           Columns     1 - 78
 Find . . . . . .    _____
*...+....1....+....2....+....3....+....4....+....5....+....6....+....7....+...
 5738SS1 V2R1M0 910524                   Job Log
  Job name . . . . . . . . . :    SFWPRT01       User . . . . :  QSPLJOB
  Job description . . . . . :    QSPLPRTW       Library . . . :  QGPL
 TIME    MSGID    SEV TYPE  MESSAGE TEXT
 140905 CPF1124   00 INFO   Job 023793/QSPLJOB/SFWPRT01 started on 05/11/92 at 14:
                            L in QSYS. Job entered system on 05/11/92 at 14:09:04.
                   RQS      -CALL QSYS/QSPWTRM1
 140912 CPA4002   99 SNDR   Verify alignment on printer SFWPRT01. ( I C G N R)
                                     Cause . . . . . :   The forms may not be aligned c
                            ine for the file is 6. Recovery . . . :   Do one of t
                            he request again. Possible choices for replying to mes
                             . . . . . . :   I - To continue printing aligned for
                            ext line of the file, type an I. C - To cancel proces
                            o continue printing aligned forms skipping to the next
                             first line again, type a G. N - To print the first 1
                             form and to verify the alignment, 1. Press Stop only i
                                                                              More...
 F3=Exit    F12=Cancel    F19=Left    F20=Right    F24=More keys
```

Immediately, the system displays the first page of the report. You can roll back and forth to see other pages, or use the Control input field to go to a specific part of the report, or use the Find input field to scan the report for a specific string of characters.

The Control field lets you shift the display window so that it begins on any given column. When you start displaying the report (which runs the DSPSPLF command) the system shows the window with column 1 on the left margin of the window. If you are using an 80-column display, you will not be able to see all of it. Even 132-column displays are limited if the report is printed with more than 132 columns. Use the **W** (window) command. To shift the window so it begins with column 41 on the left margin, for example, key in **W41** and press Enter.

To go to a specific page, key in a **P** followed by the page number. For example, **P75** takes you directly to page 75. You can go directly to the first page with the **T** (top) command, or to the bottom of the last page with the **B** (bottom) command. Other commands let you advance or back up the window by a certain number of lines. For example, **-12** takes you back 12 lines, and **+80** moves you forward 80 lines. You can always display help information by placing the cursor on the control field and pressing the Help key.

Chapter 5 - Working With Printed Output

The Find field is easy to work. You key in the string of characters you want to scan for and press F16 to scan. Each time you press F16, the scan resumes. This summary can continue until you reach the end of the report.

Changing a Report

You have already seen how to change a report so it is redirected to a different printer. You actually can change many other attributes of a report. Some attributes are unchangeable, however, such as the number of lines per page or the number of characters per inch.

The process is the same: you need to find the report first, then key in option 2 to change it. If the report is already printing, you will have to hold it first with option 3, and release it with option 6 after you have changed it.

Suppose you want to change the form type of a report (which you have already found) from *STD to *NCR2 (2-part NCR carbonless paper). You key in option 2 and roll the panel presented until you reach the form type prompt:

```
                 Change Spooled File Attributes (CHGSPLFA)

 Type choices, press Enter.

 Spooled file  . . . . . . . . . .   SQL105RG__      Name, *SELECT
 Job name  . . . . . . . . . . . .   SQL105RG__      Name, *
   User  . . . . . . . . . . . . .   QPGMR_____      Name
   Number  . . . . . . . . . . . .   025085          000000-999999
 Spooled file number . . . . . .     1___            1-9999, *ONLY, *LAST
 Printer . . . . . . . . . . . .     *OUTQ_____      Name, *SAME, *OUTQ
 Print sequence  . . . . . . . .     *SAME_____      *SAME, *NEXT
 Form type . . . . . . . . . . .     *STD_____      Form type, *SAME, *STD
 Copies  . . . . . . . . . . . .     1___            1-255, *SAME
 Restart printing  . . . . . . .     *STRPAGE        Number, *SAME, *STRPAGE...

                             Additional Parameters

 Output queue  . . . . . . . . .     PGMROUTQ__      Name, *SAME, *DEV
   Library . . . . . . . . . . .     MGTLIB____      Name, *LIBL, *CURLIB

                                                                       Bottom
 F3=Exit   F4=Prompt   F5=Refresh   F10=Additional parameters   F12=Cancel
 F13=How to use this display        F24=More keys
```

Key in *NCR2 and press Enter; the report is then changed.

This process can be tedious if there are several (or many) reports that need to be changed the same way. You can take a shortcut from either the WRKOUTQ or WRKSPLF panels: in option 2 for each report you want to change (they can be in different "pages" of the panel), move the cursor to the command line, type FORMTYPE(*NCR2), and press Enter:

```
                        Work with Output Queue

     Queue:     QPRINT          Library:    QGPL         Status:    RLS

  Type options, press Enter.
     1=Send    2=Change    3=Hold    4=Delete    5=Display    6=Release    7=Messages
     8=Attributes          9=Work with printing status

  Opt  File       User       User Data    Sts    Pages    Copies    Form Type    Pty
   2   QPJOBLOG   QSPLJOB    SFWPRT01     RDY      2        1       *STD          5
   2   QPJOBLOG   QSPLJOB    EDTDSP04P1   RDY      1        1       *STD          5
   2   QPJOBLOG   QSYS       MCRSC        RDY      1        1       *STD          5
   2   QPJOBLOG   QSYS       QBATCH       RDY      1        1       *STD          5
   2   QPJOBLOG   QSYS       QPGMR        RDY      1        1       *STD          5
   2   QPJOBLOG   QSYS       QCMN         RDY      1        1       *STD          5
   2   QPJOBLOG   QSYS       QSPL         RDY      1        1       *STD          5
   2   QPJOBLOG   QSYS       QINTER       RDY     36        1       *STD          5
   2   QPJOBLOG   QSYSOPR    QXFAUTO      RDY      1        1       *STD          5
   2   QPJOBLOG   HOFSHA     QXFSERV      RDY      1        1       *STD          5
                                                                         More...
  Parameters for options 1, 2, 3 or command
  ===> formtype(*ncr2)_____
  F3=Exit    F11=View 2    F12=Cancel    F22=Printers    F24=More keys
```

All reports you marked with option 2 are changed at once.

This shortcut works because option 2 executes the CHGSPLFA command. The parameter to change the form type is FORMTYPE. You can actually change more than one attribute at the same time, for more than one report, using the same technique. For example, if you had to change not only the form type, but also the number of copies to 3, you would again key in option 2 for each report, type FORMTYPE(*NCR2) COPIES(3) at the command line and press Enter.

Chapter 5 - Working With Printed Output

Deleting a Report

There are times when a user requests a report and then decides he does not need it, or when the system generates some printed output that you do not want. In these cases, you need to delete the reports. You can do that with the Delete Spool File (DLTSPLF) command. It is much easier, however, to use option 4 from either WRKOUTQ or WRKSPLF.

When you key in option 4 and press Enter, the system will first ask you to confirm your intentions:

```
                    Confirm Delete of Spooled Files

   Press Enter to confirm your choices for 4=Delete.
   Press F12 to return to change your choices.

                            Device or                     Total    Cur
   Opt  File       User     Queue         User Data  Sts  Pages    Page  Copy
    4   PRTKEYF    MALERN   EDTDSP05P1    PrintKey   HLD    1              1












                                                                   Bottom
   F10=View 3    F11=View 2    F12=Cancel
```

You may have entered a 4 by mistake (maybe you wanted a 5 to display the report), or you may have placed the 4 next to the wrong report. If you change your mind, press F12 to cancel your delete request. If you want to continue, press Enter again.

AS/400 Primer

Holding and Releasing

If you want to make sure that a report does not print but you do not want to delete it, you can hold it. The report will stay in the output queue, on hold, until it is released and printed or until someone deletes it.

To hold a report, you must run the Hold Spool File (HLDSPLF) command, or key in option 3 from either the WRKOUTQ or WRKSPLF command panel.

To release the report, run the Release Spool File (RLSSPLF) command, or key in option 6 from either of the panels mentioned above. Once released, the report becomes eligible for printing again and will start printing at the first page.

Restarting a Report

Restarting a report after a printer failure used to be a big chore until the release of V1R3M0 of OS/400. There used to be no direct way to make a report start printing at page 43, for example. Now that V1R3M0 is history, it may seem odd that there ever was a problem.

To restart a report at a certain page, do the following:

1. Hold the report.
2. Change the report by specifying the desired start page number in the RESTART parameter.
3. Release the report.

Once released, the report begins printing at the top of the page you specified in the second step.

Section 3: Controlling Printer Writers

There is more to controlling printed output than just changing, holding, canceling and releasing reports. You can also control the printer writers themselves.

A printer writer is a program created by the system whenever you create a new printer device description (with the CRTDEVPRT command). All printer writers have the same name as the printer device they control. The printer writer takes the information out of an output queue and into the printer itself. In essence, the printer writer is a program

Chapter 5 - Working With Printed Output

that actually and physically does the printing. You can control which output queue is processed by a certain printer writer.

The AS/400 cannot control the printer hardware itself. For example, no OS/400 command can turn a printer off or back on, or push its "on-line" button to turn it on or off-line. OS/400 can, however, control the spool writers, which is even better.

Starting and Ending Writers

The Start Printer Writer (STRPRTWTR) command starts a new job in subsystem QSPL. The spool writer runs in this new job. The End Writer (ENDWTR) command ends that QSPL job. These commands provide "hard" starts and stops for printer writers, so you should use them sparingly.

When you start a printer writer, you can specify which output queue will be processed by the writer, what message queue will receive the messages about the printer, and what forms type you want to process now. There are other choices in the STRPRTWTR command, but they are not discussed in this book.

For example, you can start the writer for printer SYSPRT01 as follows:

```
STRPRTWTR DEV(SYSPRT01)
```

Or suppose you want to start the writer for ACGPRT01 so that it prints all reports from output queue QPRINT that have forms INVOICE:

```
STRPRTWTR DEV(ACGPRT01) OUTQ(QPRINT) FORMTYPE(INVOICE)
```

To end a writer, run the ENDWTR command. You can choose when to end the writer with the OPTION parameter: immediately (*IMMED), at the end of the current spool file so it can finish printing (*FILEEND), at the end of the current page (*PAGEEND), or as soon as there are no more spool files ready (*NORDYF).

For example, consider the following:

```
ENDWTR WTR(SYSPRT01) OPTION(*IMMED)
```

The writer for printer SYSPRT01 ends immediately. Because the job is ending immediately, it is considered an abnormal end by the system and since the printer writer is a job in subsystem QSPL, the system will generate a job log when the writer ends.

Holding and Releasing Writers

As mentioned before, STRPRTWTR and ENDWTR perform "hard" starts and stops because they actually start and end a job in subsystem QSPL.

☞ If you need to start and stop the writer frequently, you should consider performing "soft" starts and stops using the Hold Writer (HLDWTR) and Release Writer (RLSWTR) commands.

HLDWTR stops activity on the printer without ending the spool writer job in QSPL. Conversely, the RLSWTR command restarts printer activity without starting a new job in QSPL.

Changing Writers

Printer writers can be changed without having to end (ENDWTR) and restart them (STRPRTWTR) with the Change Writer (CHGWTR) command. The CHGWTR command has almost the same set of options provided by the STRPRTWTR command, so you do not need to end the writer and restart it if you want to change some of the options.

You can hold the writer instead, change it, and then release it; or, you can change the writer "on the fly." For example, if the writer for printer SYSPRT01 is printing reports from output queue FRED and you want to change it so it begins printing from output queue JUNK, run the following command:

```
CHGWTR WTR(SYSPRT01) OUTQ(JUNK)
```

Replying to Printer Messages

Printer writers also communicate printer problems to the system. For example, the printer may run out of paper, have a paper jam, or be presented with a report set to a different form type than the one currently installed.

In these situations, the writer does not know what to do, so it sends a message to indicate the problem. The message goes to whatever message queue you specified in the MSGQ parameter when you created the printer device description (QSYSOPR or something else). The STRPRTWTR or CHGWTR commands can override that setting and force the writer to send the messages to a different message queue. You should not do this because it creates confusion.

☛ Under normal circumstances, new printer messages are not displayed automatically; you must run the Display Message (DSPMSG) command in order to see them.

For example, suppose that printer INVPRT01 stopped for no apparent reason. You suspect there is a problem and to confirm (or refute) your suspicion, you display messages for that printer. You have set up INVPRT01 so that its messages go to a message queue of the same name:

DSPMSG MSGQ(INVPRT01)

The message you need to reply to should be the last one, and should look something like this:

```
                             Display Messages
                                              System:    MC PGMR
 Queue . . . . . :   INVPRT01         Program . . . . :  *DSPMSG
   Library . . . :    QUSRSYS           Library . . . :
 Severity . . . :   40                 Delivery . . . :  *HOLD

 Type reply (if required), press Enter.
   Hardware failure at printer INVPRT01 (C G H I R)
     Reply . . . _____












                                                              Bottom
 F3=Exit            F11=Remove a message         F12=Cancel
 F13=Remove all     F16=Remove all except unanswered   F24=More keys
```

You can ask the system to explain the meaning of the message by moving the cursor to the line that contains the message and pressing the Help key.

To reply to the message, key in the appropriate option code and press Enter. For example, you could tell the system to ignore the error condition that caused this message by keying in an **I** and pressing Enter.

Displaying Messages Automatically

If you are signed on and want to have the system display the printer messages automatically, put the printer's message queue in break mode. For example, if you want to keep an eye on printer SYSPRT02, whose messages go to message queue PRINTERS:

```
CHGMSGQ MSGQ(PRINTERS) DLVRY(*BREAK) PGM(*DSPMSG)
```

All messages that arrive to message queue PRINTERS will cause an interruption in your interactive job, and the message will be displayed automatically. This interruption will happen no matter what the message says or is about. For example, if someone sends a message to message queue PRINTERS with the SNDMSG command, that message will also break.

If another printer uses the same message queue and that printer runs out of paper, you will get that message, as well. You can see now why it may be to your advantage to set up a different message queue for each printer.

FURTHER READING

IBM's *System Operator's Guide*.

6

Backup and Recovery

As with all other computer systems, your work on the AS/400 should be backed up periodically so you can recover lost data. Data can be lost for any of the following reasons:

- Someone accidentally deletes an item such as a file member, a program, an entire file, or a whole library.

- Someone intentionally and maliciously deletes an item. Pressing charges for sabotage and suing the person will not bring back the missing item.

- The mass-update program you created did not work as expected, so your database is mangled.

- The new Accounting clerk selected the wrong menu option, ignored all the warning panels with bells and whistles you designed to make him stop, and closed the Fiscal Year instead of the current month. The clerk will be fired for gross negligence, but you still have to restore the General Ledger.

- One of your AS/400 disk drives went down, and you will have to replace it. The manufacturer's warranty will get you a free replacement, but everything the old drive contained is irretrievable.

Each of these scenarios is disastrous if you do not have a backup of everything you could possibly lose. Better to be safe than sorry.

Section 1: Initializing

Before you back up anything to tape or diskette, you need to prepare the tape or diskette. This process is called initialization.

Initializing Tapes

To initialize a tape, you need to run the Initialize Tape (INZTAP) command. Here is an example:

```
INZTAP DEV(TAP01) NEWVOL(BACKUP) NEWOWNID(ABC_CORP) +
       VOL(*MOUNTED) CHECK(*NO) DENSITY(*DEVTYPE) +
       CODE(*EBCDIC) ENDOPT(*REWIND) CLEAR(*NO)
```

DEV(TAP01) indicates that the tape to be initialized has been mounted on tape device TAP01. You must make sure that the tape drive is on-line and that the tape is not write-protected.

NEWVOL(BACKUP) gives the tape a new volume ID of BACKUP. Volume IDs can have a maximum of six characters.

NEWOWNID(ABC_CORP) provides an owner name for this tape (such as your company name).

VOL(*MOUNTED) means that the INZTAP will initialize any tape that happens to be mounted on the drive, regardless of its current volume ID. For example, if you specify VOL(XYZ), the tape would be initialized only if it already had a volume ID of XYZ.

CHECK(*NO) indicates that the system is not to check for active files on the tape. If the tape contains data, the data is ignored and the initialization continues. You can leave the default value of *YES if you would rather be warned that the tape contains data.

DENSITY(*DEVTYPE) indicates that the tape should be initialized to whatever density is supported by the tape drive. Sometimes you can force other values, indicated in bits per inch (bpi), such as 1600, 3200, or as high as 43200.

CODE(*EBCDIC) means that the tape is initialized for EBCDIC backups. You can use the value *ASCII if you will be using that tape to restore on another system that supports ASCII.

ENDOPT(*REWIND) indicates that the tape should be rewound after the initialization is complete. You can also indicate *UNLOAD, in which case the tape is rewound and unloaded.

CLEAR(*NO) states that the tape drive is not to delete the tape of its current contents, which saves time. You can also specify *YES if you want the tape drive to erase the tape for you, but the tape will have to go all the way to the end and back.

☞ If you have a used tape and you want to erase it quickly, the best method is to pass an electromagnet by the tape a few times, then re-initialize the tape with INZTAP CLEAR(*NO). The initialization process takes just a few seconds. You can obtain electromagnets designed for this purpose from computer supply or mail-order stores.

Initializing Diskettes

To initialize a diskette, you need to run the Initialize Diskette (INZDKT) command. Here is an example:

```
INZDKT DEV(DKT01) NEWVOL(BACKUP) NEWOWNID(ABC_CORP) +
       FMT(*SAVRST) SCTSIZ(*STD) CHECK(*NO) CODE(*EBCDIC)
```

DEV(DKT01) identifies the diskette drive where you have mounted the diskette you want to initialize. Be sure to lock the drive after you insert the diskette. Also, make sure the diskette is not write-protected.

NEWVOL(BACKUP) gives the diskette a new volume ID of BACKUP. Volume IDs can have a maximum of six characters.

NEWOWNID(ABC_CORP) provides an owner name for this diskette (such as your company name).

FMT(*SAVRST) indicates that the diskette will be used for save and restore operations. This is the most versatile format and you should always use it because it lets you save objects on the AS/400 and restore them on another AS/400, S/38 or S/36. This parameter also allows other values: *DATA, 1, 2, 2D and *DATA2. *DATA is the default value. Do not bother with any of these values because they are practically useless except for basic data exchange with otherwise incompatible systems.

SCTSIZ(*STD) specifies a standard sector size for the format indicated in the FMT parameter. This is the default value, and you should use it. For the *SAVRST format, it is 1024 bytes per sector. For *DATA, 1, or 2, SCTSIZ(*STD), it gives 128 bytes per sector. For 2D or *DATA2, it gives 256. You can also indicate other sector sizes if you want to override this automatic setting: either 128, 256, 512 or 1024. For save and restore operations, only 1024 is valid.

CHECK(*NO) indicates that the system is not to check for active files on the diskette. If the diskette contains data, the data is ignored and the initialization continues. You can leave the default value of *YES if you would rather be warned that the diskette contains data.

CODE(*EBCDIC) means that the diskette is initialized for EBCDIC backups. You can use the value *ASCII if you will be using the diskette to restore on another system that supports ASCII.

☞ To quickly erase a used diskette, use the Clear Diskette (CLRDKT) command rather than the INZDKT command:

```
CLRDKT DEV(DKT01) VOL(*MOUNTED) CHECK(*NO)
```

This command clears (erases) the diskette mounted in diskette drive DKT01, regardless of its volume ID, without checking for active files. If any active files exist on the diskette, they are erased.

Section 2: Backing Up

As explained at the beginning of this chapter, backing up is a very important part of your daily AS/400 operations. OS/400 has a different save command for each type of saving operation. Most of these save commands are complicated and have many parameters. This chapter explains the basic operations in enough detail to get you started.

Always remember:

- To have enough initialized tapes or diskettes to complete your save operation. The system lets you initialize during the save operation, but doing so can be complicated.

- To give *SAVSYS special authority to the users who need to perform any kind of save or restore operation.

Most save commands have a few parameters in common:

- DEV, where you enter the name of the tape or diskette device you want to use for this save operation. You can also enter *SAVF if you would rather save to a save file on disk. Save files are described in Section 5 in this chapter.

- VOL, for the volume ID of the tape or diskette you are using. Although you can be specific, you should use *MOUNTED whenever possible. This special value literally means "whatever tape or diskette is currently mounted on the drive."

Chapter 6 - Backup and Recovery

- TGTRLS. If the restore is going to be performed on another AS/400 that is running under an earlier OS/400 release, you must use TGTRLS to indicate which release. If you have OS/400 release V2R1M0 or before, you can only specify *CURRENT or *PRV. *PRV is the release immediately prior to yours. If you are at V2R1M1 or later, you can be specific and indicate something like V1R3M0 if you want to save something to be restored in a V1R3M0 machine.

To use this option, you also must make sure that the object, when created in your system, was created with the same TGTRLS parameter in the appropriate CRTxxx command.

- ENDOPT controls what happens to the tape (not diskette) when the save operation is complete. You can choose between *REWIND (the default, which rewinds the tape but keeps it in the drive), *UNLOAD (rewinds the tape and unloads it) and *LEAVE (no rewind: the tape stays in the same spot where it ended saving).

- STG. **Do not** use STG (*FREE). The *FREE option clears the objects from your system as they are saved. If you save a file with the *FREE option, your system copies the file to the tape or diskette and clears the file as it does so which leaves you with an empty file.

☞ Backing up is no guarantee that you will be able to continue operations if something goes wrong. You should have a disaster recovery plan in place (refer to Section 4 in this chapter). At the very least, you should keep some of your backup tapes off-site, so if there is a fire or a flood, your tapes will still be usable.

Saving Libraries

You save a library with the Save Library (SAVLIB) command. When you save a library, the system copies the entire library (directory and all objects contained in it) to the tape or diskette you have specified. Here are some examples:

```
SAVLIB LIB(FRED) DEV(TAP01)
```

This command saves library FRED using tape device TAP01.

```
SAVLIB LIB(ARLIB APLIB) DEV(TAP01 TAP02)
```

This command saves libraries ARLIB and APLIB, using tape device TAP01. When the tape in TAP01 is full, the system automatically switches to TAP02 while TAP01 rewinds.

```
SAVLIB LIB(*NONSYS) DEV(TAP01)
```

This command saves all non-system libraries to TAP01. You need to end all subsystems to run this command.

```
SAVLIB LIB(*ALLUSR) DEV(TAP01) ENDOPT(*UNLOAD)
```

This command saves all user libraries to TAP01. When done, it unloads the tape from the tape drive.

☞ You also can use Operational Assistant's Backup List to automate the process of backing up your libraries on tape or diskette. For more information about Operational Assistant, see Chapter 7.

Saving Individual Objects

If it is not necessary, you do not need to save an entire library. You can save individual objects with the Save Object (SAVOBJ) command. Here are some examples:

```
SAVOBJ OBJ(EMPLOYEES) LIB(ACCTG) DEV(DKT01) OBJTYPE(*FILE)
```

This command saves file EMPLOYEES from library ACCTG to diskette. Note that the SAVOBJ command does not use qualified names in the OBJ parameter.

```
SAVOBJ OBJ(AR*) LIB(ARLIB) DEV(TAP01) OBJTYPE(*ALL)
```

This command saves all objects (regardless of type) that have names beginning in AR, in library ARLIB to tape.

```
SAVOBJ OBJ(AP001 AP002 AP003) LIB(APLIB) DEV(DKT01) +
       OBJTYPE(*DTAQ *DTAARA)
```

This command saves objects AP001, AP002 and AP003 from library APLIB to diskette, whether they are data queues or data areas.

```
SAVOBJ OBJ(QRPGSRC) LIB(PGMLIB) DEV(DKT01) OBJTYPE(*FILE) +
       FILEMBR((QRPGSRC (INV001RG INV002RG)))
```

This command saves members INV001RG and INV002RG from source file PGMLIB/QRPGSRC to diskette. The command does not save anything else and can be used for database files, as well.

Chapter 6 - Backup and Recovery

Saving Changed Objects

One way you can save time when doing your backups is by saving only the objects that have changed since the last time you performed a complete SAVLIB, or since a given date. These methods are referred to as *incremental* backup and *differential* backup, respectively. OS/400 supports these backups with the Save Changed Objects (SAVCHGOBJ) command.

The key to the SAVCHGOBJ command is in two parameters: REFDATE and REFTIME, where you enter the cutoff date and time. If an object has been changed after that date/time combination, it will be saved by the SAVCHGOBJ command.

REFDATE can contain either an actual date such as 050392 or *SAVLIB, which is the default. If you use *SAVLIB, SAVCHGOBJ saves all objects that have changed since the last complete SAVLIB.

REFTIME lets you pinpoint the cutoff time. You can enter an actual time such as 130000 for 1 o'clock in the afternoon, or use the default value, *NONE.

Here are two examples:

```
SAVCHGOBJ OBJ(*ALL) LIB(*ALLUSR) DEV(TAP01 TAP02) +
          OBJTYPE(*ALL) REFDATE(*SAVLIB) REFTIME(*NONE)
```

This command saves all objects in all user libraries that have changed since the library was saved with a complete SAVLIB to tape. Note that because you use REFDATE(*SAVLIB), the REFTIME parameter is irrelevant, and the value is *NONE.

The above command also stipulates that the save operation be performed on the tape currently mounted on tape device TAP01. When the tape ends, the save continues on tape TAP02 while TAP01 rewinds.

```
SAVCHGOBJ OBJ(PR*) LIB(DATA) DEV(TAP01) OBJTYPE(*PGM) +
          REFDATE(050392) REFTIME(083000)
```

This command saves all programs in library DATA that have names that begin in PR, if they have been changed since May 3, 1992 at 8:30 in the morning.

Saving The System

It is very important to use the Save System (SAVSYS) command to save the system regularly. The SAVSYS command saves the following items:

- Library QSYS. The save is performed in a format that makes it possible to restore the library using the operating system installation option during an attended IPL.

- All user profiles and the private authorities to objects given to each user.

- All descriptions of devices, controllers, lines, modes, classes of service, connection lists and network interfaces.

- All office distribution objects, authorization lists and authority holders you have created.

Running the SAVSYS command requires a dedicated system. A dedicated system requires that you be the only one signed on and that no other tasks be running. You must end all subsystems. Here is an example of SAVSYS:

```
SAVSYS DEV(TAP01)
```

☞ The SAVSYS command *always* should be executed on a blank tape. To avoid any problems, do not save anything else on the tape used by SAVSYS.

Saving Documents and Folders

Documents and folders reside in a special library called QDOC. You should use the Save Document Library Object (SAVDLO) command to save them to tape or diskette. Do not use SAVLIB. Here are a few examples:

```
SAVDLO DLO(*ALL) DEV(TAP01)
```

This command saves all documents and folders onto the tape mounted on drive TAP01.

```
SAVDLO DLO(SMITH.DOC) DEV(DKT01) FLR(DOCUMENT/LETTER)
```

This command saves document SMITH.DOC from folder DOCUMENT/LETTER to diskette.

```
SAVDLO DLO(*SEARCH) DEV(TAP01) REFCHGDATE(050392) +
       REFCHGTIME(144500)
```

This command searches and saves all documents that have been changed since 2:45 in the afternoon on May 3, 1992. It is similar to the SAVCHGOBJ command.

Chapter 6 - Backup and Recovery

Saving Configuration and System Values

Although configuration objects (such as device, controller and line descriptions) are saved automatically every time you perform a SAVSYS, you can save them independently of SAVSYS with the Save Configurations (SAVCFG) command. You a can save the configuration of your system if you have performed many changes (such as installing new display stations and printers) without executing a SAVSYS, which always takes a long time to process and requires a restricted system. Here is an example of SAVCFG:

```
SAVCFG DEV(TAP01) VOL(*MOUNTED) ENDOPT(*UNLOAD)
```

All configuration objects are saved to the tape currently mounted on the TAP01. When the save operation is complete, the tape is unloaded. There is no way to save individual configuration objects; it is an all-or-nothing affair.

System values, on the other hand, cannot be saved automatically by any means because they are not objects. There are two ways to solve this problem:

- Manually maintain a CL program (source code only) in a source file somewhere and call it something meaningful like SETSYSVAL (for "set system values"). Include a series of Change System Value (CHGSYSVAL) commands in this member. Include one command for each existing system value, even those you have never changed. As you change system values, you must change the corresponding statement in the CL program. You do not need to compile this program because you are not going to run it until you want to restore system values.

- Run the Work with System Values (WRKSYSVAL) command. Specify SYSVAL(*ALL) and OUTPUT(*PRINT). Then keep the printed listing in a safe place. Each time you change a system value, you must re-run the listing.

Section 3: Restoring

Restoring is the process of copying the objects you previously saved to tapes or diskettes back to the system. When you restore an object of any kind, you are recovering the object as it existed at the time it was saved. If you made some changes after you saved the object, the restored copy will not be up to date. This problem emphasizes the need to save as often as possible.

To restore an object, you use different commands depending on the type of object. This section presents the most important restore operations.

Restoring Libraries

Restoring a library means restoring the library object (*LIB) itself and all the objects contained in the library at the time you saved the library. To restore a library, use the Restore Library (RSTLIB) command. Here are some examples:

RSTLIB SAVLIB(ARLIB) DEV(TAP01)

This command restores library ARLIB from the tape mounted in tape drive TAP01. Note that the name of the library, ARLIB, goes in parameter SAVLIB. Although confusing, this is the way the RSTLIB command has been designed. Remember that ARLIB is the name of the library that was saved.

RSTLIB SAVLIB(ARLIB) DEV(TAP01) RSTLIB(ARDATA)

This command is a variation of the previous one. The tape contains library ARLIB (the saved library, SAVLIB), but you want to restore the library into the system (RSTLIB) with the name ARDATA. In other words, library ARLIB is restored with a different name. When the RSTLIB command ends, you will have a library called ARDATA in your system.

RSTLIB SAVLIB(ARLIB) DEV(TAP01) OPTION(*ALL)

This command is identical to the first one because the OPTION parameter defaults to *ALL. All objects in the saved library, ARLIB, are restored to your system, whether or not your system's ARLIB library already contains the objects.

In other words, your system has a library named ARLIB on disk that contains file A but does not have file B. The version of ARLIB you have on the tape contains both files, A and B. When you restore ARLIB with OPTION(*ALL), both files are restored. File A is overwritten and file B is created.

RSTLIB SAVLIB(ARLIB) DEV(TAP01) OPTION(*NEW)

This command operates like the previous one except that only file B would be restored because A already exists in your system's ARLIB. The OPTION parameter can also have value *OLD (its meaning is opposite of *NEW) and *FREE. *FREE is used only when you saved a library with STG(*FREE), which is usually not recommended.

RSTLIB SAVLIB(*NONSYS) DEV(TAP01 TAP02)

This command restores all non-system libraries contained in the tape mounted on TAP01. When that tape is exhausted, the system automatically continues with TAP02 while TAP01 rewinds.

Restoring Individual Objects

You do not have to restore a whole library if you need only a few of the objects contained in it. With the Restore Object (RSTOBJ) command you can restore individual objects. Here are a few examples:

```
RSTOBJ OBJ(*ALL) SAVLIB(ARLIB) DEV(TAP01) OBJTYPE(*DTAARA)
```

This command restores all data areas that were saved from library ARLIB. The system uses the tape drive TAP01 for the restore.

```
RSTOBJ OBJ(AR001CL AR001RG) SAVLIB(ARLIB) DEV(DKT01) +
       OBJTYPE(*ALL)
```

This command restores objects AR001CL and AR001RG (no matter what their type) from the diskette mounted in DKT01.

```
RSTOBJ OBJ(QRPGSRC) SAVLIB(PGMLIB) DEV(DKT01) +
       OBJTYPE(*FILE) FILEMBR((QRPGSRC (MBR1 MBR2))) +
       MBROPT(*ALL)
```

This command restores members MBR1 and MBR2 from file QRPGSRC, as saved in library PGMLIB in diskette DKT01.

Restoring Documents and Folders

Use the Restore Document Library Object (RSTDLO) to restore documents and folders from tape or diskette. Here are two examples:

```
RSTDLO DLO(*ALL) DEV(TAP01)
```

This command restores all documents and folders previously saved on the tape mounted in TAP01.

```
RSTDLO DLO(FRANKIE.DOC) DEV(DKT01) SAVFLR(*ANY) +
       RENAME(FRANK.DOC) RSTFLR(MEMOS/PERSONAL)
```

This command assumes that the diskette in DKT01 contains a document named FRANKIE.DOC (in any folder) that you want to restore. Once the document is restored, however, its name is changed to FRANK.DOC, and it is placed in folder MEMOS/PERSONAL.

Restoring Configuration Objects

If you have a tape where you have saved the configuration objects (such as device descriptions and controllers), either with the SAVSYS or SAVCFG command, you can restore individual configuration objects from that tape using the Restore Configuration (RSTCFG) command. For example:

RSTCFG OBJ(DSP32 DSP35 PRT02) OBJTYPE(*DEVD) ENDOPT(*UNLOAD)

This command restores the device descriptions DSP32, DSP35 and PRT02. When the restore is completed, the tape is unloaded.

RSTCFG OBJ(*ALL) ENDOPT(*UNLOAD) OUTPUT(*PRINT)

This command restores all configuration objects from the tape. It also prints a report that lists all objects that were successfully restored, those that were not restored, and those that were excluded.

Restoring System Values

Restoring system values is impossible. The previous section describes two methods to "save" system values: by writing a CL program that contains a series of CHGSYSVAL commands or by printing a list of the values and saving the printout.

- If you maintained the CL program, all you need to do is compile and execute it. When the program ends, you should consider IPLing the system to make sure that all system values have become effective. Some system values like QSECURITY require an IPL before they activate.

- If you opted for the printed list, run the WRKSYSVAL command and enter option 2 for all system values to change them. Then key in the values shown on the listing. When you are done, IPL the system.

Section 4: Disaster Recovery Planning

No one is safe from disaster. A disaster can be a fire that burns your company building to the ground, a flood, an earthquake, a major system failure, or even sabotage.

Backing up is not enough to protect yourself from disaster. In the event of a fire or earthquake, having tapes with everything you ever had on the system does not do you

Chapter 6 - Backup and Recovery

any good if you do not have a system to restore them to. Therefore you must devise a safe and sound disaster recovery plan.

A discussion of such a plan (or even a complete definition) is beyond the scope of this book. There are firms whose primary business is providing a disaster recovery plan for computer users. You should get in touch with one of them immediately.

A well-implemented disaster recovery plan can offer you a replacement system that will be available if your system become unusable. The disaster recovery supplier charges a fee for this service, but you can look at it as a form of insurance. The provider works with you and helps you design a good disaster recovery plan.

☞ Once you have a plan in place, follow its guidelines religiously and test it thoroughly. Sometimes you think the plan is foolproof, and yet later you discover that there are holes.

Section 5: Using Save Files

What Are Save Files?

When you perform save and restore operations, you can use save files instead of tapes or diskettes.

Save files are objects of type *FILE that reside on disk. They offer faster backups than those provided by tapes or diskettes because a save operation to a save file is a copy from disk to disk. In addition, they do not require operator intervention as when a tape (or diskette) ends, and you have to mount the next.

On the other hand, save files use up (at least temporarily) space on your disk drives.

Using Save Files

To use a save file instead of tape or diskette, you must create the save file first using the Create Save File (CRTSAVF) command. For example:

```
CRTSAVF FILE(MYLIB/MYSAVF) TEXT('Save file for backups')
```

To save to the save file, execute the usual save command, except specify DEV(*SAVF) and the name of the save file in the SAVF parameter. Note that the SAVSYS command does not accept DEV(*SAVF). For example:

```
LIB(ACCTG) DEV(*SAVF) SAVF(MYLIB/MYSAVF)
```

This command saves the entire ACCTG library in save file MYSAVF in library MYLIB. It goes in a compressed format; it is not a byte-by-byte copy.

At your leisure, some time after this SAVLIB command ends, you can save the save file to tape or diskette and clear the save file, which frees precious disk space:

```
SAVF(MYLIB/MYSAVF) DEV(SYSTAP01)

FILE(MYLIB/MYSAVF)
```

If you need to restore the ACCTG library from this tape, you use the regular RSTLIB command. The system will not care that you used a save file in the process.

If you can afford the space on your disk, you can leave the save file full of data and never perform the backup to tape. In this case, the RSTLIB command would have to specify DEV(*SAVF) SAVF(MYLIB/MYSAVF). However, with this method you do not have an external backup that you can keep in a safe place. If your disk crashes and needs to be replaced, the backup in the save file will be lost too.

Section 6: AS/400 & S/36 Media Exchange

As is explained in Chapter 25, the AS/400 includes the System/36 Execution Environment (abbreviated S/36EE or S/36E), which lets you administer, operate and program the AS/400 as if it were an S/36.

Even though the S/36E provides the real S/36 procedures to save and restore, you will not be able to save a file on the S/36 and restore it on the AS/400's S/36E with the predictable SAVE and RESTORE procedures. It will not work.

From S/36 to AS/400

On the S/36 side, use the usual commands such as SAVE and FROMLIBR. On the AS/400 side, however, you must use the native commands:

RSTS36F. Restores a S/36 file that was backed up by the S/36 with the SAVE procedure.

RSTS36LIBM. Restores one or more S/36 library members that were backed by the S/36 with the FROMLIBR procedure.

From AS/400 to S/36

The opposite also is true. You must save the files or library members with the AS/400 native commands:

SAVS36F. Saves an AS/400 file to tape or diskette in a format that will make it possible for the S/36 to restore it with the RESTORE procedure.

SAVS36LIBM. Saves one or more library members, as defined in the S/36E, to tape or diskette. This tape or diskette can then be processed by the S/36 with the TOLIBR procedure.

FURTHER READING

IBM's *Backup and Recovery Guide*.

7

Operational Assistant

The System/38 is the AS/400's predecessor. CPF, the S/38's operating system, has always been considered sophisticated and difficult to use. When developers at IBM designed the AS/400, they incorporated many of the ease-of-use features of the System/36. The AS/400 is a sophisticated system, but it is still not easy enough to operate.

IBM developed Operational Assistant (OA) and made it part of the AS/400's operating system. OA is comprised of a series of menus, help displays and prompt displays that guide the system operator through some of the most obscure system commands. OA has also recently been enhanced to include features such as the automatic power schedule and the automatic backup schedule, which automate these processes tremendously.

OA is available on every AS/400. You should investigate and use it, at least until you become familiar with OS/400 (although there is no reason to stop using it when you become an expert).

Section 1: Accessing OA

Organization of OA

OA is organized in menus. OA's main menu is called ASSIST, but there are other menus you can reach by taking numbered options from the ASSIST menu or by going directly to them from any other menu.

Starting Up OA

You can start up OA in two different ways:

- Pressing the Attention (Attn) key. This method works if your user profile has been created or changed with the parameter ATNPGM(*ASSIST). If you want to be able to start up OA by pressing the Attention key, you should change your user profile's ATNPGM parameter to *ASSIST.

- Going to one of the OA menus directly by running the GO command. For example, GO ASSIST takes you to the main OA menu.

OA is not a program that keeps running in the background, so there is no performance penalty for using it. You can leave OA anytime by exiting from the OA menus by pressing F3.

Section 2: OA Menus

Operational Assistant is entirely menu-driven. To appreciate it, you should look at the menus it presents. Remember that you can go to any of these menus directly by executing the GO command followed by the menu name.

All menus have two items in common. They all provide option 80 to disconnect your job, which is a "soft" sign-off. All menus also provide F9 to open up a window from which you can execute any OS/400 commands.

Chapter 7 - Operational Assistant

ASSIST: The Main Menu

The main menu presents some general-purpose options to start tasks that you may find yourself performing over and over. Here is the main menu (ASSIST):

```
ASSIST              AS/400 Operational Assistant (TM) Menu
                                                     System:   MC PGMR
To select one of the following, type its number below and press Enter:

    1. Work with printer output
    2. Work with jobs
    3. Work with messages
    4. Send messages
    5. Change your password

   10. Manage your system, users, and devices
   11. Customize your system, users, and devices

   75. Information and problem handling

   80. Temporary sign-off


Type a menu option below


F1=Help    F3=Exit    F9=Command line    F12=Cancel
```

Each option does the following tasks:

1. WRKSLPF. Lets you work with your own spool files. Using this command, you can easily control what is printed and how.

2. WRKUSRJOB. Lets you work with your own jobs. It lets you see what your jobs are doing, and lets you change your jobs.

3. WRKMSG. Displays messages that others have sent to you, and lets you reply to inquiry messages or remove messages.

4. Calls a program that presents a panel from which you can select what kind of message to send and to whom. Depending on your input, the system executes the SNDMSG or the SNDBRKMSG command.

AS/400 Primer

5. CHGPWD. With this command you can change your password.

10. GO MANAGESYS. Takes you to OA's MANAGESYS menu.

11. GO SETUP. Displays OA's SETUP menu.

75. GO USERHELP. Takes you to OA's USERHELP menu.

80. DSCJOB. Disconnects your job from the system.

BACKUP: Backup Tasks

The Backup Tasks menu gives you options to easily perform backups of your libraries or of the system, and to initialize tapes for use during the backup.

```
BACKUP                      Backup Tasks
                                                   System:   MC PGMR
To select one of the following, type its number below and press Enter:

     1. Run backup
     2. Display backup status

    10. Set up backup

    20. Initialize a tape
    21. Initialize a tape set




Type a menu option below


F1=Help    F3=Exit    F9=Command line    F12=Cancel
```

The options perform the following tasks:

1. GO RUNBCKUP. Takes you to OA's RUNBCKUP menu.

Chapter 7 - Operational Assistant

2. Displays the status of the backup.

10. GO SETUPBCKUP. Takes you to OA's SETUPBCKUP menu.

20. Runs a program that lets you initialize tapes.

30. Runs a program that lets you initialize a set of tapes.

CLEANUP: Cleanup Tasks

Automatic cleanup is a special job the system runs periodically (as you indicate). The job deletes unnecessary objects in order to keep your system as clean and free from garbage as possible.

```
CLEANUP                    Cleanup Tasks
                                                    System:    MC PGMR
To select one of the following, type its number below and press Enter:

    1. Change cleanup options
    2. Start cleanup at scheduled time
    3. Start cleanup immediately
    4. End cleanup








Type a menu option below

F1=Help    F3=Exit    F9=Command line    F12=Cancel
```

The options do the following tasks:

1. CHGCLNUP. With this command, you can change the cleanup job options, such as when to start cleanup automatically, and what to do during cleanup.

2. STRCLNUP OPTION(*SCHED). Allows automatic cleanup to start, all by itself, at the time you specified option 1.

3. STRCLNUP OPTION(*IMMED). The cleanup job starts immediately. This way you can run the cleanup job on demand instead of waiting for its scheduled time.

4. ENDCLNUP. If the cleanup job is running or waiting on the job queue, option 4 terminates it immediately.

CMNCFG: Communications Configuration Tasks

This menu helps you configure communications on your system.

```
CMNCFG                  Communications Configuration Tasks
                                                      System:    MC PGMR
To configure one of the following, type its number below and press Enter:

     1. Remote work station controllers and devices
     2. Remote systems
     3. Remote systems using printed instructions











Type a menu option below


F1=Help    F3=Exit    F9=Command line    F12=Cancel
```

The menu options perform the following tasks:

1. Configures workstation controllers, display stations and printers that communicate with your system via a telephone line.

2. Configures your system to enable it to communicate with another system.

3. Similar to option 2, except using a printed instruction sheet.

Chapter 7 - Operational Assistant

DEVICESTS: Device Status Menu

The DEVICESTS menu contains options that let you work with all kinds of physical devices. You can use these options whenever you need to know the status of a device or solve a problem related to it.

```
DEVICESTS                    Device Status Tasks
                                                     System:   MC PGMR
To select one of the following, type its number below and press Enter:

    1. Work with display devices
    2. Work with printer devices
    3. Work with tape devices
    4. Work with diskette devices

   10. Print local device addresses









Type a menu option below


F1=Help   F3=Exit    F9=Command line    F12=Cancel
```

The menu options perform the following tasks:

1. WRKDEVD DEVD(*DSP). Shows all display devices currently installed on the system.

2. WRKDEVD DEVD(*PRT). Shows all printer devices.

3. WRKDEVD DEVD(*TAP). Shows all tape devices.

4. WRKDEVD DEVD(*DKT). Shows all diskette devices.

10. PRTDEVADR. It asks you for the name of a workstation controller (typically named CTL01) and then prints a grid containing all of the local displays and printers you have configured. Each cell of the grid has the port number and switch setting as coordinates.

DISKTASKS: Disk Space Tasks

The DISKTASKS menu contains options that let you control your disk (auxiliary storage) usage.

```
DISKTASKS                    Disk Space Tasks
                                                         System:    MC PGMR
  To select one of the following, type its number below and press Enter:

       1. Collect disk space information
       2. Print disk space information

      10. Work with libraries
      11. Work with folders
      12. Work with objects by owner







  Type a menu option below


  F1=Help    F3=Exit    F9=Command line    F12=Cancel
```

The options perform the following tasks:

1. Runs a program that gathers information about the disk space used on your system. This option takes a long time to run.

2. Prints a report using the information collected by option 1.

10. WRKLIB. Lists libraries on your system, and lets you manipulate them.

11. WRKFLR. Lists folders on your system.

12. WRKOBJOWN. Lists objects owned by a particular user. For users who own many objects (such as QSECOFR), this command can take a long time to process.

Chapter 7 - Operational Assistant

INFO: Information Assistant Options

You can use this menu when you are not sure what to do.

```
INFO                 Information Assistant Options
                                                          System: MC_PGMR
 To select one of the following, type its number below and press Enter:

    1. Where do I look for information?
    2. How can I comment on information?

   10. What's new this release?
   11. What's coming in the next release?

   20. Start InfoSeeker (BookManager)
   21. Start online education

   23. Work with problems
   24. Start search index




 Type a menu option below


 F1=Help    F3=Exit    F9=Command line    F12=Cancel
 (C) COPYRIGHT IBM CORP. 1980, 1994.
```

The INFO menu options do the following:

1. Displays a series of panels that list IBM manuals you can use.

2. Tells you how you can give IBM your opinion of its manuals.

10. Lists the improvements IBM made to the new OS/400 release.

11. This option does not list what is coming up. It only tells you there will be a PTF available at the same time the next release becomes available. When you apply the PTF, option 11 will list what is coming up.

20. STRINFSKR. Lets you display the AS/400 manuals right on your terminal's screen. Although it's a neat idea in theory, it is unbearably slow in practice. You should use the PC version of BookManager, which has many more features and runs considerably faster.

21. STREDU. Starts the on-line education software if it is installed on your system.

23. WRKPRB. Lists problem logs and lets you work with them.

24. STRSCHIDX. Lets you use the system's search index object, which allows you to look for specific information. See Chapter 9, Section 5, for more information about the search index function.

MANAGESYS: The System Management Menu

The MANAGESYS menu contains several options you can use to help you manage your system. This is what the MANAGESYS menu looks like:

```
MANAGESYS              Manage Your System, Users, and Devices
                                                      System:    MC PGMR
To select one of the following, type its number below and press Enter:

    1. Display system status
    2. Run a backup
    3. Work with system operator messages

   10. Work with printer output
   11. Work with jobs
   12. Work with signed-on users

   20. Device status tasks

   60. Customize your system, users, and devices




Type a menu option below


F1=Help    F3=Exit    F9=Command line    F12=Cancel
```

Each option does the following:

1. DSPSYSSTS. Displays important status information about your system.

2. GO RUNBCKUP. Takes you to OA's RUNBCKUP menu.

Chapter 7 - Operational Assistant

3. WRKMSGQSYSOPR. Displays system operator messages.

10. WRKSPLF Lets you control reports that are ready to print or are already printing.

11. WRKUSRJOB.Lets you control jobs that are running on the system.

12. WRKUSRJOB. Displays a list of users who are currently signed on.

20. GO DEVICESTS. Takes you to OA's DEVICESTS menu.

60. GO SETUP. Takes you to OA's SETUP menu.

POWER: Power On/Off Tasks

As the name implies, the Power On/Off Tasks menu helps you power off the system and use the Power On/Off Schedule.

```
POWER                    Power On and Off Tasks
                                              System:   MC PGMR
To select one of the following, type its number below and press Enter:

   1. Display power on and off schedule
   2. Change power on and off schedule
   3. Power off the system immediately
   4. Power off the system immediately and then power on




















Type a menu option below


F1=Help    F3=Exit    F9=Command line    F12=Cancel
```

The options of the POWER menu perform the following tasks:

AS/400 Primer

1. DSPPWRSCD. Shows what the Power On/Off Schedule looks like at this time.

2. CHGPWRSCD. Lets you change the Power On/Off Schedule. With this facility, you can instruct the system to power itself on or off at specific times on the dates you specify. There is no guesswork. It is a giant step forward from the QIPLDATTIM system value.

3. PWRDWNSYS OPTION(*IMMED) RESTART(*NO). Ends all subsystems immediately and shuts off the system immediately. "Immediately" does not actually mean "right now," because the AS/400 always performs some housekeeping tasks. If you need to shut down the system this very second, use the emergency switch located on the CPU. You should be aware that this is for true emergencies only. The next IPL you perform can take an extremely long time.

4. PWRDWNSYS OPTION(*IMMED) RESTART(*YES). This option IPLs the system immediately. Again, "immediately" does not mean "right now."

RUNBCKUP: Run Backup

The Run Backup menu executes periodic backups according to what you have set up via the SETUPBCKUP menu for each option.

```
RUNBCKUP                        Run Backup
                                                        System:   MC PGMR
To select one of the following, type its number below and press Enter:

    1. Run daily backup
    2. Run weekly backup
    3. Run monthly backup

   10. Back up IBM-supplied libraries
   11. Back up the entire system




Type a menu option below


F1=Help    F3=Exit    F9=Command line    F12=Cancel
```

Chapter 7 - Operational Assistant

The menu options perform the following:

1. Backs up your system according to your daily backup options.

2. Backs up your system according to your weekly backup options.

3. Backs up your system according to your monthly backup options.

10. SAVLIB LIB(*IBM). Saves all libraries that were provided by IBM. This backup includes most libraries with names beginning in Q, except QSYS.

11. SAVSYS. Saves QSYS and a few other items. For a complete description of SAVSYS, refer to Chapter 6.

SETUP: Customize Your System, Users, and Devices

Most system configuration and user setup options can be executed from this menu and its related submenus.

```
SETUP               Customize Your System, Users, and Devices
                                                    System:   MC PGMR
To select an option, type its number below and press Enter:

    1. Change system options
    2. Cleanup tasks
    3. Power on and off tasks
    4. Disk space tasks
    5. Backup tasks

   10. Work with user enrollment
   11. Change passwords for IBM-supplied users

   20. Communications configuration tasks




Type a menu option below


F1=Help   F3=Exit   F9=Command line   F12=Cancel
```

The options perform the following functions:

1. Lets you change system configuration options (system values) using a simplified method.

2. GO CLEANUP. Takes you to the CLEANUP menu.

3. GO POWER. Takes you to the POWER menu.

4. GO DISKTASKS. Takes you to the DISKTASKS menu.

5. GO BACKUP. Takes you to the BACKUP menu.

10. WRKUSRPRF. Lists all user profiles and lets you perform different functions on them.

11. Runs a program that prompts you for new passwords for all IBM-supplied user profiles, such as QSECOFR, QSYSOPR and QSRV.

20. GO CMNCFG. Takes you to the CMNCFG menu.

SETUPBCKUP: Set Up Backup

With this menu you can customize the automated backup function of OA.

```
SETUPBCKUP                    Set Up Backup
                                                    System:   MC PGMR
To select one of the following, type its number below and press Enter:

    1. Change daily backup options
    2. Change weekly backup options
    3. Change monthly backup options

   10. Change library backup list
   11. Change folder backup list

   20. Change backup schedule




Type a menu option below


F1=Help   F3=Exit   F9=Command line   F12=Cancel
```

The options in this menu do the following:

1. Changes the options for your daily backups.

2. Changes the options for your weekly backups.

3. Changes the options for your monthly backups.

10. Runs a program that lets you maintain the backup list for libraries. With this option, you can tailor the backup list to include the libraries you need to have.

11. Runs a program to maintain the backup list for folders. Similar to option 10.

20. Maintains the backup schedule.

AS/400 Primer

TECHHELP: Technical Support Tasks

When you call IBM, you use this menu to help IBM's technical assistant solve problems. Occasionally, IBM's technicians will use this menu when they come in to solve problems.

```
TECHHELP                  Technical Support Tasks
                                                    System:   MC PGMR
 To select one of the following, type its number below and press Enter:

    1. Display messages for the system operator

   10. Work with problems with the system
   11. Work with PTF(s)
   12. Copy your screen on another display station
   13. Stop copying your screen

   20. Connect to technical support
   21. Disconnect from technical support

   80. Temporary sign-off




 Type a menu option below


 F1=Help    F3=Exit    F9=Command line    F12=Cancel
 (C) COPYRIGHT IBM CORP. 1980, 1992.
```

TECHHELP's options do the following:

1. DSPMSG MSGQ(QSYSOPR). Displays messages from the system operator's message queue. The system logs many problems in the form of messages in QSYSOPR. QSYSOPR is also the destination of all inquiry messages issued by the system when it encounters a problem it cannot resolve.

10. WRKPRB. Lists all problems that have been logged.

11. WRKPTF. Lists all Program Temporary Fixes (PTFs) that have been loaded and/or applied to your system.

12. STRCPYSCN SRCDEV(*REQUESTER). Begins copying images of your display station's screen into another display station or into a database file. The IBM technician may ask you to do this, so he can see the same things you are seeing.

Chapter 7 - Operational Assistant

13. ENDCPYSCN. Ends the copy process, so you have privacy again.

20. STRRMTSPS: Starts a technical support session using the ECS modem to connect to IBM's mainframe.

21. ENDRMTSPT: Ends the communication with IBM's technical support mainframe.

USERHELP: Documentation & Problem Handling

The Documentation and Problem Handling menu explains the basics and helps you to solve problems that may arise with your system.

```
USERHELP                Information and Problem Handling
                                                    System:   MC PGMR
To select one of the following, type its number below and press Enter:

    1. How to use help
    2. Information Assistant options
    3. Display work station user

   10. Save information to help resolve a problem
   11. Technical support tasks

   80. Temporary sign-off




Type a menu option below


F1=Help    F3=Exit    F9=Command line    F12=Cancel
(C) COPYRIGHT IBM CORP. 1980, 1992.
```

The options perform the following tasks:

1. Runs a program that presents panels that explain how to use the system's help support.

2. GO INFO. Takes you to OA's INFO menu.

AS/400 Primer

3. DSPWSUSR. This command presents a panel that identifies the user who is signed on, the display station, and other items of general-purpose information.

10. Runs a program that leads you to collect and provide information that can be submitted to IBM electronically, whenever you have a problem with your system.

11. GO TECHHELP. Takes you to OA's TECHHELP menu.

FURTHER READING

IBM's *System Operator's Guide*.

IBM's *New User's Guide*.

8

User Messages

A message is a kind of free-form communication between any two entities. When you talk to another person, you and the other person are actually exchanging messages. You are taking turns transmitting one message at a time in the form of speech.

In computer terms, a message is also a form of communication between the computer and a user, between two users, or between two computer programs. While all three forms of messages have their specific uses (and are equally important), this chapter deals exclusively with messages exchanged between two users. Many of the techniques described here can also be applied to other kinds of messages.

Section 1: Sending Messages

You might want to send a message to another user for many reasons. For example, you may need to inform the user that his report has finished printing and is ready for pick-up in the computer room. Or you may need to tell all users that the system will be shut down at 4:30 p.m. for a release upgrade.

Whatever the case, sending a user message helps you convey these ideas or announcements to your users. To send a message, you need to run the Send Message (SNDMSG) command.

The SNDMSG Command

The SNDMSG command has five parameters, but for most practical purposes you need to concern yourself only with the first three. With these three parameters you indicate who should receive the message and what the message should say.

For example, suppose you want to send a message to user LARRY, to tell him that the inventory master parts list he requested has printed. This is what you do:

```
SNDMSG MSG('Your inventory master parts list is printed.') +
       TOUSR(LARRY)
```

Note that you have used two parameters: MSG, to spell out the text of the message, and TOUSR, which indicates what user receives the message. Alternatively, you could have used the TOMSGQ parameter (instead of TOUSR). The disadvantage is that then you must know the name of the message queue that has been assigned to user LARRY. By using the TOUSR parameter, however, you the system performs that search for you.

Sending to Multiple Users

The TOUSR parameter has one limitation that is not shared by the TOMSGQ parameter: it can accept only one name. Using the TOMSGQ parameter you can send the same message to several users. Or, more accurately, to several message queues:

```
SNDMSG MSG('Time to start our meeting in the Computer +
       Room.') TOMSGQ(JODY JIM JENNIFER JUSTIN)
```

In this case, the same message would be sent to message queues JODY, JIM, JENNIFER and JUSTIN: "Time to start our meeting in the computer room." (You have scheduled a meeting with this group of people and want to send a message to remind them of it.)

The distinction between user and message queue is important. When the security administrator creates a user profile, he has to assign a message queue for the new user. The name of the message queue defaults to the user profile name. A user named JUSTIN would have a message queue of the same name. In this case, it makes no difference whether you use the TOUSR or the TOMSGQ parameter, because the names are identical. Keep in mind, however, that this similarity is not necessarily so.

Chapter 8 - User Messages

Sending Messages to Special Users

The SNDMSG command allows you to send a message to the system operator without having to remember the name of its user profile or message queue. All you need to do is specify TOUSR(*SYSOPR) or TOMSGQ(*SYSOPR). Again, you can see the similarity between TOUSR and TOMSGQ. The system operator's profile name is QSYSOPR and so is the name of its message queue.

You can also specify TOUSR(*ALLACT) if you want to broadcast the message to all users currently signed on. Finally, you can specify TOUSR(*REQUESTER) if you want to send a message to yourself. You can use a message to yourself to write a reminder of things to do the next day, just before you sign off and go home in the evening.

Sending Inquiry Messages

Another use of the SNDMSG command has not been discussed yet: that of sending an *inquiry* message. An inquiry message is a type of message you send when you want the recipient to acknowledge it and give you an answer. The system uses inquiry messages liberally. You can take advantage of them too.

For example, you can send the following inquiry message to user LARRY:

```
SNDMSG MSG('I need to shut down the system. How much +
         longer are you going to use it?') +
       TOUSR(LARRY) +
       MSGTYPE(*INQ)
```

When LARRY sees this message, the system provides an input field that goes all the way across the screen, right below the message text. LARRY can then type the answer and press Enter; when he does that, you get the answer at your terminal.

You can even specify where to receive the reply, with the help of the RPYMSGQ parameter. This parameter always defaults to *WRKSTN, which means that your display station's message queue receives the reply. However, there is nothing to prevent you from entering a different value in the RPYMSGQ parameter if, for instance, you want your supervisor GEORGE to receive the reply. In this case you would indicate RPYMSGQ(GEORGE).

Sending inquiry messages has two restrictions, however. You cannot specify TOUSR(*ALLACT) or indicate more than one name in the TOMSGQ parameter because you would not want the answer to come from all recipients at once, or from any one of them.

Section 2: Displaying Messages

Just because you send a message to someone does not guarantee that the other person is going to read the message. For example, the other person may not be signed on, or may be away from his display station. Even if the recipient is signed on and using the display station, under normal circumstances, the system does not automatically display the message.

The recipient is notified of the message by a beep, and the "message waiting" indicator on the screen turns on. The recipient can then request to display the message at a convenient time.

The DSPMSG Command

Run the Display Message (DSPMSG) command to display the contents of a message queue. You specify which message queue with the MSGQ parameter. If you do not specify which message queue you want to display, DSPMSG uses the default value *WRKUSR, which gives you both your own user profile's and your display station's message queues. This feature is convenient because it lets you display your own messages by keying in DSPMSG and pressing Enter. When you run DSPMSG you see the following panel:

```
                        Display Messages
                                          System:      MC PGMR
   Queue . . . . . :   MALERN            Program . . . . :   MONMSG
     Library . . . :     QUSRSYS           Library . . . :     MGTLIB
   Severity . . . :   00                 Delivery . . . :   *BREAK

   Type reply (if required), press Enter.
     From . . . :   QSECOFR      05/24/92    12:56:36
      I have given you *READ access to file INVENTORY per your request.




                                                              Bottom
   F3=Exit          F11=Remove a message              F12=Cancel
   F13=Remove all   F16=Remove all except unanswered  F24=More keys
```

Chapter 8 - User Messages

Although you also can use special values *USRPRF and *WRKSTN to display either (but not both) your own user profile's and your display station's message queues, these special values are seldom used. It is much easier to let DSPMSG give you both queues by not keying in any value.

You can enter any message queue name you want (and have authorization to) in the MSGQ parameter, including QSYSOPR. You also can display QSYSOPR's message queue by keying in the value QSYSOPR or *SYSOPR. Because an asterisk is harder to type than the letter Q (the asterisk requires the Shift key), *SYSOPR is not of much value.

You can use other parameters in the DSPMSG command, but they are not as important as the MSGQ parameter. For example, you can specify where to begin displaying the messages. You can display at the top or at the bottom of the message queue using the START parameter's *FIRST and *LAST values. The default value is *LAST.

Function Keys in DSPMSG Panel

The DSPMSG command panel offers several function keys, including three to remove messages from the message queue. Use these function keys carefully.

- F11: If you move the cursor to a message and press F11, the system removes that particular message from the message queue. Do not do this on an inquiry message that has not been replied to already, or you will lose your opportunity to reply to the message.

- F13: Removes all messages without exception, including non-replied inquiry messages. All non-replied inquiry messages are replied to with the default reply, which may be inappropriate. The system then removes both the original message and the reply. You have no way of knowing what the system did. Avoid using F13 at all costs.

- F16: Removes all messages, except non-replied inquiry messages. This key is the safest way to clean up the message queue. You should get in the habit of pressing it as soon as you read newly arrived messages.

Section 3: Sending Break Messages

Because messages are not displayed the moment they are sent, there can be a delay (of unknown length) between the time you send a message and the time the recipient actually reads it. If your message is urgent, you should consider sending your message as a *break* message. Break messages interrupt the recipient's interactive job and display the message immediately.

The SNDBRKMSG Command

To send a break message, use the Send Break Message (SNDBRKMSG) command. The SNDBRKMSG command is similar to SNDMSG, except that it has a few restrictions.

You cannot send a break message to a user's message queue. You can only send it to a display station message queue, which means that if you want to send a break message to user FRANNIE, you must first find out where FRANNIE is signed on. For example:

WRKUSRJOB USER(FRANNIE) STATUS(*ACTIVE)

With the Work with User Jobs (WRKUSRJOB) command you can find out the names of the active jobs that user FRANNIE is running. You could omit the STATUS parameter, but in that case you would get all of FRANNIE's jobs (she may have dozens of jobs that are either completed or waiting in a job queue, and you are not interested in those). When the system shows you the list of jobs, you can visually scan it for interactive jobs (type INT). The job name is always equal to the display station name.

With this knowledge, you can now run the SNDBRKMSG command to send Frannie a break message. For example:

SNDBRKMSG MSG('Hey, let''s do lunch.') TOMSGQ(INVDSP03)

Like SNDMSG, you can send the same break message to more than one place. The TOMSGQ parameter accepts a list of display station names (to send the same break message to several specific display stations) or even *ALLWS, which sends the message to all workstations, whether they are in use or not. IBM does not, however, provide an *ALLACT value ("all active") as it does for the SNDMSG command. The utility command SNDBRKACT solves this problem. SNDBRKACT sends the same break message to all active display stations. (i.e., those display stations that have someone signed on).

SNDBRKMSG also can send an inquiry message. Specify MSGTYPE(*INQ) to only one display station at a time. Just like the SNDMSG command, you can indicate what message queue is to receive the reply.

Chapter 8 - User Messages

Handling Break Messages

Break messages can be annoying because they interrupt whatever the recipient is doing at the display station. Break messages are descriptive; just like when two people are engaged in a conversation and someone walks by and breaks right in without waiting for a pause in the conversation. Therefore, you should send as few break messages as possible.

On the other hand, you may prefer break messages and wish there were a way you could force the system to treat all your incoming messages as break messages. Then you would be sure not to miss any messages at all.

You can do that with the Change Message Queue (CHGMSGQ) command, as follows:

```
CHGMSGQ MSGQ(...) DLVRY(*BREAK) PGM(*DSPMSG)
```

DLVRY(*BREAK) changes the way the system handles your incoming messages: now they will break into your job. When this happens, the system runs a program named in the PGM parameter. In this case, the special value *DSPMSG means that the system will run the DSPMSG command. The result is that when someone sends you a message (with SNDMSG or SNDBRKMSG), you will receive the message in break mode and the system will run the DSPMSG command for you automatically.

You can create your own break-handling program and put its name in the PGM parameter instead of *DSPMSG. This way, you can "monitor" your message queue and invoke your break-handling program automatically every time a new message arrives. Here is an example of a break-handling program:

```
MSG2LIN24: +
   PGM PARM(&MSGQ &MSGQLIB &MSGKEY)

   DCL VAR(&MSGDTA)      TYPE(*CHAR) LEN(132)
   DCL VAR(&MSGKEY)      TYPE(*CHAR) LEN(4)
   DCL VAR(&MSGQ)        TYPE(*CHAR) LEN(10)
   DCL VAR(&MSGQLIB)     TYPE(*CHAR) LEN(10)

   RCVMSG MSGQ(&MSGQLIB/&MSGQ) MSGKEY(&MSGKEY) RMV(*NO) MSG(&MSGDTA)
   MONMSG MSGID(CPF0000)
   SNDPGMMSG MSGID(CPF9897) MSGF(QCPFMSG) MSGDTA(&MSGDTA) +
      TOPGMQ(*EXT) MSGTYPE(*STATUS)

   ENDPGM
```

To compile: `CRTCLPGM PGM(xxx/MSG2LIN24) SRCFILE(xxx/QCLSRC)`

Key the program into source physical file QCLSRC in one of your libraries (represented by xxx), then compile the program by executing the CRTCLPGM as indicated. Now run the following command:

`CHGMSGQ MSGQ(...) DLVRY(*BREAK) PGM(xxx/MSG2LIN24)`

Because you are instructing the system to run MSG2LIN24 as your break-handling program, MSG2LIN24 will run whenever a new message arrives to your message queue. MSG2LIN24 receives the message from your message queue and sends it again as a status message that appears at the bottom of your screen.

FURTHER READING

IBM's *New User's Guide*.

9

Commands and System Help

OS/400 is a complex operating system that is driven by commands. No matter what you need to do, you do it by executing the command that carries out the task at hand.

Section 1: Command Names

Most computers have operating systems with control commands that make no sense. The S/36, for example, has a command named LIBRLIBR. If you do not know the S/36's operating system idiosyncrasies, you might think "library-library." The name does not convey the purpose of the command, which is to copy a library member.

The CICS transaction code, CSSF, that is used in the System/370 to sign off from the system is cryptic. You cannot look at CSSF and say, "Oh yes, that means sign off."

OS/400 Command Name Structure

OS/400, on the other hand, uses a standard set of abbreviations that are always followed. The vast majority of OS/400 commands adhere to the following naming scheme:

1. First, a 3-letter abbreviation for a verb, such as create, remove, print, or send.

2. Last, a series of abbreviations for modifiers, such as file, program, job queue, or user profile. These abbreviations are usually 3 letters long, but there are many exceptions.

This naming scheme makes OS/400 command names easy to guess. If you know the abbreviations used by IBM, all you need to do is put them together, and you are likely to be right.

Some Abbreviations

- Verbs:
CRT	Create.
CHT	Change.
DLT	Delete.
ADD	Add.
RMV	Remove.
DSP	Display.
WRK	Work with.
STR	Start.
END	End.

- Modifiers:
F	File.
PF	Physical File.
LF	Logical File.
SRCF	Source File.
CLPGM	CL Program.
RPGPGM	RPG Program.
MSGQ	Message Queue.
OUTQ	Output Queue.
JOBQ	Job Queue.
DTAQ	Data Queue.
DTAARA	Data Area.
SBS	Subsystem.

A Few Examples

Suppose you need to create a new message queue. What command would you use? If you look at the list of verbs, you will see that the verb create is abbreviated CRT. In the

Chapter 9 - Commands and System Help

list of modifiers, message queue is abbreviated MSGQ. Putting them together you obtain CRTMSGQ, which is correct.

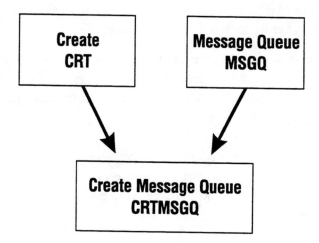

Now, suppose you want to display a data area. Display is DSP and data area is DTAARA. The command, then, is DSPDTAARA. Correct again.

Finally, suppose you want to create an RPG program and then you want to delete a CL program. Create is CRT and RPG program is RPGPGM, so the command should be CRTRPGPGM (correct). To delete a CL program, however, you do not run the DLTCLPGM. That command does not exist. You run the DLTPGM command. The system does not care what language you used to create the program when you are going to delete it. Although you use CRTPF to create a physical file, you use DLTF (delete file) to delete it. It makes no difference to the system what kind of file it is.

Section 2: Finding a Command

Sometimes you need to execute a command but you cannot remember what it is, and the naming system does not really help if you do not know what you are looking for. OS/400 provides two different ways to look up unknown commands: the Select Command (SLTCMD) command and the menus.

The SLTCMD Command

The SLTCMD command presents a list of commands as they are found in a particular library. You need to specify *ALL, a generic name, or a specific name, and the name of the library where you want to search for the command.

For example, suppose you want to display the contents of a file. You try DSPF (which seems logical) but there is no such command. Then you try DSPPF (which seems logical too), but there is no such command either. To find the command, do the following:

```
SLTCMD CMD(QSYS/DSP*)
```

This command will show you a list of all the QSYS commands that begin in the letters DSP. There will be dozens of them so you need to go through the list, rolling forward if necessary, until you find the command that seems likely. It turns out that the command you needed is DSPPFM.

Chapter 9 - Commands and System Help

Command Menus

Another feature of OS/400 is its menus. OS/400 has hundreds of menus. The main menu is called MAIN. You can display this menu by executing the following command:

GO MENU(MAIN)

```
MAIN                       AS/400 Main Menu
                                                      System:    MC_PGMR
  Select one of the following:

     1. User tasks
     2. Office tasks
     3. General system tasks
     4. Files, libraries, and folders
     5. Programming
     6. Communications
     7. Define or change the system
     8. Problem handling
     9. Display a menu
    10. Information Assistant options
    11. Client Access tasks

    90. Sign off

  Selection or command
  ===> _____

  F3=Exit    F4=Prompt    F9=Retrieve    F12=Cancel    F13=Information Assistant
  F23=Set initial menu
  (C) COPYRIGHT IBM CORP. 1980, 1994.
```

The GO command is used throughout OS/400 to go to a particular menu. From the MAIN menu, you can select options by keying in the appropriate number and pressing Enter, to take you to another menu. Or you can execute a command or program. Try the following command:

GO MENU(MAJOR)

AS/400 Primer

```
 MAJOR                        Major Command Groups
                                                     System:   MC PGMR
   Select one of the following:

         1.  Select Command by Name                      SLTCMD
         2.  Verb Commands                               VERB
         3.  Subject Commands                            SUBJECT
         4.  Object Management Commands                  CMDOBJMGT
         5.  File Commands                               CMDFILE
         6.  Save and Restore Commands                   CMDSAVRST
         7.  Work Management Commands                    CMDWRKMGT
         8.  Data Management Commands                    CMDDTAMGT
         9.  Security Commands                           CMDSEC
        10.  Print Commands                              CMDPRT
        11.  Spooling Commands                           CMDSPL
        12.  System Control Commands                     CMDSYSCTL
        13.  Program Commands                            CMDPGM
                                                            More...
   Selection or command
   ===> _____

 F3=Exit    F4=Prompt    F9=Retrieve    F12=Cancel    F13=Information Assistant
 F16=AS/400 Main menu
 (C) COPYRIGHT IBM CORP. 1980, 1993.
```

From here, you can go to other menus:

- VERB, which lists all the OS/400 verbs (such as create, print, submit and receive). Each option in the VERB menu takes you to another menu, called CMDxxx (where xxx is the verb's abbreviation). From this menu, you can find a command. For example, the CMDDSP menu shows all OS/400 commands that perform some kind of displaying action.

Chapter 9 - Commands and System Help

```
VERB                          Verb Commands

Select one of the following:

    1.  Add Commands                                    CMDADD
    2.  Allocate Commands                               CMDALC
    3.  Answer Commands                                 CMDANS
    4.  Analyze Commands                                CMDANZ
    5.  Apply Commands                                  CMDAPY
    6.  Ask Commands                                    CMDASK
    7.  Auditing Commands                               CMDAUD
    8.  Call Commands                                   CMDCALL
    9.  Configuration Commands                          CMDCFG
   10.  Change Commands                                 CMDCHG
   11.  Check Commands                                  CMDCHK
   12.  Close Commands                                  CMDCLO
   13.  Cleanup Commands                                CMDCLNUP
   14.  Clear Commands                                  CMDCLR
                                                        More...
Selection or command
===> _____

F3=Exit    F4=Prompt    F9=Retrieve    F12=Cancel    F16=Major menu
(C) COPYRIGHT IBM CORP. 1980, 1993.
```

- SUBJECT, which lists all the OS/400 modifiers (such as output queue and file). Again, each option in the SUBJECT menu takes you to another menu, called CMDxxx (where xxx is the modifier's abbreviation), from which you can find a command. For example, the CMDOUTQ menu lists all commands that relate to output queues such as: create, delete and work with.

```
SUBJECT                    Subject Commands

 Select one of the following:

         1. Abnormal Commands                      CMDABN
         2. Abstract Syntax Commands               CMDABSN
         3. Access Code Commands                   CMDACC
         4. Access Group Commands                  CMDACCGRP
         5. Accounting Commands                    CMDACG
         6. Action Commands                        CMDACN
         7. Action Entry Commands                  CMDACNE
         8. Active Commands                        CMDACT
         9. Adjacent Node Commands                 CMDADJN
        10. Application Dev Mgr/400 Cmds           CMDADM
        11. Adopt Commands                         CMDADP
        12. Address Commands                       CMDADR

        14. AFP Commands                           CMDAFP
                                                     More...
 Selection or command
 ===> _____

 F3=Exit   F4=Prompt   F9=Retrieve   F12=Cancel   F16=Major menu
 (C) COPYRIGHT IBM CORP. 1980, 1993.
```

Remember that the GO command can be used with any menu. For example, you have seen that there is a menu named CMDOUTQ. You can go there directly by executing:

GO MENU(CMDOUTQ)

Chapter 9 - Commands and System Help

```
CMDOUTQ                    Output Queue Commands

Select one of the following:

 Commands
   1. Change Output Queue                                 CHGOUTQ
   2. Clear Output Queue                                  CLROUTQ
   3. Create Output Queue                                 CRTOUTQ
   4. Delete Output Queue                                 DLTOUTQ
   5. Hold Output Queue                                   HLDOUTQ
   6. Release Output Queue                                RLSOUTQ
   7. Work with Output Queue                              WRKOUTQ

 Related Command Menus
   8. Output Queue Descr Commands                         CMDOUTQD
   9. Spooling Commands                                   CMDSPL
  10. Spooled File Commands                               CMDSPLF
  11. Writer Commands                                     CMDWTR
                                                            Bottom
Selection or command
===> _____


F3=Exit    F4=Prompt    F9=Retrieve    F12=Cancel    F16=Major menu
(C) COPYRIGHT IBM CORP. 1980, 1991.
```

Section 3: Customizing IBM Commands

IBM-supplied commands have many parameters that can accept a wide variety of values. This design allows you to operate and program the system with a fraction of the total number of commands you would need if each individual task required a separate command.

Most optional parameters have default values. Although IBM's choice for default values is sensible, they cannot possibly foresee all the environments in which the AS/400 is used. The result is that in many cases, the default parameters are not what you would want them to be.

Fortunately, you can change the default value for any parameter in any command if:

- The parameter already has a default value. You cannot assign a default value to a parameter that is defined as mandatory, nor to one that shows no parameter at all when you invoke the command prompter.

- The parameter is not a list parameter.

☛ To change the default value of a parameter, run the Change Command Default (CHGCMDDFT command.

The Simple Approach

The simplest way to change an IBM-supplied command is to change the command itself in QSYS. For example, suppose you often use the Work with Output Queues (WRKOUTQ) command to display the contents of output queue QPRINT. WRKOUTQ's OUTQ parameter defaults to *ALL, which takes long to process and is not what you want.

You can change WRKOUTQ's default for the OUTQ parameter, so that QPRINT is assumed if no value is entered. This change would allow you to work with QPRINT by typing WRKOUTQ and pressing Enter. To change the default:

```
CHGCMDDFT CMD(QSYS/WRKOUTQ) NEWDFT('OUTQ(QPRINT)')
```

This method works, but it has one rather serious disadvantage. When you upgrade to a new release of OS/400, or sometimes even when you apply certain PTFs, you will lose your new default values and the system will not alert you to it. If this is not a problem for you, it is okay to change QSYS commands directly. If it is a problem, read the next subheading.

The Learned Approach

A safer approach to changing command defaults is by first making a copy of the original QSYS command and then changing the copy, not the original. Here is the process:

1. Create a user library where you can place your copies of QSYS objects. You can name it ALTQSY (for Alternative QSYS):

   ```
   CRTLIB LIB(ALTQSYS) TEXT('Alternative QSYS')
   ```

2. Place this library ahead of QSYS in the system portion of the library list. This change guarantees that your copies of the objects will be used instead of the QSYS originals:

   ```
   WRKSYSVAL SYSVAL(QSYSLIBL)
   Select option 2.
   Insert ALTQSYS before QSYS.
   ```

3. Copy the QSYS command you want to change into ALTQSYS:

```
CRTDUPOBJ OBJ(WRKOUTQ) OBJTYPE(*CMD) FROMLIB(QSYS) +
          TOLIB(ALTQSYS)
```

4. Change the copy's defaults as you see fit:

```
CHGCMDDFT CMD(ALTQSYS/WRKOUTQ) +
          NEWDFT('OUTQ(QPRINT)')
```

Document Your Changes

Document all the changes you make to command parameters in a CL program. For each command with changed defaults, include the following section of code in the CL program:

```
/* Regenerate command xxx */
        DLTCMD    CMD(ALTQSYS/xxx)
        MONMSG    MSGID(CPF0000)
        CRTDUPOBJ OBJ(xxx) OBJTYPE(*CMD) FROMLIB(QSYS) +
                  TOLIB(ALTQSYS)
        CHGCMDDFT CMD(ALTQSYS/xxx) NEWDFT(...)
```

The xxx represents the name of the command you have changed. When you upgrade your system to a new release or apply PTFs that may change the definition of the original QSYS commands, you should compile this CL program and execute it.

First, it deletes the ALTQSYS command and creates a new one from QSYS. The ALTQSYS command then always will reflect the latest changes made by IBM (such as added parameters). Finally, it changes the default value in the ALTQSYS copy.

Section 4: The Command Prompter

Most OS/400 commands have parameters to fine-tune the purpose or the task to be performed by the command. For instance, the Display Message (DSPMSG) command uses a parameter to determine what messages to display. If parameters did not exist, you would need a different command for each message queue, which would be impractical.

AS/400 Primer

Invoking the Command Prompter

The command prompter can be activated by keying in the name of the command at the command line and pressing F4 instead of Enter. When you do this, the system presents the prompt panel for that command. For example, you can invoke the prompter for the Change Library List (CHGLIBL) command as follows:

CHGLIBL   ... press F4:

```
                     Change Library List (CHGLIBL)

 Type choices, press Enter.

 Libraries for current job  . . .    $MALERN___     Name, *SAME, *NONE
                                     UTILITY___
                                     MGTLIB____
                                     QGPL_____
                                     MCRSCLIB__
             + for more values       QTEMP_____
 Current library  . . . . . . . .    *CRTDFT        Name, *SAME, *CRTDFT




                                                                     Bottom
 F3=Exit   F4=Prompt   F5=Refresh   F12=Cancel   F13=How to use this display
 F24=More keys
```

You also can invoke the command prompter by typing a question mark (?) at the command line immediately followed by the command name and pressing the Enter key.

Command Parameters

In the previous illustration, the CHGLIBL command has two parameters. The first parameter ("Libraries for current job") is a list, while the second parameter ("Current library") is a normal parameter.

Chapter 9 - Commands and System Help

The command prompter gives you input fields so you can change the values of the parameters. On the right-hand side, it shows you what values are acceptable. For example, the first parameter allows entry of a name, *SAME or *NONE. The second parameter allows a name, *SAME or *CRTDFT.

The command parameter names are not shown unless you press F11 or change your user profile with USROPT(*CLKWD). The first parameter has a keyword of LIBL, and the second parameter's keyword is CURLIB.

Changing Parameter Values

Simple parameters like CURLIB are easy to change, by typing over the old value (which shows *CRTDFT in the example above). List parameters like LIBL are more difficult

If you only need to replace one element in the list for another, proceed as you would with a simple parameter: type over the old value and press Enter.

If you want to remove one of the elements of the list, blank it out and press Enter. Optionally, you can type a less-than (<) character, at least one space, and press Enter. Both methods yield the same result.

If you want to insert a new element to the list, somewhere in the middle, type a greater-than (>) symbol in the input field before which you want to insert, at least one space, and press Enter. The command prompter will present a different panel where you can type one or more new elements. When you are done inserting, press Enter. The system returns to the command prompter with the new values already inserted.

If you want to add a new element at the bottom of the list, type a plus (+) sign and at least one space on any of the elements of the list and press Enter. The system will present a different panel to let you type the new elements to be inserted. When you are done, press Enter again and the system takes you back to the command prompter, with the new values already appended at the end of the list.

Sometimes you need to type more characters than will fit in the input field provided by the prompter. This happens when you are entering a CL program and one of the parameters is an expression rather than a variable name. To lengthen the input field, type an ampersand (&) and at least one space and press Enter. The command prompter will lengthen the input field to the next higher length it provides.

Although this process of lengthening a parameter's input field can be repeated several times (until the input field reaches its maximum length of 512 spaces), it does not guarantee that the command prompter is going to accept that many characters. For example, the Display User Profile (DSPUSRPRF) command expects a user profile name in the USRPRF parameter. Because it is a name, it can be up to 10 characters long. You can lengthen the input field to 32 characters and even type 32 characters in the input field. When you press Enter, however, the prompter will reject your input because it is too long.

Requesting Help

The command prompter provides help. You can press F13 to display instructions about using the command prompter if you are not sure about all the features you have at your fingertips.

☞ The Help Key also is available. It provides cursor-sensitive help text that explains the purpose, allowed values and special rules about all parameters. If you move the cursor above the first parameter and press Help, the system displays help text to explain the purpose of the command itself.

While the cursor is on an input field, you can also press F4 (or type a question mark (?) and at least one space, then press Enter) to obtain a list of allowed values for the parameter in question.

Function Keys

This section discusses the most important function keys available with the command prompter. F1 works like the Help key. F2 is allowed only while help is active, to display the extended help. Extended help shows all help available for the command. F3 and F12 cancel the command prompter.

F4 lists the allowed values for a parameter. If the parameter expects a command string (such as the THEN parameter of the IF command, or the CMD parameter of the SBMJOB command), F4 can be used to invoke the command prompter for the command you are entering.

For example, suppose you need to submit the DSPLIB command to batch. You begin by typing SBMJOB at the command line and then you press F4 to prompt the SBMJOB command. The first parameter, CMD, is where you enter the command you want to submit for batch execution. You type DSPLIB and press F4 again. The system prompts the DSPLIB command. It is one prompt within another. The following diagram illustrates this process:

Chapter 9 - Commands and System Help

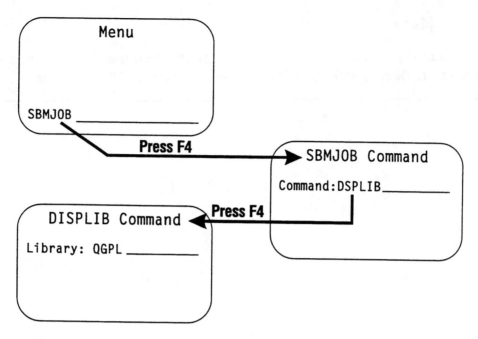

F5 returns all parameters to their original default values (if you have changed them but not yet pressed Enter). If you lengthened any parameter input fields with the & character, F5 returns the input fields to their original length.

F10 is not always available. When it is, it displays additional parameters not normally shown at first because they are seldom used.

F11 displays the parameter keywords or omits them if they are already present. You can change your user profile to USROPT(*CLKWD) if you would rather see the keywords all the time.

F14 displays the entire command string, including all the parameters to which you have given values. The string is displayed the way the command would look if you had entered it manually at the command line or included it in a CL program. This function key is helpful for documentation purposes.

Section 5: System Help

The system provides many layers of help, in the form of help entry panels, help text, and a utility called the search index. Usually, you can press the Help Key to display additional information.

AS/400 Primer

The Support Menu

In OS/400 menus, you can use F13 as a quick way to access the SUPPORT menu. You also can go there directly with the GO command. This is the SUPPORT menu:

```
SUPPORT                 User Support and Education
                                                    System:    MC PGMR
 Select one of the following:

    1. How to use help
    2. Search system help index
    3. How to use commands
    4. Question and answer
    5. AS/400 publications
    6. IBM product information
    7. How to handle system problems
    8. Problem handling
    9. Online education




 Selection or command
 ===> _____

 F3=Exit    F4=Prompt   F9=Retrieve   F12=Cancel   F16=AS/400 Main menu
 (C) COPYRIGHT IBM CORP. 1980, 1991.
```

The purpose of the SUPPORT menu is to provide information and general-purpose help. For example, if you choose option 1, you access a series of panels that explain how to use the system help facility:

Chapter 9 - Commands and System Help

```
Help                       How to Use Help

  Help is provided for all AS/400 displays. The type of help provided
  depends on the location of the cursor.

   o  For all displays, the following information is provided:

      -  What the display is used for
      -  How to use the display
      -  How to use the command line if there is one
      -  How to use the entry fields and parameter line if any
      -  What function keys are active and what they do

   o  The following information is also provided for specific areas,
      depending on the type of information being displayed:

      -  Menus:  Meaning of each option
      -  Entry (prompting) displays:  Meanings and use of all values
         for each entry field
      -  List displays:  Meaning and use of each column
                                                              More...
 F3=Exit help     F10=Move to top    F11=InfoSeeker   F12=Cancel
 F13=Information Assistant           F14=Print help
```

The Search Index

The search index support lets you find information by just typing a few words and pressing the Enter key. You can start the search index either by selecting option 2 from the SUPPORT menu or by executing the Start Search Index (STRSCHIDX) command. Here is what you get:

AS/400 Primer

```
                         InfoSeeker

Type options, press Enter. (+ indicates an expandable topic)
   5=Display topic   6=Print topic   7=Expand topic   8=Compress topic

Opt   Topic
      AS/400 System Information
  _   + AS/400 Query Management
  _   + AS/400 Structured Query Language (SQL)
  _   + Communication and connectivity
  _   + Customer support and education
  _   + Debug topics
  _   + Glossary
  _   + Interactive Data Definition Utility (IDDU)
  _   + Operating System/400 CL commands
  _   + Questions and Answers
  _   + REXX
                                                         More...
Or type search words and press Enter. (* indicates a topic match)
_____

F3=Exit help    F5=All topics    F6=Main topics    F11=Hide structure
F12=Cancel      F13=Information Assistant    F18=More indexes    F24=More keys
```

Now, suppose you want to learn about system values. You do not know what they are, or how they are controlled. All it takes is typing "system value" and pressing Enter:

Chapter 9 - Commands and System Help

```
                         InfoSeeker

Type options, press Enter. (+ indicates an expandable topic)
  5=Display topic   6=Print topic   7=Expand topic   8=Compress topic

Opt   Topic
      AS/400 System Information
 _      + Communication and connectivity
 _        + Configuration
 _          Work management
 _            Changing system values for device configuration
 _    *         Changing QAUTOCFG system value
 _    *         Changing QDEVNAMING system value
 _    *         Changing QPRTDEV system value
 _      + Glossary
 _        + C
 _    *     Callable interface
                                                         More...
Or type search words and press Enter. (* indicates a topic match)
system value_____

F3=Exit help    F5=All topics    F6=Main topics    F11=Hide structure
F12=Cancel      F13=Information Assistant    F18=More indexes    F24=More keys
```

You can select any of the entries listed (all of which are related to system values in some way). To display one of them, enter an option 5 next to it and press Enter. If you would rather print the information, use option 6 instead.

Some topics are so extensive that you may find many entries that will not fit a on single screen. In that case, the system displays the "More" indicator and lets you use the Roll keys to page forward or backward.

Other options you can select include 7 to expand a topic (flagged with a + sign, such as "Configuration" on the second line) and 8 to collapse an expanded topic. The indentation of the titles reveals the hierarchy of the topics.

If you enter option 5 on the fifth line ("Changing QAUTOCFG system value") and press Enter, you will see the following:

121

AS/400 Primer

```
┌──────────────────────────────────────────────────────────────────┐
│  Help                    Changing QAUTOCFG system value         │
│                                                                  │
│    A system value called QAUTOCFG controls whether or not your system │
│    automatically configures any new local twinaxial or ASCII    │
│    controllers, tape controllers, local twinaxial devices, tape units, │
│    or diskette units that are added to your system. It is set to │
│    QAUTOCFG(1) (which means automatic configuration is on) unless you │
│    specified N (No) to the automatic configuration option on the Set │
│    Major System Options display or unless someone has changed the │
│    system value to QAUTOCFG(0) (which means off).               │
│                                                                  │
│    If you change the system value to QAUTOCFG(0) (which means off) you │
│    will have to manually configure any new local twinaxial or ASCII │
│    controllers, tape controllers, local twinaxial devices, tape units, │
│    or diskette units that you add to your system. However, you can │
│    choose to change the system value back to QAUTOCFG(1), (which means │
│    on) at any time.                                             │
│                                                                  │
│    To change the QAUTOCFG system value:                         │
│      1. Select option 7 (Define or change the system) on the system │
│                                                         More... │
│  F3=Exit help    F10=Move to top    F12=Cancel    F13=Information Assistant │
│  F14=Print help                                                 │
└──────────────────────────────────────────────────────────────────┘
```

The system displays information about how to change the QAUTOCFG system value. The text presented describes the purpose of the QAUTOCFG system value, and what happens when it is given every valid value. Because the information is longer than would fit on a single screen, the system has placed the "More" indicator at the bottom of the screen. You can then use the Roll keys to see the remaining pages of information.

FURTHER READING

IBM's *New User's Guide*.

IBM's *System Operator's Guide*.

IBM's *CL Reference*.

Part III:
Administration

10

System Values

Section 1: Overview

What Are System Values?

Much of the overall behavior of the system is dictated by what are known as system values. System values are not objects like programs and files because they cannot be created or deleted; they can only be changed and displayed.

There are nearly 100 system values. Some of them control system performance, others control security, others provide defaults to common settings. A complete discussion of system values is beyond the scope of this book, which concentrates only on a few of the most important ones.

System Value References

Many commands accept *SYSVAL as a valid value in certain parameters. *SYSVAL is a reference to a system value. When you use *SYSVAL, the system uses the current system value.

For example, in the Create User Profile (CRTUSRPRF) command one of the parameters is ATNPGM, which determines what program to run when the user presses the Attention key (Attn). ATNPGM accepts *SYSVAL. If you choose *SYSVAL, the user profile points to the appropriate system value which is named QATNPGM, and contains the name of the program required in the CRTUSRPRF's ATNPGM parameter.

The advantage to using *SYSVAL is obvious. If you want to give most of your users the same attention-key program, you would be better off plugging its name in system value QATNPGM and using ATNPGM(*SYSVAL) in the user profiles. That way, you can change all those users with a single keystroke by only changing the system value.

Section 2: Managing System Values

As mentioned at the beginning of this chapter, system values cannot be created or deleted because they are not objects. For the same reason, they cannot be secured either. Only three operations are allowed on system values: listing, displaying and changing.

Each system value has a name. In most cases the name is made up using a method similar to that of naming commands: by putting together several abbreviations. This method makes system value names easy to remember. All system value names begin with the letter Q.

Listing System Values

The Work with System Values (WRKSYSVAL) command lists system values either on the display or on the printer.

If you select the printer, you get a report with the system values listed alphabetically by name along with their description, current value, and the value they had originally when the system was shipped to you. The report also marks the system values that no longer have the original value.

Whether you select a displayed or printed listing, you can select either all system values, a certain group of them, or a single one. All you need to do is provide a different value to the SYSVAL parameter. For example, you can print a list that includes all system values as follows:

```
WRKSYSVAL SYSVAL(*ALL) OUTPUT(*PRINT)
```

You can also display a list of all security-related system values:

```
WRKSYSVAL SYSVAL(*SEC) OUTPUT(*)
```

☛ You should obtain a printed list of all system values immediately after you change any of them even slightly. You should keep this listing in a safe place. By doing this, you can restore your system values to the way you had them, if they become corrupted. System values can become corrupted, in the sense that they change values unexpectedly when you upgrade your AS/400 to a new release of the operating system.

Displaying System Values

Use the Display System Value (DSPSYSVAL) command to display individual system values. You need to know the name of the system value. For example, you can check the system date by displaying system value QDATE:

```
DSPSYSVAL SYSVAL(QDATE)
```

If you do not know the name of the system value, you can use WRKSYSVAL to list them on the screen. Then you can use the Roll keys until you find the system value you need. At that point, you can key in option 5 and press Enter.

If you use the DSPSYSVAL command, you also can direct the output to the printer by specifying OUTPUT(*PRINT), as follows:

```
DSPSYSVAL SYSVAL(QDATE) OUTPUT(*PRINT)
```

Remember that if you want to print all system values or those that belong in a particular group, you can use WRKSYSVAL.

Changing System Values

Use the Change System Value (CHGSYSVAL) command to change an individual system value. You need to know the name of the system value and the type of value it expects. Most system values contain character data.

Changing a system value can change the way the system operates. Some changes to system values take effect immediately, others become effective the next time a user signs on, and others do not become effective until you IPL the system.

☛ A much easier way to change system values is by using the WRKSYSVAL command, finding the proper system value, and keying in option 2. The panel informs you about the values and their meanings. If you use the CHGSYSVAL command, the command prompter gives you a generic input field and no information about the system value you are about to change.

Section 3: Date, Time And Edit System Values

The system clock has two parts: a system date and a system time. Both parts are controlled by system values, and changing these system values takes effect immediately. All date and time system values are in character format.

System Date

The system date is contained in system value QDATE. The system date is subdivided in three parts: day, month, and year, which are contained in system values QDAY, QMONTH and QYEAR. System value QDATFMT dictates in what order these subdivisions are put together in QDATE.

If you live in the United States, you probably want to set QDATFMT to the value MDY. This causes May 3, 1993 to appear as 05/03/93. If you live in Mexico, however, QDATFMT should be set to DMY. The same date would then appear as 03/05/93. Other valid values are YMD (so the year appears first) and JUL (for pseudo-Julian dates YYDDD, where YY is the year and DDD is a sequential number between 1 and 366).

One additional system value related to the system date is QDATSEP. There are several options, and each one uses a different character as the separator. For example, if you put a value of '1' in QDATSEP, the system date appears as 05/03/93. If you use '2', it would appear as 05-03-93. You have three other choices: a period, a comma, or a blank space.

System Time

The system time is contained in system value QTIME. Like the system date, the system time also is subdivided in three parts: hours (QHOUR), minutes (QMINUTE) and seconds (QSECOND). System time differs from system date, however, in that there are no options for formatting the system time because the format HHMMSS is used throughout the world. There is, however, a system value that controls what character is used to separate the subdivisions: QTIMSEP.

QTIMSEP has four options. For example, '1' causes the system to use a colon (:), so noon appears as 12:00:00. You can also select a period, a comma, or a blank space.

☞ Because changing the date and time system values takes effect immediately, you can reset your system clock by changing the appropriate system value.

For example, when Daylight Savings Time begins, you can adjust the time by changing QHOUR. You do not have to change the whole system time (QTIME), just the hour:

```
CHGSYSVAL SYSVAL(QHOUR) VALUE('07')
```

This command changes the hour portion to 07. When Daylight Savings Time ends, you can change QHOUR again.

Editing System Values

In addition to QDATFMT, QDATSEP and QTIMSEP, which edit dates and times, there are two other editing system values:

- QCURSYM, which contains a single character that will be used as the currency symbol in application programs.

- QDECFMT, which controls what character is used for the decimal mark. You can select between a blank (period for decimal, zero suppression), I (comma for decimal, zero suppression) and J (comma for decimal, one leading zero).

Section 4: Security System Values

Many of the most important system values fall in the category of security system values. These system values are important because they control the workings of the system-supplied security such as authorizations, auditing, and password management. A system value can have five different values.

Security Level

Of all security system values, the most important is QSECURITY. QSECURITY controls the level of system security provided by OS/400. It can have five different values:

- 10: The system has no security whatsoever. Anyone can sign on without being set up first. The system asks for a user profile name at the sign-on display, but you can enter anything. No password is required or allowed. Once someone is in the system, he can do everything.

- 20: The system requires entry of a valid user profile name and a password when the user signs on. The user profile must have been created beforehand. Once someone is in the system, however, he can do everything.

- 30: User profile name and password are required to sign on. After signing on, the system checks authorities every time the user attempts to start a task. Level 30 is the recommended security level.

- 40: Similar to level 30, but the system does not allow access to system objects except through "proper channels." Level 40 gives the system administrator tighter security which protects the system from enterprising MI programmers and computer hackers.

- 50: Somewhat tighter than 40. System objects are protected not only by invalidating unsupported interfaces, but by enforcing proper parameter values in those interfaces that are supported.

☞ In order to change from one security level to another, you must change QSECURITY and perform an IPL. The new security level does not become effective until after the IPL.

Default Public Authority Upon Creation

Beginning with V2R1, OS/400 lets you customize the public authority given by default when an object is created in a library. All create (CRTxxx) commands have an AUT parameter, which now supports special value *LIBCRTAUT. This special value points to the CRTAUT parameter of the library where you are creating the object.

For example, suppose you want to create a data area in library MYLIB. When you created MYLIB, you specified CRTAUT(*USE). If you now specify AUT(*LIBCRTAUT) when you create the data area in MYLIB, the data area will have a public authority of *USE:

```
CRTLIB LIB(MYLIB) CRTAUT(*USE)
CRTDTAARA DTAARA(MYLIB/MYDTAARA) ... AUT(*LIBCRTAUT)
```

Library MYLIB also could have been created with CRTAUT(*SYSVAL). In this case, the CRTLIB command references system value QCRTAUT:

Chapter 10 - System Values

```
CHGSYSVAL SYSVAL(QCRTAUT) VALUE('*USE')
CRTLIB LIB(MYLIB) CRTAUT(*SYSVAL)
CRTDTAARA DTAARA(MYLIB/MYDTAARA) ... AUT(*LIBCRTAUT)
```

The Create Data Area (CRTDTAARA) command looks up the library's CRTAUT parameter, which is *SYSVAL. This makes the system look up system value QCRTAUT, where it finds *USE. The net result is that the public authority for the data area is *USE.

Initially, QCRTAUT has the value *CHANGE. This default value is good in most cases, so you really should think twice before you change it.

If you are working in the S/36 environment, be sure to create your files library (QS36F or otherwise) with CRTAUT(*ALL). You should do this because S/36E software creates and deletes work files liberally. If one user creates a work file and another user had to delete it, you would run into trouble.

Idle Display Stations

When a user signs on to a display station and walks away without signing off, the display station is ready for use by anyone who happens to walk by. This situation poses a security risk The severity of this risk depends on the security classification and authorities of the user who signed on.

Consider what would happen if QSECOFR (who can do everything) left a display station unattended. Anyone would be able to do anything from that display station! If you want to keep security tight on your system, you need to control these unattended display stations.

System value QINACTITV determines how long a display station is allowed to remain inactive (no function keys or Enter pressed). When the specified time interval (in minutes) passes, the system takes an action that is controlled by system value QINACTMSGO.

QINACTMSGQ can contain the qualified name of a message queue. In this case, the system sends a message to that message queue. QINACTMSGQ can also have two special values: *ENDJOB and *DSCJOB. If you choose *ENDJOB, the system ends the interactive job of the inactive display station (i.e. the system signs it off automatically). If you choose *DSCJOB, the system disconnects the display station. Here is an example:

```
CHGSYSVAL SYSVAL(QINACTITV) VALUE('30')
CHGSYSVAL SYSVAL(QINATCMSGQ) VALUE('*DSCJOB')
```

With these settings, the system waits 30 minutes for the user to press a function key or Enter. If the user does not do so, the system disconnects the display station and shows the sign-on display. A message appears at the bottom, saying that user QSYS disconnected the job. When the user returns, he will have to enter the User profile name and password again, but the system will take the user back where he left off, with everything intact.

☛ You should consider activating this feature with the *DSCJOB option. All things considered, the message queue alone does not give you much security (the display station remains signed on, although there are complicated ways you can improve on this). On the other hand, the *ENDJOB option seems too harsh and can result in lost data if the user was in the middle of a complicated transaction when he went on his coffee break.

An additional system value, QDSCJOBITV, controls how long a job can remain disconnected before the system ends it. You can use this system value in conjunction with the *DSCJOB option to follow-up on jobs the system disconnected for being inactive. For example, you can set QDSCJOBITV to 60 minutes:

```
CHGSYSVAL SYSVAL(QDSCJOBITV) VALUE('60')
```

Password Management

Several system values control passwords. These system values are:

- QPWDEXPITV controls how long the user can keep his password without being forced to change it. It defaults to *NOMAX, which means that the system does not care how long this duration is. You should consider setting this system value to a value no greater than 60, although 30 may be safer.

- QPWDMINLEN and QPWDMAXLEN control the minimum and maximum lengths allowed for a password. When the system is shipped to you, these system values are set to 1 and 10, respectively. Passwords that consist of a single character are not very difficult to guess. Consider changing QPWDMINLEN to at least 4 or 5. If you work on both a S/36 and an AS/400 and want to use the same password on both systems, then you can force users to have 4-character passwords (all passwords on the S/36 are 4 characters) by changing both QPWDMINLEN and QPWDMAXLEN to 4.

- QPWDLMTAJC can be set to '1' if you do not want your users to have passwords with more than one digit in a row.

Chapter 10 - System Values

- QPWDLMTCHR can contain a string of characters. None of the characters in the string will be allowed in passwords. For example, if you set QPWDLMTCHR to 'DOG,' passwords will not be allowed to contain the letters D, O or G.

- QPWDLMTREP will not allow repeated characters in a password if you set it to '1.' This prevents users from using easily guessed passwords such as XXXX.

- QPWDPOSDIF can be set to '1' if you do not want users to change to a new password with characters in the same position as the old one. Each character in the new password must differ from the same positional character in the old one. For example, if the user has a password of BUTTERFLY, he cannot change it to HATCHET because both passwords have a T in the third position.

- QPWDRQDDGT forces the user to use at least one digit (0 to 9) in the password. Passwords containing digits are less significant, and therefore less likely to be guessed.

- QPWDRQDDIF forbids the user to re-use a password. The system keeps track of the last 32 passwords each user has had. Users can begin recycling passwords after the 32nd.

- QPWDVLDPGM can contain the qualified name of a program that you can create to perform additional validation checking on new passwords, if the password is being changed with the Change Password (CHGPWD) command.

Sign-On Control

The system also has a few system values that control signing on. These system values provide an additional layer of security, and you should consider implementing them.

- QDSPSGNINF, when set to '1,' displays a panel each time a user signs on. This panel informs the user the last time he signed on, and whether there have been any invalid sign-on attempts using his user profile name. This panel is useful when you suspect there is someone who is signing on with your name. You can activate this feature at the user profile level, so some users get the information panel and others do not. Change the user profile with DSPSGNINF(*YES). If you choose *SYSVAL, the system uses this system value to determine whether or not to display the panel.

- QLMTDEVSSN can be set to '1' if you do not want your users to be able to sign on to more than one display station. This can discourage users from leaving their own terminals signed on, but it can also prevent a user from signing on to another display station when there is a legitimate need for it.

- QLMTSECOFR can be set to '1' if you want to restrict QSECOFR to sign on to the system console only. It is a good idea to leave this system value with its default value of '0' so QSECOFR can sign on anywhere.

- QMAXSIGN indicates how many times a user is allowed to make mistakes during sign-on. This system value is originally set to 15, which is exceedingly high. This value offers ample chance for someone to try to sign on by guessing someone else's password. You should consider reducing this value to five attempts (at most). A value of three is probably even better.

- QMAXSGNACN controls what happens when the maximum number of invalid sign-ons (indicated by QMAXSIGN) is reached. A value of '1' varies off the display station. A value of '2' disables the user profile. A value of '3' does both.

    ☞ A value of '1' is dangerous when your AS/400 is in a restricted state ("dedicated") and only the system console is varied on. If you make mistakes when signing on, you may lose the system console and be forced to IPL the system to regain it. Using a value of '2' is safer.

Section 5: Library List System Values

Two system values control the library list initially assigned to new jobs. System value QSYSLIBL is always used to determine the system portion of the library list. QUSRLIBL, however, is used only if the job description used to start the job has *SYSVAL in the INLLIBL parameter. For example, when a user signs on, the job description used is the one referenced in the user profile's JOBD parameter. When you submit a job to batch with the SBMJOB command, the JOBD parameter names the job description.

System Portion

System value QSYSLIBL can contain a list of up to 15 library names. These libraries are considered to be in the system portion of the library list. QSYSLIBL should always contain library QSYS.

If you change QSYSLIBL, existing jobs are not affected. New jobs started after the change, however, will use the new system portion of the library list.

☞ You should consider creating a user library (call it ALTQSYS) and place it before QSYS in the system portion of the library list. Then you can place objects you have duplicated from QSYS and changed in this library. Your copies will be used instead

Chapter 10 - System Values

of the original objects from QSYS. Using this technique you can modify commands and other system objects without actually changing the originals.

User Portion

System value QUSRLIBL can contain up to 25 library names, which will make up the user portion of the library list. If you use QUSRLIBL, make sure the job descriptions reference INLLIBL(*SYSVAL).

Different users have different library list requirements so as a general rule it is better to use job descriptions to control the user portion of the library list.

Section 6: System Control System Values

Many aspects of the system configuration and control are maintained through system values. These system values are very important, and in some cases are not changeable.

Some Unchangeable System Values

There are a few system values you can display but cannot change:

- QABNORMSW indicates how the system was ended last time.
- QIPLSTS shows what kind of IPL was performed last time.
- QMODEL contains the AS/400 model of your system, such as B10, D45 or E90.
- QSRLNBR contains the serial number of the CPU of your system.
- QSTRPRTWTR indicates whether to start printer writers at IPL. The only way you can change this system value is by performing an attended IPL because the system asks if you want to start printer writers at that time.

Device-Related System Values

The following system values are related to devices (displays and printers) in some way.

AS/400 Primer

- QAUTOCFG determines whether the system can configure new devices automatically. When you set this system value to '1,' the system creates a device description for any new local display or printer device that is connected and powered on.

  Although you do not have to run the Create Device (CRTDEVxxx) command yourself, the disadvantage is that you relinquish control over the device name. See system value QDEVNAMING, below.

- QCONSOLE cannot be changed. It contains the name of the display device you have connected to port 0, address 0 of the first workstation controller. This display is also known as the system console. If you want to rename the system console, you need to vary off the console, delete its device description, create a new one, and vary it back on. The next time you IPL the system, QCONSOLE reflects the change in name.

- QDEVNAMING indicates what naming convention the system uses when configuring local devices automatically (per QAUTOCFG, explained above).

  *NORMAL gives new local devices names like DSPxx and PRTxx, where xx is a sequential number from 01 to 99. This is the default setting.

  *DEVADR gives new local devices names based on their address (workstation controller, port number and switch setting). The device names are DSPccppss (or PRTccppss), where **cc** is a two-digit number that represents the workstation controller, **pp** is another two-digit number that represents the port number, and **ss** is a third two-digit number representing the switch setting. For example, DSP010305 is the display station connected to the first workstation controller, port 3, switch setting 5.

  *S36 gives new local device names following the System/36 naming convention of only two characters: **Wn** for display stations and **Pn** for printers, where **n** is usually a digit (although it does not have to be).

- QDSCJOBITV controls how long (in minutes) a disconnected job can remain active until the system automatically ends it. If your users have a bad habit of disconnecting their jobs and forgetting about them, you can set QDSCJOBITV to 60 so that your users have a full hour to reconnect before they lose their interactive job. If this sounds harsh, remember that each job (even disconnected ones) has to be maintained by the system, and therefore reduces the overall performance of the system.

- QPRTDEV contains the name of the system printer. You can change this system value anytime. This system value is referenced by the user profile, job, or job description's PRTDEV parameters when it has the value *SYSVAL.

Power Up and Down System Values

The behavior of the system during power up and power down is controlled by a few system values:

- QCTLSBSD contains the qualified name of the controlling subsystem description. During IPL, the system starts the controlling subsystem and runs the start-up program. By default, this system value has the value QBASE. You should consider changing it to QCTL in order to better control performance of your system. See Chapter 4 for more information about subsystems.

- QIPLDATTIM can contain a date and time when you want the system to automatically power on and IPL itself. For example, you can change this system value to '070192   053000' and then power off the system. At 5:30 a.m. on July 1, 1992, the system will power on and IPL by itself.

    Operational Assitant now provides an automatic power up/down schedule, which has rendered this system value useless for manual (direct) manipulation. See Chapter 2 for more information.

- QPWRDWNLMT controls how long the system will wait for jobs to finish when executing a PWRDWNSYS OPTION(*IMMED). The default is 600 seconds (10 minutes). If jobs are still executing when this time interval expires, the system performs an abnormal system termination. This abnormal system termination is recorded in system value QABNORMSW. The next IPL will take much longer than usual.

- QSTRUPPGM contains the qualified name of a program. The system runs this program during IPL. When the system is shipped to you, this system value contains the name QSYS/QSTRUP. You can create your own start-up program (in CL, because you will need to run commands) and change QSTRUPPGM to contain the qualified name of your program.

Interactive Job System Values

When a user signs on, some of the attributes for the interactive job are drawn from a job description, from the user profile, or both. If any of these attributes is set to *SYSVAL, the appropriate system value is referenced.

- QASTLVL indicates how much assistance to provide the user in certain system-related commands such as Display Message (DSPMSG). QASTLVL can contain *BASIC (give the user as much assistance as possible), *INTERMED (minimal assistance) or *ADVANCED (no assistance).

At first, you should leave this system value to *BASIC. As you and your users gain experience, you can change it to *INTERMED or *ADVANCED. This attribute can be controlled at the user profile level with the ASTLVL parameter of the Create User Profile (CRTUSRPRF) or Change User Profile (CHGUSRPRF) commands.

- QATNPGM contains the qualified name of a program. The system executes this program when the user presses the Attention (Attn) key. You can control this attribute at the user profile level, too. If you use the value *ASSIST, the Attention key displays Operational Assistant's main menu. A value of *NONE disables the Attention key (it does nothing).

- QPRTKEYFMT indicates what format to use for the printed output when the user presses the Print key. *PRTHDR prints a header which identifies the user who pressed the Print key. *PRTBDR prints a rectangular border around the screen facsimile, with scales and line numbers. *PRTALL prints both the header and the border. *NONE only prints the facsimile itself. You should consider using *PRTALL, or at least *PRTHDR. This attribute can be controlled at the job level.

- QSPCENV controls which environment the user's interactive job is run in. *NONE runs the job in native environment. *S36 runs the interactive job in the System/36 environment. When you select *S36, the user is taken to the S/36 environment upon sign-on, and out of it when signing off. This attribute can be controlled at the user profile level.

FURTHER READING

IBM's *Work Management Guide.*

11

Elements Of Security and Configuration

System security is a very serious matter. When security is well implemented, your system is relatively safe from sabotage (intentional or not). At the same time, security prevents unauthorized users from becoming privy to such as employee records and secret financial or manufacturing data.

Security is a complex topic that deserves a whole book by itself. This chapter contains only basic information and does not attempt to paint a complete picture. You should refer to the AS/400's *Security Concepts and Planning Guide* for a more extensive treatment of the matter.

Section 1: Introduction

Authorities

AS/400 security is based on the concept of authority. Authority links an object (such as a file or a program) to a user (such as yourself or QSYSOPR). The authority determines whether the user can be given access to the object, and what kind of access he may have.

For example, if you have a file named EMPLOYEES in a given library, you can instruct the system to allow user JOSIE (who manages the Personnel department) full access to it. JOSIE would then be able to read EMPLOYEES, update it, delete records, reorganize the records, and perform all other operations to the file. At the same time, user PETER could be given only enough authority to read EMPLOYEES, but make no changes. If PETER runs a program that attempts to add a new employee to the file, the program ends with an error. You can also say that all other users should have no authority at all. In this case, user STEVE can neither read nor update the file.

Here is a brief summary of all the object authorities you can use:

Authority	Description
*OBJOPR	Object Operational. Allows the user to operate the object according to the data authorities that may be given (*READ, *ADD, *UPD and *DLT). It also allows the user to look at the description of the object.
*OBJMGT	Object Management. Allows the user to manage the object; i.e., to maintain security for the object, move it to another library (MOVOBJ), or rename it (RNMOBJ). If the object is a database file, the user can also add members to it (ADDPFM, ADDLFM).
*OBJEXIST	Object Existence. Allows the user to control the existence of the object and who should be its owner. The user can run the following commands on the object: DLTxxx, SAVOBJ with STG(*FREE), SAVOBJ, RSTOBJ and CHGOBJOWN. Note that if the user already has *SAVSYS special authority (defined later), he does not need *OBJEXIST to save or restore any objects.
*OBJALTER	New in V3R1. Used to control who can alter the attributes of database files and SQL packages, such as maintaining triggers, referential integrity, or other attributes.
*OBJREF	New in V3R1. Used only for database files. It authorizes the user to reference an object from another.
*READ	Data authority required to display the contents of an object. For a database file, *READ is required to read records.
*ADD	Data authority required to add entries to an object. For a database file, *ADD is required to write new records.

Chapter 11 - Elements Of Security and Configuration

Authority	Description
*UPD	Data authority required to change entries in an object. For a database file, *UPD is required to update existing records.
*DLT	Data authority required to remove entries from an object. For a database file, *DLT is required to delete existing records.
*EXECUTE	New in V3R1. It allows the user to locate an object in a library, and to run a program.

For your convenience, you can also use standard "combinations" provided by IBM. These combinations come in handy:

Combination	Description
*ALL	Equivalent to all object authorities together: *OBJOPR, *OBJMGT, *OBJEXIST, *OBJALTER, *OBJREF, *READ, *ADD, *UPD, *DLT, and *EXECUTE. The user can do anything with the object, except whatever can only be done by the object's owner or controlled by an authorization list. When a user creates an object, that user automatically acquires *ALL authority to the object.
*CHANGE	Equivalent to *OBJOPR, *READ, *ADD, *UPD, *DLT, and *EXECUTE.
*USE	Equivalent to *OBJOPR, *READ, and *EXECUTE.
*EXCLUDE	No authorities whatsoever. The user cannot do anything with the object. He cannot even look at it.

Private Authorities

Authorities can be assigned to specific users. For example, the security administrator can give user CHARLIE enough authority to *READ the inventory master file, without allowing him to change or delete existing records or add new ones. This is called a *private* authority because it applies to one user and one only.

Private authorities are given by entering an actual user profile name (such as CHARLIE).

Public Authorities

In contrast with private authorities, *public* authorities are those given to the users in general. When an object such as a file is created, the creator (or the security administrator) decides what authority to give the public. Usually (although not necessarily), this authority is *CHANGE, which means that the user can read, update, or delete records from the file.

When the security administrator begins assigning private authorities to individual users, these private authorities override the public authority, they become exceptions to the rule.

For example, a programmer creates a file named ORDERS and gives the public *CHANGE authority. Then the security administrator grants user FRED *READ authority, and user FRANK *EXCLUDE authority.

When user JEREMY signs on, he has *CHANGE authority because he has not been given any private authority to file ORDERS, so he enjoys the public's authority. When user FRANK signs on, he has *EXCLUDE authority because the security administrator specifically gave him that authority.

Special Authorities

Special authorities are different from private and public authorities. Special authorities give the user authorization to perform certain system-related functions, while private/public authorities give the user authorization to manipulate objects.

There are six different special authorities. Users can have one or more of them in any combination; they also can have none at all.

Special Authority	Description
*SAVSYS	Save System. Gives the user authorization to perform any save or restore operation, even on objects to which the user is not authorized through private or public authorities. For example, a system operator may not be authorized to read the Employee master file, but if he has *SAVSYS authority he can perform all the necessary save and restore operations to have a proper backup.

Chapter 11 - Elements Of Security and Configuration

Special Authority	Description
*JOBCTL	Job Control. Gives the user authorization to maintain other user's jobs. System operators need this special authority. The user can display or change all jobs, and manipulate all printed output if the reports are in output queues that have OPRCTL(*YES). *JOBCTL also gives the user the authorization to reload the operating system, perform an IPL, and control printer writers and subsystems.
*ALLOBJ	All Objects. Gives the user authority to perform any operation on any object. This special authority overrides all private/public authorities on the system, so you must make sure which users really need it. Once they have *ALLOBJ, users can read, change or delete any file, execute any program or command, add, update and delete records from any file, etc. Do not give *ALLOBJ authority unnecessarily.
*SECADM	Security Administrator. Gives the user authority to maintain user profiles if the user has private/public authority to the Create, Change and Delete User Profile commands (CRTUSRPRF, CHGUSRPRF and DLTUSRPRF), and private/public authority to the user profile object (*USRPRF) being maintained. The user also can only grant those special authorities he has himself. Therefore, a security administrator who does not have *ALLJOB cannot give *ALLJOB to another user.
*SERVICE	Service. Gives a user the authority to run the service functions such as the System Service Tools (SST). Do not give *SERVICE special authority to anyone without first determining that the user really needs it to fulfill his duties. Only key system operators should have *SERVICE authority.
*SPLCTL	Spool Control. Gives the user the authority to control printed output in any output queue. Before you decide to give *SPLCTL to a user, think about confidential reports waiting in output queues. A user with *SPLCTL authority is able to display them.
*AUDIT	Auditing. Gives the user the necessary authority to perform auditing functions such as changing QAUDxxx system values and changing user profile or object auditing.
*IOSYSCFG	New in V3R1. Created to control access to new commands, also added in V3R1, to configure communictations. *IOSYSCFG gives the user authorization to change how the system is configured.

☞ Do not give your users more authority than they need to perform their jobs. Although it would simplify your job to give every user *ALLOBJ special authority, for example, it also would completely negate security level 30 and provide open doors everywhere.

Security Levels

OS/400 provides five levels of security called 10, 20, 30, 40 and 50 in order of increasing security.

When you install the AS/400, it comes with security level 10, which provides no security at all. Under level 10, the sign-on display does not even ask for a password; all the user has to do is type a user profile name, and he can enter any name because the computer does not check it for accuracy. Because of this extreme lassitude, security level 10 is not recommended unless you are a software developer working at home (with the AS/400 sitting next to your desk) and the system is not accessible by anyone either physically or remotely by telephone.

Level 20 is somewhat better. When you change the level to 20, the sign-on display requires a password to sign on in addition to the user name. Both are checked for accuracy, and the correct password must be entered for the right user profile name. However, once you pass the sign-on display barrier, the system imposes no other obstacles on you. You can do anything you want and so can anyone else who signs on successfully. Any user can create or change other users, configure the system or gain access to all database files.

Level 20 is better than 10, but still is not enough security in most cases. Level 20 is acceptable for installations where users are never given a chance to enter commands but are forced to select options from a menu (which has been designed so that it contains only the required options). Even then there are possible security risks involved.

Level 30 probably is the best security level. Not only is the user forced to supply a valid user profile name and password, but the system checks authorities every time the user attempts to perform a task. Level 30 involves more work for the security administrator because he or she has to define the authorities for all users, but the system is considerably more secure than at level 20. If your company ever experiences a security audit, your AS/400 will fail the test if it is at level 20.

Level 30 seems like a tremendous amount of work, but there are many tools in OS/400 that simplify the management and maintenance of object authorities. There are also many techniques that can simplify the task considerably.

Chapter 11 - Elements Of Security and Configuration

Level 40 is almost identical to level 30 except that under level 40, programs cannot access objects except through "proper channels." When an MI program attempts to access a "system" object (as opposed to a "user" object), the MI program fails. For this reason, IBM claims that security level 40 affords system integrity. This feature is also why level 40 probably can thwart most computer hackers.

Many utility software packages on the market perform extremely useful functions, but they all are invalidated if your system runs under level 40. Unless your system can fall in the hands of MI programmers, level 40 will not do you much good.

Level 50 is even more restrictive than level 40. Under level 40, you can still access some system objects via "supported interfaces," by supplying reserved or invalid parameter values to IBM-supplied programs or APIs. Level 50 blocks this avenue as well.

Changing Security Levels

To go from one security level to another (to either increase or decrease security), you only need to perform two tasks: change system value QSECURITY to the new value and then IPL the system.

For example, suppose your system is running under level 20 and you wish to change it to level 30. Do the following:

PWRDWNSYS RESTART(*YES)

When IPL completes, the system will be running under level 30. Note that the level number is enclosed in single quotes.

Section 2: User Profiles

User profiles are important objects (type *USRPRF) because they identify a user to the system. The name of this object is the name the user needs to type at the sign-on display under "User profile."

User profiles are also the vehicle the system uses to set up an interactive environment when the user signs on. User profiles contain many attribute settings such as the name of the output queue or printer used by default, the name of the Attention key handling program and job description.

☞ Never allow two people to share a user profile. Although you cannot be expected to play police and keep people from disclosing each other's passwords or using each other's user profiles, you can take steps to minimize this practice. Specifically, do not give two or more people the same user profile.

Naming User Profiles

All user profiles must reside in QSYS. Therefore, there can be no duplicate user profiles in the system. You should decide, before you install the system (if possible) on a convenient naming system for your user profiles.

Resist the temptation to name the user profiles with the user's first or last name or a nickname. The system will not object if you create a user profile named JOHN, but you are likely to have more than one person named John in your company, and the system accepts no duplicates.

Using last names reduces the risk of duplication, but does not eliminate it. Even if two or more people are not related in any way, they may share the same last name.

In reality, there is no bulletproof method to avoid duplication unless you use some unique identification that cannot be repeated in your company, such as employee numbers or Social Security Numbers. However, people other than employees may need access to your computer (such as a consultant or someone who rents computer time from you), so the employee number idea will not work. Social Security Numbers are unique, but people might resent being identified by numbers. Users are people, and people want names.

The following naming system can be used with satisfactory results: Combine the last name and the first name into the user profile. Pick the first three letters of each name and put them together. For example, if a user is called Dorian Gray, his user profile would be GRADOR. Florence Nightingale's user profile would be NIGFLO. If you decide to use this naming system, be aware that once in a while you may create a user profile name that is not acceptable when spoken. Always say the new name aloud before you cast it in stone.

Maintaining User Profiles

User profiles can be created, changed, deleted and displayed. OS/400 provides several commands for the security administrator's use. CRTUSRPRF creates a new user profile.

Chapter 11 - Elements Of Security and Configuration

CHGUSRPRF changes an existing profile. DLTUSRPRF deletes an existing user. DSPUSRPRF shows a user profile's information on the screen or on paper, and Work with User Profiles (WRKUSRPRF), presents a list of user profiles on the screen (sorted by name). You can easily run any of the other commands from this panel as well.

The CRTUSRPRF and CHGUSRPRF commands have many parameters. This book will not attempt to describe them. Instead, you should review the information presented in either the *Security Concepts and Planning Guide* or the *CL Reference Guide*.

Let's review the most important parameters of the CRTUSRPRF command to give you an idea of how it is used.

The USRPRF parameter actually gives the user profile its name. PASSWORD assigns the sign-on password. When you create a new user profile, you should assign the new user a standard password such as TEMP, or make the password equal to the user profile name. However, you should specify PWDEXP(*YES), which tells the system that the user's password is expired. PWDEXP(*YES) forces the new user to change the password right after he signs on for the first time.

Two parameters, USRCLS (user class) and SPCAUT (special authority) are interrelated. Actually, SPCAUT is the one parameter that counts when the new user is given authority to perform system-type activities such as saving and restoring or controlling jobs or printers. For instance, SPCAUT(*JOBCTL) informs the system that the new user is allowed to display and change information pertaining to other users' jobs. The user actually can cancel jobs unconditionally. If you specify SPCAUT(*USRCLS), however, the system looks at the USRCLS parameter to determine how much special authority it needs to give the user. This is the only time the USRCLS parameter is referenced. If you specify any value other than *USRCLS in the SPCAUT parameter, the USRCLS parameter does nothing.

For example, suppose you create a user profile with USRCLS(*SECOFR) SPCAUT(*NONE). Although the user has been classified as a security officer, he has no special authority at all because the SPCAUT parameter takes precedence over USRCLS.

INLPGM (initial program) determines what program to run when the user signs on. CURLIB (current library) indicates which library will be considered the "current" library for the user when he signs on. INLMNU (initial menu) determines what menu to show when the user signs on, after the INLPGM finishes. If you specify INLMNU(*SIGNOFF), the user is signed off automatically when the INLPGM ends.

LMTCPB (limited capabilities) tells the system that the user must be restricted in certain ways. LMTCPB(*YES) will not let the user override his INLPGM, CURLIB or INLMNU by typing different values at the sign-on display. The user also cannot run most commands from the command line, except such innocuous commands like DSPMSG, DSPJOB, DSPJOBLOG, SNDMSG and SIGNOFF.

MSGQ (message queue) names the message queue that is to accumulate the messages sent to the user. It is a good idea to leave the default value so the message queue is named after the user profile itself. Using the default simplifies your job considerably.

OUTQ (output queue) and PRTDEV (printer device) control where the system sends reports requested by the user. The OUTQ parameter is more important. Unless OUTQ(*DEV) is specified, the PRTDEV parameter does nothing.

ATNPGM (Attention key handling program) names the program to execute when the user presses the Attention key.

☛ Finally, the TEXT parameter is optional, but you should get into the habit of using it as if it were mandatory. Enter the user's full name and department in the TEXT parameter to document your users.

Section 3: Group Profiles And Authorization Lists

You could have your user profiles scattered all over the place, without organization, however, a nightmarish situation occurs when you have to maintain authorities on dozens of individual user profiles.

Group profiles and authorization lists are two ways to simplify the administrative part of system security. Group profiles and authorization lists let you make sets of users (or objects) and manipulate authorities as a group at the set level.

Even if you never plan to go to security level 30, group profiles let you group your users and achieve some amount of organization.

The concepts of group profiles and authorization lists are complex. A full discussion of these topics is beyond the scope of this book.

Group Profiles

A *group profile* is a user profile like any other, which you create with the CRTUSRPRF command. What makes group profiles different from "regular" user profiles is that a group profile appears in the GRPPRF parameter of one or more other user profiles.

Chapter 11 - Elements Of Security and Configuration

Group profiles can be given any name. If you want to use a naming convention for your group profiles, consider giving them names that begin with the characters GRP (for "group"), followed by some significant name like ACG for Accounting or SAL for Sales.

This example creates a group profile for the Human Resources department. You can call it GRP_HUM. Note that the underscore character (_) is used to make the group profile name more readable:

```
CRTUSRPRF USRPRF (GRP_HUM) PASSWORD(*NONE) GRPPRF(NONE)   +
          TEXT('Group profile for Human Resources')
```

PASSWORD(*NONE) guarantees that no one will be able to sign on using the GRP_HUM profile, which forces users to sign on as themselves. GRPPRF(*NONE) is a requirement for all group profiles because group profiles cannot belong to another group profile. Because the GRPPRF parameter defaults to *NONE, normally you do not have to key in this parameter at all.

Now change users MARIA, LOURDES and WANDA, so they reference GRP_HUM as their group profile. Because all three users work in the Human Resources department; they reference GRP_HUM.

```
CHGUSRPRF USRPRF(MARIA)   GRPPRF(GRP_HUM)
CHGUSRPRF USRPRF(LOURDES) GRPPRF(GRP_HUM)
CHGUSRPRF USRPRF(WANDA)   GRPPRF(GRP_HUM)
```

From now on, you can authorize all three users to the same objects, in a single stroke, by authorizing their group profile, GRP_HUM.

There are two commands that come in handy when working with group profiles. First, you can list the users that belong to a group profile with the DSPUSRPRF TYPE(*GRPMBR):

```
DSPUSRPRF USRPRF(GRP_HUM) TYPE(*GRPMBR)
```

Then, you can list all user profiles, broken down by group profile in which they belong, with the DSPAUTUSR SEQ(*GRPPRF) command:

```
DSPAUTUSR SEQ(*GRPPRF) OUTPUT(*PRINT)
```

Authorization Lists

Authorization lists are objects of type *AUTL that always reside in QSYS. You can create them, delete them, and maintain their contents.

An authorization list can secure any number of objects by attaching the authorization list to the object it secures. Within the authorization list there are entries. Each entry contains a user profile name (or group profile) and an authority value such as *USE or *CHANGE.

By attaching the authorization list to an object, the object adopts the list of users and authorities contained within. For example, secure output queue QPRINT with an authorization list, which you can call AUTL_ONE, as follows:

```
CRTAUTLAUTL(AUTL_ONE)  AUT(*EXCLUDE)
GRTOBJAUT OBJ(QPRINT)  OBJTYPE(*OUTQ)  AUTL(AUTL_ONE)
```

The first command creates the authorization list. AUT(*EXCLUDE) ensures that no one except QSECOFR is allowed to maintain the authorization list.

The second command attaches QPRINT to AUTL_ONE. Up to this point, however, AUTL_ONE has been empty. A few entries are added as follows:

```
ADDAUTLE  AUTL(AUTL_ONE)  USER(VICKY)  AUT(*USE)
ADDAUTLE  AUTL(AUTL_ONE)  USER(GREG)   AUT(*CHANGE)
ADDAUTLE  AUTL(AUTL_ONE)  USER(KIM)    AUT(*ALL)
```

Because users VICKY, GREG and KIM are in the authorization list with *USE, *CHANGE and *ALL authorities (respectively), all objects secured with AUTL_ONE will share those authorities.

You can remove authorization list entries with the RMVAUTLE command, or use the Edit Authorization List (EDTAUTL) command to work interactively and visually (which is better).

There are two handy commands to work with authorization lists. The first one, DSPAUTL, displays the entries (user name and authority) contained in the authorization list. The second one, DSPAUTLOBJ, lists what objects are secured with a given authorization list.

Section 4: Device Descriptions

Device descriptions are objects (type *DEVD) that the system uses to store information about a peripheral device such as a display station, a printer, or a tape drive. This section will concentrate on the display stations and printers.

Chapter 11 - Elements Of Security and Configuration

Naming Device Descriptions

Device descriptions need to have reasonable names just as much as user profiles. If you use IBM's naming system (which is enforced when you use automatic configuration), you end up with entirely meaningless device description names such as DSP17 or PRT010203.

If you see a message at the system console that informs you that someone has attempted to sign on at display station DSP23 using an invalid user profile name, you probably will not know where is DSP23. It could be right next to you or at the other end of the building.

The following is a more meaningful naming system for display stations and printers (and even for all other device descriptions). The system uses three letters to abbreviate the location of the device, plus DSP or PRT, plus two digits for sequencing. The number 01 is always reserved for the department's manager.

Location abbreviations are entirely up to you. For example, you could use ACG for Accounting and INV for Inventory. The main printer in Accounting would then be ACGPRT01 and the Accounting manager's display station is ACGDSP01. Here are some suggestions for your device description names:

Location	Description
ACG	Accounting
ASY	Final Assembly
CNF	Conference Room
CSV	Customer Service
ENG	Engineering
FIN	Finance
HUM	Human Resources
INV	Inventory Control
LAB	Laboratory
LBY	Lobby (reception area)
MGT	Management
MKT	Marketing
MIS	Data Processing
OFC	General Office
OPS	Operations
PRD	Production Control
PUR	Purchasing
QLT	Quality Control
RCV	Receiving
SAL	Sales

```
SHM        Sheet Metal
SHP        Shipping
SYS        System (computer room)
WHS        Warehouse
```

There are few device types:

```
Device     Description
DKT        Diskette
DSP        Display
PRT        Printer
TAP        Tape
```

You can name your system console SYSDSP01 and your system printer SYSPRT01. The main tape drive can be SYSTAP01.

Maintaining Device Descriptions

You can create, change, delete and display device descriptions at any time. Whatever changes you make become effective immediately. The system does not require you to IPL it or perform any other major chore for your changes to be accepted. If at any time of the day you receive a call because the Marketing department needs an additional display station, you can plug it in, turn it on, connect it to the system, and begin using it.

If system value QAUTOCFG is set to '1', the system automatically takes care of the configuration of your local device descriptions, which are those that communicate with the system by regular cables and do not require telephone lines. In this case, you do not have to worry about creating the device descriptions. You only connect the new device, turn it on, wait less than a minute, and the system configures it for you, makes it ready, and presents the sign-on display. If the device is a printer, it will be ready to print.

The trouble with automatic configuration is that the system creates meaningless names for the devices. The first display station is named DSP01; the second station, DSP02; and so on. There also is a more subtle problem with automatic configuration: if you swap two different devices (for example a 5251 model 11 display station and a 3196 display station), the system sometimes deletes the old display stations and creates new ones because it senses that the models do not match anymore. This changes the old names of the two display stations. Instead of being DSP12 and DSP15, for example, they may become DSP38 and DSP39.

Chapter 11 - Elements Of Security and Configuration

☞ You are better off disengaging automatic configuration as soon as you become familiar with the commands used to configure devices manually. These commands are the Create Device Description commands (CRTDEVxxx), where xxx is DSP for display stations and PRT for printers. There are other possible values for xxx, but they are beyond the scope of this book.

You can change many (but not all) of the settings of a device description once it is created by using the corresponding Change Device Description (CHGDEV) command. Again, xxx can be replaced by DSP or PRT. You can also display a device description with the DSPDEVD command or delete the device descriptions with the Delete Device Description (DLTDEVD) command. Neither has xxx variations.

☞ You can also rename a device description with the Rename Object (RNMOBJ) command. The device description's message queue is automatically renamed. This provides a way to change the meaningless names given device descriptions by automatic configuration. Be sure to vary off the device before running RNMOBJ, and to vary it back on afterwards.

For example, if automatic configuration created DSP42 and you want to name it OFCDSP03, run the following command:

```
RNMOBJ OBJ(DSP42) OBJTYPE(*DEVD) NEWNAME(OFCDSP03)
```

Taking charge of this maintenance is not as bad as it seems. There is a Work with Device Descriptions (WRKDEVD) command that lists all available device descriptions. You can perform any of the device description commands from here, including making a copy with option 3. This copy function is great when you have just configured a new device description and you realize that now you must configure another one that is almost identical.

When you create a new local display device description, pay attention to the following parameters: TYPE and MODEL, which define the type of machine (for example, a 3477 model FC); CTL, PORT and SWTSET, which indicate where the new display is connected. CTL is the name of the workstation controller, which is usually CTL01. PORT is a number from 0 to 7, and SWTSET is a number from 0 to 6. OUTQ and PRTDEV name the default output queue and printer for whatever print jobs are requested from this display, and AUT tells the system what authority to give the public. Unless you have special security requirements, use a value of *CHANGE so that anyone can use the new display station.

Printers are somewhat different. They do not have OUTQ and PRTDEV parameters, but they have a MSGQ parameter, which names the message queue that is to receive the messages the system issues when something goes wrong with the printer (such as running out of paper or having a ribbon jam). You need to decide where you want to send these messages. Here are three suggestions:

1. Use QSYSOPR, which allows you to have a centralized message queue where you can see all the messages related to printers. Possible disadvantages are that QSYSOPR may be overly busy already without the additional burden of printer messages, and that the system operator may not be near the printer to correct the problem.

2. Use one message queue (other than QSYSOPR) for all printers. Doing this relieves QSYSOPR from that burden. Because any user with enough authority can display messages from the message queue, anyone can take corrective action (especially someone near the printer). A disadvantage of this scheme is that it provides little security. By replying to inquiry messages in this message queue, anyone authorized to do so would indirectly control all printers.

3. Create a separate message queue for each printer. Separate message queues give the best possible control, and is not as bad as it sounds, especially if you name the message queue after the printer it controls. If the Receiving department's printer is called RCVPRT01, create a message queue called RCVPRT01 and make it the message queue for the printer. When you need to display messages for RCVPRT01, you will know what message queue to display.

Listing Device Descriptions

Often, you will need to obtain a list of device descriptions. You can do so in three different ways:

- Run the Display Object Description (DSPOBJD) command, and specify OBJ(QSYS/*ALL) OBJTYPE(*DEVD). You can direct the output to the display (by default) or to the printer, by specifying OUTPUT(*PRINT). The main problem with DSPOBJD is that it generates a list that shows only the device description names and text descriptions. It does not show any of their configuration settings.

- Run the Print Device Address (PRTDEVADR) command. This command produces a printed grid that lists all device descriptions attached to a particular local workstation controller. The command only has one parameter, CTL, where you must name the workstation controller you need to see. Supply a value like CTL01.

- Run the Work with Configuration Status (WRKCFGSTS) command, specifying CFGTYPE(*DEVD) CFGD(*ALL). Like the DSPOBJD command, you can direct the output to the display or to the printer by entering * or *PRINT in the OUTPUT parameter.

Chapter 11 - Elements Of Security and Configuration

None of these commands gives you much information about the actual configuration of the devices. OS/400 has no built-in commands that give you this information.

However, armed with a list of device descriptions (like the one produced by the first or third method), you can run the DSPDEVD command individually for each device. there is a shortcut you can take:

1. Run the WRKDEVDcommand, and specify DEVD(*ALL). This command does not allow output to a printer, but that does not matter.

2. Key in an option 5 (display) next to each device description listed, rolling through all the pages without pressing Enter.

3. Move the cursor to the command line and type OUTPUT(*PRINT). Then press Enter. The WRKDEVD command then processes all your option 5 requests. Option 5 runs the DSPDEVD command, which accepts OUTPUT(*PRINT) as a parameter. Thus, OUTPUT(*PRINT) is appended to all option 5 requests, which results in a multiple execution of DSPDEVD to print.

Section 5: Job Descriptions

One of the system objects you are likely to find difficult to understand is the job description.

What Is a Job Description?

A job description is an object (type *JOBD) that you can create and maintain in any library. Job descriptions are a set of job attributes that have been given a name for easy reference. When a job enters the system, it adopts many of its attributes from a given job description.

Job descriptions contain settings for many attributes, and many of them are too advanced to discuss in this book. Here are the most important attributes:

- Job queue (JOBQ). When you submit another job to batch, this setting determines what job queue you use by default in the Submit Job (SBMJOB) command.

- Output Queue (OUTQ). Unless otherwise indicated, all printed output produced by this job goes to the output queue named here. If OUTQ(*DEV) is specified, all printed output goes to the printer device named in the PRTDEV attribute.

- Initial Library List (INLLIBL). Lists the libraries to be included in this job's user portion of the library list. You can enter up to 25 library names.

- Message Logging (LOG). Controls the production of a job log when the job ends.

Benefits of Job Descriptions

Job descriptions are handy objects. They allow you to provide useful, initial settings for all kinds of jobs. Job descriptions can be referenced in the SBMJOB command, so that the batch job you are creating starts with a particular set of attributes. Job descriptions can also be referenced in user profiles, so that when a user signs on, his job's attributes are set accordingly.

Referencing job descriptions in user profiles gives you control over jobs. For example, if all your users in the Accounting department need to have libraries GLLIB, APLIB and ARLIB in their library list, you could create a job description that includes these library names in the INLLIBL parameter, Then you would change each Accounting user to reference the job description in his user profile, as follows:

```
CRTJOBD JOBD(MGTLIB/ACCTG) INLLIBL(GLLIB APLIB ARLIB) +
        TEXT('Job Description for Accounting')

CHGUSRPRF USRPRF(KAYE) JOBD(MGTLIB/ACCTG)
CHGUSRPRF USRPRF(BOB) JOBD(MGTLIB/ACCTG)
CHGUSRPRF USRPRF(TRISHA) JOBD(MGTLIB/ACCTG)
```

From now on, users KAYE, BOB and TRISHA (of Accounting) will use job description ACCTG in library MGTLIB. When they sign on, that job description automatically sets their library list to GLLIB (General Ledger), APLIB (Accounts Payable) and ARLIB (Accounts Receivable).

Naming Job Descriptions

If you are going to create job descriptions for each department, consider naming each job description after the department for which it is intended.

You should consider creating a different job description for each programmer in your organization, because it is likely that they will need different settings depending on what project they happen to be working on at any given time. Programmers, therefore, should have individual job descriptions. Name the job description after the user profile of the programmer who is going to useit.

Chapter 11 - Elements Of Security and Configuration

You could create a different job description for every user on your system, but that would be overkill.

Maintaining Job Descriptions

You can create a job description with the Create Job Description (CRTJOBD) command. After you have created it, you can display it with DSPJOBD, change it with CHGJOBD, delete it with DLTJOBD, and work with several job descriptions with WRKJOBD.

Be sure to use the command prompter when you change a job description. The command prompter will bring the current values for all the parameters to the screen. All you need to do is type over these values and press Enter to change them.

For example, to change job description ACCTG:

```
CHGJOBD JOBD(ACCTG)     ...and press F4.
```

Section 6: Output Queues

Output queues are holding areas for all the reports requested by your users. Reports (a generic term that could apply to a Print key image or to a 2,000-page A/R Aging) are generated within an output queue and wait for their turn to be printed.

The system comes equipped with a number of output queues. QPRINT is the most obvious example. You do not have to use IBM's output queues, although you could.

You should investigate the possibility of creating your own output queues and classify your reports by assigning them to different output queues according to the requirements of your company.

For example, you probably should have a separate output queue for the Personnel (Human Resources) department. This output queue could be secured with a public authority of *EXCLUDE. Then you could give the users in the Personnel department *CHANGE authority. The net result is that only the users in the Personnel department could produce reports in their output queue, and no one but Personnel employees would be able to display them. Confidential information then would be protected.

Naming Output Queues

Output queues can have non-systematic names because it is unlikely that you will have a great deal of them. If you create an output queue for miscellaneous reports that users put on hold, you could name it ONHOLD. Remember that output queues can be placed in any library.

☛ The system automatically creates an output queue for each printer device at the time you create the device description for the printer (with the CRTDEVPRT command). This is the simplest way to direct printed output because the output queue and the printer have the same name. You should consider using these printer-related output queues whenever possible.

Maintaining Output Queues

The commands used to maintain output queues are all easy to remember. You create an output queue with the Create Output Queue (CRTOUTQ) command, change it with CHGOUTQ, delete it with DLTOUTQ. However, you do not work with output queues with the WRKOUTQ command. That command is reserved for working with the contents of output queues, not for working with the objects themselves.

To select an output queue for maintenance, use the Work with Output Queue Description (WRKOUTQD) command.

Assigning Output Queues to Users

You can assign an output queue to a user by changing his user profile's OUTQ parameter. For example, if user FRED needs all his reports to go to output queue SPECIAL, run the following command:

```
CHGUSRPRF USRPRF(FRED) OUTQ(SPECIAL)
```

Another way to achieve the same result is to go through a job description. This approach is better if several users need to use the same output queue. For example, suppose that both FRED and MARY want their reports in output queue SPECIAL:

```
CRTJOBD  JOBD(MGTLIB/XYZ)  OUTQ(SPECIAL)
CHGUSRPRF USRPRF(FRED)  JOBD(MGTLIB/XYZ)  OUTQ(*JOBD)
CHGUSRPRF USRPRF(MARY)  JOBD(MGTLIB/XYZ)  OUTQ(*JOBD)
```

Chapter 11 - Elements Of Security and Configuration

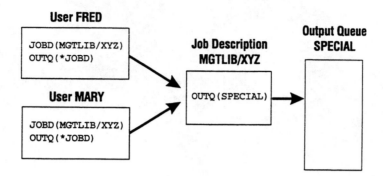

Note that the user profile's OUTQ parameter has been set to *JOBD. This points to the job description and means "get the name of the output queue from the job description assigned to this user." Because the job description is XYZ in MGTLIB, the system goes to that job description where it finds that the output queue parameter is SPECIAL. Both FRED's and MARY's output queue, then, is SPECIAL.

FURTHER READING

IBM's *Security Concepts and Planning*.

IBM's *Device Configuration Guide*.

12

Printing

This chapter explains how to manage printers and output queues in such a way that users can always get their work done without compromising security. Because the administrative side of printing is so closely related to security features, this chapter can be considered a continuation of the previous chapter.

Section 1: Output Queues

Printed output always goes to an output queue. It never goes to a printer, aside from a few exceptional cases. For all intents and purposes, you should concern yourself primarily with output queues when you manage printed output.

Output Queues You Can Use

Besides the system-provided output queues (such as QPRINT), you can use the following output queues:

- Output queues named after each printer device. These output queues are created automatically when you run the Create Device Printer (CRTDEVPRT) command to configure a new printer. You then can direct output to those output queues whenever you want the output to be printed at that specific printer.

- Output queues named after some departments. A few departments in your organization may need to collect reports in separate areas, such as output queues. Any department that produces confidential information is a good candidate; for example, Human Resources and Finance. Give these output queues meaningful names such as HUMRES or FINANCE.

- Output queues for your programmers. Programmers generate a great deal of printed output, most of which they do not really use. For example, all compiles produce printed output, and yet all the programmer may need to see is the end of it, where the system lists the errors. These can be displayed instead of printed. You can save an enormous amount of paper by creating output queues for your programmers. Name these output queues after the programmer's user profile, or use something like PGMROUTQ if you would rather have only one.

- An output queue for reports to be held for long periods of time. Some companies need to generate reports at month-end, but do not want to print them right away. These reports would be kept on hold, but doing so clutters the output queue and there is always danger of someone deleting the report by accident. With an output queue destined solely for the purpose of storing held reports, you avoid this danger. Name this output queue ONHOLD.

- By the same token, you could have an output queue for reports that have been printed and are saved for the same reasons. Name it SAVED or something of that nature.

Where to Keep These Output Queues

Aside from the output queues created for each printer device, you can place your output queues in the same library. The library you choose is entirely up to you. Use any library that is in everyone's library list if you want to save your users the effort of qualifying the name.

☞ A viable suggestion would be to create a special library for company-wide objects that help manage the system. You can name it COMPANY or something like MGTLIB (Management Library).

Chapter 12 - Printing

Output Queue Security

Always keep an eye on system security. If the Human Resources department requests to print a report that lists the salaries of all employees and directs that report to their own output queue, anyone with sufficient authority can still display the report at any display station, or even change the report so it prints somewhere else. Think about this.

Because your system operators need *JOBCTL special authority to perform their duties, they are, by default, authorized to manipulate all printed output in every form. You need to take special measures to protect sensitive reports from being pried upon (either by accident or intentionally).

Use the following parameters of the Create Output Queue (CRTOUTQ) or Change Output Queue (CHGOUTQ) command to protect certain output queues:

- DSPDTA (display data). A value of *YES means that anyone can use option 5 to display any spool file contained in the output queue. A value of *NO (the default) means that the only people authorized to use option 5 are the creator of the report and users who have *JOBCTL or *SPLCTL special authority in their user profiles, such as system operators.

- OPRCTL (operator control). A value of *YES (the default) means that users with *JOBCTL special authority can control all spool files contained in the output queue. Users can change, display, delete them, and put them on hold. A value of *NO means that the creator of the report and users with *SPLCTL special authority are the only users who can perform these functions.

- AUTCHK (authority to check). A value of *OWNER (the default) means that a user will not be able to perform any commands that check the authority to the output queue unless he is the owner of the output queue, belongs to a group profile which includes the owner, or is running a program that adopts the authority of the owner. A value of *DTAAUT, on the other hand, is more lenient, and therefore more security-loose. Any user who is authorized to read, add or delete in the output queue can perform the commands that check output queue authority.

Securing Output Queues

Remember that output queues are objects like any other. You can secure these objects in the usual fashion with the Grant Object Authority (GRTOBJAUT), Revoke Object Authority (RVKOBJAUT), and Edit Object Authority (EDTOBJAUT) commands.

Do not forget public authority. A user enjoys public authority when he has not been personally granted or revoked authority to an object. If the public authority to an output queue is *USE (as it is by default), the user can display its contents and perform certain basic manipulations such as placing reports on hold.

☞ If you need to have an output queue that absolutely no one (except a few people) can have access to, you must give it a public authority of *EXCLUDE and then grant the few people *USE authority to it.

For example, suppose your Human Resources prints payroll checks by sending the output to output queue HUMRES. Users MARIA and LOURDES should be the only two Human Resources employees who can access the queue. This is what you do:

```
GRTOBJAUT   OBJ(HUMRES) OBJTYPE(*OUTQ) USER(*PUBLIC) +
            AUT(*EXCLUDE)
GRTOBJAUT   OBJ(HUMRES) OBJTYPE(*OUTQ) USER(MARIA LOURDES) +
            AUT(*USE)
```

The first command gives *EXCLUDE authority to the public. The second command gives *USE authority to MARIA and LOURDES. The net result enables only MARIA and LOURDES to use the output queue.

Section 2: Printers

Before you can use a printer, you must connect it to the AS/400. Before that, you have to configure the printer. The configuration process can be left to the system if you are using automatic configuration (system value QAUTOCFTG set to '1'), or you can create the device description yourself.

Creating a device description for a printer involves the use of the CRTDEVPRT command. Many parameters will have to receive values based on what the printer is, or where you are connecting it. Other parameters can be set to different values depending on how you want to control the printers. This section deals with these management parameters.

Automatic On-Line (ONLINE)

The ONLINE parameter determines whether the system automatically varies on the printer at IPL time. It defaults to *YES. ONLINE should be left to its default value unless there is a compelling reason to change it to *NO.

If ONLINE(*NO) is specified, the system operator (or the user who normally controls the printer) will have to manually vary on the printer and start its printer writer before users can get any printing done. This action seems like an additional burden for no immediate advantage.

Message Queue (MSGQ)

Printers run into trouble now and then. For example, a printer may be printing reports on standard paper for hours until a user requests purchase orders, which must be printed on special preprinted forms. When the system begins to send the purchase order spool file, the printer realizes that the forms it has installed and the new spool file forms do not match.

Perhaps your printer's ribbon jams, or someone turns it off by accident, or it runs out of paper. Any of these situations require operator intervention, and the only way your printer can communicate this fact is by sending a message. The MSGQ parameter names the message queue where this message is sent.

MSGQ defaults to QSYSOPR, but this is a poor choice in many cases. QSYSOPR is a very busy message queue, especially in large AS/400 installations because QSYSOPR receives many messages from all kinds of jobs running on the system.

☞ You should designate a message queue other than QSYSOPR to receive the printer messages. You can use a single message queue for all your printer devices, or group them together so that some (but not all) printers share a message queue, or you can give each printer a separate message queue.

- If you use a single message queue, you will know where to look without having to think. You could name this unique message queue a significant name such as PRINTERS and put it in a library where you can always find it using the library list support. You would check on printer messages by executing the command:

```
DSPMSG MSGQ(PRINTERS)
```

The disadvantage of a single message queue is obvious. It is almost as bad as using QSYSOPR itself. PRINTERS will receive messages from all printers, and you will have to be especially careful that you do not confuse one with another.

- Grouping printers by message queue is somewhat better. You could create a message queue for the Accounting department and use it for all printers located in that department. The danger of misinterpreting a message is less than if you had a single message queue, but it still exists.

- Using a separate message queue for each printer works best, and you can simplify the setup by giving the message queue the same name as the printer device it services. This way, if printer PURPRT01 (in Purchasing) has stopped printing, you can display messages as follows:

```
DSPMSG MSGQ(PURPRT01)
```

Printer Error Messages (PRTERRMSG)

Some messages are important and others are not. The PRTERRMSG parameter determines how the system handles recoverable error situations. If you specify *INQ (the default value), the system sends an inquiry message. Someone must reply to this message before the printer can continue. If you specify *INFO, however, the message is sent but printing continues.

Assigning a Printer to a User

With the proper combination of parameter values, you can set up your users in such a way that all their printed output goes to a specific printer, no matter where they have signed on.

The proper combination is one of the following (xxx is the name of the desired printer):

- OUTQ(*DEV) PRTDEV(xxx) in their job description.
- OUTQ(*USRPRF) in their job description, and OUTQ(*DEV) PRTDEV(xxx) in their user profile.

Section 3: Workstations

Some parameters of the Create Device Display (CRTDEVDSP) affect printing. They are OUTQ, PRTDEV and PRTFILE.

Output Queue (OUTQ) and Printer Device (PRTDEV)

Beginning with V2R1M0 of OS/400, the workstation can determine where to send all printed output generated by any user who uses the workstation. This feature is closer to the System/36's normal way of functioning.

To enable this feature, do one of the following:

- Set your users' job descriptions to OUTQ(*WRKSTN).

- Set your users' job descriptions to OUTQ(*USRPRF) and their user profiles to OUTQ(*WRKSTN).

Then, use the OUTQ and PRTDEV parameters in the workstation (the display device) to direct output to a given output queue or printer device. For example, you can set the parameters so that all output goes to output queue QPRINT with the following command:

```
CHGDEVDSP DEVD(xxx) OUTQ(QPRINT)
```

You also can set the parameters so that all printed output goes to printer SYSPRT01, as follows:

```
CHGDEVDSP DEVD(xxx) OUTQ(*DEV) PRTDEV(SYSPRT01)
```

This technique is convenient in some environments. For example, you may have users who sign on to a number of workstations and request reports or press the Print key. If you use the technique described above, the user will have the printouts he requested at the printer that you assigned to the workstation (which is, hopefully, the closest one).

Printer File (PRTFILE)

The PRTFILE parameter determines what printer file is used by the system when the user presses the Print key. By default, PRTFILE has a value of QSYSPRT. QSYSPRT is a printer file located in QSYS that is provided by IBM.

You can create your own printer files and assign them to workstations. Because printer files contain a number of attributes (such as form type, form size and print text), you can make your Print key do all sorts of things.

For example, you could create a printer file called PRTKEY as follows:

```
CRTDUPOBJ OBJ(QSYSPRT) FROM LIB(QSYS) OBJTYPE(*FILE)   +
          TOLIB(xxx) NEWOBJ(PRTKEY)
```

This command creates a clone of QSYSPRT, names it PRTKEY, and places it in library xxx (one of your own libraries). Now change your new printer file as follows:

```
CHGPRTF FILE(PRTKEY) HOLD(*YES) USRDTA('Print Key')
```

Finally, assign this printer file to your display station. DSP01 is used in this example:

```
CHGDEVDSP DEVD(DSP01) PRTFILE(PRTKEY)
```

From now on, anyone who signs on to DSP01 and presses the Print key will produce a screen image that is automatically on hold and has a user data of 'Print Key.' If you changed all workstations (in addition to DSP01) the same way, all presses of the Print key, regardless of user, would have the same attributes.

Because it is automatically on hold, the screen image would not print if, for example, the user pressed the Print key by mistake. He may have intended to press the Help key, for example. Having a user data of 'Print Key' would allow you to list all of the screen images with a single command:

```
WRKSPLF SELECT(*ALL *ALL *ALL 'Print Key')
```

Section 4: Where Output Goes

OS/400 was designed for flexibility, but sometimes this flexibility seems to be taken to impractical extremes. For example, the system provides several levels of settings for directly printed output, and some seem to directly contradict others.

The Path for Settings

Actually, although OS/400 is complex, it is not so complex that it is impossible to understand. The system follows a long but fixed (and predictable) path to determine where to send output. If you know the path, you always will be able to determine the destination of your reports. You also will be able to make the system work the way you want it to.

All levels of settings have two settings: one to name an output queue (always called OUTQ) and one to name a printer device (called PRTDEV or DEV). The OUTQ setting is the more important of the two. The other setting only matters if OUTQ(*DEV) has been specified.

Either attribute can have special values such as *JOB and *SYSVAL. In this case, the system jumps directly to the appropriate level, and skips all others. For example, a file override (top level) may specify OUTQ(*DEV) PRTDEV(*SYSVAL). *SYSVAL stands for "system value," which is the bottom level. The system jumps to the system value level directly; it skips all other levels.

- File Overrides: To start the process, the system checks to see if there are any active file overrides for the printer file you use to generate your printed output. If the file's OUTQ or PRTDEV settings have been overridden (with the Override Printer File [OVRPRTF] command), the override settings are used and no more checking is performed. If there are no overrides for the printer file, the system continues checking with the next level.

- The Printer File: The next level is the printer file itself. All printer files have an OUTQ and a DEV attribute. If they name an actual output queue or printer device, the search stops. If not, the search continues.

- The running job (*JOB): The job that is producing the printed output has a number of settings. It has an OUTQ and a PRTDEV attribute among them. These attributes are used to determine where to send the printed output.

- The job description (*JOBD): The system then examines the job description used in the job that produces the output. The job description contains the same two settings: OUTQ and PRTDEV.

- The user profile (*USRPRF): The user profile also contains the same two settings: OUTQ and PRTDEV, which are examined next.

- The workstation (*WRKSTN): The display station device description contains the same two settings: OUTQ and PRTDEV. This level was added with V2R1M0.

- The system value (*SYSVAL): System value QPRTDEV contains the name of the system printer. There is no system value for an output queue. The search for a destination ends at this level.

FURTHER READING

IBM's *System Operator's Guide*.

IBM's *Device Configuration Guide*.

IBM's *Security Concepts and Planning*.

13

Maintenance

Section 1: Mechanical

Computers are machines; they require maintenance when something breaks down. To minimize the time your system is unavailable due to a breakdown, you need to perform periodic preventive maintenance on your system

☛ All mechanical (including electronic) maintenance should be performed by a qualified technician. The person who fixes the personal computers or the telephone system at work is not the person to take care of your AS/400. Not all computers are created equal. The PC repairman may be an expert on PCs, but that does not give him the proper credentials for repairing an AS/400. The reverse is also true.

The advice given in the previous paragraph applies to you, too. Unless you have been trained as an AS/400 technician, you are not qualified to repair the machine, no matter how many electronics courses you took in college. Never tinker with the AS/400.

IBM or Third Party?

You may be tempted to believe that because the machine has the IBM name, only IBM can perform repairs. This is not true. Many companies can service your AS/400 because they have fully trained technicians, many of whom are former IBM employees.

Usually, these third-party service providers charge less than IBM to attract customers. After all, computer repairs can add up to a considerable amount of money, not only in labor (many hours) but in spare parts.

Do not be fooled into believing, however, that any third-party company that provides service is good and reputable. That is not true. As in any other business, there are good companies and crooks.

Maintenance Agreements

All service providers (IBM or third-party) will ask you to sign a maintenance agreement with them. A maintenance agreement is a form of insurance, but is only necessary after IBM's first-year warranty has expired. During the warranty period, you should always call IBM for repairs, no matter who sold you the system.

Before the warranty is over you should investigate several service providers (including IBM) and compare them. If you think you will enjoy peace of mind by having IBM's service, go for it. But always compare the following:

- Professionalism. How are you greeted on the phone when you call? If the other person is not available at the moment do they call you back when they promised. Do they treat you like a VIP, or like a burden?

- Quick turnaround. How long after you call does someone show up to fix the computer? Can they guarantee one-hour turnaround?

- Quality of service. Does the technician have the proper tools to perform his job, or is he using the same Phillips-head screwdriver for everything? Does he treat the machines with care and avoid jarring and violent movements?

- Knowledgeability. Does the technician have the manuals required to perform his job? Has he been trained properly (perhaps by IBM)?

- Price. Price should always be the last consideration because it is the least important. If your computer goes down for a long period of time because the technician cannot fix it, it will not matter that you saved a substantial sum of money in monthly charges. Your firm will lose revenues, and you may lose your job.

Chapter 13 - Maintenance

Section 2: IPLing Regularly

One thing you can do to keep your AS/400 in shape is to IPL it regularly. You do not need to IPL it every day or even every week, but make a point to reserve some time to IPL at least twice a year. An IPL each month may be the optimum frequency.

During IPL, the system performs a number of "housekeeping" chores it cannot do at any other time. It rebuilds the access paths to keyed files and reclaims space that was previously used by spooled files. IPLing also makes certain changes (such as a change to system value QSECURITY) effective.

Performing an Unattended IPL

The easiest type of IPL is the unattended IPL. Set the key lock of the CPU front panel to Normal, sign on to the system console, and follow the steps described in Chapter 2, in the sections titled "Ending Subsystems" and "Power Down the System."

IPL will take time. It is not possible to predict how long because a lot depends on how long ago you performed the last IPL, and whether any jobs or the system ended abnormally.

☛ You can easily schedule automatic power up and power down with Operational Assistant's power scheduler. See Chapter 2 for additional information.

Section 3: Reclaiming Storage

Besides IPLing regularly, there is something else you can do to keep your AS/400 in good shape: run the various Reclaim (RCLxxx) commands.

Reclaim Storage (RCLSTG)

The Reclaim Storage (RCLSTG) command is one of the few OS/400 commands without parameters. It performs only one function and allows no variations.

The RCLSTG command checks all auxiliary (DASD) storage and performs the following clean-up tasks:

- It collects all objects that have fallen outside of a library in library QRCL (which is created if it does not exist). Because all objects must be within libraries, this is an abnormal situation. RCLSTG takes care of it.

- If RCLSTG finds an object without an owner, an object whose owner does not exist, or an object whose owner's user profile is damaged, it assigns an owner of QDFTOWN. QDFTOWN is one of the IBM-provided user profiles.

- Damaged or destroyed objects are deleted.

- If an object is protected by a damaged, destroyed or otherwise unusable authorization list, the system secures the object with authorization list QRCLAUTL, which is part of QSYS.

- If keyed database files have been damaged, RCLSTG rebuilds their access paths.

RCLSTG must be run interactively from the system console, with all subsystems ended (including the controlling subsystem). You cannot submit RCLSTG to batch. All corrective actions taken by RCLSTG are recorded in message queue QSYSOPR and in the system log, QHST.

RCLSTG can take a long time, especially if you have not run it in a while. Always schedule downtime for off-hours or during the weekend.

☞ You must make room for a periodic run of RCLSTG, even if your system must stay up and running all the time. If you do not run RCLSTG periodically, the system may start to give you trouble.

Reclaim Documents (RCLDLO)

The Reclaim Document Library Objects (RCLDLO) command is similar to RCLSTG in that it also reclaims space occupied by unusable objects. RCLDLO reclaims space from folders and documents in QDOC. If you use Office Vision and maintain many folders and documents, you should run RCLDLO periodically.

Unlike RCLSTG, however, RCLDLO does not require a dedicated system; however, you probably should run RCLDLO that way in order to avoid lock contention on objects that may be in use.

When RCLDLO runs, it creates two folders named QRCLnnn.DOC and QRCLnnn.FLR, where it places folders and documents that were found in error. When RCLDLO finishes, check these folders. If they contain any objects, you will have to move the objects to their appropriate place; then you should delete both folders from the system.

Chapter 13 - Maintenance

Section 4: DASD Saving Techniques

The AS/400 uses vast amounts of disk space. It is not unusual for an AS/400 to start choking because of lack of space. QSYSOPR receives message CPF0907, "Serious storage condition may exist" whenever there is less than 10% of space left in your DASD. Do not wait to get this message.

Monitoring Available Space

You can check how much space is left available. All you need to do is run the Work with System Status (WRKSYSSTS) or Display System Status (DSPSYSSTS) command. The system presents a panel that looks like this:

```
                      Work with System Status              MC  PGMR
                                                 10/28/93  21:06:25
   % CPU used . . . . . . . :      1.5    Auxiliary storage:
   Elapsed time . . . . . . :  00:01:00   System ASP . . . . . . :    2234 M
   Jobs in system . . . . . :      190    % system ASP used  . . :    78.6161
   % addresses used:                      Total  . . . . . . . . :    2234 M
      Permanent  . . . . . . :     3.316  Current unprotect used :     452 M
      Temporary  . . . . . . :      .108  Maximum unprotect  . . :     460 M

   Type changes (if allowed), press Enter.

   System   Pool     Reserved    Max    - - -DB- - -    - -Non-DB- -
    Pool    Size (K) Size (K)   Active  Fault   Pages   Fault   Pages
     1       __3750    2497      +++     .0      .0      .4      .9
     2       __4342       0      __5     .0      .0      .0      .2
     3       ___100       0      __1     .0      .0      .0      .0
     4       __8192       0      _13     .0      .0      .7     3.5

                                                                 Bottom
   Command
   ===> _____
   F3=Exit     F4=Prompt            F5=Refresh    F9=Retrieve   F10=Restart
   F11=Display transition data      F12=Cancel    F24=More keys
```

The only difference between WRKSYSSTS and DSPSYSSTS is that DSPSYSSTS does not let you change any of the information presented such as pool sizes and maximum active.

You will notice that near the top-right corner there is a caption that reads "% used." In the illustration, the value is 78.6161 percent. If your system shows 78 percent used, it means there is 22 percent left. You should start worrying as soon as the percentage used gets beyond 80 or 85. If you wait longer, the system will not perform as well. Do not let your system run at over 95 percent for long periods of time.

Recovering Disk Space

You can do several things to decrease your system's usage of DASD. If these techniques do not help enough, then it is time to buy additional DASD and upgrade your system.

- Reclaim storage. Run the RCLSTG command as explained earlier in this chapter. This alone can free up a considerable amount of DASD.

- Reclaim documents and folders. Run the RCLDLO command, as explained in this chapter.

- Reclaim spool storage. Run the Reclaim Spool Storage (RCLSPLSTG) command to reclaim the storage taken up by unused spool file members where spool file data is kept. You will be asked how many days worth of unused space to keep. The following example reclaims all spool storage that has not been used in the last seven days.

  ```
  RCLSPLSTG DAYS(7)
  ```

- Delete history logs. When the system log (QHST) fills up, the system copies its contents to a database file in QSYS whose name begins with QHST. Then the system clears the system log and starts over. These old history logs accumulate and are never automatically deleted. Periodically, you should delete them. You can start with the following command:

  ```
  WRKF FILE(QSYS/QHST*)
  ```

  Then you should analyze the list presented. The text description tells what period of time they cover. The text description contains a string of characters as follows:

  ```
  CYYMMDDHHMMSSCYYMMDDHHMMSS
  ```

  This string represents the starting date and time (CYYMMDDHHMMSS) and the ending date and time, in the same format.

- Delete problem logs. As soon as the system detects a hardware problem, it creates a problem log. Like history logs, problem logs accumulate and must be deleted manually. Start with the Work with Problems (WRKPRB) command and see what problem logs you can delete with option 4. Then you need to run the Reorganize

Chapter 13 - Maintenance

Physical File Member (RGZPFM) command on all physical files in QSYS that have names beginning withQASX.

- Delete old spool files, job logs, user profiles and device descriptions that may have accumulated and you no longer need.

- Apply PTFs permanently. See Chapter 29 for a description of PTF management which includes applying PTFs permanently.

- Clear libraries QRCL and QRPLOBJ periodically. These libraries are a kind of trash can.

- Keep your database files reorganized to remove deleted records. Use the Reorganize Physical File Member (RGZPFM) command, which reorganizes one member at a time.

- Delete libraries you do not use. Pay very close attention to what you do because deleting a library is serious business. Ask other people in your organization if the libraries that you suspect are useless are indeed useless. Do not delete libraries with names that begin with the letter Q. These libraries are IBM-supplied libraries. To delete a library, run the Delete Library (DLTLIB) command in batch:

```
SBMJOB CMD(DLTLIB LIB(OLDSTUFF)) JOB(DLTLIB)
```

- Compress objects that have not been used for the last few days. First you need to determine the number of days. You can start by using 15 days as an approximation:

```
SBMJOB CMD(CPROBJ OBJ(*ALL/*ALL) OBJTYPE(*ALL) +
        DAYS(14)) JOB(CPROBJ)
```

This command can take a considerable amount of time to complete.

Most of these tasks can be automated by Operational Assistant's Automatic Cleanup. Run the following command to display the CLEANUP menu:

```
GO CLEANUP
```

```
CLEANUP                       Cleanup Tasks
                                                    System:     MC PGMR
To select one of the following, type its number below and press Enter:

     1. Change cleanup options
     2. Start cleanup at scheduled time
     3. Start cleanup immediately
     4. End cleanup




Type a menu option below
     _

F1=Help    F3=Exit    F9=Command line    F12=Cancel
```

More information about this menu can be found in Chapter 7.

FURTHER READING

IBM's *System Operator's Guide*.

IBM's *CL Reference*.

Midrange Computing's *DASD Saver*.

14

Manuals

Section 1: IBM's Manuals

IBM publishes an impressive array of manuals for the AS/400 which cover all aspects of the machine. There is no reason for you to obtain all of these manuals because you are not likely to have all the products installed on your system. For example, there are manuals for communications. If you do not use communications, those manuals are of no use to you. Manuals come in two forms: printed or computerized.

Printed Manuals

Printed manuals cost money. IBM charges a fee for most manuals, except for a few that are distributed free with the AS/400. IBM provides three-ring binders in which you can insert the printed material (with holes already punched for quick insertion in the binder).

Each manual has an identification code such as SC41-8082-0. When you order manuals, IBM will ask you to provide the identification code. Section 2 in this chapter lists some of the important manuals available from IBM and their identification codes.

Printed manuals are bulky and heavy, but easy to work with. You can see two whole pages at a glance, you can browse the manuals quickly by flipping the pages, and you can have as many on your desk (all open at once) as space allows.

Computerized Manuals

IBM also provides the manuals in computerized form. You can use any PC with an attached compact disc (CD ROM) drive. IBM sells software called READ/DOS or Book Manager and a CD that contains all the manuals.

The advantages of the CD ROM are obvious. You have all the AS/400 manuals published by IBM, and you can carry them with you in your briefcase, ready for use any time you have a PC with a CD ROM drive and Book Manager at your destination point. Even this limitation may not be a real problem because you can purchase a laptop PC and attach a CD ROM drive to it.

The Book Manager software has search capabilities. You can search a single book or all books contained in a "bookshelf," which is a set of books you maintain. If you need to find out about commitment control but are not sure where to look, you can search all books for "commit" and let the Book Manager find all references for you.

The computerized manuals have one disadvantage, however. The Book Manager does not provide a graphical user interface. The program has a rather primitive text-based application program which can only display 24 lines by 80 columns. You cannot see a whole page at a glance; you are given a 24x80 window that you must shift horizontally and vertically. The text portion of the books presents no problems because it has been formatted with this limitation in mind. The diagrams and figures can be a problem, however.

Recently, IBM released a Windows-based version of its Softcopy Library Reader (a subset of BookManager), which solves many of the problems and inconveniences that plagued the DOS version. Because it's a Windows application, you get a full graphical user interface, complete with mouse support, cut, paste—everything. It even lets you have more than one book open at once.

Section 2: Some Important Manuals

This section describes some of the manuals IBM has published for the AS/400. There are far too many to provide a complete listing. For your convenience, the list is broken down in two major categories: programming and operations/administration. The numbers in parentheses after the title are the identification codes for Version 2.

Programming Manuals

C/400 User's Guide. A must for C programmers on the AS/400. It provides a comprehensive description of the implementation of C on the AS/400.

CL Programmer's Guide. All programmers should have this book because all programmers have to use CL at one point or another. This book also explains a great deal more than just CL.

COBOL/400 Reference. A must for COBOL programmers. It has complete syntax diagrams for all the COBOL verbs, divisions, sections and paragraphs.

COBOL/400 User's Guide. If you program in COBOL, you must have this book, which shows you all the features of the language with examples.

Concepts and Programmer's Guide for the System/36 Environment. If your system runs in the S/36 Environment and you are unfamiliar with S/36 concepts, this book explains them in detail.

Database Guide. Contains a great deal of information about the structure of database files, as well as how to design and use them.

DDS Reference. This book is must for any programmer. It contains all the necessary information to code Data Description Specifications (DDS) with accuracy.

DFU User's Guide and Reference. Teaches you how to use the Database File Utility (DFU) on the AS/400.

Guide To Programming For Displays. Shows you how to design application programs that communicate with the user through the display station.

Guide To Programming For Printing. Shows you how to design application programs that produce printed output.

PDM User's Guide and Reference. Teaches you how to use the Program Development Manager (PDM) on the AS/400.

Procedures Language (REXX) Programmer's Guide. REXX is a "procedures language" you can use in many platforms including the AS/400. REXX has many features you can put to good use, and it is part of OS/400. This book teaches you about the language and its AS/400 implementation.

Procedures Language (REXX) Reference. If you plan to do any programming in REXX, you should get this book. It describes all the features of the language in great detail.

Query Management/400 Programmer's Guide. A descriptive book about Query Management/400. You should be able to learn about the product with this book. Required if you have Query Management/400.

Query Management/400 Reference. Reference manual for Query Management/400. Required if you have Query Management/400.

RLU User's Guide and Reference. Teaches you how to use the Report Layout Utility (RLU) on the AS/400.

RPG/400 Reference. Another must for every RPG/400 programmer. It contains reference material, such as the syntax for each operation code and the rules that govern each RPG specification.

RPG/400 User's Guide. This book is a must if you program in RPG/400. It shows you the features of the language and has plenty of examples.

SAA C Reference. C programmers should have this book. It contains complete reference material and includes function descriptions.

SDA User's Guide and Reference. Teaches you how to use the Screen Design Aid (SDA) on the AS/400.

SEU User's Guide and Reference. Teaches you how to use the Source Entry Utility (SEU) on the AS/400.

Sort User's Guide and Reference. Shows you how to sort database files using the Format Data (FMTDTA) command.

SQL/400 Programmer's Guide. Required if you have SQL/400. This book contains basic information about the product.

SQL/400 Reference. Required if you have SQL/400. This book is a reference manual that includes the complete syntax of each SQL statement.

System Programmer's Interface Reference. This book explains in detail each Application Program Interface (API) provided by IBM. APIs offer ways to retrieve system information (not database) in a direct manner with better performance than other methods.

System Reference for the System/36 Environment. This manual has a complete description of every S/36E procedure, command and OCL statement available. A must for S/36E programmers.

Chapter 14 - Manuals

System/36-Compatible RPG II User's Guide and Reference. S/36E programmers who work with RPG II need this manual.

Operations & Administration Manuals

Backup and Recovery Guide. Do not wait until you need this book to order it. The book shows you, in depth, how to perform efficient backups and what to do to recover from data loss.

CL Reference. The CL Reference consists of three large volumes. Be sure to get this book. It explains everything you need to know about each of the commands provided with OS/400 (about 1,000 of them). The book may be as boring as a telephone directory, but it can be just as useful if you need it.

Device Configuration Guide. This book shows you how to configure any device to your system. You should get this book even if you plan to use automatic configuration.

Licensed Programs & New Release Installation Guide. This book can help you through the process of installing software products and new releases of the operating system.

New User's Guide. This book describes very basic operations, such as how to sign on and the use of function keys and menus. It has plenty of illustrations.

PC Support/400 User's Guide for DOS and *PC Support/400 User's Guide for OS/2.* These two manuals explain the workings of PC Support on the AS/400 from the user's perspective. The first manual applies to PCs that run MS-DOS. The second manual applies to PCs that run IBM's OS/2.

PC Support/400 DOS Installation and Administration Guide and *PC Support/400 OS/2 Installation and Administration Guide.* These two manuals explain how to install and maintain PC Support on the AS/400. The first manual applies to PCs that run MS-DOS. The second manual applies to PCs that run IBM's OS/2.

Physical Planning Guide and Reference. Use this manual to plan the physical installation of the AS/400. This manual contains a great deal of information about the physical aspect of the AS/400 machinery.

Security Concepts and Planning. This book is a must for every AS/400 installation. It explains all the concepts related to system security, and how to implement and maintain security.

System Operator's Guide. Every AS/400 installation should have this book. It contains invaluable information for the system operator and includes troubleshooting.

Work Management Guide. The Work Management Guide shows you how work (jobs) is processed by the system. It goes into fine detail when describing subsystems, system values, and other concepts such as routing. Although it is not light reading, it is important.

FURTHER READING

IBM's *Publications Guide*.

15

Upgrading To a New Release

Other than recovering from a disaster, few system activities are as intricate as upgrading the operating system to a new release. This chapter presents the general steps you have to take to upgrade.

Section 1: Why Upgrade?

The first question you need to ask yourself is: why bother upgrading to a new release? Upgrading to a new release is a complicated process during which many things can go wrong. To make matters worse, the new release of the operating system may not be entirely compatible with some of your programs. In this case, those programs will stop working or will yield invalid information.

To justify the upgrade, you need to address the following concerns. Only you can be the judge of them, but evaluate them carefully:

- IBM will not support an old release forever. If you do not upgrade to new releases within a reasonable amount of time after they are available, you will be on your own if you discover a bug in the operating system or one of the software products. For example, one installation may have stayed with OS/400 Version 1, Release 1, Modification 0 (V1R1M0), the first release of OS/400, which was announced in 1988 along with the AS/400 hardware. If such an installation found a bug in the operating system, IBM would force them to upgrade to a later release (probably the latest) before they would even touch the problem.

- New releases often bring support for new display stations, printers, tape drives, disk drives and other hardware. They also bring added functionality and features to the operating system, programming languages and utilities. IBM does not add new features to old releases.

- Job applicants for system operator, programmer or administrator positions for your Data Processing department may be turned off when they find out that your system is lagging behind. The best applicants will ask you what OS/400 release your system is running.

- New software that is developed by software firms may require a fairly recent release of OS/400 in order to work. New software may use some of the features that were added to the operating system or programming languages. If your system is still using an old release, you may not be able to install that software.

Section 2: Preparation

Before you start the release upgrade, you need to prepare yourself, your users and the system for this traumatic event. This section contains a basic outline of the steps you should take to prepare for the upgrade.

Order the New Release

The first step is to order the new release of the operating system. When a new release comes out, you should get a form you can fill out and return to place your order. If you have not received it, call your IBM SE (or your system provider).

The time it takes for the tapes to arrive depends on the backlog of orders IBM is receiving. Always place your order at least a month before you plan to install the new release. A month gives you enough time to plan the upgrade carefully and also gives IBM time to fill your order.

Never upgrade to a new release immediately after it has been announced. All new releases have bugs that require fixes (PTFs). If you upgrade your system too soon, you will be IBM's guinea pig. It is always better to let someone else find the bugs. This may take a few months.

Chapter 15 - Upgrading To a New Release

Read IBM's Documentation

Among the materials IBM sends with your new release, there will be complete instructions about how to install it. Be sure to read these instructions from beginning to end. Save these instructions even after the release upgrade is complete, in case you need to refer to them again.

☛ IBM's documentation always has the last word about a procedure. If you do not understand something in the documentation, call IBM and ask for clarification.

Take Inventory of Tapes Received

Your new release order should also include a packing list which shows what tapes you should have received. Always check this packing list against the actual tapes you received to verify that your order is complete. Sometimes the shipment is not complete, and IBM sends you the backlogged tapes at a later date.

Do not perform the upgrade until you have received all the tapes. If you do not receive the missing ones (if any) after a reasonable period of time, call IBM and demand them.

Check that the tapes are in good condition. Sometimes the tapes are faulty, and there is nothing worse than discovering it in the middle of the upgrade. Although there are no 100% sure-fire methods to check that the tapes will be usable, you can at least check that they are readable.

To check if a tape is readable, run the Display Tape (DSPTAP) command and direct the output to *PRINT. You can run the command in batch for better efficiency, as follows:

```
SBMJOB CMD(DSPTAP DEV(SYSTAP01) DATA(*LABELS) +
       OUTPUT(*PRINT)) JOB(DSPTAP)
```

If the tape is unreadable, the job aborts with an error message sent to QSYSOPR. If you find unreadable tapes, get new ones from IBM immediately.

Get Cume PTF Tapes for New Release

New releases are usually shipped with a tape that contains a cumulative PTF tape (or "cume PTF tape"). This tape contains fixes for all the bugs users have already discovered in the new release.

Even if you receive this tape, make sure that there are no more recent cume tapes. You may have to send an order for a newer cume PTF tape package or for new HIPER PTFs that may have been issued. Hopefully, however there will not be any.

Estimate Downtime

The upgrade process takes a considerable amount of time. Sometimes IBM will indicate how long it should take (of course, it is an approximation only). Never plan on finishing in less than six hours.

Depending on how much you have to back up (which depends on how large your system is) and how many problems you encounter, the upgrade may take between eight and forty hours. The average (and most likely number) is around twelve hours.

Schedule Downtime

Because the upgrade takes such a long time, you need to select a good time to carry it out. Weekends are the logical choice. Even if something goes seriously awry, you usually can assure your users that the system will be operational by Monday morning.

Select a weekend that is convenient for your users, your IBM SE, and you. Then announce the upgrade to your users so they know well in advance that the system will not be available for use. Then stick to your schedule.

Get SE's Home Phone Number

It would be to your advantage to obtain your IBM SE's home phone number or pager in case you need to be rescued sometime during the upgrade process. If you cannot get it, obtain the home phone number of a fellow AS/400 professional who has done an upgrade before. The first upgrade you do is likely to be traumatic and troublesome.

Initialize Lots of Tapes

One of the steps you will have to take before the release upgrade is backing up the system. Make doubly sure you have enough initialized tapes for this backup. Now is a good time to initialize a few dozen.

Chapter 15 - Upgrading To a New Release

Section 3: Execution

The tricky part of the release upgrade is actually doing it. Remember for your own protection that IBM's documentation always has the last word, and the procedure IBM suggests should be followed even if it is in conflict with advice you get from other sources (including this book).

Backing Up

The very first step you need to perform is to back up your entire system. Do not omit anything. Here is what you need to do (xxx represents the name of your tape device):

1. End all subsystems from the system console, in order to obtain a dedicated system.

2. Save the system:

    SAVSYS DEV(xxx) ENDOPT(*UNLOAD)

3. Save all non-system libraries:

    SAVLIB LIB(*NONSYS) DEV(xxx) ENDOPT(*UNLOAD)

4. Save all documents and folders:

    SAVDLO DLO(*ALL) DEV(xxx) ENDOPT(*UNLOAD)

☞ Throughout the back up process, you should clean your tape drive to make sure you are creating a good backup. Clean the tape drive before using each tape, even continuation tapes for the steps that require more than one. It is better to waste a little time now (by doing something that may be useless) than to waste hours later (because you lost data, and your backups were useless).

Saving Configuration and System Values

Chapter 6 contains an explanation of how you can save your system configuration (devices, controllers and lines) and your system values. It is a very short procedure and can save you from trouble if something goes wrong.

The reason to save the system values is that sometimes new releases incorporate new system values. The existing system values should not be changed, but it is better to be safe than sorry.

Print Subsystem Descriptions

Sometimes new releases make changes in the internal structure of subsystem descriptions, and sometimes they are changed without your knowledge. To save yourself headaches, you should print the description of all your subsystems and save the printouts.

First, run the Work with Subsystem Descriptions (WRKSBSD) command, as follows:

```
WRKSBSD SBSD(*ALL/*ALL)
```

This command presents a list of all subsystem descriptions in existence. Then enter an option 5 (display) next to each one (do not press Enter yet, but do press Roll Up to display more pages, if any). When you are done entering a 5 next to all subsystem names, move the cursor to the command line and type the following:

```
OUTPUT(*PRINT)
```

Then press Enter. Option 5 runs the Display Subsystem Description (DSPSBSD) command for each subsystem. When combined with OUTPUT(*PRINT), the description is printed instead of displayed.

Keep the listing in a safe place. It will be voluminous.

Have IBM's Documentation Ready

Get the manual IBM sent with the tapes and find where it explains how to install the new release of OS/400. Keep this manual open and ready next to you throughout the installation process. Check off the steps as you execute them.

Get a Dedicated System

If you do not have a dedicated system by now, end all subsystems to make sure that no one is using the system. You will already have a dedicated system if you backed up your entire system today, as indicated at the beginning of this section. If not, do:

```
ENDSBS SBS(*ALL) OPTION(*IMMED)
```

Now make sure you do not need to back up again! Has anyone been on the system and made any changes to the database or to the system?

Chapter 15 - Upgrading To a New Release

Apply PTFs Permanently

Before you start the upgrade, you need to run the Apply PTF (APYPTF) command to permanently apply all the PTFs you have temporarily applied to your current release. Then you need to IPL the system:

```
APYPTF LICPGM(*ALL) APY(*PERM) DELAYED(*YES)

PWRDWNSYS OPTION(*IMMED) RESTART(*YES)
```

This step can be skipped if you have plenty of available disk space. There is no way to tell for sure how much "plenty" is. When in doubt, perform this step.

Start Upgrade

Now follow IBM's instructions to install the new release of the operating system. Follow the instructions in IBM's book carefully.

☞ You will have to mount tapes in a certain order. Be sure you mount the proper tape, and be sure to clean your tape drive after *each tape*.

Load Any Cume PTF Tapes

Next, you need to load the PTFs included in the cumulative ("cume") tape IBM sent you with the new release (if there is one). Follow the instructions provided by IBM. This tape contains fixes for all the bugs that users have discovered in the operating system and system products.

You will be using the Load PTF (LODPTF) command.

Apply PTFs Temporarily

Now apply all the PTFs you have loaded from the cume tape. You will use the APYPTF command as indicated in the instructions provided by IBM. Then IPL your system again to make sure that all PTFs are applied successfully.

Your system is now running the new release of the operating system.

Verify Configuration, System Values and Subsystems

Compare the listings you obtained (of system values and subsystems) against the real thing to check system values and subsystem descriptions. Configuration objects should not have changed; if they have, you can run the Restore Configuration (RSTCFG) command if the changes introduced by the release upgrade are for the worse. In making this evaluation, always keep in mind that the release upgrade may have introduced changes to support new features not available in the previous release. Do not undo these changes by accident.

Reapply Changes to System Objects

If you changed some system (QSYS) objects before the upgrade, your changes are gone. You will have to perform all your changes again.

Usually it is a better idea to create duplicates of QSYS objects and place them in a user library that you place at the top of the system portion of the library list, so the system uses your copies instead of the original QSYS objects. In this case, be sure to delete your copies from your user library, make fresh copies from QSYS again (which will incorporate the new features or other changes they may have), and perform your changes on the duplicates.

Make System Available

Finally, if everything went okay, you can now make the system available for use. Depending on what changes you had to re-do on system values or other settings, you may need to IPL the system to make sure all the changes are effective. It is a good idea to IPL the system once again just to be sure:

```
PWRDWNSYS OPTION(*IMMED) RESTART(*YES)
```

FURTHER READING

IBM's *Licensed Programs & New Release Installation Guide*.

Part IV:
System Architecture

16

Libraries, Objects and Library List

Section 1: Review of Concepts

The System Architecture

The AS/400 has a complex architecture. In order to effectively operate, administer and program this machine, you need to understand the main concepts about this architecture. This chapter explains them.

Before you start, you should know that the AS/400 architecture is derived from the System/38's. If you are familiar with the S/38, you already know a great deal about the AS/400. You probably even know enough to be able to skip most of this chapter.

Single-Level Storage

The AS/400 is a single-level storage machine. To the operating system, both memory and DASD (Direct Access Storage Device, or "disk") are treated the same. When a program runs and it needs to retrieve a piece of information, all the program needs to know is a single address. The operating system uses this address to retrieve the information whether it is in memory or DASD.

In addition, the AS/400 does not need to store an object in a single, continuous space on DASD. If you have a large file, for example, the file may be split in dozens or hundreds of small pieces and spread across several physical DASD units.

The advantage is immediate: neither the operating system nor the person who uses the system needs to worry about reserving enough space for objects because the system automatically uses whatever space is available, even if the pieces are many and far apart.

Along with this advantage, there is a price to pay. If one of the DASD units breaks down, you have a long and complicated recovery procedure ahead of you. The reason is because many thousands of objects could be affected. All these objects could have small splinters of their information in the DASD unit that failed and have the rest of their information in the other units. Consequently, none of the DASD units (except maybe one or two, if you are incredibly lucky) would have complete and usable objects.

Libraries

The most important concept in AS/400 architecture is that of a *library*. A library is just a container with a name. In other systems, a library is called a folder or a directory; on the AS/400, it is called a library.

Libraries can contain any number of objects, but they cannot contain other libraries. The only exception to this limitation is library QSYS, which is discussed later in this chapter.

Objects

Libraries contain objects. Objects come in many types, depending on their function. For example, there are files, programs, commands, job queues, message queues, data areas and panel groups. Each type of object has an object type identifier; files, for example, have an object type identifier of *FILE.

All identifiers begin with an asterisk, and have a standard abbreviation following the asterisk, such as PGM for program. You will learn more about object types in Section 5 later in this chapter.

Other System Storage

Libraries and objects are not everything. The AS/400 also uses DASD to store the system microcode, PTFs applied temporarily, system values, and all the QTEMP libraries. None of these items is stored in any library.

The system also occasionally places objects (such as files or programs) outside of any library. This is an abnormal situation, but it happens now and then, and is corrected with the Reclaim Storage (RCLSTG) command.

The Work with System Status (WRKSYSSTS) command displays the total amount of DASD in use. If you add up the sizes of all the objects in all the libraries, plus the sizes of the libraries themselves, you will not obtain the number shown by WRKSYSSTS. The difference is equal to the sum of all the items that are outside of libraries.

Section 2: IBM Libraries

IBM ships AS/400s with some libraries already installed. All IBM-supplied libraries have names beginning with the letter Q. The reverse ("all libraries that have names beginning with Q are IBM's) is not necessarily true because you can use the Create Library (CRTLIB) command to create a user library and give it any name you want (even if it begins with Q). However:

- Do not give your own libraries names beginning with the letter Q. You can name objects any way you want (even with Q at the beginning) but not libraries.

- *Never*, under any circumstances, delete an IBM-supplied library with the Delete Library (DLTLIB) command. If you absolutely have to get rid of one of them, you should treat the process as a deinstallation of a licensed program. Run the GO LICPGM command to get to the Licensed Programs menu, then select the option that deinstalls them. The system presents a list of all licensed products currently installed. Enter option 4 next to the item you want to delete and press Enter twice. You do not need a dedicated system to perform this task.

The rest of this section contains a brief description of some of IBM's libraries.

QSYS

QSYS is the most important library in the system. QSYS contains OS/400, the operating system, and it also contains all other libraries. You cannot operate an AS/400 without QSYS.

There are several types of objects that cannot be placed anywhere but in QSYS. Three examples are: user profiles, device descriptions and authorization lists.

QSYS has a number of unusual traits. You cannot save it with the Save Library (SAVLIB) command or restore with the Restore Library (RSTLIB) command. You cannot save any of its objects with the Save Object (SAVOBJ) or Save Changed Objects (SAVCHGOBJ) command. Consequently, you cannot restore them with Restore Object (RSTOBJ) either.

☞ You should *never*, under any circumstances, delete objects from QSYS. The various Delete (DLTxxx) commands will not stop you if you have enough authority, but the result could be disastrous. As you have read in the previous paragraph, you cannot save or restore QSYS objects. The only way to save QSYS is by running the Save System (SAVSYS) command. Except for a few exceptions, you cannot restore any QSYS objects except by reloading the entire operating system over again.

You can delete QSYS objects only if there are specialized commands for that purpose. For example, user profiles always reside in QSYS. You can delete user profiles (even though they are in QSYS) because there is a Delete User Profile (DLTUSRPRF) command. You must use the specialized command to perform the deletion.

On the other hand, there is no specialized command to delete a file from QSYS. The Delete File (DLTF) command is generic for all libraries.

☞ *Never*, under any circumstances, create one of your own objects into QSYS, or move one of your own objects from any library into QSYS. Leave QSYS for IBM-supplied objects.

QUSRSYS

QUSRSYS is a library where you can place user objects and still consider them, more or less, "system" objects. Typically, QUSRSYS contains message queues for user profiles, and some data files used by the system (which you can delete in most cases).

QUSRSYS, however, is a "normal" library. You can save it and restore it (as well as its contents) in the normal fashion.

Chapter 16 - Libraries, Objects and Library List

QHLPSYS

QHLPSYS contains all the help information (which is extensive) that is provided by the system at the touch of the Help Key. QHLPSYS contains most of this information in the form of panel group and search index objects.

QHLPSYS is not essential to run the system if you do not mind not having help available. The system-supplied help support is so convenient, however, that it is easy to take it for granted.

QGPL

QGPL's name stands for *General Purpose Library*. As this name implies, QGPL contains a potpourri of miscellaneous objects that can be used either by the system or by you at various times. QGPL contains objects such as job queues, subsystem descriptions, source physical files and output queues.

QGPL should not be cluttered with user objects. Do not use it to store your own objects unless there is a compelling reason to do so. Keep this advice in mind whenever you create an object.

☞ Most Create (CRTxxx) commands default the library to *CURLIB (whatever library happens to be your current library). However, if you do not have any library as current, the object is placed in QGPL.

QSPL

QSPL (spooling library) contains several database files used by the system to store reports and other printed output waiting to be printed. The database files in QSPL actually make up the system's spooling support.

☞ *Do not* ever, under any circumstances, manipulate these database files in any way. Do not even display them! The Display Physical File Member (DSPPFM) command locks the file and member you are displaying, but the system's spooling support needs these files to be free of any locks.

QDOC

Office Vision/400 and PC Support are licensed products that use folders and documents. Folders and documents cannot be stored just anywhere, they must created and maintained in library QDOC.

You should not save QDOC with the SAVLIB command or restore it with RSTLIB. The system has two specialized commands for QDOC: Save Document Library Objects (SAVDLO) and Restore Document Library Objects (RSTDLO).

Do not put any user objects in QDOC.

Product Libraries

IBM licensed program products are self-contained software packages. Each comes in a separate library (a product library).

For example, the Application Development Tools program product, also known as PDM (Program Development Manager), comes in library QPDA. The RPG/400 compiler and RPG/400 support come in library QRPG.

Special Environments

The AS/400 supports a System/36 and a System/38 environment. Both environments are contained in libraries.

The S/38 environment is contained in library QSYS38. QSYS38 contains all the commands used on the S/38 that can still be supported on the AS/400. Certain features such as card devices are no longer supported.

Besides QSYS38, the S/38 environment optionally can include libraries for some S/38 licensed program products such as RPG III support in library QPRPG38.

The S/36 environment is contained in several libraries. The main library is QSSP, which contains the S/36 SSP procedures, utility programs, control commands, and OCL interpreter. #LIBRARY is provided so you can place user objects you would have placed in #LIBRARY in a real-life S/36.

In addition to QSSP and #LIBRARY, the S/36 environment has QS36F, a library that contains all the database files used in the environment, and other libraries for licensed program products, such as #RPGLIB for RPG II support, or #SDALIBfor S/36 SDA support.

Chapter 16 - Libraries, Objects and Library List

Section 3: User Libraries

Aside from system libraries, the AS/400 can have any number of libraries you create. These libraries are referred to as user libraries.

Working with Libraries

The Work with Libraries (WRKLIB) command gives you a list of libraries. In the LIB parameter, you can specify what library or libraries you want to work with. For example, you could work with all user libraries on the system by executing:

```
WRKLIB LIB(*ALLUSR)
```

This command automatically filters out IBM-supplied libraries. Or, you could work with all libraries that have names beginning in Q by executing:

```
WRKLIB LIB(Q*)
```

If you have PDM installed on your system, you can also use the Work with Libraries using PDM (WRKLIBPDM) command, which provides a few additional features not available in WRKLIB.

Creating Libraries

Creating a library is easy. You run the CRTLIB command, and specify a few parameters. The LIB parameter, in particular, accepts the name you want to give the library.

☞ Do not choose a name that begins with the letter Q because this letter is reserved for IBM libraries.

Here are some examples:

```
CRTLIB LIB(MYLIB) TEXT('My library')
```

This command creates a library called MYLIB and gives it a text description of "My library."

```
CRTLIB LIB(SCRATCH) TYPE(*TEST) TEXT('Scratch work library')
```

This command creates a library called SCRATCH with a text description. The TYPE parameter is *TEST, which indicates that this library contains only test objects.

A test library (*TEST) does not protect its database files during debugging sessions, even if the programmer runs the Start Debug (STRDBG) command with UPDPROD(*NO), which normally would protect database files from updates.

Production libraries (*PROD), on the other hand, are protected from updates during debugging sessions if the programmer specifies UPDPROD(*NO) in the STRDBG command.

When you create a library, the system assumes TYPE(*PROD) by default.

```
CRTLIB LIB(PROJECT) AUT(*USE)
```

This command creates a library called PROJECT, and gives the library a public authority of *USE. This public authority means that all users, unless otherwise authorized, can use the library.

```
CRTLIB LIB(PROJECT) AUT(*USE) CRTAUT(*EXCLUDE)
```

The effect of this command is similar to the previous example. The only difference is that all objects created within library PROJECT will have a public authority of *EXCLUDE (by default). For example, if a user creates a data area and does not specify a public authority for it, the data area adopts the *EXCLUDE public authority specified in the library's CRTAUT parameter.

Displaying Libraries

Some time after creating the library, you may be curious about what objects are contained in it. You can quickly determine that using the Display Library (DSPLILB) command.

The DSPLIB command presents a list of objects and gives the size of each object. If you send this list to the screen, that information is all you get. If you send the list to the printer, however, the listing also contains the total of all the object sizes. Beware that this is not the size of the library, but only the total size of the objects contained in it. You still have to add the size of the library object itself to this number.

Here is an example of the DSPLIB command:

```
DSPLIB LIB(ARLIB) OUTPUT(*PRINT)
```

Chapter 16 - Libraries, Objects and Library List

Working with Objects

You can use two commands to work with objects within libraries: Work with Objects (WRKOBJ) and Work with Objects using PDM (WRKOBJPDM). The latter is available only if you have PDM installed on your system.

Both commands let you select the objects you want to work with. You indicate the name of the library (or libraries), the type of object, and the name of the objects (which can be generic). Here is an example:

```
WRKOBJ OBJ(*ALLUSR/CR*) OBJTYPE(*DTAARA)
```

This command shows all data area objects contained in any user library that have names which begin in CR. Once you have the list of objects on the screen, you can select a number of options. The option you pick depends on the kind of action you want to perform. For example, you can select option 4 to delete an object shown on the list.

Deleting Libraries

Deleting a library is a drastic action. Deleting a library not only deletes the library itself, but all the objects contained in it. For this reason, the process of deleting a library can take a considerable amount of time.

To delete a library, you need to run the DLTLIB command. This command only requires one parameter: the name of the library you want to delete.

☞ Rather than executing DLTLIB interactively, consider executing it in batch mode. Running DLTLIB in batch gives you better performance and does not lock up your display station:

```
SBMJOB CMD(DLTLIB LIB(MYLIB)) JOB(MYLIB)
```

If the library contains just a few objects (or is empty altogether), there is no harm in executing the DLTLIB command interactively:

```
DLTLIB LIB(MYLIB)
```

☞ *Never*, under any circumstances, delete an IBM library (name beginning in Q). If you want to delete a licensed product, use the Delete Licensed Program (DLTLICPGM) instead, or use the LICPGM menu, as follows:

```
GO LICPGM
```

```
LICPGM                  Work with Licensed Programs
                                                          System:    MC PGMR
  Select one of the following:

    Manual Install
       1. Install all

    Licensed Programs
      10. Display installed licensed programs
      11. Install licensed programs
      12. Delete licensed programs
      13. Save licensed programs

    Secondary Languages
      20. Display installed secondary languages
      21. Install secondary languages
      22. Delete secondary languages
                                                                More...
  Selection or command
  ===> 12_____

  F3=Exit    F4=Prompt    F9=Retrieve    F12=Cancel    F13=Information Assistant
  F16=AS/400 Main menu
  (C) COPYRIGHT IBM CORP. 1980, 1993.
```

Chapter 16 - Libraries, Objects and Library List

Select option 12 to delete licensed programs:

```
                        Delete Licensed Programs
                                                      System:    MC_PGMR
 Type options, press Enter.
   4=Delete

             Licensed                                              Installed
 Option      Program     Description                               Release
    _        5763SS1     OS/400 - Online Information               V3R1M0
    _        5763SS1     OS/400 - S/36 and S/38 Migration          V3R1M0
    _        5763SS1     OS/400 - System/36 Environment            V3R1M0
    _        5763SS1     OS/400 - Example Tools Library            V3R1M0
    _        5763SS1     OS/400 - AFP Compatibility Fonts          V3R1M0
    _        5763SS1     OS/400 - Host Servers                     V3R1M0
    _        5763SS1     OS/400 - GDDM                             V3R1M0
    _        5763SS1     OS/400 - Print Services Facility/400      V3R1M0
    _        5763AF1     Advanced Function Printing Utilities/400  V3R1M0
    _        5763CB1     Integrated Language Environment COBOL/400 V3R1M0
    _        5763CB1     ILE COBOL/400 - *PRV COBOL/400            V3R1M0
    _        5763CB1     ILE COBOL/400 - COBOL/400                 V3R1M0
    _        5763CD1     CoOperative Development Environment/400   V3R1M0
    _        5763CM1     Communications Utilities/400              V3R1M0
                                                                       More...
 F3=Exit    F12=Cancel
 (C) COPYRIGHT IBM CORP. 1980, 1994.
```

Now you can enter an option 4 next to each licensed program that you want to delete. Deleting the licensed program will delete the associated library; for example, if you choose to delete RPG/400, the system will delete library QRPG. This process does not require a dedicated system.

Section 4: QTEMP

QTEMP is not one library, but many. There is one QTEMP library per job on the system. Each time you sign on, the system creates one QTEMP library for your interactive job. When you submit a job to batch, the system creates another QTEMP library for the job you have just submitted. QTEMP's existence ends when the job ends.

QTEMP is an ephemeral library. You cannot create it or delete it with the standard CRTLIB or DLTLIB commands, but you can perform any of the other tasks related to libraries, including clearing it with the CLRLIB command.

The Privacy Act

Because there is a separate QTEMP library for each job, you cannot look at someone else's QTEMP library. If you run the DSPLIB command to display QTEMP, you will always see your own job's QTEMP. You cannot manipulate another job's QTEMP library in any way.

Automatic Delete

Always remember that the objects in QTEMP, as well as the library itself, are of a temporary nature. If you sign on and create an object in QTEMP, the object and the library exist until you sign off. When you sign off, both the objects and the library are automatically deleted from the system.

Using QTEMP

QTEMP is the ideal place to put objects that you need on a temporary basis only. Perhaps the best example is that of work files needed to gather information from several other files to prepare data to print a report. Once the report is printed, the work files are no longer needed.

If you create these work files in any other library, the files would remain on the system until you deleted them. In this case, you may forget, or the system may not have a chance to do under program control if the program aborts due to an error condition.

Rather than risking the job's continued existence (which could affect other jobs coming after it), it is much safer to create temporary objects in QTEMP and let the system delete them when the job ends. The job will end sooner or later, and the objects go with it, even if the job ends abnormally for any reason.

QTEMP and SBMJOB

The Submit Job (SBMJOB) command starts a brand new job and places it in a job queue. Because the job created by SBMJOB is completely separate from the original job, it has a different QTEMP library.

Therefore, you cannot create objects in your interactive job's QTEMP, submit a job to batch, and expect the batch job to use the objects you placed in QTEMP. It is the wrong QTEMP. The batch job's QTEMP is empty until that job, by itself, creates objects in it.

You must create objects in permanent libraries if you need to share those objects between two or more jobs.

Section 5: Objects

The AS/400 architecture supports a great variety of objects. Each object has a type identifier. The type identifier always begins with an asterisk and is followed by an abbreviated name, such as PGM for program. Therefore, the object type for a program is *PGM.

The rest of this section only describes some of the most important object types because there are far too many to describe them all.

Authorization List (*AUTL)

Authorization lists are objects you can create to simplify maintenance of object authorities. You can learn more about them in Chapter 11. All authorization lists must exist in QSYS.

Command (*CMD)

Commands are objects used to give an order to the system. When the system receives the command, it starts a particular task. All commands have an associated program object (*PGM), called the command processing program, which is the object that actually performs all the work. The command object acts as an interface between the user and the program.

Controller Description (*CTLD)

Controller descriptions must reside in QSYS. They are objects (such as a local workstation controller) that describe a controller device to the system.

Device Description (*DEVD)

Device descriptions must reside in QSYS. They are objects that describe a physical (although sometimes logical) device to the system. For example, when you configure a new printer, you create a device description for that printer.

Document (*DOC)

Documents can only exist in QDOC, and they must be processed either by Office Vision, by a PC through PC Support, or by APIs. Documents usually are word processing documents.

Data Area (*DTAARA)

Data areas are objects you can create to store small bits of information that are not repetitive in nature (a file would be overkill). Think of a data area as a file that has only one record. They are ideal for storing constants such as report titles and headings, or company names that could change someday.

Data Queue (*DTAQ)

Data queues are similar to data areas, except that they can contain multiple entries. They are the most efficient way to pass information between two programs. Data queues can be accessed by many programs at once. Some programs may be writing data and others may be reading. The main difference between a data queue and a file is that the latter has an internal structure known to the system (via DDS), while the former has no structure at all. Also, entries in a file can be read any number of times; entries in a data queue are usually deleted automatically as soon as they are read, unless system API QMHRDQM is used to read the data queue.

File (*FILE)

Files come in several subtypes, but all have something in common: they can contain many entries ("records"). The records remain until intentionally deleted, and the records have a template that defines data items ("fields"). Files are ideal for permanent (or at least long-term) storage of information.

Chapter 16 - Libraries, Objects and Library List

The file subtypes are:

- Physical database files. These are the files you normally think of as "files." They are permanent, and they contain data.

- Physical source files. Source files contain the source code for your programs, file definitions and commands.

- Logical files. Logical files are alternative views of physical files (either database or source). By "view" the system means a different sequencing of the records or a different selection of records (with some records omitted). To some extent, the System/36's alternative index files are logical files.

- Device files. Device files describe the data passed for input and output between the system and a physical device, such as a display station or a printer. If the device file describes a display station, it is often called a display file. If the device file describes a printer, it is usually called a printer file. There are also diskette files and tape files.

Folder (*FLR)

Folders, like libraries, are containers that have a name. The difference is that libraries contain objects, while folders can only contain other folders or documents. Libraries also cannot contain other libraries (except QSYS), but any folder can contain another folder. All folders reside in library QDOC.

Folders are processed by Office Vision and PC Support. In particular, PC Support treats folders as PC subdirectories.

Job Description (*JOBD)

Job descriptions are objects used to provide a set of attributes to a job that is about to begin. When you submit a job to batch, for example, you can attach a job description that provides the submitted job with things such as a library list and a default output queue. Job descriptions are described in detail in Chapter 11.

Job Queue (*JOBQ)

Job queues are objects you can create and maintain. When you submit a job to batch, the job must enter a subsystem (where the job's work is eventually performed) by passing through a job queue. The job may have to wait in the job queue for its turn to start. The system can have any number of job queues, and job queues may bring jobs to the subsystem in a single thread (one job at a time), or in groups of any size.

Journal and Journal Receiver (*JRN & *JRNRCV)

Journaling is a task that records events in journal receivers. Any event can be journaled, but in most cases it is a database file operation such as adding or changing a record. These events must go through a journal object. The journal channels the recording of the event into one or more journal receivers. Journaling is described in detail in Chapter 23.

Library (*LIB)

Libraries have been described already. They are mentioned again to reinforce the concept that they are just another type of object to the system.

Line Description (*LIND)

Line descriptions are objects used to describe a telecommunications line to the system. All line descriptions reside in QSYS.

Menu (*MENU)

Menus are objects used to start activities by selecting one of the options presented on the screen. A menu "ties" together a display file with either a message file or a program.

Message File (*MSGF)

Message files are not *FILE objects, but *MSGF. You cannot store data in them or use them to pass data between a program and a device. Message files can only contain message descriptions which are predefined messages with a fixed text and characteristics. The most important message file is QSYS/QCPFMSG which contains all the operating system's messages.

Message Queue (*MSGQ)

Message queues are repositories of messages that are waiting to be received by the user to which they are destined. The system automatically creates message queues for user profiles, but you can create your own.

Module (*Module)*MODULE

New in V2R3 is the *MODULE object. ILE (Integrated Language Environment) imposes the creation of modules from language-specific source code, which have to be bound together into a program before they can be executed.

Output Queue (*OUTQ)

Output queues are repositories for reports that are waiting to be printed. They are described in detail in Chapter 11.

Program (*PGM)

Programs are extremely important objects. They are the objects that actually perform work on the AS/400. Programs are created by a compiler when you run the compiler on a piece of source code that contains no syntax errors.

Programs are all in machine language. The source code (contained in source files) is what is written in languages like RPG/400, CL, COBOL or PL/I.

Panel Group (*PNLGRP)

Panel groups are objects used to present information on the screen. They are similar to display files, but have a different structure and somewhat different uses. All IBM-supplied OS/400 displays (except for a few) are panel groups.

Subsystem Description (*SBSD)

Subsystem descriptions are objects used to describe a subsystem. A subsystem is the place where work is actually performed. The subsystem (as controlled by the subsystem description) allocates resources and manipulates system objects in order to carry out the work intended for the jobs.

Service Program (*SRVPGM)

New in V2R3 is the *SRVPGM object. it is a collection of "utility"-type modules, each of which can be statically called from any program or module.

S/36 Machine Description (*S36)

There is only one object of type *S36, named QS36ENV in library #LIBRARY. This object contains the description of the System/36 environment. It contains all the systemwide settings the S/36 would have maintained with the CNFIGSSP procedure. For example it contains the default forms number, default session library, and other items such as the names of the physical devices.

User Profile (*USRPRF)

User profiles describe a computer user. They were described in detail in Chapter 11. They must reside in QSYS.

Section 6: Library List

Definition

OS/400 has a unique way to locate objects in the system: the library list. The library list is, as the name implies, a list of libraries. When you manipulate an object with any command but do not tell the system which library it resides in, the system uses the library list to find an object with a matching name.

The library list can have a maximum of 40 names and is always scanned from top to bottom. As soon as the system finds the object it is looking for in one of the libraries in the list, it searches no further. Therefore, the scanning process always stops at the first match.

Chapter 16 - Libraries, Objects and Library List

Structure

The library list consists of two parts: the system portion and the user portion. In addition, there can be two libraries sitting in between. These two libraries are called the product library and the current library. The setup is as follows:

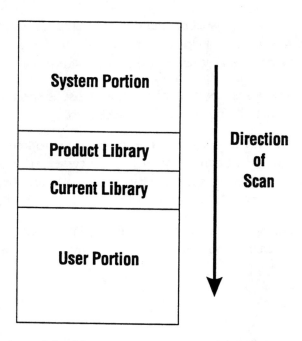

- The system portion of the library list must always exist, and must always contain at least QSYS. The system portion never can be empty, nor can it contain more than 15 names.

- The product library can become part of the library list on a temporary basis, while the system runs a command that uses a product library, or by displaying a menu (with the GO command) that uses a product library. The product library is removed from the library list as soon as the command ends, or as soon as the user exits the menu.

- The current library also can become part of the library list, but it can be a permanent part of it. The current library can be set with the CURLIB parameter of the user profile, or job description, or by executing the Change Current Library (CHGCURLIB) command.

  Many commands point to the current library with the special value *CURLIB instead of a library name. If your library list has a current library, that library name is substituted. If you do not have a current library, the system uses QGPL.

- The user portion of the library list can contain up to 25 names, but it also can be empty; it is completely optional.

The System Portion

The system portion of the library list is maintained by changing system value QSYSLIBL. The system portion of the library list does not exist anywhere else and is a system-wide setting that cannot be customized by user profile, workstation, or job description.

☞ You should keep the system portion of the library list as short as possible. Place in it only the libraries that all your users need access to.

Another good use for the system portion of the library list is to keep objects duplicated from QSYS (that later may have been changed), so the system uses your versions of the objects instead of those in QSYS. This is done by creating a library (which can be named ALTQSYS) and placing it above QSYS in the system portion of the library list.

Remember that the change you make in system value QSYSLIBL does not affect jobs that are already running. The change only affects new jobs initiated from that moment on.

The User Portion

The user portion of the library list should be used for libraries that depend on the nature of the job being performed. Each user can have a different set of libraries in the user portion of the library list. If you want to provide a system wide default set, use system value QUSRLIBL.

For example, you could create job descriptions for different people, and provide a different set of libraries in the INLLIBL parameter which lists the user portion of the library list only. The INLLIBL parameter can have special value *SYSVAL. In this case, the system uses the default set in system value QUSRLIBL for INLLIBL.

Changing the Library List

At any time during the life of a job, the library list can be changed with the Change Library List (CHGLIBL) or Edit Library List (EDTLIBL) command. These commands replace the whole set of the user portion of the library list in a single stroke.

Chapter 16 - Libraries, Objects and Library List

For subtler changes (such as adding or removing a library), use the Add Library List Entry (ADDLIBLE) or Remove Library List Entry (RMVLIBLE) command. The ADDLIBLE command lets you indicate where within the list you want to add the library.

You also can alter your job's copy of the system portion of the library list with the Change System Library List (CHGSYSLBL) command. When you execute this command, only your job is affected. All the others remain intact. The CHGSYSLIBL command lets you add a library at the very top of the system portion of the library list, or remove a library from it. You cannot control where in the system portion you are adding the library. The library always goes to the top.

Using the Library List

When you manipulate objects, you need to tell the system which library contains the object you are manipulating. For example, suppose you want to delete a data area named COMPANY. The system could have any number of data areas all named COMPANY, located in different libraries. How would the system know which one to delete?

There are two ways to reach the right data area: by qualifying its name with the name of the library where it resides, or by qualifying it with *LIBL, as follows:

```
DLTDTAARA DTAARA(MYLIB/COMPANY)
-or-
DLTDTAARA DTAARA(*LIBL/COMPANY)
```

In the first case, the system expects to find data area COMPANY in library MYLIB. If COMPANY is not there, the DLTDTAARA command ends in error.

In the second instance, the system scans the libraries in the library list for the job, from top to bottom, until it finds a data area named COMPANY. When the system finds the job, it deletes the data area and stops the scan. If the system runs out of libraries without finding COMPANY in the library list, the DLTDTAARA command ends in error.

You also can use *CURLIB, if you want to manipulate an object you know is in the current library, as follows:

```
DLTDTAARA DTAARA(*CURLIB/COMPANY)
```

Finally, you can omit the library qualifier altogether, as follows:

```
DLTDTAARA DTAARA(COMPANY)
```

This is equivalent to using *LIBL because the library name defaults to *LIBL in the DLTDTAARA command. Some commands default to *CURLIB. You should always make sure you know what the default value is before you use it.

FURTHER READING

IBM's *CL Programmer's Guide*.

17

Everything About Files

Files are objects (type *FILE) contained in libraries. Because of their importance, files deserve detailed coverage. Although this chapter is titled "Everything About Files," remember that the nature of this book is to provide the basics of the AS/400. You should interpret the title, therefore, as "everything a beginner needs to know about files."

Section 1: Classification of Files

There are many types of files. Before you continue reading about them, it is important that you recognize the following file types:

- Physical files. Physical files contain data and are subdivided into database and source physical files.

- Logical files. Logical files are objects that let you access the records in physical files using different views such as a different sequence, or omitting certain records. Logical files can also be used to join several physical files together.

- Device files. Device files are objects used for communications between a program and a physical device, such as a display station. The device file contains a layout of the data that is coming into or going out of the program. Device files are subdivided by device type, so there are display, printer, tape and diskette device files. The word "device" is frequently removed in these cases. For example, display device files are referred to as display files.

- Message files are not actual files; they have a different object type (*MSGF instead of *FILE).

Section 2: Physical Files

A physical file is the only type of file that actually contains data. They are used for permanent storage of information when the information is of repetitive nature. Physical files are used when there can be any number of identically-formatted entries (each entry being a record).

To display basic information about physical files, you can run the Display File Description (DSPFD) command.

Record Formats

A record format is a template that defines the fields contained in each record. This template has the name of the fields, their type, length, and other characteristics.

Physical files can contain only one record format. If your background is on the System/36, you are probably wondering how you can migrate all your multi-format files to the AS/400. There are two options.

1. Use a single database file that contains a single-character field as long as the record. You can then define the record within your programs as you did on the S/36. This method negates the advantages of the external file definition which is convenient to use.

2. Keep each record type in a separate physical file and put them together with a simple logical file. This method lets you keep the external file definition, but it involves more work.

Record formats are coded in Data Description Specifications (DDS), which are described in Chapter 18.

To display the record format of a physical file, use the Display File Field Description (DSPFFD) command. This command can send its output either to the display or to the printer.

File Members

A file is not necessarily composed of one piece. Physical files can be divided into file *members*. Each member of the file uses the same record format, but can contain a different set of records.

For example, one member of your General Ledger file could contain the journal entries for the month of April, while another member could contain those for May. In fact, you could have a separate member for each month of the year.

You can put members to many uses, but they do have an inherent risk. Most file operations assume you want to work with the first member of the file (which is the only member if there is only one). In order to process any other member of the file, you have to override the file. The file override points to a different member in the file.

Picture the following scenario. Your company has several manufacturing plants, and you want to use separate members in each of the files where you keep their data. You write a program that processes several of these files. You accidentally neglect to override one of them, and your program then processes the correct information for all but one of the files. The program still reads (and possibly updates) the records in the first member instead of the correct member.

☛ File members are a good concept, but you probably should avoid them. Instead of using multi-member database files, consider using separate files in different libraries.

Database Files

Physical files can be database files or source files. Database files contain information such as accounts receivable, open shop orders, hotel reservations, and the like. Database files are the types of files you would use to keep your company records.

Database files can have two different organizations: arrival sequence or keyed sequence. In System/36 terms, these are sequential and indexed files (direct files as such are not supported).

Here are some of the commands you can use with database files:

- Create Physical File (CRTPF). Use this command to create a new physical file. You can give this command a record length (with the RCDLEN parameter) or the name of a source file member that contains the DDS for the record format.

If you use RCDLEN, the file contains only one character field, as long as the record, with the same name as the file. This is the "flat file" concept. To use this kind of file, you need to define the internal fields in each program that uses the file.

If you use DDS, the file contains the fields described in the DDS, and if the DDS describe key fields, the file is considered of keyed organization (indexed). You cannot create a keyed file without DDS, except with the BLDINDEX procedure in the System/36 Environment.

When you use the CRTPF command, you also can specify how many members you want to allow as maximum (MAXMBRS parameter) and the maximum number of records (SIZE). Consider specifying SIZE(*NOMAX) for all physical files you create because it will save you headaches.

- Delete File (DLTF). Deletes a file and all its members. You cannot delete a physical file if you have created logical files based on it. You must first delete all the logical files based on the physical files and then delete the physical files themselves.

- Clear Physical File Member (CLRPFM). Deletes all records contained in a member of a physical file.

- Reorganize Physical File Member (RGZPFM). Removes all the deleted records from a physical file member, and optionally resequences the records. The RGZPFM command can be run without deleting logical files that may be built on top of the physical file.

- Change Physical File (CHGPF). Allows you to change some of the characteristics of a physical file, such as maximum number of members or records within a member.

- Add Physical File Member (ADDPFM) and Remove Member (RMVM). You can use these commands to add (or remove) a member in a physical file.

- Rename Member (RNMM). Used to change the name of a member.

- Display Physical File Member (DSPPFM). Lets you see the records contained in a physical file member. You can send the output to the screen or the printer.

- Copy File (CPYF). Use the CPYF command to copy from one file into another. If you specify TOFILE(*PRINT) or TOFILE(QSYSPRT), the CPYF command prints the list of records. CPYF has several parameters that let you select which records to copy.

Source Files

Source files are similar to database files, except that they are used to store the source code programmers use for programs, commands, file definitions, and the like.

Source files differ from database files in the following aspects:

- You cannot use DDS to define a record format. The record format is predefined as having three fields: SRCSEQ (sequence number, 6 characters), SRCDAT (date the record was last maintained, 6 characters) and SRCDTA (source data, any number of characters).

- You create a source file with the Create Source Physical File (CRTSRCPF) command instead of CRTPF. When you do so, you specify a record length in the RCDLEN parameter. If you want your source statements to allow n characters per statement, specify a record length of $n+12$. The record length defaults to 92, which lets you code statements up to 80 characters long.

- When you create a source file, it defaults to *NOMAX for the maximum number of members and *NONE for the name of the first member, which means there will not yet be any members.

- Source files are always of arrival sequence. They are never keyed. If you want to build a key, you need to create a logical file based on the source file.

- Use the Copy Source File (CPYSRCF) instead of CPYF to copy from one source file to another, or from a database file to a source file or vice-versa. Also, CPYSRCF gives you a better printout than CPYF if you specify TOFILE(*PRINT).

For source files, you can use any of the other listed commands for database files.

Section 3: Simple Logical Files

Logical files are objects (type *FILE) you can create over one or more physical files to access records differently. Although this is usually called a different view of the file, the system actually creates a different access path through the records. Logical files do not contain any actual data. Each "record" in a logical file is nothing but a pointer to the actual record in the physical file.

Logical files are divided in two major categories: simple and join. Simple logical files are covered in this section. Join logicals are covered in the next section.

AS/400 Primer

Creating a Simple Logical File

Simple logical files can be created over one or more physical files which can have entirely different record structures and may have no fields in common at all. Unless you choose to omit records, a simple logical file contains the sum of all the records in all the physical files it references.

To create the logical file, you must first write DDS specifications and compile them with the Create Logical File (CRTLF) command. The CRTLF command contains two parameters that cause confusion:

- MBR (Member). This parameter receives the name of the member, in the logical file, to be created along with the file. It defaults to *FILE, which means that the logical file is created with one member named like the file.

- DTAMBRS (Data Members). This parameter receives the names of the physical files and physical file members from which the logical file will draw data to create the member named in the MBR parameter. This parameter defaults to *ALL, which means that the logical file member named in MBR will be based on all the files and all the members in each file that have been referenced in the DDS of the logical file.

Adding and Removing Members

After creation, you can add members to a logical file with the Add Logical File Member (ADDLFM) command or remove members with the Remove Member (RMVM) command.

The ADDLFM command contains the same pair of MBR and DTAMBRS parameters, and they mean the same as they do for the CRTLF command.

Using Simple Logical Files

Simple logical files have many uses:

- They can provide a key to an arrival sequence file. Often, it is more convenient (and efficient) to create physical files without a key (in other words, arrival sequence files). Using logical files is a good idea especially if the file contains many records or will undergo much maintenance. For example, a transaction history file (such as inventory) can have several hundred thousand records (or even millions of records).

- They can provide a different key to a keyed file. Sometimes you have a keyed file, but for the purposes of an application program, you need to access the records using a different key field. Logical files let you do that.

- They let you omit records from a file. If an application program can only use records that follow a certain pattern, you can create a logical file that include only the records that follow the pattern. The application program then does not need to make the selections. As far as the program is concerned, it needs to process all records.

- They let you redefine the key. If the key to the file is on a character field that can contain uppercase and lowercase letters, a logical file is capable of disregarding the distinction between upper- and lowercase.

- They let you combine the records of more than one member, or more than one physical file together. Logical files can have multiple record formats.

- They let you exclude fields from the record layout of the physical file. This is useful for files that contain sensitive or confidential information. For example, you can define a logical file on top of the Employee Master (physical) file that has the same or different key. The logical file could exclude pay rate and other confidential data. Even if all users were allowed to read the file, the confidentiality would not be compromised.

To the application program, a logical file looks just like a physical file. You code the same file description and operations you would code for a physical file.

Section 4: Join Logical Files

Join logical files are similar to simple logical files both in concept and in manipulation. However, record structure and update capability are some differences that are worth analyzing.

Record Structure in Join Logicals

Join logical files can combine fields from several physical files in a single record format. The system only requires that the physical files have equivalent fields in each file. The fields must also have equal values through which to join the two records.

For example, consider the following case. You have three files: COM (customer order master), COLI (customer order line items) and IM (item master).

COM contains the following fields:

```
COORD#      Customer order number
COCUST      Customer number
COPO#       Purchase order number
```

COLI contains the following fields:

```
LIORD#      Customer order number
LIITEM      Item number
LIQTY       Quantity ordered
```

IM contains the following fields:

```
IMITEM      Item number
IMDESC      Description
IMCOST      Unit cost
```

Through a join logical, you can combine all fields into a single record format (a single file containing all the fields) because COM and COLI have the order number in common, and COLI and IM have the item number in common. The join logical would therefore have the following fields:

```
JFORD#      Customer order number
JFCUST      Customer number
JFPO#       Purchase order number
JFITEM      Item number
JFQTY       Quantity ordered
JFDESC      Description
JFCOST      Unit cost
```

All this information would be contained in a single join logical file. Next time you need to create a program to print a report based on these fields, you would have to process only one file (the join logical).

Updating Data

Join logicals cannot be used to update the data fields they have joined. Join logical files can only be used to read data. If you want to change the contents of any of the fields in the join logical file's record, you must perform the update through the appropriate physical file.

Section 5: Display and Printer Files

Display and printer files are two of the types of device files supported by the AS/400. They are as important as physical and logical files because they provide an avenue through which a program communicates with the user.

In theory, both display and printer files can be created with or without DDS. In practice, however, display files are almost useless if they are created without DDS. Printer files, on the other hand, are equally useful either way if you program mainly in RPG/400. In other languages, printer files are much easier to handle if they are created with DDS.

The remainder of this section assumes that you create your display and printer files with DDS.

Common Features

Both display and printer files support the following features:

- They usually contain more than one record format. A display file can use one record format to ask the user to enter a customer number, and a different record format to display the customer's information. A printer file can use one record format for report headings and a different one for columnar data.

- Both support constant fields. Constant fields, as their name implies, are fields that never change in value. In a display file, a constant field could be the title that is centered at the top, or the legend that informs the user to press F3 to exit the program.

- Fields can be conditioned with indicators. You can condition the inclusion of a field in a record format, so that the field is part of the record only if a set of indicators match a certain pattern (off-on-off, for example). You can also condition some of the attributes of a field, such as making it appear underlined. Indicators are logical variables (switches) that can have only two values: on or off.

Display Files

You create a display file by writing the DDS and running the Create Display File (CRTDSPF) command. Display files offer a variety of functions:

- Data can go into or out of the program because the fields can be defined as input, output, or both.

- The display file can sense when the user has pressed a function key (F1 to F24, Enter, Roll Up, Roll Down) and notify the program through an indicator.

- The display file can also sense many things about the input entered by the user and can act upon them. For example, you can define an input field in such a way that it only accepts the values 'A' or 'B.' If the user enters a 'C,' the display file rejects the input. The program does not get involved.

- You can define subfiles within the display file. A subfile is a group of similar records that can be displayed at once on the screen and make columns of data. You can use arrays to simulate these columns, but subfiles simplify some of the coding (although they complicate other things).

The utility called Screen Design Aid (SDA) simplifies the design and maintenance of display files. SDA is described in Chapter 22.

Printer Files

Technically speaking, a printer file does not pass information from the program to the printer, but to a spool file in an output queue. In order to avoid unnecessary confusion, however, the popular "printer file" term will be used.

Printer files do more than pass information to a printer. They also format the data by adhering to the record format definition. They also contain a number of printer settings necessary to print the report successfully.

For example, you can create a printer file for printing purchase order forms. When you create the printer file (with the Create Printer File [CRTPRTF] command), you tell the system what form type to use, how many lines long the form is, how many characters wide, whether to skip unprintable characters, and the name of the default output queue or printer device.

From then on, each time you run a program that writes to that printer file, the system remembers all the printer settings and automatically generates a spool file that matches them. You do not have to remember the settings.

Printer files do not offer as many bells and whistles as display files because printers are not capable of receiving input or presenting text in blinking characters, for example. Printer files can still simplify the generation of bar codes and provide two special effects: underline and highlighting (by printing more than once on the same spot).

Chapter 17 - Everything About Files

You can design printer files by entering the DDS specifications directly with SEU, but there is another way using Report Layout Utility (RLU). Some programmers find RLU more trouble than it is worth, and others swear by it. You need to make your own decision by trying out the utility.

Section 6: Sharing Files

Open Data Paths

Each time you open a file, the system creates what is called an *open data path* (ODP). You can think of the ODP as a tunnel between your program and the file you are using. Each time you open a file, the system has to dig open a new tunnel.

If you have an application that consists of several programs that call one another, there is a good chance that more than one program will use the same file. In this case, the system digs open one tunnel (ODP) when it runs the first program. When it runs the second program that uses the same file, it digs another tunnel, even though the first one is already open and is not in use. All this digging is a lot of unnecessary work.

Sharing files means sharing the ODP. When you share files, the system creates a single ODP for each file, which can substantially improve performance. However, ODPs cannot be shared across different jobs. ODP's can only be shared among the programs that run in the same job. This limitation also means that your interactive job cannot share an ODP with a job you submit to batch because the interactive and the batch jobs are different.

Coding Files For Sharing

You can force the system to always share a file by using the SHARE*YES parameter in either the Create (CRTxxxF) or Change (CHGxxxF) command. For example, if you have a physical file you suspect always will need to be shared, you can change the file to SHARE(*YES) with the Change Physical File (CHGPF) command, as follows:

```
CHGPF FILE(...) SHARE(*YES)
```

More often than not, however, you need to control when a file is available for share and when it is not. Because of this, the SHARE parameter defaults to *NO in all commands.

If you create a file with SHARE(*NO) and want to be able to share its open data path, do not change it to SHARE(*YES) and back. Instead, use the Override File (OVRxxxF) command with SHARE(*YES) in the CL program that controls your job. As you will learn in the following section, file overrides provide a way to produce a localized change (as opposed to a permanent, system wide change) in the characteristics of a file.

When you no longer want to share the ODP to the file, you can either override the file again to SHARE(*NO) or delete the override.

Disadvantages of Sharing

Sharing ODPs can cause problems. If programs A and B share the ODP of a database file and program A calls program B, the following abnormal situation can occur:

Program A reads record 347 randomly by record number, then calls program B. Program B issues a read prior operation on the same file. The file pointer changes to 346; then program B returns control to A. Program A updates the record in the file. Because the file pointer changed position, the wrong record is updated.

☛ Whenever you share ODPs, you must make sure you are processing the record you think you are processing. Read the record again if in doubt.

Section 7: Overriding Files

The Concept

Files always are processed with certain assumptions. Certain conditions are taken for granted. For example, when you execute a program that reads records from a database file, the system feeds the program the first member of the file, no matter how many members are in the file.

These assumptions may not reflect what you want to do, however. In some cases you could change the file with one of the CHGxxxF commands, but doing so would change the file for all jobs on the system and, unless you change the file back, the file stays changed forever.

The alternative is to override the file. A file override is a temporary and localized change in the file. When you override a file, the change you are making is taken into account only by the job you are running. The file itself is not changed. Other jobs that are running are not affected.

Override File Commands (OVRxxxF)

There are a number of OVRxxxF commands; practically one for each type of file. For example, there is an OVRDSPF command to override display files, and OVRPRTF to override printer files. There is no OVRPF or OVRLF for physical files and logical files, however. They are combined into the Override Database File (OVRDBF) command.

Each override file command has a different set of parameters because each type of file has different requirements and attributes that can be overridden. For example, although it makes sense to override a database file so that member ABC is used instead of the first one, it would not make sense to perform an identical override to a display file because display files have no members. Therefore, the OVRDBF file has a MBR parameter, but the OVRDSPF does not.

Scope of the Override

File overrides begin when you execute the appropriate OVRxxxF command and end when the program (or request level) ends. For example, if you run a CL program that performs an OVRDBF command, the override stays in effect until the CL program ends. Note that it remains in effect in any program the CL program may call.

If program A overrides file X and then calls program B, file X is still overridden throughout the execution of B. When control returns to A, the file is still overridden. When program A ends, the file is no longer overridden.

Another way to end an override is by executing the Delete Override (DLTOVR) command. This command deletes all overrides you have performed on a file, or on all files.

Accumulating Overrides

Overrides also accumulate from one program level to the next. For instance, program A overrides database file INVENTORY so that member CHICAGO is processed:

```
OVRDBF FILE(INVENTORY) MBR(CHICAGO)
```

Program A now calls program B, which overrides the same file to block sequential reads in chunks of 100 records:

```
OVRDBF FILE(INVENTORY) SEQONLY(*YES 100)
```

By then, file INVENTORY has two overrides in effect: MBR(CHICAGO) and SEQONLY(*YES 100). Both overrides have accumulated. If you want the second override to replace the first rather than accumulate, you need to add the SECURE(*YES) parameter to the second OVRDBF.

A Few Gotchas to Watch Out For

Overriding files is a tricky business. File overrides do not always work as you might anticipate. Here are some things to watch out for:

- If the same program issues two OVRxxxF commands to the same file, the first override is completely ignored. For example, if you override a printer file (OVRPRTF) first with LPI(4) and then with CPI(15), CPI(15) is the result.

- If program A calls program B and both programs override the same attribute of the same file, the override issued by program B is ignored. For example, if program A overrides a printer file with LPI(4) and program B overrides it with LPI(8), the result is LPI(4). Both programs are overriding the same attribute (LPI). If you want to make sure that program B's override applies, add SECURE*YES to the override command.

- If program A calls program B and they override different attributes of the same file, the overrides accumulate. If you want to isolate B's overrides instead of accumulating the overrides of both programs, add SECURE(*YES).

- If program A calls program B and A overrides a file, program B cannot use the Delete Override (DLTOVR) command to remove the overrides because B did not issue them.

Some OVRDBF Uses

The OVRDBF command has quite a few parameters. The following lists some of them and their uses.

- TOFILE. If you have a program that uses file ACCOUNT but you want the program to process file ACCTG, override the file as follows:

Chapter 17 - Everything About Files

```
OVRDBF FILE(ACCOUNT) TOFILE(ACCTG)
```

The TOFILE parameter contains the real name of the file you will be processing. The FILE parameter is the name with which the program knows the file. The TOFILE parameter can also be used to point to a particular library so the system does not use the library list to locate the file. This can be handy in situations where the same file exists in two or more libraries and you want to process one of them but are not sure if it is the first one in the library list. Code the following override:

```
OVRDBF FILE(ACCOUNT) TOFILE(ARLIB/ACCOUNT)
```

This command ensures that the program processes the ACCOUNT file located in library ARLIB and no other.

- MBR. Normally, the system processes the first member in a file, no matter how many members there are in the file. If you want to process any member other than the first, you must override the file. Name the member you want to process in the MBR parameter, as follows:

```
OVRDBF FILE(ACCOUNT) MBR(SANDIEGO)
```

You can even specify MBR(*ALL) if you want your program to process all records in all the files. If you use such a file in RPG, the LR indicator will not turn on until all records in all members have been read.

- POSITION. This parameter lets you set the file pointer in a particular position, ready for a read operation. For example, *FIRST positions the file pointer at the first record. *RRN and a record number place the pointer at that record. Further, there are several values you can use to position the file pointer using keys, such as *KEYAE for "key after or equal" to a particular value. This parameter is especially useful when reading a database file in a CL program. With the POSITION parameter, a CL program can read a file randomly by record number, or randomly or sequentially by key.

- SHARE. Lets you share the open data path (ODP) of a database file. See the preceding section for a description of file sharing.

- SEQONLY. If your programs are going to read a file sequentially only, you can improve performance by blocking the records in chunks of a certain number of records, such as SEQONLY(*YES 500). With a file overridden this way, the first read operation in the program would bring 500 records into the input buffer. The following 499 reads would pull the records from the buffer which, being in memory, is much faster than a disk I/O.

Knowing how many records to block can be tricky. As a general rule, block your records so that each block is about 28KB. For example, suppose you are going to process a file sequentially, and that its record length is 300 bytes. Because 28KB is 28672 bytes, divide that number by 300 (the record length). It turns out that the optimum block size should have 95 records. You would, therefore, use SEQONLY(*YES 95).

FURTHER READING

IBM's *Database Guide*.

IBM's *CL Reference*.

Part V: Programming

18

DDS

Section 1: General Overview

What Is DDS?

DDS stands for **D**ata **D**escription **S**pecifications. DDS is a programming language that originated with the System/38. DDS is used to describe records in files by giving a name to the record and listing all the fields that will be considered part of the record.

You can also describe the file inside each program that uses it. Older systems often describe files this way because there is no other choice. The problem with these program-described files (as they are often called) is that they have a tendency toward lack of standardization. For example, the first field of the file (which holds a vendor number) may be called VNDNBR in one program, VENDOR in another, and VENDNO in a third.

Because each program must contain the entire definition for the record, the effort is multiplied by whatever number of programs use the same file. Although using compiler directives such as /COPY in RPG alleviates the problem, files created with DDS are fully defined to the system. The system knows what fields make up the record, so it can make use of this definition everywhere a file is used. For example:

- CL programs have no compiler directive to copy source code (like /COPY in RPG). If you use a file in CL, you have to declare each field separately or at least know its absolute position within the record. If the file were created with DDS, however, the CL program already knows the definition of the file.

- Products and features such as Query/400, SQL/400, OPNQRYF and Query Management also can make use of the definition of the file provided by DDS. Without this file definition, it would be impractical (to say the least) to use any of these products, except Query/400 which can use IDDU file definitions.

Coding DDS

DDS is coded in source file members like any other piece of programming code. IBM suggests you use source physical file QDDSSRC in whatever library you are programming. You do not have to, however; if you feel better having one source physical file (call it SOURCE), you can do that too.

The source type depends on the type of file for which you are coding DDS: PF for physical files, LF for logical files (including join logicals), DSPF for display files, and PRTF for printer files.

SEU supports DDS. For example, SEU has predefined prompts for entering DDS. These prompts are: PF (physical files), LF (logical files) and DP (display or printer files).

The A-Specs

DDS is coded by entering letters and numbers in the A-specifications ("A-specs"), which are like RPG's various specifications. The main difference is that the A-specs have an **A** in column 6. If you are familiar with RPG, you probably would have guessed as much.

☞ Throughout this chapter, a reference such as "1-5" means "columns 1 to 5." A simple "27" means "column 27."

The A-specs have the following structure:

Sequence number. 1-5 can contain an optional sequence number. This number is rarely (if ever) used because it does nothing but clutter the code with useless information (the compiler never uses it).

Specification type. 6 is where you code the letter **A** that identifies this statement as an A-spec. However, this entry is optional. You do not have to code an **A** because all specifications in a DDS source member are always A-specs. The compiler does not need this entry, but you still may want to code it for documentation.

Comments, AND or OR. 7 can contain an asterisk (*) to indicate that the current line is a comment. If 7 contains an **A** (AND) or an **O** (OR), then the indicators coded in 8-16 of this line are logically connected (with AND or OR) to those of the previous line. It works like RPG's AN and OR entries in 7-8 of the C-specs.

Conditioning indicators. 8-16 can contain one, two or three indicators that condition the entire line. Some types of files such as physical and logical files do not allow indicators.

Type. In some cases, 17 must contain a particular entry to identify records (**R**), key fields (**K**), or the conditions under which records are selected (**S**) or omitted (**O**) from a logical file. In join logical files, a **J** indicates the beginning of join specifications (how to join the files). In display files, an **H** marks the beginning of help specifications. The most common entry, however, is a blank. Blanks are used to define fields within records and in many other cases.

Name. 19-28 are used to code the name of a record or field within a record. Pay particular attention to the fact that you are given 10 characters to name the record or field you are coding. You can always define records and fields with up to 10 characters in the name, but if you use RPG/400 as your main programming language, you will have to rename the fields inside the program. Doing this takes away most of the advantages of defining the file externally to the program. Practical considerations (for RPG/400 users only) suggest that you restrict names to six characters.

Reference. If you code an **R** in 29, it means that the field named in 19-28 (see above) is defined by referencing another field, usually a field of the same name in a different file (although this is not always the case). This eliminates the need to define the same field over again in many files. When you define by reference you do not have to provide any other definition options unless you want to override some of them.

Length. 30-34 contain the length of the field named in 19-28.

Data type. 35 is used to indicate what type of data is associated with the field named in 19-28. For example, a **P** indicates packed decimal and an **A** indicates alphanumeric. Another frequent entry is **S** for zoned decimal.

Decimal positions. 36-37 are used for numeric fields only. From the number of digits indicated in 30-34, 36-37 indicate how many are to the right of the decimal mark. So, if 30-34 have a 7 and 36-37 have a 2, the field in 19-28 is defined as 7 digits long with 2 decimal places. Therefore, it can hold a number as large as 99,999.99.

Usage. 38 indicates how the field in 19-28 is used. It can be defined for input only (**I**), output only (**O**) or both (**B**). There are other entries you can code here.

Location. Display and printer files (only) require that you indicate where to place the field in 19-28. You can do this by coding a line number in 39-41 and a column number in 42-44.

Functions. 45-80 can contain constants or optional DDS keywords that give additional information about the fields or records being defined elsewhere. For example, if you define a numeric field that is to contain a date, you can code EDTCDE(Y) anywhere in the functions area to indicate that the field should be edited with an edit code Y.

Complexity of DDS

DDS is one of the most complex and least intuitive programming languages available on the AS/400. Because the intent of this book is to present the basics of the AS/400, it does not attempt to mention anything but the essentials you need to get started. Undoubtedly, you will want more information and you should refer to IBM's *DDS Reference* manual (SC41-9620-00).

Section 2: Physical Files

Physical files are easy to describe in DDS because their structure is simple. Only one record format is allowed in a physical file. A physical file definition consists of little besides a record name, a series of field descriptions and an optional key definition (if the file is keyed).

After you have coded the DDS for a physical file in a source member (type PF), you compile the source (create the file) with the Create Physical File (CRTPF) command.

A Simple Example

Here is an example of a physical file, described with DDS. It is called VNDMST (vendor master):

Chapter 18 - DDS

```
....1....+....2....+....3....+....4....+....5....+....6....+....7....+
A                                       UNIQUE
A *
A          R VNDREC                     TEXT('Vendor record')
A            VNVEND         6A          TEXT('Vendor number')
A                                       COLHDG('Vendor' 'Number')
A            VNNAME        30A          COLHDG('Vendor' 'Name')
A            VNADR1        30A          COLHDG('Address' 'Line 1')
A            VNADR2        30A          COLHDG('Address' 'Line 2')
A            VNCITY        20A          COLHDG('City')
A            VNSTE          2A          COLHDG('State Code')
A            VNZIP          5P 0        COLHDG('Zip Code')
A                                       RANGE(00000 99999)
A            VNDUE          9P 2        COLHDG('Amount' 'Due')
A                                       EDTCDE(J $)
A *
A          K VNVEND
```

DDS keyword UNIQUE has been coded before any record in the file is defined. That makes this keyword applicable to the whole file. Keywords that apply to the entire file are said to be file-level keywords. UNIQUE indicates that the file is keyed and that the key should be unique. No duplicate keys are allowed. If you omit UNIQUE, the file can have duplicate keys.

Two comment lines are indicated by an asterisk in 7. These lines are only used to separate groups of lines that belong together.

The third line describes record (**R** in 17) named VNDREC. Note that the TEXT keyword appears on the same line, which makes TEXT a record-level keyword. In this case, it describes the purpose of the record.

The A-specs that follow describe the fields contained in record VNDREC: VNVEND (6 bytes alphanumeric), VNNAME, VNADR1 and VNADR2 (30 bytes alphanumeric), VNCITY (20 bytes alphanumeric), VNSTE (2 bytes alphanumeric), VNZIP (5 digits, no decimals, packed decimal), and VNDUE (9 digits, 2 decimals, packed decimal). Finally, the key to the file (**K** in 17) is defined as consisting of field VNVEND only.

Look at the definition of field VNVEND. The line contains not only the name of the field (VNVEND) and its definition, but also keyword TEXT which, in this case, is a field-level keyword because it applies to that field only. The next line also applies to field VNVEND. The line gives the field a column heading of 'Vendor' and 'Number' (stacked on two consecutive lines) when printed or displayed by Query/400 or SQL/400.

Field VNZIP also has a column heading, but it also has the DDS keyword RANGE which indicates that the zip code must have a value between 00000 and 99999. This range excludes negative numbers, of course. Although the physical file does not complain if you write a zip code that is out of range, it is useful to include these keywords. When you reference VNZIP in a display file, for example, the display file will not allow the user to enter values outside of that range, and you will not have to code anything in your data entry program to make it happen.

Finally, field VNDUE has keyword EDTCDE (edit code). The first value is the edit code itself (J). The second (optional) value indicates a floating currency symbol. Again, the physical file does not use this information, but it is there ready for reference by display and printer files. When the amount you owe to the vendor is displayed or printed, it will automatically have a floating currency symbol and will be edited with commas and a trailing sign (edit code J). You will not have to do anything in your program. You also will not have to remember to code this in your display or printer file.

Defining by Reference

Of the variations to the basic example shown above, the most important is defining a record or a field by reference to another record or field elsewhere. For example, suppose you want to create another physical file that has the same record layout without any changes. You can do so by coding a one-line DDS member, as follows:

```
....1....+....2....+....3....+....4....+....5....+....6....+....7....+
A          R VNDREC                    FORMAT(VNDMST)
```

You can call this the SUPPLIER file. Note that the record name (VNDREC) is the same. The FORMAT keyword references the name of the file serving as a model. As you can see, this method is very inflexible. You must name the new record the same as the existing one, and you must include all fields with identical names and attributes.

Another more flexible method to define by reference involves the REF and the REFFLD keywords. Suppose you need to create a file called VNDCONT (vendor contacts) that must include the vendor number, the name of a person to contact and a phone number. Here is what the DDS could look like:

Chapter 18 - DDS

```
....1....+....2....+....3....+....4....+....5....+....6....+....7....+
A                                       REF(VNDMST)
 *
A          R VCRCD                      TEXT('Vendor contact record')
A            VCVEND      R              REFFLD(VNVEND)
A            VCNAME      R              REFFLD(VNNAME)
A                                       COLHDG('Contact' 'Name')
A            VCPHNE     15A             COLHDG('Contact' 'Phone No.')
 *
A          K VCVEND
```

The REF(VNDMST) keyword indicates that this member can define fields by referencing fields contained in the VNDMST file. That technique is used to define fields VCVEND and VCNAME.

VCVEND is the vendor number. You could have kept the name VNVEND, but if you work with RPG/400, you almost need to give all fields a different name across files. The **R** in 29 indicates that this field is defined by reference, so there is no indication of length or data type. The REFFLD(VNVEND) keyword indicates that field VNVEND serves as the model. Keywords associated with VNVEND in file VNDMST automatically apply to the new field, VCVEND. In this case, VCVEND will have the same column headings.

Field VCNAME also is defined by reference. It copies the definition of field VNNAME. Because VNNAME has column headings that read "Vendor Name," you need to override that. Therefore, the COLHDG keyword follows on the next line.

The last field in the record is new, so you cannot define it by reference. Note that the key is now field VCVEND (not VNVEND). Because the UNIQUE key was not included in this file's definition, the file allows duplicate keys, which is good because there can be more than one contact for each vendor.

☞ Defining by reference is a powerful technique. It not only saves work, but it makes your database more consistent. You define a piece of data in only one place, then you use that definition everywhere else it is needed.

Section 3: Simple Logical Files

Logical files do not contain data. They are nothing but a file of pointers. Each pointer contains the address of a record in a physical file that contains the data. Logical files can be used to create a new access path over existing data. For example, you can create a logical file to define a different key and/or to omit records from a file.

Logical files also can be used to join two or more files together. This technique is explained in Section 4.

The DDS for a logical file is entered in a source file member (type LF). When you are done coding it, you can compile the source (creating the file) with the Create Logical File (CRTLF command.

Defining Another Key

Go back to the VNDMST physical file defined in Section 2. You may need to process its records, not by vendor number (the physical file key), but by the zip code, if you are going to do a massive mailing campaign on all your vendors. Suppose you want to send Christmas cards to all your vendors. You choose a zip code sequence to take advantage of discounts offered by the postal service. Here is the DDS for a logical file, keyed by zip code:

```
....1....+....2....+....3....+....4....+....5....+....6....+....7....+
A          R VZLREC                   PFILE(VNDMST)
 *
A          K VNZIP
```

The record-level keyword PFILE names the physical file (VNDMST in this case) over which you are building this logical file. Following that, you name the new key field (or fields) to the file.

If you need to process the vendor records by reverse zip code order (beginning with 99999 and ending with 00000), add the DESCEND keyword on the line that defines the key field, as follows:

```
....1....+....2....+....3....+....4....+....5....+....6....+....7....+
A          R VZLREC                   PFILE(VNDMST)
 *
A          K VNZIP                    DESCEND
```

☛ In both cases, the file will allow duplicate keys because there is no UNIQUE keyword. Most logical files use duplicate keys because they provide a key that is different from the physical file key (which usually identifies a record).

Selecting And Omitting Records

Logical files also can select and omit records from the access path. If you wanted to send Christmas cards to all vendors to whom you owe $5,000 or more, code the following:

```
....1....+....2....+....3....+....4....+....5....+....6....+....7....+
A          R VZLREC                   PFILE(VNDMST)
 *
A          K VNZIP
 *
A          S VNDUE                    COMP(GE 5000.00)
```

The **S** in 17 defines a select specification. It defines which records to include in the access path of the logical file. The records included will be those whose VNDUE field is greater than or equal to 5000.00. The COMP keyword compares the field value against the literal included within.

☞ Note that the comparison operator is GE, not *GE as it would be in CL (i.e., there is no asterisk).

If you wanted to include vendors to whom you owe $5,000 or more, but not more than $10,000, code the following:

```
....1....+....2....+....3....+....4....+....5....+....6....+....7....+
A          R VZLREC                   PFILE(VNDMST)
 *
A          K VNZIP
 *
A          S VNDUE                    COMP(GE 5000.00)
A            VNDUE                    COMP(LE 10000.00)
```

In this case, there are two selection specifications. The absence of an **S** on the second one means that the two comparisons are combined with an AND. Therefore, the selection means "select records with VNDUE greater than or equal to 5000, and less than or equal to 10000." If you had placed an **S** on the second line, the two lines would have been connected with an OR operator.

Because you are describing a range of values you want to consider valid for VNDUE, you can shorten the code by using the RANGE keyword instead:

```
    ....1....+....2....+....3....+....4....+....5....+....6....+....7....+
    A          R VZLREC                   PFILE(VNDMST)
    *
    A          K VNZIP
    *
    A          S VNDUE                    RANGE(5000.00 10000.00)
```

Now, suppose you still want this selection, but you do not want to include vendors in California, Oregon and Washington (state codes CA, OR and WA). You can code the following:

```
    ....1....+....2....+....3....+....4....+....5....+....6....+....7....+
    A          R VZLREC                   PFILE(VNDMST)
    *
    A          K VNZIP
    *
    A          S VNDUE                    RANGE(5000.00 10000.00)
    A          O VNSTE                    VALUES('CA' 'OR' 'WA')
```

The **O** (the letter, not a zero) in 17 describes an omission specification. All records having CA, OR or WA in VNSTE will be omitted.

Section 4: Join Logical Files

What Is a Join File?

Join files are a special kind of logical file you can use to combine, in a single record, the fields contained in two or more records (in files elsewhere). Join files have the following limitations:

- You cannot open a join file for update or output. You can only open a join file for input. In other words, you can only read a join file.

- A join file can contain only one record format, as opposed to non-join logicals, which can contain many record formats.

- You can join two records only if the joining fields have the same type length and have equal values.

Chapter 18 - DDS

- If you define key fields for a join file, all key fields that make up the key must come from the first file listed in the JFILE keyword (see below).

An Example of Join File

In Section 2, two physical files were defined: a vendor master (VNDMST) and a vendor contact (VNDCONT) file. Join the two files using the vendor number (common in both files) as the join field.

```
....1....+....2....+....3....+....4....+....5....+....6....+....7....+
A          R JFREC                      JFILE(VNDMST VNDCONT)
 *
A          J                            JOIN(VNDMST VNDCONT)
A                                       JFLD(VNVEND VCVEND)
A            VNVEND
A            VNNAME
A            VNADR1
A            VNADR2
A            VNCITY
A            VNSTE
A            VNZIP
A            VCNAME
A            VCPHNE
 *
A          K VNVEND
```

Take note of the following points:

- The record definition contains the keyword JFILE that lists the files being joined.

- Immediately following is a line with a **J** in 17. This line defines the method for joining the files. The JOIN keyword lists the two files being joined. The next line indicates which fields are used for joining. In this case, field VNVEND and VCVEND are being used for joining. Because the JOIN keyword has VNDMST first, the VNVEND in JFLD (which is also first) is assumed to be coming from VNDMST. The same can be said about VCVEND, but it is coming from the second file.

- As opposed to simple logical files, in which you do not have to specify the fields that make up the record, join files do require that you specify the fields. In this case, you have included every field from both files (except for VNDUE from VNDMST because you do not need it). There is no need to include every field; you only need to include the fields you need to process for the task at hand.

- This logical file is keyed by vendor number. Because there is no UNIQUE keyword, it can contain multiple records with the same key value.

You may be wondering why you have to repeat the names of the files being joined (first in the JFILE keyword) then in JOIN. You must do this because you can join more than two files. When you join more than two files, you name them all in JFILE (three, four, however many). But then, each JOIN keyword can only contain two files. The example below clarifies this concept.

Joining Three Files

Imagine that there is a third physical file (Vendor activity file VNDACT) that contains vendor information and also includes a vendor number field (called VAVEND in this third file). You can join all three files as follows:

```
....1....+....2....+....3....+....4....+....5....+....6....+....7....+
A          R JFREC                   JFILE(VNDMST VNDCONT VNDACT)
 *
A          J                         JOIN(VNDMST VNDCONT)
A                                    JFLD(VNVEND VCVEND)
 *
A          J                         JOIN(VNDCONT VNDACT)
A                                    JFLD(VCVEND VAVEND)
A ... (list of fields follows)
```

This example shows the difference between the JFILE and the JOIN keywords. In JFILE, you list all files being joined, regardless of how many there are.

Then, you need to join all files in groups of two. The first **J** specification (**J** in 17, keywords JOIN and JFLD) joins VNDMST with VNDCONT by vendor number.

The second **J** specification also joins by vendor number VNDCONT (which is already joined to VNDMST) with VNDACT. The net result is that all three files are joined by vendor number. The list of fields can include fields from any or all three files.

Section 5: Multi-Format Logical Files

Physical files can contain only one record format, but logical files can contain many. If you need to combine the records contained in several files into a single file (whether or not they have the same record layout), you can use a multi-format logical file. This technique is especially useful when databases are converted from an S/36.

☞ The difference between a join logical file and a multi-format logical file is that join logicals have one record format that contains the fields from more than one file, while multi-format logicals are an accumulation of different record formats. Each format is from a separate physical file.

General Overview

To build a multi-format logical file, you need to do the following:

- Get the names of all the physical files and their record formats that you are combining.

- Decide what field or fields you are going to use as key to the multi-format logical file. All multi-format logicals must be keyed.

- Write the DDS and compile it with the CRTLF command to create the file.

A Simple Example

Let's create a multi-format logical file that will contain the records from the following two physical files:

Item Master File (ITMMST):

```
....1....+....2....+....3....+....4....+....5....+....6....+....7....+
A          R IMREC
A            IMITEM        15A        TEXT('Item number')
A            IMRCD          1A        TEXT('Record type A')
A            IMDESC        30A        TEXT('Item description')
A            IMCLAS         2A        TEXT('Item class')
 *
A          K IMITEM
A          K IMRCD
```

Item Balance File (ITMBAL):

```
....1....+....2....+....3....+....4....+....5....+....6....+....7....+
A          R IBREC
A            IBITEM        15A         TEXT('Item number')
A            IBRCD          1A         TEXT('Record type B')
A            IBQOH          9P 0       TEXT('Quantity on hand')
A            IBUM           2A         TEXT('Unit of measure')
 *
A          K IBITEM
A          K IBRCD
```

Here is the DDS for the multi-format logical file. It is called INVMST (Inventory Master):

```
....1....+....2....+....3....+....4....+....5....+....6....+....7....+
A          R IMREC                     PFILE(ITMMST)
A          K IMITEM
A          K IMRCD
 *
A          R IBREC                     PFILE(ITMBAL)
A          K IBITEM
A          K IBRCD
```

Remember the rules:

- The record formats in the multi-format logical must have the same names as they do in the physical file from which they come. That restriction forces us to use record format names IMREC and IBREC in the multi-format logical file.

- Each record format must have a reference to the physical file from which it comes, via the PFILE keyword.

- Each record format must have a key.

Using the Multi-Format Logical

An RPG/400 program can use a multi-format logical file the same way it uses a simple logical file or a join file. The F-specs do not change at all. However, keep in mind that:

- When you write a new record, you must move the field values to the fields contained in the appropriate record format, then issue the WRITE operation with the record format name in Factor 2.

- To read a record, use a KLIST/KFLD operation group to define the key, then CHAIN to the record by specifying the record format name in Factor 2.

- To update or delete a record, read it first, then issue an UPDAT or DELET operation, referencing the record format name in Factor 2.

If you cannot use record names in the WRITE, CHAIN, UPDAT or DELET operations, you can use a format selector program. Format selector programs are described below.

Using a Format Selector Program

Format selector programs let you perform operations on multi-format logical files without referencing the record format name. In essence, you are letting the format selector program determine what record format is applicable. This technique is particularly useful for databases that have been brought over from the S/36 into the AS/400's S/36 Environment.

The format selector program can be written in any language, including CL. It must have two parameters:

- A character string that contains the unformatted ("flat") record data at least up to and including the field that distinguishes one record format from all others (the "record ID" field).

- A 10-byte character string that the format selector program uses to return the name of the record format to be used.

For example, suppose you have created a multi-format logical file named LGLFILE that uses a 2-byte record ID field located in positions 11 and 12 of the record. Here is how you could code the format selector program in CL:

```
PGM1:      PGM        PARM(&DATA &FORMAT)

           DCL        VAR(&DATA) TYPE(*CHAR) LEN(12)
           DCL        VAR(&FORMAT) TYPE(*CHAR) LEN(10)
           DCL        VAR(&RCD_ID) TYPE(*CHAR) LEN(2)

           CHGVAR     VAR(&RCD_ID) VALUE(%SST(&DATA 11 2))

           IF         COND(&RCD_ID *EQ 'AA') THEN( +
                        CHGVAR VAR(&FORMAT) VALUE('AAREC'))
           ELSE       CMD(IF COND(&RCDID_ID *EQ 'BB') THEN( +
```

```
                        CHGVAR VAR(&FORMAT) VALUE('BBREC')))
            ELSE        CMD(CHGVAR VAR(&FORMAT) VALUE(' '))

            ENDPGM
```

This program, PGM1, receives the record data (up to the 12th byte, which includes the record ID field). The program could have received the entire record, however; it really makes no difference. The first CHGVAR statement extracts the record ID field into CL variable &RCD_ID.

The first IF compares that against 'AA.' If equal, the program assigns 'AAREC' to the record format name (in variable &FORMAT). This value is the name you coded in the DDS of the logical file. If the record ID field contains 'BB,' however, &FORMAT is assigned the value 'BBREC.' If neither is true, &FORMAT is blanked out which represents an error condition.

☞ To use this program, you must specify its qualified name in the FMTSLR parameter of the CRTLF or CHGLF command for the logical file. The format selector program then becomes, for all intents and purposes, part of the file itself.

Section 6: Display Files

As explained at the beginning of the chapter, DDS is the least intuitive and the most difficult programming language on the AS/400. Display files are so difficult that at this early stage you should not attempt to code DDS for display files yourself. You should let SDA do the work. Later, when you gain confidence and experience, you can start coding DDS manually (using SEU) if you prefer.

SDA is by far the easiest way to design display files on the AS/400. You can see everything you are designing right on the screen, including special attributes such as underline, color, and the like. You also have access to all features of display files, except the windowing DDS keywords. These keywords are too advanced to be discussed here, so SDA will work out for you, no matter what you attempt to do.

Because the DDS for display files is so complicated, and SDA eliminates the need to learn all the intricacies, concepts rather than code syntax will be discussed.

Record Formats

Each display panel is a separate *record format* in the display file. However, these records do not have to paint the entire screen. The records can paint only a small area if you prefer. If you omit the INDARA keyword at the file level, the record includes one byte per indicator used for conditioning or otherwise; each indicator actually goes into the record data itself. If you include INDARA, however, the indicators go into a separate area (the indicator area) at the rate of one byte per indicator.

Function Keys

To enable a particular function key, you must include a keyword that is appropriate for the key. For example, you can enable the F3 key by including either CA03 or CF03 at the file level or at the record level.

If you want to enable a particular function key in all record formats, place the appropriate DDS keyword at the file level (before the first record is defined). If you want to enable it only in certain (but not all) records, do not put the DDS keyword at the file level, but at the record level. You must put the DDS keyword once on each record that must have it enabled.

For the F1 to F24 keys, use keywords CA01 to CA24, or CF01 to CF24. The difference between CAxx and CFxx is that the CAxx keywords ignore all input the user may have entered, while CFxx keywords accept it. Because the F3 key means "Exit" and is used to terminate a program, it should probably always be coded with a CA03 key. On the other hand, F4 usually means "Prompt," which requires input from the user. CF04 would be appropriate in this case.

The Roll keys use DDS keywords ROLLUP and ROLLDOWN, or alternatively, PAGE-DOWN and PAGEUP, respectively. Note that the UP and DOWN directions are reversed: ROLLUP and PAGEDOWN are the same thing. The name "roll keys" comes from the 5250-type display stations. The name "page keys," on the other hand, come from the PC world. The trend is to use "page" instead of "roll" nowadays, but you can use either.

The DDS keyword should include an indicator within parentheses (although it is not required for CAxx and CFxx keywords). This indicator turns on when the user presses the corresponding function key. The application program using the display file can, therefore, sense that the function key was pressed.

For example, CA03(17) enables F3. If the user presses F3, indicator 17 turns on. If the user presses any other key (including Enter), indicator 17 turns off.

Do Not Forget PRINT and BLINK

The PRINT keyword must be included at either the file level or the record level to allow the user to press the Print key and obtain a facsimile of the screen. If you omit PRINT, the user gets an error message when he presses Print. This error can be a problem if the user needs to copy the screen. Unless you have a compelling reason for disabling PRINT in certain record formats, consider placing it at the file level so all records can use it.

IBM-supplied panels (including the sign-on displays) always blink the cursor. To do the same, you must use the BLINK keyword. Unfortunately, BLINK cannot be placed at the file level, so you need to repeat it on each record. BLINK is not a requirement but is a little cosmetic feature that makes your screens more IBM-like.

Displaying Variables and Constants

You can display the contents of a variable by coding the name of the variable in 19-28 and its location (beginning row and column) in 39-41 and 42-44, respectively. In addition, the variable must be defined either directly or by reference.

☞ Constants can be displayed by coding their location (their beginning row and column) and the actual text of the constant in 45-80 (enclosed in single quotes). If you need more space, you can put a + or - sign at the end and continue on the next line.

In the following example, a display file record prompts for field UNIT. Note that the text "Unit of Measure" appears on row 5, column 2. The letter U in "Unit of Measure" falls on column 2. The field itself has a location of +1 in the column specification. This number indicates that field UNIT is located after the constant "Unit of Measure" in such a way that there is one space in between the two.

```
....1....+....2....+....3....+....4....+....5....+....6....+....7....+
A                                         5 2'Unit of Measure'
A             UNIT        R                +1
```

Input Validation Basics

AS/400 display files let you specify DDS keywords that can control what user input is acceptable. This process relieves the application program from performing much validation checking.

Chapter 18 - DDS

For example, you can design a display file that, among other things, prompts for a code. If you want the display file to accept only certain values, you can do so by using the VALUES keyword at the field level.

Other keywords are:

- CHECK. You can allow blanks (AB) or demand that the user enter a valid name (VN). Example: CHECK(VN).

- COMP. Lets you specify a comparison, such as COMP(GT 20). The user must then enter a numeric value greater than 20.

- RANGE. Lets you specify a range of valid values, such as RANGE('A' 'M'). The user must then enter a character between A and M.

- VALUES. As already explained, it lets you specify what values are considered valid, such as VALUES(1 2 3 5 9). The field will then accept values of 1, 2, 3, 5 or 9 and no other.

If the workstation user enters a value that does not meet the criteria you have selected, the workstation controller sends a generic error message, highlights the offending field, and locks the keyboard. The user must press Reset, correct the error, and try again.

Using the Display File

In RPG/400, display files are used in the following way:

- Define the file in the F-spec as Combined Full-Procedural, place an E in 19 (to use the external definition provided by DDS), and WORKSTN beginning in 40. If needed, you can code one or more continuation F-specs to use the INFDS, for example.

- To display a panel, use the WRITE operation (for output only) or the EXFMT operation (for output immediately followed by input), with the record name in Factor 2. You will use EXFMT more often than WRITE because normally you want to present a panel, wait for input, and process the input. You can also use a WRITE immediately followed by a READ, but why go to the trouble?

- To determine if the user has pressed any function keys, test the response indicators associated with such function keys. For example, if the display file contains CF04(82), indicator 82 turns on if the user presses F4. You can then check if *IN82 is on ('1') in your program and take whatever action is appropriate in that case. If none of the function key response indicators is on, it means that the user pressed the Enter key.

- If you have conditioned fields, display attributes (such as high intensity or color) or error messages with indicators, you can activate them by turning on the associated indicator before presenting the panel. For example, suppose you have conditioned the COLOR(RED) keyword with indicator 17. If you want to display the field in normal color (green), turn off indicator 17 before the WRITE or EXFMT operation is issued. If you want to show the field in red, however, turn on indicator 17.

Displaying Error Messages

There are many ways to display error messages. You can use one particularly simple method for the time being. At a later time you then can investigate other more sophisticated methods.

The method in question involves the use of the ERRMSG or the ERRMSGID keywords at the field level and the ERRSFL keyword at the file level. Here is an example:

```
....1....+....2....+....3....+....4....+....5....+....6....+....7....+
A                                     ERRSFL
 *
A          R PANEL
A            CODE          1A  B  5 10VALUES('A' 'B' 'C')
A 91                                   ERRMSG('Invalid code' 91)
A            AMOUNT        9P 2B  7 10COMP(LT 950.75)
A 92                                   ERRMSG('Invalid amount' 92)
```

Record PANEL prompts for two fields: CODE (which accepts only the letters A, B or C) and AMOUNT (which must be less than 950.75). The user sees the panel, enters D for CODE and 1000 for AMOUNT, and presses Enter.

At that point, the workstation controller realizes that both fields are incorrect. It turns on indicators 91 and 92 and displays the error messages included in the ERRMSG keywords in a subfile. If you had omitted ERRSFL, the system would have shown only the first error message. In this case, only half the errors made by the user would have been reported.

To make this technique work, you must make sure to use the same indicator (as indicator 91 is used above) twice in the ERRMSG line: first as a conditioning indicator (left-hand side) and then inside the ERRMSG keyword.

Chapter 18 - DDS

CUA Standards

Display files are noticeable because the user actually sees them on the screen. If you want to design application programs or other software to look like IBM's, you need to adhere to the Common User Access (CUA) standards because the panels presented by OS/400 adhere to CUA.

In particular:

- All panels must have a title that is centered in high intensity (white color) at the top (line 1). This title must briefly describe the purpose of the panel.

- If any special instructions for the user are required, enter them beginning on line 3, left-adjusted, in blue color. You undoubtedly have seen IBM's "Type options, press Enter" in that spot many times.

- The available function keys (and their purpose) must be documented on line 23, left-adjusted, in blue. If you need more space than line 23 provides, use line 22 and 23. The general format is:

  Fx=Description

- Leave line 24 for error messages, which should always appear in high intensity (white color).

Most function keys also have a standard meaning. The most important ones are:

- F1: Equivalent to the Help key. The user should be allowed to press either Help or F1 to request help. Although it wastes a function key, it is the standard. The system can equate for you F1 (or any other key) to the Help key. You need to use the ALTHELP keyword in the DDS of the display file.

- F3: Exit. Ends the program immediately.

- F4: Prompt. If a field accepts many values, you can define F4 to present a list of the allowed values.

- F5: Refresh. Restores the panel as it was when it was presented first. If the user has entered anything, input is ignored.

- F12: Cancel. Takes you back to the previous panel (if there is one). If there is no previous panel, it performs the same function as F3.

Section 7: Printer Files

Printer files are not as complicated as display files. For one thing, printed material can go on for hundreds of lines, even if you disregard the perforation between pages or the physical end of one sheet in laser printers. Displayed information, on the other hand, has to be designed so that it fits the limitations of the display device. This limitation means the programmer needs to be concerned with Roll keys or use subfiles or other techniques to overcome these difficulties.

Much of the difficulty of display files is due to their ability to accept user input. Printer files, on the other hand, are strictly for output which simplifies their design and coding enormously.

☞ RLU, a tool equivalent to SDA, can be used to design printer files on the screen. The problem with RLU is its interface. While SDA provides a WYSIWYG (what you see is what you get) approach, RLU does not. RLU's display helps, but what you see on the screen is not what you will get. Using RLU is not as easy and intuitive as SDA.

RLU can be too cumbersome to be of value. A faster approach is direct entry of printer file DDS through SEU. You should investigate both methods and decide for yourself which method works best for you.

General Overview

To design printed output, you need to concern yourself with different record formats. Imagine a typical file listing report, such as one that lists all vendors in a master file.

The report needs to have a title line that usually contains the title of the report ("Vendor Master Listing") and other information such as date run, page number, and some identification code. Then, you need another record that contains the column headings, so that each column of data is identified. Finally, you need another record that contains the information for each vendor in the file.

When do you need to write each record? The title record and the column heading record are required only once per page when the page begins. The data record, however, has to be printed many times on each page, line after line until you reach the end of the page.

Because this simple report does not need to differentiate between the title record and the column heading record (both contain constants only, and both are printed at the same time), you could simplify coding by combining the two into a single record.

Sample Report

In Section 2, physical file, VNDMST was defined. It contains basic information about vendors. Let's use that example again to design a sample report that lists all records in VNDMST. For your convenience, here is the DDS of VNDMST:

```
....1....+....2....+....3....+....4....+....5....+....6....+....7....+
A                                       UNIQUE
A*
A          R VNDREC                     TEXT('Vendor record')
A            VNVEND        6A           TEXT('Vendor number')
A                                       COLHDG('Vendor' 'Number')
A            VNNAME       30A           COLHDG('Vendor' 'Name')
A            VNADR1       30A           COLHDG('Address' 'Line 1')
A            VNADR2       30A           COLHDG('Address' 'Line 2')
A            VNCITY       20A           COLHDG('City')
A            VNSTE         2A           COLHDG('State Code')
A            VNZIP         5P 0         COLHDG('Zip Code')
A                                       RANGE(00000 99999)
A            VNDUE         9P 2         COLHDG('Amount' 'Due')
A                                       EDTCDE(J $)
A*
A          K VNVEND
```

Here is what the DDS for the printer file (let's call it VNDLST) might look like:

```
....1....+....2....+....3....+....4....+....5....+....6....+....7....+
A                                       REF(VNDMST)
A*
A          R HEADER                     SKIPB(3)
A                                        1DATE EDTCDE(Y)
A                                       55'Vendor Master Listing'
A                                      124'Page'
A                                       +1PAGNBR EDTCDE(3)
A                                          SPACEA(3)
A*
A                                       11'Number'
A                                       21'Name and Address'
A                                       56'City, State and Zip'
A                                       91'Amount Due'
A                                          SPACEA(2)
```

```
     *
     A              R DETAIL
     A                VNVEND     R            11
     A                VNNAME     R            21
     A                VNCITY     R            56
     A                VNSTE      R            +1
     A                VNZIP      R            +1
     A                VNDUE      R            91SPACEA(1)
     *
     A                VNADR1     R            21SPACEA(1)
     *
     A                VNADR2     R            21SPACEA(2)
```

Only two records have been defined: HEADER (with the report title and column headings) and DETAIL (with the data from each vendor). First, notice the REF keyword at the file level that references file VNDMST. Note also that all fields in record DETAIL are defined by reference, without the REFFLD keyword. Because REFFLD is missing, the data fields in the printer file will have the same names as the fields in the physical file.

Next, there are several spacing keywords. The HEADER record has SKIPB(3) at the record level. This skips 3 lines before writing the record (i.e., the heading will begin on line 4) Then there are SPACEA(3) and SPACEA(2), also in the HEADER record, which provide space after (3 lines or 2 lines). This makes the printer leave blank lines. For example, SPACEA(2) advances two lines after printing which leaves one blank line.

The DETAIL record prints the vendor number, the name, city, state, zip code, and amount due, then advances one line. On the next line, it prints the first line of address immediately below the name (previous line), then advances to the next line and prints the second line of address. After that, the detail record advances two lines. The next DETAIL record you write will be separated from the previous one by a blank line.

Finally, note the presence of a DATE keyword in the HEADER record that is immediately followed by EDTCDE(Y). This retrieves the current job date (not the system date), and edits it with a Y edit code. It is equivalent to the UDATE field in RPG/400. There also is a TIME keyword, but it is not include in this report. On the other hand, a PAGNBR keyword, followed by EDTCDE(3) has been included. This retrieves the current page number and edits it by removing leading zeros. Again, it is equivalent to the PAGE field in RPG/400.

☞ When you use the TIME keyword, remember that it does not need editing the way DATE and PAGNBR do. You will have to get used to this irregularity.

Using the Printer File

Here is what you could code in RPG/400 to print a list of vendors, using the previous example:

```
....1....+....2....+....3....+....4....+....5....+....6....+....7....+
FVNDMST  IP  E            K            DISK
FVNDLST  O   E                 99      PRINTER
 *
C                  *IN99     IFEQ '1'
C                            WRITEHEADER
C                            MOVE '0'      *IN99
C                            END
 *
C                            WRITEDETAIL
 *
C                  *INZSR    BEGSR
C                            WRITEHEADER
C                            ENDSR
```

Both files are described externally to the program. The K in 31 of the VNDMST F-spec indicates that the file is to be read sequentially by key. The 99 in 33-34 of the printer file's F-spec is the overflow indicator. All externally described indicators must use numeric (01-99) indicators.

Before the program does anything else, it runs the *INZSR subroutine that writes the HEADER record and prints the report title and column headings for the first page of the report. As all indicators are at the beginning of the program, Indicator 99 (*IN99) is off at this time.

Each cycle checks *IN99. If it is on, overflow has occurred. In this case the WRITE operation outputs the HEADER record again which starts a new page. Then *IN99 is turned off manually (the RPG cycle does not do it for you). Following suit, once per cycle, you write the DETAIL record, which outputs the vendor data to the printer file.

You do not have to move data between the physical file and the printer file because the data fields are identically named; RPG also takes care of that.

FURTHER READING

IBM's *Database Guide*.

IBM's *DDS Reference*.

IBM's *Guide To Programming For Displays*.

IBM's *Guide To Programming For Printing*.

19

CL

Section 1: General Overview

Control Language (CL) is the most important programming language on the AS/400 because every AS/400 must have it. CL is an integral part of the operating system, and it is the way you control the AS/400.

CL was born with the S/38's operating system, CPF. Since CPF Release 1.0, CL has undergone a series of improvements that continue to the present day.

Commands and Parameters

CL is comprised of commands, and commands are comprised of a command name and a list of parameters. Therefore, CL has a particular look that is not shared by everyday programming languages.

For example, the addition of numeric variables A, B and C (storing the result in R) would be expressed in a language like C as follows:

```
r = a + b + c;
```

CL expresses the same statement in a form that looks entirely different at first sight:

```
CHGVAR VAR(&R) VALUE(&A + &B + &C)
```

The name of the command is Change Variable (CHGVAR) and it has two parameters, which have keywords (names) VAR and VALUE. The value of the VAR parameter is &R, which is a variable. The value of the VALUE parameter is the expression &A + &B + &C.

CL commands can be written into a source file member (source type CLP) and the member compiled into a program with the Create CL Program (CRTCLPGM) command.

When to Use CL

You must use CL whenever you need your program to start a system activity through a command. For example, you could create a CL program that would present a menu to the user. When the user selects the option marked "start printer," the CL program would run the Start Printer Writer (STRPRTWTR) or the Release Writer (RLSWTR) command.

You can write CL programs that execute almost every one of the commands available in OS/400. Along with some rudimentary program flow control commands, a CL program can automate the operation of your AS/400 by eliminating the need for you to execute commands manually.

☞ CL should not be used for regular data processing activities because it is not suited for that task. CL is somewhat slower than other languages like RPG or COBOL and it provides only the most rudimentary support to process database files. CL can only read from database programs; one file per program.

Parts of a CL Program

All CL programs have the same general outline:

1. The Program (PGM) command at the very top of the program. The PGM command marks the beginning of the program. If any parameters are to be received by this program, they are listed in the PARM parameter.

2. A series of Declare (DCL) commands to define all the variables used in the program. All variables must be declared before the program does anything else. Consequently, all DCL commands must be grouped together right after the PGM command. If the

CL program uses a file, it must be declared here as well with the Declare File (DCLF) command.

3. An optional, global error trap with the Monitor Message (MONMSG) command. This is described in more detail in Section 3.

4. The body of the program, which executes whatever commands are necessary to perform the task you have in mind. You can insert program flow control commands to alter the order in which the commands are executed. Program flow control commands are described in Section 2.

5. The End Program (ENDPGM) command to mark the end of the program.

CL Variables

CL supports three types of variables: character, decimal and logical.

- Character variables are declared with TYPE(*CHAR). They can have any length between 1 and 9999 characters. They can be given any value at all, including hexadecimal values such as X'01'.

- Decimal variables are declared with TYPE(*DEC). They can have any length between 1 and 15 digits and have between 0 and 9 decimal positions. They can contain any numeric value that falls within those limits, whether it is positive, zero or negative.

- Logical variables are declared with TYPE(*LGL). They are always 1-byte long, and can only have two values: true ('1') or false ('0').

☞ All variable names must begin with an ampersand (&). The ampersand is what makes the rest of the name the name of a variable.

The rest of the name must conform to the following rules:

- The first character must be a letter (A to Z) or the characters @, #, or $.

- Following characters in the name can be letters, the characters @, #, $ or _ (underscore), or digits (0 to 9).

- At least one character must follow the & character.

- No more than 10 characters can follow the & character.

Giving Values to Variables

CL variables can obtain a value in three different ways:

- If the variable is a parameter passed to your CL program, the variable receives a value from the caller.

- By being declared with an initial value. The DCL command can have an optional parameter, VALUE, in which you can specify any initial value you want to give the variable. If you do not specify VALUE, character variables default to blank, decimal variables default to zero, and logical variables default to false.

- From the Change Variable (CHGVAR) command, which is CL's assignment command. If you want to assign variable &X the value 'ABC,' you code it in a CHGVAR command:

```
CHGVAR VAR(&X) VALUE('ABC')
```

The VALUE parameter can contain a single constant, a variable, or an expression that consists of many variables and/or constants, as in:

```
CHGVAR VAR(&NUMBER) VALUE(3 * (&COUNTER + 2))
```

Besides the usual four arithmetic operations (which you can perform on decimal variables only), you can use the following operations on character strings:

- Concatenation. There are three types of concatenation: *CAT (splicing together the two strings as they are, keeping trailing and leading blanks), *BCAT (removes the trailing blanks at the end of the first string and then inserts a single blank space between the two) and *TCAT (removes trailing blanks at the end of the first string and then joins them).

    For example, if variable &FIRST is 10 characters long and contains 'John' and &LAST is 10 characters long and contains 'Smith,' &FIRST *CAT &LAST yields 'John   Smith' (six blanks in between) because *CAT keeps the trailing blanks in &FIRST. &FIRST *BCAT &LAST would yield 'John Smith' (one blank), and &FIRST *TCAT &LAST yields 'JohnSmith.'

- Substring. The substring function lets you extract part of a string and place the result into another string variable. The substring function is referenced as %SST or %SUBSTRING. If you want to extract the first three characters of &FIRST, code %SST(&FIRST 1 3). The "1" indicates the beginning position for the extraction and the "3" indicates how many characters to extract.

Example:

```
CHGVAR VAR(&NAME) VALUE(&FIRST *BCAT %SST(&LAST 1 4))
```

This CHGVAR command concatenates (with a single space in between) variable &FIRST and the first four characters of &LAST. If &FIRST contains 'John' and &LAST contains 'Smith,' &NAME is given the value 'John Smith.'

Section 2: Control Commands

All programming languages need to use statements that control the execution of the program because, in most cases, it is not desirable to execute the statements in a program sequentially. Programs always have loops, decisions and jumps.

CL is rather poor in these features. As a matter of fact, it has lagged behind the rest of the languages and provides no looping features or subroutines of any kind.

If this lack of structured programming constructs bothers you, perhaps you should consider using CL/free, a precompiler that runs on the PC and was designed by Picante Software of Eugene, Oregon. CL/free has DO loops, WHILE, UNTIL, subroutines, and other useful constructs. The PC translates all structures into IFs and GOTOs. The IFS and GOTOs can then be compiled by the AS/400's CRTCLPGM command.

IF and ELSE Commands

All decision making is performed by the IF command. The general form is:

```
IF COND(...) THEN(...)
ELSE CMD(...)
```

The condition enclosed in the COND parameter is evaluated first. If it is true, the program executes the statement contained in the THEN parameter. If it is false, it executes the statement in the ELSE's CMD parameter. The ELSE command is optional.

If you have more than one statement to execute in either or both cases of the decision, you can use the DO/ENDDO command pair, as follows:

```
IF COND(...) THEN(DO)
    :
    :
    ENDDO
    ELSE CMD(DO)
    :
    :
    ENDDO
```

In this case, the program executes the statements embedded in the first DO/ENDDO pair if the condition is true, or the second DO/ENDDO if false.

The COND parameter can contain any expression that yields a true or false result, such as:

```
IF COND(&A *EQ &B)
```

In this example, both &A and &B are variables of the same type (character, decimal or logical). The *EQ operator compares them for equality. The following table shows all of the available comparison operators:

Operator	Description
*EQ	Equal
*NE	Not equal
*LT	Less than
*LE	Less than or equal to
*NL	Not less than (same as *GE)
*GT	Greater than
*GE	Greater than or equal to
*NG	Not greater than (same as *LE)

You also can combine these comparisons with *AND, *OR and *NOT, using parentheses, if necessary. CL allows very complicated conditions in the COND parameter.

GOTO Command

The GOTO statement is practically taboo in most programming languages, yet it is still used in CL. CL has no other way to jump from one place of the program to another, so it must rely on GOTO exclusively.

The GOTO statement always transfers control to a label (or "tag") in the CL program. A label is a name followed by a colon (:) that is written before a command name. For example:

```
GOTO CMDLBL(HERE)
:
:
HERE: CHGVAR ...
```

The GOTO statement transfers control to label HERE, which points to the CHGVAR statement.

CALL Command

Another control command is the CALL command. With CALL you can call another program (which can be written in any language) and pass parameters. When the other program ends, the system automatically returns control to your CL program. The CL program resumes execution at the statement immediately following the CALL.

You can pass either variables or constants as parameters. In general, passing parameters as constants is tricky. There are ways to make it work, but that discussion is beyond the scope of this book. A good starting point would be for you to pass parameters as variables all the time. When you gain experience, you can begin experimenting with constants.

The caller and the called program must agree in number of parameters. If program A calls program B, the CALL command in program A must list the same number of parameters as program B expects at its entry point.

Parameters must also agree in type and length, although some languages are less strict about this than others. When in doubt, make them agree. If program A calls B listing a 10-character string variable and a 7-digit numeric variable, be sure that program B expects the same.

When the called program ends, the parameters are returned to the caller. The parameters may have been changed by the program you called.

ENDPGM and RETURN

The ENDPGM and RETURN commands can be used to signal the end of a program. ENDPGM must be the very last statement in a CL program, but RETURN can be anywhere. While there can be only one ENDPGM statement, there can be any number of RETURNs scattered throughout the CL program.

The commands perform the same function; there is no difference at all. You can use RETURN to terminate a program no matter where within the program you may be. This command saves you from having to code a GOTO command to take you to the ENDPGM.

If the CL program you are running was called from another, either ENDPGM or RETURN can be used to return control to the caller.

Section 3: Dealing With Errors

One of the strengths of CL is its ability to handle error situations gracefully. In this respect, it cannot be surpassed.

*ESCAPE Messages

Every time the system finds a problem with a command you run, it sends an *ESCAPE message. A complete explanation of AS/400 messages is not provided in this book of basics. Messages are of different types, and one of those types is *ESCAPE. ESCAPE messages are only issued when there is an error serious enough to merit canceling the command you requested to run.

For example, you type the following command at the command line:

```
DSPLIB LIB(XYZ) OUTPUT(*PRINT)
```

When the system receives this request, it checks to see that library XYZ exists. If it does, the DSPLIB command runs without trouble. If it does not, the system sends an *ESCAPE message.

Because you are running the DSPLIB command from the keyboard, you see the message and you think, "Oh, I must have made a mistake." Then you try again. Perhaps the name of the library was not XYZ but XXX.

CL programs are not so fortunate. If the DSPLIB command shown above were part of a CL program, and you execute the program, the DSPLIB command would fail just as quickly, and issue the same *ESCAPE message. This *ESCAPE message would force your CL program to abort.

The MONMSG Command

You can use the MONMSG command to trap *ESCAPE messages and take care of the problem gracefully. To use this command, you need to do the following:

1. Find out what message ID the system issues for the error condition you want to be ready for. For example, the Delete File (DLTF) command issues message CPF2105 (the message ID) if the file does not exist.

2. Code a MONMSG command immediately after the statement you think will issue the *ESCAPE message. For example, you would code a MONMSG command after the DLTF command if you think that the file will not exist when the DLTF command is executed.

Here is an example of what the sequence looks like:

```
DLTF FILE(MYLIB/MYFILE)
MONMSG MSGID(CPF2105) EXEC(...)
```

The MONMSG command shown above has two parameters: MSGID, which lists the message IDs you want to watch out for (you actually can include several) and the EXEC parameter, which should contain a command you want to run if CPF2105 is issued.

You can omit the EXEC parameter if you do not want to do anything, such as if you want to ignore the *ESCAPE message. Alternatively, you can also put a DO command in the EXEC parameter if you want to execute several commands. In this case, the sequence of commands will have to be terminated with an ENDDO command:

```
DLTF FILE(MYLIB/MYFILE)
MONMSG MSGID(CPF2105) EXEC(DO)
 :
 :
ENDDO
```

Global MONMSG Command

The MONMSG command can also be placed at the top of the CL program, immediately after the DCL/DCLF commands. If placed there, MONMSG acts as a blanket that covers the entire program. Every statement in the CL program is "protected" by the MONMSG command. This arrangement is usually called a "global" or program-level MONMSG.

The global MONMSG can include only a GOTO command in its EXEC parameter, or have the EXEC parameter missing. Usually the global MONMSG is used for catch-all situations. In this case, it is common practice to monitor for CPF0000.

CPF0000 is a wild card. It is the same as saying "monitor for any CPFxxxx error message." The CL program will be protected from any CPFxxxx error message. Another blanket message ID is any message ID ending in two zeros, such as CPF1400. CPF1400 would cover any message between CPF1401 and CPF14FF.

Section 4: Retrieving Data

One of CL's specialties is its ability to retrieve data from system objects such as user profiles, data areas and system values.

Data Areas

Data areas are objects contained in libraries of type *DTAARA which you can use to store small pieces of information, such as report headings or the name of your company.

Manually, you can create, change, delete, and display data areas. You use the obvious commands CRTDTAARA, CHGDTAARA, DLTDTAARA and DSPDTAARA. These commands can be placed easily in CL programs.

Whenever you manipulate a data area, you need to reference the beginning position and the length of the data. For example, you may want to change the contents of the data area. You use the CHGDTAARA command, and specify in what position to begin changing, and how many characters:

```
CHGDTAARA DTAARA(ABC (25 3)) VALUE('***')
```

This command changes positions 25, 26 and 27 of data area ABC to asterisks.

CL allows you to retrieve their contents and place them in a CL variable. It is akin to reading a file. To retrieve the contents of a data area into a CL variable, you use the Retrieve Data Area (RTVDTAARA) command. The name of the CL variable goes into the RTNVAR parameter, as follows:

```
RTVDTAARA DTAARA(ABC (16 5)) RTNVAR(&VALUE)
```

In this example, variable &VALUE receives the value contained in positions 16 to 20 of data area ABC.

System Values

System values are very important entities used to configure the system. You can find more information on system values in Chapter 10. CL programs can contain the Display, Change and Work with System Values (DSPSYSVAL, CHGSYSVAL and WRKSYSVAL) commands used to manipulate them. This means that a CL program is capable of changing the configuration of the system if the person who runs the program has sufficient authority.

CL programs can also retrieve the current value of system values with the Retrieve System Value (RTVSYSVAL) command. Depending on which system value you are retrieving, the value must be given to a character or decimal variable. The value must also be a particular length which also depends on the system value.

For example, your CL program can retrieve the value of QTIME, the system value that holds the system time, as follows:

```
RTVSYSVAL SYSVAL(QTIME) RTNVAR(&SYSTIM)
```

This statement assumes that &SYSTIM is a six-character string variable. When RTVSYSVAL executes, &SYSTIM will contain the time of day of the moment RTVSYSVAL was executed, in the format HHMMSS.

Other Information

You can retrieve a lot more information into CL variables with other Retrieve (RTVxxx) commands. Among them, the two most important are:

- RTVJOBA. The Retrieve Job Attributes command lets you find out about the settings of your own job (the one in which the CL program is running). For example, you can retrieve the name of the current output queue with the OUTQ and OUTQLIB parameters, or the name of the display station from which you are running the command (if running interactively) with the JOB parameter. The TYPE parameter returns '0' if the job is running in batch or '1' otherwise.

- RTVUSRPRF. The Retrieve User Profile command allows you to retrieve important information about any user profile. If you do not specify which, your own is assumed.

If you wish, you can find other RTVxxx commands available in OS/400 by executing the following command:

```
SLTCMD CMD(QSYS/RTV*)
```

Section 5: Using Files

CL programs are weak in file processing. In fact, CL programs can only process three types of files: database, source, and display.

Database and source files can only be read from (never written to) by a CL program. CL lacks the ability to write new records, update existing ones, or delete records.

Display files can be either read or written. CL does not support all display file features. For example, there is no support in CL for subfiles, except message subfiles.

☛ As if these limitations weren't enough, CL can only process one file. It cannot open one file, process it, close it, and process a different one. It can process only one file. Period.

The DCLF Command

Before you process a file in CL, you must declare it with the DCLF command. The DCLF command must be placed at the beginning of the program, either before or after (or amid) the DCL commands.

The DCLF command has two parameters: FILE, which identifies the file you want to process in the CL program, and RCDFMT, which names the record formats you will use in the program. The parameter defaults to *ALL, and you should leave it alone until you understand more about record formats.

The DCLF command actually pulls the eternal definition of the file and creates CL variables using the DDS names prefixed with the ampersand (&) symbol. For example, if the file has a variable called INPUT, the DCLF command creates a CL variable called &INPUT with the same type and length as defined in the DDS of the file.

☞ If the file was not created with DDS (i.e., if it is a "flat" file), the DCLF command creates a single character variable equal in length to the record in the file, named the same as the file. For example, if the file is called MASTER, DCLF creates a CL variable called &MASTER.

Display file indicators also become CL variables. Their names are &INxx, where xx is the indicator number. For example, if a display file uses indicator 03, the DCLF command creates a CL variable named &IN03, which will be declared as TYPE(*LGL) [logical].

Other Commands

CL provides three commands to process files record by record:

- RCVF. The Receive File command reads a record from the file. If there are no more records in the file, the RCVF command ends with *ESCAPE message CPF0864. If you are processing a display file, you must indicate the name of the record format you are reading from (if there is more than one).

- SNDF. The Send File command writes a record to the file. You can use SNDF only on display files, and you must indicate the name of the record format you are writing, if there is more than one.

- SNDRCVF. The Send/Receive File writes a record and then reads it back. Like SNDF, it can be used only on display files and you must specify the name of the record format to process, if there is more than one.

FURTHER READING

IBM's *CL Programmer's Guide*.

IBM's *CL Reference*.

Midrange Computing's *Complete CL*.

Midrange Computing's *Creating Commands*.

20

RPG/400

It is hard to imagine an IBM midrange computer professional that is not at least acquainted with the language known as **R**eport **P**rogram **G**enerator, or RPG. This is because RPG is widespread among all the members of the midrange computer family, beginning with System/3 all the way to the AS/400, where it receives the name RPG/400.

In spite of its humble beginnings (when RPG was used for little else than creating report-type programs), RPG on the AS/400 is a full-fledged high-level language that is capable of performing complex database operations, interactive applications that supports subfiles, and heavy mass-update programs. Of course, RPG also creates report programs, thereby living up to its name.

IBM publishes two large volumes that explain RPG/400 in great detail. If you need any information not provided in this chapter (which is just a presentation of the language, not a treatise on it), you should refer to IBM's manuals.

Because most AS/400 programmers that code in RPG are still likely to use the RPG III version (as opposed to RPG IV, the ILE version), all references to fixed columns, limits, features, and so on, apply to RPG III—the "traditional" RPG/400—unless otherwise noted.

Section 1: General Overview

RPG Specifications

RPG/400 is remarkably different from most other languages. While other languages are written on a blank sheet of paper, so to speak, RPG/400 is written on preprinted forms where the programmer fills out the blanks with letters and numbers. This is an allegorical way of describing RPG, but it depicts the truth. In the early days, RPG programmers did indeed use preprinted forms (called coding sheets) that were given to a keypunch operator to prepare a deck of punched cards, ready to be submitted to the System/3 or System/360. Nowadays, no one would think of using coding sheets, but the concept remains.

An RPG/400 program consists of a series of statements that are each exactly one physical line long, In RPG/400 there is no such thing as a true continuation line. The purpose of each statement is determined by the specification ID, which is a single letter located in column 6. RPG/400 supports the following specifications:

- **H** (header, also called control). A program can have only one H-spec or none. If present, the H-spec must be the first statement in the program. The H-spec provides some global options that apply to the entire program, such as a currency symbol or an option to omit unprintable characters.

- **F** (file). Each F-spec defines a single file to the program. The F-spec indicates the name of the file, whether it is opened for input, output, update or combined I/O, and other file-level details.

- **E** (extension). E-specs are used to define arrays and tables and to provide additional information that may be required for certain files.

- **L** (line counter). L-specs are practically obsolete. They were used in earlier systems to provide the length of the printed page (in lines) and to indicate where in the page to process overflow. CL is much better suited for this; it can run an Override Printer File (OVRPRTF) command before it calls the RPG/400 program, or you can place all the printer attributes in the printer file object.

- **I** (input). I-specs can be included to define the fields contained within each file record (if you choose not to use the file's external definition). I-specs can also be used to define data structures and named constants.

- **C** (calculation). The C-specs are the meat and potatoes of the RPG/400 program. C-specs are where the action takes place. Each C-spec is an operation such as addition, reading a record, decision, subroutine call, etc.

- **O** (output). Like the I-specs, O-specs can be used to define output if you choose not to use external file definition. Unlike the I-specs, however, the O-specs cannot be used for anything else.

☞ The specifications must be entered into the source program in the order in which they are listed above. If there is as much as one specification out of sequence, the compilation aborts.

Because most programmers agree in using the external file definition, it is not unlikely to have RPG/400 programs without H-, I- and O-specs. L-specs are practically never used, but I-specs are still used for data structures and named constants. All that is left is F-, E-, I- and C-specs.

Fixed Format

RPG/400 is unique in another aspect: it has a fixed format. You cannot code your program statements anywhere you like. The RPG compiler forces you to utilize predefined spaces. If you do not use those spaces, the RPG compiler may not recognize your code as valid, or may misinterpret it.

For example, an **F** in column 16 of the F-specs means that the file is full-procedural (an RPG term meaning that the file is manipulated manually with READ and WRITE operations). Shift that **F** three columns to the right (column 19) and its meaning changes. An **F** in column 19 means that the file has a fixed-length record and that the program is not to use its eternal definition. Of course an **F** in column 6 identifies the statement as an F-spec.

Although it is true that the fixed format presents problems and limitations, it is also true that most business application programs can be coded in fixed format without undue hardship.

Some enterprising programmers have developed precompilers that accept free-format RPG statements. By far the most popular is RPG/free, developed by Picante Software of Eugene, Oregon. The PC version is distributed free of charge if you include a small fee for distribution costs, shipping and handling. In addition, the PC version can be downloaded from bulletin board services (BBSs). Although at first it is hard to break the habit of coding RPG in fixed format, you may find that you like the free format better. it is worth a try, and the price is certainly right.

RPG Names

RPG/400 has one limitation of a different nature: the names it supports. While all other programming languages allow use of at least 10-character names on files, records, labels and variables (and many more than 10 characters in most cases), RPG/400 never allows more than eight characters. In fact, files and records have a maximum length of eight characters, while labels and variables are not allowed names longer than six characters. This limitation usually presents difficulties to programmers who have backgrounds in other languages.

There is no way to circumvent this limitation, but you can adopt strict naming standards that reduce the likelihood of getting into trouble. This 6-character variable name limit makes RPG/400 programs harder to read because you cannot cram much meaning into such a short name. You have to abbreviate everything, and no two programmers would choose the same abbreviations. Therefore, strict naming standards are necessary.

All RPG/400 names must begin with a letter of the alphabet (A to Z) or the symbols @, # and $. The remaining characters can be more of the same or any of the 10 digits (0 to 9). All other symbols are invalid.

RPG IV (the ILE version of RPG) supports names of up to 10 characters, all of which can be written in uppercase, lowercase, or mixed case. Besides the characters listed above, RPG IV names can also contain the underscore (_) character anywhere except the first position.

Indicators

Indicators are just logical variables with a different name. An indicator can be either on (true) or off (false). While other languages provide standard names for logical variables, RPG provides two-character codes for indicators, including two-digit numeric codes from 01 to 99.

The 01-99 indicators are usually called general-purpose indicators. You can use them for anything, including communicating with display and printer files. Other indicators have special functions:

- H1-H9 (halt indicators) are an obsolete feature that can be more trouble than it is worth. Do not use halt indicators in your program.

- KA-KN and KP-KY (function key indicators) can be used to sense when the user has pressed one of the function keys (F1 to F24) during the execution of an interactive program.

- L0-L9 (control level indicators) are used to detect changes in certain fields while the Primary file is being processed record by record. You can use them to sense these changes and do things like printing subtotals.

- LR (last record indicator) is used to signal the end of the execution of the program. If you have a Primary file, LR turns on when the last record is read. You can also turn it on manually.

- MR (matching record indicator) is used when processing a Primary and a Secondary file with the matching record technique. MR turns on when the corresponding fields in the two files have the same values.

- OA-OG and OV (overflow indicators) are used to sense the end of a physical page while writing to a printer file. You can use these indicators to control skipping to a new page and printing headings.

- 1P (first page indicator) is on only at the beginning of the program, when the printer file is at the first page. You can use it, for example, to print different information on the first page.

Although the current tendency among programmers is to avoid the use of indicators whenever possible, RPG/400 still requires indicators in some circumstances. For example, the READ, CHAIN and LOKUP operations all require an indicator. If you need to control the appearance of your interactive program's display file, you need to do so through indicators (the same indicator is coded in the DDS to condition display attributes such as high intensity and is coded in the program to turn on or off).

☞ The indiscriminate use of indicators can reduce the readability of your program considerably because indicators have completely meaningless names. An indicator such as '43' could mean "record not found" or "character scan ended abnormally," just to name two possibilities. Try to reduce indicator usage to only the absolutely essential ones.

The RPG Cycle

RPG/400 is unique in yet another way. RPG/400 is the only language that provides a built-in processing cycle. Because most business application programs need to perform input, calculations and output, the RPG compiler provides this process automatically in the RPG cycle.

A file can be designated as Primary. When you use a Primary file, the RPG cycle automatically reads it, performs the calculations coded in the C-specs, and then performs whatever output you indicate (to itself, if the file is being updated, or to a different file such as a printer file).

In addition, the RPG cycle offers other effort-saving features. You can code control-level breaks by using L1-L9 indicators on the I-specs that define certain fields of the Primary file. When the system reads a record (automatically, because you are using the cycle), and it detects that those fields have changed, it turns on the indicator. You can use that indicator to command the program to print subtotals or to perform other operations.

The RPG cycle cannot be disengaged. Even if you do not use a Primary file, the cycle is still active and you must indicate to the program when to end by turning on the LR indicator. In fact, the compiler will not create a program object unless you include a way to turn on LR, either using the cycle, if there is a Primary file, or manually.

Section 2: The C-Specs

As mentioned before, the C-specs is where everything happens. It is therefore important that you understand the workings of the C-specs.

Each C-spec executes an operation (such as add, multiply, read a record, turn off an indicator, or compare two variables for equality). This operation has a five-character operation code (RPG programmers usually call it "opcode"), which is coded in columns 28-32. Some operations have opcodes that do not use all five characters allotted to them.

Anatomy of a C-Spec

C-specs have a rather simple organization. They are divided into a few fields that never vary in meaning or purpose. C-specs differ from the I-specs, for example, which are used for many different things. Here is what the C-spec contains:

- The specification ID (C) in column 6. There is no escaping this requirement. All C-specs must have a letter **C** in column 6.

- A control level indicator in columns 7-8, which is used if you want to perform an operation during the total time that control-level indicator is on. C-specs that have a control-level indicator in columns 7-8 must be coded at the end of the C-specs. This entry is optional.

Chapter 20 - RPG/400

- Up to three conditioning indicatiors in columns 9-11, 12-14 and 15-17. All three entries are optional. The presence of indicators in these columns conditions the C-spec so that it is executed only if all three conditions are met.

- An entry labeled Factor 1 in columns 18-27. This entry may be mandatory or optional, depending on the opcode entered in columns 28-32.

- An opcode in columns 28-32. This entry is mandatory.

- An entry labeled Factor 2 in columns 33-42. Like Factor 1, it can be mandatory or optional, depending on the opcode used.

- A result field in columns 43-48. Again, it can be either mandatory, optional, or can even be prohibited.

- Result field definition. Columns 49-51 contain the length of the result field and, if numeric, column 52 contains the number of decimal places.

- An operation extender in column 53. Certain numeric operations allow use of an **H** to round the result rather than truncate it. String operations allow the use of a **P** to blank the result field before loading it with the result of the operation. Database file input operations allow use of an **N** to avoid locking the record (if the file is open for update).

- Resulting indicators in columns 54-55, 56-57 and 58-59. All are optional, although certain operations require at least one of them. Other operations do not allow any.

- Comments in columns beyond 59. You can enter anything you want if you think it will help you understand what the C-spec is doing.

File I/O Operations

RPG/400 provides a rich set of file I/O operations. Here are some of them:

- READ. Reads the next record from the file specified in Factor 2. Factor 2 can also contain a record name if you are using externally described files.

- READP. Reads the previous record. Similar to READ.

- READE. Read the next record that has the same key value.

- REDPE. Read the previous record that has the same key value.

- CHAIN. Read a record randomly by record number or key value.

275

- WRITE. Write a new record to an externally described file.
- UPDAT. Update the last record read from an externally described file.
- DELET. Delete the last record read from an externally described file.
- EXCPT. Perform exception output on program-described files.

Structured Operations

RPG/400 provides several structures you can use for decision making within your program:

- IFxx/ELSE/ENDIF. The IFxx operation compares the variables in Factor 1 and Factor 2. How they are compared depends on the value of xx. If you code EQ (which makes the opcode "IFEQ"), they are compared for equality. Other values are NE (not equal), LT (less than), LE (less than or equal to), GT (greater than) and GE (greater than or equal to). Here is an example:

```
....1.... ....2.... ....3.... ....4.... ....5.... ....6.... ....7
C          CSTNBR    IFGT 500
C                    WRITENEWREC
C                    ELSE
C                    UPDATOLDREC
C                    ENDIF
```

This code executes the WRITE operation if CSTNBR is greater than 500. If not, the ELSE operation dictates that the UPDAT operation be executed. The ENDIF marks the end of the decision group. If you are running a release of OS/400 prior to V2R1M0, you will have to use END instead of ENDIF.

- ANDxx and ORxx. You can add these operations immediately after an IFxx operation to combine more than one comparison. Here is an example:

```
....1.... ....2.... ....3.... ....4.... ....5.... ....6.... ....7
C          CSTNBR    IFGT 500
C          CRDCDE    OREQ 'T'
C                    WRITENEWREC
C                    ELSE
C                    UPDATOLDREC
C                    ENDIF
```

This example is a modification of the last one. The WRITE operation is executed if CSTNBR is greater than 500 or if CRDCDE is equal to 'T.' In any other case, (CSTNBR less than or equal to 500 and CRDCDE not equal to 'T'), the program executes the UPDAT operation.

- DO/ENDDO. The DO operation causes the repetition of all the statements between it and the ENDDO that follows. That repetition is performed for increasing values of a control variable (the Result field), from the value indicated in Factor 1 to the value in Factor 2. Each repetition increases the control variable by 1, unless indicated in Factor 2 of the related ENDDO.

  If Factor 1 or Factor 2 is omitted, a value of 1 is assumed. If the Result field is omitted, the compiler uses an internal control variable.

- DOWxx/ENDDO and DOUxx/ENDDO. The DOWxx and DOUxx operations are similar to IFxx in that they too accept a two-letter modifier like EQ and NE. DOWxx (do while) repeats the statements enclosed between it and the ENDDO that follows, for as long as the comparison between Factor 1 and Factor 2 is true. DOUxx (do until) repeats the statements until the comparison is true. Like IFxx, DOWxx and DOUxx accept ANDxx and ORxx modifiers. Here is an example:

```
.... ....1.... ....2.... ....3.... ....4.... ....5.... ....6.... ....7
     C           CMPLT     DOUEQ'Y'
     C                     :
     C                     :
     C                     ENDDO
```

This piece of code executes the statements between the DOUEQ and the ENDDO until CMPLT is equal to 'Y.' Because the DOUxx operations perform the test at the ENDDO, the statements included would be executed at least once, even if CMPLT were equal to 'Y' to begin with. On the other hand, the DOWxx operations perform the comparison immediately before they start the sequence of statements included. If the comparison does not hold true the first time, the statements included would not be executed at all (not even once).

- ITER and LEAVE. These two operations can be included in any DO, DOWxx or DOUxx group. LEAVE (as the name suggests) leaves the group immediately, transferring control to the statement that follows ENDDO. You can use LEAVE when you have accomplished what you wanted to do in the DO, DOWxx or DOUxx group and need to get out of it.

  ITER (iterate) is different. ITER transfers control to the statement that performs the comparison. If that test yields a positive result, execution continues. ITER can be used to skip the rest of the current execution of the loop, in order to go to the next one.

- EXSR. Use EXSR (execute subroutine) to execute a subroutine coded within the program. The subroutine must begin with BEGSR (begin subroutine) and end with ENDSR (end subroutine). The subroutine can contain EXSR statements to execute other subroutines. When the program executes the ENDSR operation, control returns to the statement immediately after the EXSR.

- CALL and PARM. You can use the CALL operation (followed by optional PARM operations) to execute a different program from within your RPG program. It works like EXSR, except that the statements executed are not within your program, but in another. PARMs allow you to pass parameter data to the called program and/or obtain information back from it.

- SELEC, WHxx, OTHER, and ENDSL. The IFxx operation, when combined with ELSE, performs a two-pronged decision fork. Execution can follow one path or the other. If you need more than two paths, you need to use the SELEC operation group, as the following example shows. Note that any of the WHxx operations could have been combined with ANDxx or ORxx:

```
....1.... ....2.... ....3.... ....4.... ....5.... ....6.... ....7
C                        SELEC
C          CODE          WHEQ 'A'
C                        :
C                        : Segment 1
C                        :
C          CODE          WHEQ 'B'
C                        :
C                        : Segment 2
C                        :
C          CODE          WHEQ 'C'
C                        :
C                        : Segment 3
C                        :
C                        OTHER
C                        :
C                        : Segment 4
C                        :
C                        ENDSL
```

This piece of code executes segment 1 when CODE equals 'A,' or executes segment 2 when CODE equals 'B,' or segment 3 when CODE equals 'C.' OTHERwise (if none of the WHxx tests holds true), it executes segment 4.

Unstructured Operations to Avoid

Unfortunately, RPG/400 still supports old and outdated opcodes that do not follow structured programming guidelines. You should avoid these operations whenever possible:

- COMP. The Compare operation was used in early versions of RPG that did not have the IFxx operation. COMP compares Factor 1 and Factor 2 and then turns the indicators coded in columns 54-55, 56-57 and 58-59 on or off depending on the result of the test.

  If Factor 1 is greater than Factor 2, the indicator in 54-55 is turned on (and the other two, if present, are turned off). If Factor 1 is less than Factor 2, the indicator in 56-57 turns on (and the other two, if present, turn off). If Factor 1 is equal to Factor 2, the indicator in 58-59 turns on (and the other two, if present, turn off).

☞ Now that you have the IFxx operation, there is no reason to use COMP at all. IFxx is more explicit than COMP, which results in code that is easier to understand.

- GOTO and TAG. The GOTO statement transfers control to the TAG statement. Both GOTO and TAG reference a label name; this label name links the GOTO with the TAG you want to reach.

  GOTOs and TAGs are particularly pernicious. They encourage the kind of programming style that results in "spaghetti" code which is a bunch of code segments that have no apparent connection. "Spaghetti" code forces you to constantly jump from one place to another.

☞ Use the GOTO and TAG pair operations only when absolutely necessary (sometimes they actually make the code clearer). Keep your definition of "absolutely necessary" as tight and strict as possible, however.

- CABxx. The xx can represent EQ, NE, LT, LE, GT or GE. CABxx compares Factor 1 and Factor 2. If the condition is met, it control transfers to the tag indicated in the Result field. CABxx basically is another form of GOTO.

FURTHER READING

IBM's *RPG/400 User's Guide*.

IBM's *RPG/400 Reference*.

21

Sorting Data

More often than not, the records in a database file will not be in the sequence you need them for a particular application program. For example, you may have an Inventory Transaction History file which is defined as an arrival sequence file. Records are added all the time in the order the transactions are posted to Inventory.

If you want to print a report that lists transactions sorted by warehouse number and, within each warehouse, sorted by item number, you clearly need to sort (rearrange the order of) the file. Once the file is sorted the way you need it, you would be able to print the report you want.

Later, someone else may need to print a different report based on the same file. The new report requires that the records be listed in reverse order of their transaction value, and pick up only sales transactions (but exclude other types of transactions such as inventory adjustments and purchases). This points out another common requirement while sorting: specifying which records to include (and of course which records to exclude).

Section 1: Using a Logical File

Logical Files

Logical files are one of the methods available for sorting records. Logical files are a path the system can use to access the records in a physical file by using a different sequence and optionally selecting/omitting some records.

☛ Logical file does not contain any records. The logical file only contains pointers to the records in the physical file. Therefore, when you say that the logical file alters the sequence of the records, you are really saying that, through the logical file, the records seem to be in a different sequence. This is the reason why logical files are usually referred to as different "views" of the database.

Also remember that if you use a logical file for sorting and/or selecting or omitting records, the logical file uses a fixed sort sequence and fixed criteria for selection and omission. The specifications are coded in the DDS in the form of key fields or constants that you cannot change after the logical file is created. If you need flexibility, consider using OPNQRYF instead of logical files.

Specifying Sequence

To change the sequence of the records, you need to create a logical file whose key fields describe the order in which you want to process the physical file's records. For example, if the Inventory Transaction History file has two fields named ITWHSE (the warehouse number) and ITITEM (the item number), you should use these two fields as the keys to the logical file to sort the physical file by warehouse number and item number.

The key can be specified to be in descending sequence by adding the DDS keyword DESCEND. That keyword seems to satisfy the requirement for the second report described in the opening paragraphs. To sort the Inventory Transaction History file in descending order of transaction value, you would specify a key field of ITTVAL (assuming that is the name of the transaction value field) with DESCEND. Of course, if there are two transactions on file that have identical values, the system will not know what order to put those in.

Including and Omitting Records

Logical files also are capable of specifying which records to include and which records to omit from the view. For more information about coding, see Chapter 18, Section 3.

CRTLF Options and Performance

The process of creating a logical file is described in Chapter 18. You should review the subheading that deals with the Create Logical File (CRTLF) command and pay particular attention to the MAINT and RECOVER parameters.

These parameters, particularly MAINT, have an impact on system performance. As you continue to create more and more logical files over the same physical file, the system starts to slow down if MAINT (IMMED) has been specified on all of them. The more logicals you have with MAINT(*IMMED), the more work the system has to do when records are added, changed or deleted from the physical file.

☞ You therefore should use MAINT(*IMMED) only with logical files you use constantly or those that have unique keys (DDS keyword UNIQUE). The other two options, MAINT(*REBLD) and MAINT(DLY), maintain the access path only when the logical file is used. The difference between the two is that *REBLD forces the system to rebuild the access path for the entire logical file, while *DLY makes the system update the access path for the records that have been added, changed or deleted since the last time the logical file was opened.

*DLY therefore is preferable over *REBLD for those files you do not need to open very frequently. However, when the number of records that have been added, changed or deleted since the last open exceeds 10 percent of the total, the system rebuilds the entire access path (*REBLD-style) even if *DLY is specified. For example, you could have a logical file with an access path for 1000 records and MAINT(*DLY). You opened it last week, but since then you have added 250 records, which is 25 percent of the size it had the last time you opened it. When you open the file today, the system rebuilds the entire access path (for all 1250 records), and treats the file as if it were created with MAINT(*REBLD).

Using the Logical File

Using logical files in your application programs is very easy. All you need to do is code the name of the logical file instead of the name of the physical file, and define the file as having keyed access. Your application program then reads the file sequentially by key (or randomly by key, if that is how you need to read the file).

To the application program, the logical file contains all the data records. You do not have to reference the physical file anywhere.

Section 2: Using OPNQRYF

The OPNQRYF Command

The Open Query File (OPNQRYF) command creates a temporary open data path "on the fly" according to your specifications. Think of it as creating a logical file for you to use once and delete afterwards, but without the trouble of coding DDS for it and without the overhead of the CRTLF and DLTF commands.

The OPNQRYF command has enough parameters to deserve a book of its own. This book will only describe a small fraction of its capabilities. This information should be enough, however, to get you started using OPNQRYF.

The first parameter is FILE. You have to give the name of the physical or logical file you want to sort. You can (optionally) include the library name and the name of the member you want to process. For example:

```
OPNQRYF FILE((*LIBL/CUSTOMER))
```

This command would sort file CUSTOMER using the library list to find it. You can omit the *LIBL qualifier and the library list would still be used.

Sorting Records

To indicate how you want to sort the records, use the KEYFLD parameter. In KEYFLD, you can name up to 50 fields you want to use as key fields for the sorting. Any of them can be in descending sequence if you specify *DESCEND. If the field is numeric, you can ignore its sign (positive or negative) by specifying *ABSVAL. For example:

```
KEYFLD((ITWHSE) (ITITEM))
```

This parameter specifies that the file should be sorted first by ITWHSE. If more than one record has the same value in ITWHSE, those should be sorted by ITITEM. Both will be sorted in ascending sequence.

```
KEYFLD((ITTVAL *DESCEND))
```

With this parameter, the file is sorted in descending value by ITTVAL.

```
KEYFLD((ITWHSE) (ITITEM) (ITTVAL *ABSVAL))
```

This version combines the two. First, sort by ITWHSE in ascending sequence. If several records have the same value in ITWHSE, sort them by ITITEM, then by ITTVAL, ignoring the sign of the numeric value (which means that -3 and +3 are considered equal, and that -4 is considered greater than +3).

The KEYFLD can also have special values *NONE (do not sort the records in any particular order) and *FILE (use the same order in which the records appear in the original file).

Selecting and Omitting Records

OPNQRYF indicates the selection/omission of records with the QRYSLT parameter. QRYSLT must contain a character string that describes a condition which can be either true or false. If the condition is a true value for a particular record, the record is included in the access path built by OPNQRYF. If the condition is a false value, it is omitted.

For example, suppose you have an Accounts Receivable file (ACTRCV) and you want to extract only open invoices dated December 31, 1991 or before. The invoice is considered open if field ARSTAT contains an **O**, and the date is contained in field ARDATE in YYMMDD format. Here is how you code it:

```
QRYSLT('ARSTAT *EQ ''O'' *AND ARDATE *EQ 911231')
```

First of all, note that the entire expression is contained within single quotes. This makes the expression a character string as OPNQRYF requires. Next, note that because you need to compare ARSTAT for equality with the letter **O**, the letter **O** must be enclosed in quotes. Because the entire string is already enclosed in quotes, the inner quotes must be doubled. Note the double quotes around the letter **O**.

ARDATE, on the other hand, is being compared against a numeric value, so 911231 does not have any quotes around it. Finally, notice that the expression uses the same operators (*EQ and *AND) used in CL. You can also use symbolic operators (= and &) if you prefer.

QRYSLT in CL Programs

Under normal circumstances, you would not execute OPNQRYF manually from the keyboard, but from within a CL program. In that case, you frequently have to code the QRYSLT parameter in such a way that the values used for comparison are contained in CL variables instead of being constants. For example, you may have coded the following line in your CL program:

```
QRYSLT('ARSTAT *EQ ''O'' *AND ARDATE *EQ 911231')
```

Then you may want to give your CL program some flexibility by letting it compare ARSTAT to values other than **O** and ARDATE to dates other than 911231. Using variables is natural, so you may be tempted to code:

```
QRYSLT('ARSTAT *EQ &STAT *AND ARDATE *EQ &DATE')
```

This line, however, is invalid. OPNQRYF will attempt to compare field ARSTAT against constant '&STAT' and it will not be able to compare ARDATE against constant '&DATE' because ARDATE is numeric and '&DATE' is character. The reason this command does not work is because the entire string is contained in single quotes, and is being interpreted as-is, without recognizing &STAT and &DATE as variables. The string mistakes the variables for character constants.

To solve this problem, you need to break up the QRYSLT parameter value into pieces and concatenate them with the *CAT, *BCAT and *TCAT CL operators, as follows:

```
QRYSLT('ARSTAT *EQ ''' *TCAT &STAT *TCAT ''' *AND ARDATE +
    *EQ' *BCAT &DATE)
```

To understand this expression, let's look at one piece at a time. First, there is the constant 'ARSTAT *EQ '''. This string ends by including a single quote, so that the system will see it as:

```
ARSTAT *EQ '
```

Next, the *TCAT operator concatenates the value contained in &STAT without any intervening spaces. Assuming that &STAT contains a letter **O**, the system now sees
```
ARSTAT *EQ 'O
```

You concatenate, again without any intervening spaces, the following piece, which is ''' *AND ARDATE *EQ'. The system now sees:

```
ARSTAT *EQ 'O' *AND ARDATE *EQ
```

Finally, you concatenate (with one intervening blank, as mandated by *BCAT) the value in character variable &DATE. The date must be contained in a character variable (even though dates are usually numeric) because the concatenation operators require character variables to work. Assuming that variable &DATE contains the value 911231, the system finally sees:

```
ARSTAT *EQ 'O' *AND ARDATE *EQ 911231
```

which is a valid expression the system can evaluate as true or false.

Using OPNQRYF

To use OPNQRYF in your application programs, you must do the following:

- Override the file being sorted (the file you named in the FILE parameter) with the Override Database File (OVRDBF) command, specifying SHARE(YES).

- Run the OPNQRYF command as required.

- Call the program that uses the sorted file. This program must reference the original file (as named in the FILE parameter) and declare it as having keyed access.

- Close the file with the CLOF command.

- Delete the override with the DLTOVER command.

For example:

```
OVRDBF     FILE(CUSTOMER) SHARE(*YES)
OPNQRYF    FILE((CUSTOMER)) QRYSLT(...) KEYFLD(...)
CALL       PGM(...)
CLOF       FILE(CUSTOMER)
DLTOVR     FILE(CUSTOMER)
```

Section 3: Using FMTDTA

Instead of logical files or OPNQRYF, you can use the Format Data (FMTDTA) command to sort a database file. FMTDTA offers better performance than logicals or OPNQRYF when the file to be sorted is very large (such as more than 100,000 records).

FMTDTA uses sort specifications to define the order of sorting and what records are included or omitted in the process. The sort specifications are identical to the #GSORT specifications of the S/36.

Drawbacks of FMTDTA

FMTDTA is an old-fashioned technique. The only advantage it has is its better performance when sorting very large files. The rest of its characteristics are disadvantages.

- FMTDTA does not use the external file definition of the file being sorted. You have to code beginning and ending positions for the fields you need to reference. For example, if you want to sort a customer master file by customer number (which happens to occupy positions 1 to 7), you instruct FMTDTA to sort by whatever is stored in bytes 1 to 7. Neither you nor FMTDTA knows what is there.

  Because OS/400 encourages file design with external definitions (DDS), you may not even know the absolute positions of the fields you need to reference. You can obtain this information with the Display File Field Description (DSPFFD) command.

- FMTDTA actually produces an output file (containing the sorted records), but this file must exist before you run FMTDTA. It is easy to forget that requirement. You have to code DDS for the output file and create it, or make a duplicate of an existing file that may serve as a model.

- You cannot give the sort specifications "on the fly." FMTDTA requires that you enter the sort specifications in a source member, which is referenced in parameters SRCFILE and SRCMBR of the FMTDTA command. These sort specifications do not allow any form of parameter passing or substitution or variations of any form.

An Example of Use

Because FMTDTA presents so many obstacles, programmers usually shy away from it. Either OPNQRYF or logical files provide much easier coding and more flexibility. Still, you may have good reasons for using FMTDTA some day. One example of its use will explain the workings of FMTDTA.

Suppose that you have a huge Inventory Transaction History File that contains approximately 500,000 records. You need to prepare a summary report, sorted by item number, of all sales transactions that have taken place between January 1, 1991 and December 31, 1991. Your Inventory Transaction History File (ITH) has the following DDS (simplified for this example):

```
....1....+....2....+....3....+....4....+....5....+....6....+....7....+
A          R ITHREC
A            ITITEM        15A          COLHDG('Item Number')
A            ITWHSE         2A          COLHDG('Warehouse' 'Code')
A            ITTRAN         3A          COLHDG('Transaction' 'Type')
A            ITQTY          7P 0        COLHDG('Quantity')
A                                       EDTCDE(J)
A            ITDATE         6P 0        COLHDG('Transaction' 'Date')
A                                       EDTCDE(Y)
A            ITORDR         7A          COLHDG('Order' 'Number')
A            ITREF         10A          COLHDG('Reference')
```

From this DDS, you can conclude that the item number begins on byte 1 and ends on byte 15 of the record. The transaction type ("SAL" for sales) begins on 18 and ends on 20. And the transaction date begins on 25 and ends on 28. Therefore, the sort specifications you need are:

```
....1....+....2....+....3....+....4....+....5....+....6....+....7....+
HSORTR     15A          X
*
I C   18   20EQCSAL              Include sales transactions
IAP   25   28GEC910101            Date >= 910101
IAP   25   28LEC911231            Date <= 911231
*
FNC   1    15                    Sort by item number
FDC   1    45                    Entire record
```

This example uses the "tag along" sort, which is not particularly efficient, but it is somewhat easier to follow.

The H-spec says that the sort control field has a total length of 15 bytes (which agrees with the length of the item number field, which is the field you will use to sort the records). The **A** means ascending sequence. The **X** prevents FMTDTA from writing the sort field to the output record automatically.

The I-specs describe what records to include. Note that there is no mention of the names of the fields. The comments beginning at column 40 are your way to remember what you are doing. The first I-spec says that a record should be included if there is SAL in bytes 18 through 20 of the record. The transaction type happens to be at this location, and you are interested in sales transactions only.

The second and third I-specs have an **A** (and) which ties them to the first one with an AND operator. The packed decimal value in bytes 25 to 28 (transaction date) must be greater than or equal to 910101 and less than or equal to 911231.

Finally, the first F-spec indicates in what order to sort the records. The **N** means normal sort (which agrees with the **A** in the H-spec, therefore sorting in ascending sequence). The numbers next to that reference the sort field (item number). The next F-spec directs the output file to receive the data (that is the **D** in column 7) contained between bytes 1 and 45, which happens to be the entire input record.

Suppose that now you enter these sort specifications into member XYZ of source file MYLIB/QFMTSRC. By the way, IBM recommends using source file QFMTSRC, but you do not have to. The following fragment of a CL program would carry out the sort:

```
CRTDUPOBJ   OBJ(ITH) OBJTYPE(*FILE) FROMLIB(MYLIB) +
              TOLIB(QTEMP) NEWOBJ(ITH) DATA(*NO)
FMTDTA      INFILE((MYLIB/ITH)) OUTFILE(QTEMP/ITH) +
              SRCFILE(MYLIB/QFMTSRC) SRCMBR(XYZ)
OVRDBF      FILE(ITH) TOFILE(QTEMP/ITH) +
              SEQONLY(*YES 1000)
CALL        PGM(...)
DLTOVR      FILE(ITH)
```

The CRTDUPOBJ command creates an empty file [DATA(*NO)] that has the same record layout as the original file. The empty file is also named ITH, but it goes into QTEMP.

The FMTDTA command sorts MYLIB/ITH (the original file) and writes to QTEMP/ITH, using the sort specifications you have just written.

The OVRDBF command overrides file ITH to make sure that the program that follows processes the file in QTEMP and not the original (unsorted) file. The SEQONLY(*YES 1000) parameter ensures that the program will read the records (in blocks of 1000 records each to add a bit of efficiency).

FURTHER READING

IBM's *Database Guide*.

IBM's *DDS Reference*.

IBM's *CL Reference*.

IBM's *Sort User's Guide and Reference*.

Midrange Computing's *Open Query File Magic*.

22

IBM Utilities

IBM has several utilities to help the programmer do a better and more organized job. This chapter will quickly review three of them. They are:

- Program Development Manager (PDM)
- Source Entry Utility (SEU)
- Screen Design Aid (SDA)

Section 1: PDM

PDM stands for **P**rogram **D**evelopment **M**anager. The main purpose of PDM is to provide an easy interface between the programmer and the system. To reach this goal, PDM presents lists of items in typical "Work with" panels from which you can perform actions by entering options and pressing function keys.

PDM's Main Menu

When you execute the Start PDM (STRPDM) command, you will see the PDM main menu, which looks like this:

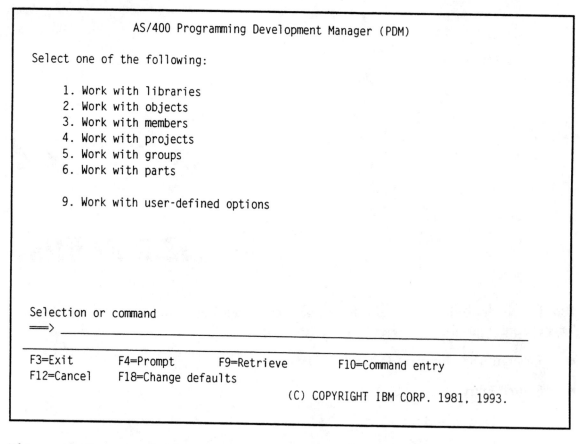

```
                  AS/400 Programming Development Manager (PDM)

   Select one of the following:

        1. Work with libraries
        2. Work with objects
        3. Work with members
        4. Work with projects
        5. Work with groups
        6. Work with parts

        9. Work with user-defined options




   Selection or command
   ===> _____

   F3=Exit      F4=Prompt      F9=Retrieve      F10=Command entry
   F12=Cancel   F18=Change defaults
                                         (C) COPYRIGHT IBM CORP. 1981, 1993.
```

This menu illustrates the three methods you can follow to use PDM:

1. Working with libraries. This option runs the Work with Libraries using PDM (WRKLIBPDM) command, which is explained later.

2. Working with objects. This option runs the Work with Objects using PDM (WRKOBJPDM) command, which also is explained later.

3. Working with file members. This option runs the Work with Members using PDM (WRKMBRPDM) command, which also is explained later.

Options 4, 5, and 6 will not be covered here. Option 9 is a shortcut to maintain user-defined options for PDM. PDM allows you to define your own options to make your work more productive.

Working with Libraries

When you run the WRKLIBPDM command (either manually or by selecting option 1 from the PDM main menu), you can select which libraries you want to work with.

If you run the WRKLIBPDM command manually, you can do so by pressing F4, which invokes the command prompter. If you select option 1 from the PDM main menu, the following panel appears:

```
                    Specify Libraries to Work With

  Type choices, press Enter.

       Library . . . . . . . . . .   mgtlib____    *CURLIB, name

       Object:
         Name . . . . . . . . . .   *ALL_____    *ALL, name, *generic*
         Type . . . . . . . . . .   *ALL_____    *ALL, *type
         Attribute  . . . . . . .   *ALL_____    *ALL, attribute, *generic*,
                                                  *BLANK










  F3=Exit      F5=Refresh     F12=Cancel
```

You can enter different values depending on which libraries you want to work with:

- Enter *LIBL to work with all the libraries contained in your library list.

- Enter a specific name if you want to work with only one library, and you know its name.

- Enter a generic name if you know part of the name, and you want to have a list of the libraries whose names match your entry. This generic name can contain an asterisk (*) at the beginning, in the middle, at the end, or at both the beginning and the end. When you press Enter, PDM considers the asterisk a wild card.

- Enter *ALL if you want a list of all libraries on the system.

- Enter *ALLUSR for a list of all user libraries. This option eliminates the IBM-supplied libraries such as QSYS.

- *USRLIBL works like *LIBL, except that you get only the libraries contained in the user portion of the library list.

- Enter *CURLIB if you want to work with your current library.

When you press Enter, PDM follows your selection instructions and shows a list of the libraries that meet your selection criteria. This is a sample of what your system might present if you selected *ALLUSR:

```
                    Work with Libraries Using PDM

 List type  . . . . . . .   *ALLUSR___    Position to . . . . .  _____

 Type options, press Enter.
    2=Change         3=Copy                  4=Delete          5=Display
    7=Rename         8=Display description   9=Save           10=Restore ...

 Opt  Library     Type      Text
 __   $HOFSHA     *PROD     Project library - Sharon Hoffman
 __   $JONMIK     *PROD     Project Library - Mike Jones
 __   $MALERN     *PROD     Project Library - Ernie Malaga
 __   $SHARIC     *PROD     Project library - Richard Shaler
 __   #LIBRARY    *PROD
 __
 __   ALTQSYS     *PROD     Alternate QSYS:  Duplicate commands, etc.
 __   ALTQSYSSDD  *PROD     Alternate QSYS for SDD.
 __   BBSLIB      *PROD     Programs for Bulletin Board System
                                                                    More...
 Parameters or command
 ===> _____
 F3=Exit            F4=Prompt          F5=Refresh         F6=Create
 F9=Retrieve        F10=Command entry  F23=More options   F24=More keys
```

The actual libraries listed will depend, of course, on the libraries you have on your system. From this panel (the main WRKLIBPDM panel), you can do several things:

- You can change your mind and select another option for library search. As you can see at the top, the list type says *ALLUSR which reflects what you selected. You can move the cursor, change this value, and press Enter.

Chapter 22 - IBM Utilities

- If the list contains many libraries, you can use the "Position to" field (at the top) to shift the list at any point you want. For example, if you type an M and press Enter, WRKLIBPDM starts the list of libraries with the first library with a name that begins with M. If there is not any, it begins with the library immediately prior to that point (it could be a library named LYNN, for example).

- You can move the cursor to one of the input fields on the left column, type an option number (from the option numbers listed near the top, such as 4=Delete) and press Enter. The option you selected is carried out. Each option performs a different task and, as you can see after 10=Restore, there are 3 dots (...). These dots mean that there are more options and you can press F23 to display them.

- You can press any of the function keys available, such as F3 to exit WRKLIBPDM or F6 to create a new library. F24 is available to display more function keys because all of them could not fit in the available space provided.

One of the options you can select on a library is 12. Option 12 starts the WRKOBJPDM command for that library and displays all the objects contained in it.

Working with Objects

The WRKOBJPDM command lets you work with the objects contained in a library. When you run WRKOBJPDM, you can specify which objects you want to work with. If you run WRKOBJPDM manually, you can narrow down your selection by pressing F4 to invoke the command prompter. If you select option 2 from the PDM main menu, the following panel appears:

AS/400 Primer

```
                    Specify Objects to Work With

 Type choices, press Enter.

     Library  . . . . . . . . . .   mcrsclib__   *CURLIB, name

     Object:
       Name . . . . . . . . . . .   *ALL_____   *ALL, name, *generic*
       Type . . . . . . . . . . .   *ALL_____   *ALL, *type
       Attribute  . . . . . . . .   *ALL_____   *ALL, attribute, *generic*,
                                                 *BLANK










 F3=Exit      F5=Refresh      F12=Cancel
```

WRKOBJPDM lets you select the library, the name of the object, its type, and its attribute. In the example provided above, you would get a list of all objects (regardless of name, type or attribute) contained in library MCRSCLIB.

The Type input field lets you select objects by their type. You can enter a value like *PGM or *DTAQ or any other valid object type.

The Attribute input field lets you further narrow down your search. Program objects (*PGM), for example, can have different attributes depending on the language that was used to write them. Program objects, therefore, can have an attribute of CLP if CL was used, or RPG if you used RPG/400.

If you press Enter from the panel shown above, PDM presents the main WRKOBJPDM panel, which looks like this:

Chapter 22 - IBM Utilities

```
                    Work with Objects Using PDM
     Library . . . . .  MGTLIB____      Position to . . . . . . . . _____
                                        Position to type . . . . .  _____

  Type options, press Enter.
     2=Change          3=Copy           4=Delete        5=Display       7=Rename
     8=Display description              9=Save         10=Restore      11=Move ...

  Opt  Object       Type        Attribute    Text
  __   ACT002CL     *PGM        CLP          CPP for LSTACTUSR command
  __   ARA001RG     *PGM        RPG          CPP for DSPARACDE command
  __   ATNKEYPGM    *PGM        CLP          Attention Key Program
  __   ATN001CL     *PGM        CLP          VCP for CHGATNPGM command
  __   ATN001CLA    *PGM        CLP          CPP for CHGATNPGM command
  __   BACKUPD20    *PGM        CLP          Backup D20 AS/400 (SAVLIB *ALLUSR & S
  __   BACK001CL    *PGM        CLP          CPP for STRBACKUP
  __   BACK002CL    *PGM        CLP          CPP for UPDBACKUP command
                                                                         More...
  Parameters or command
  ===>  _____
  F3=Exit            F4=Prompt              F5=Refresh            F6=Create
  F9=Retrieve        F10=Command entry      F23=More options      F24=More keys
```

The actual items you see on the screen depends on what library you choose and what objects are in that library.

You will note that this panel is virtually a duplicate of the WRKLIBPDM main panel. This panel shows one of the strong points about PDM: its consistency of interface. The only differences are those necessitated by the fact that now you are working with objects and not with libraries. Consequently, the numbered options you can select have changed.

Now there are two "Position" input fields at the top-right corner. One of them lets you reposition the list at a particular name, and the other lets you reposition the list at a particular object type. For example, now the list shows program objects (*PGM). If you want to look at files, you would enter the value *FILE in the "Position to type" input field and press Enter.

One of the numeric options you can select on a *FILE object is 12. Option 12 runs the WRKMBRPDM command on that file and lists all its members.

Working with File Members

The WRKMBRPDM command lets you work with the members contained in a file. Contrary to popular belief, you can use WRKMBRPDM on either a database file or a source file. For the most part, however, you will use it on source files.

When you run WRKMBRPDM, you can specify which members you want to work with. If you run the command manually, you can narrow down your selection by pressing F4 to invoke the command prompter. If you select option 3 from the PDM main menu, the following panel appears:

```
                   Specify Members to Work With

 Type choices, press Enter.

   File  . . . . . . . . . .   qrpgsrc___   Name, F4 for list
    Library . . . . . . . .    mcrsclib__   *LIBL, *CURLIB, name
   Member:
     Name  . . . . . . . . .   *ALL_____    *ALL, name, *generic*
     Type  . . . . . . . . .   *ALL_____    *ALL, type, *generic*, *BLANK










 F3=Exit     F4=Prompt     F5=Refresh     F12=Cancel
```

In this example, you will obtain a list of all members (regardless of name or type) that are contained in file MCRSCLIB/QRPGSRC. You can narrow down the list by selecting members by name (usually a generic name is used because you may not remember the actual member name). You can also narrow down the list by member type, such as RPG for RPG/400 source members or DSPF for display file DDS source members.

If you do not change the values shown above, you get the following list in the WRKMBRPDM main panel:

```
                    Work with Members Using PDM

   File . . . . . . SOURCE____
      Library . . . .  MGTLIB____         Position to . . . . . _____

   Type options, press Enter.
     2=Edit          3=Copy         4=Delete        5=Display      6=Print
     7=Rename        8=Display description          9=Save        13=Change text ...

   Opt  Member      Type      Text
   __   #CONFIGURE  CL        Configuration as of 2/25/93
   __   ACT002CL    CLP       CPP for LSTACTUSR command
   __   ARACDE      PF        Area Code Master
   __   ARA001DF    DSPF      Display file for DSPARACDE command
   __   ARA001RG    RPG       CPP for DSPARACDE command
   __   ASNMAGTXT   CMD       Assign Magazine Source Text
   __   ASNTOPSEQ   CMD       Assign Topic Sequence
   __   ATNKEYPGM   CLP       Attention Key Program for Rolling Menus
                                                                   More...
   Parameters or command
   ===> _____

   F3=Exit         F4=Prompt         F5=Refresh          F6=Create
   F9=Retrieve     F10=Command entry F23=More options    F24=More keys
```

Once again, you see PDM's consistency at work. This panel has the same features you have already seen in WRKLIBPDM and WRKOBJPDM.

Changing Defaults

PDM is customizable. Each programmer can use it differently depending on his needs. From any of the three main panels: (WRKLIBPDM, WRKOBJPDM or WRKMBRPDM), you can press F18 to reach the following panel:

```
                          Change Defaults

 Type choices, press Enter.

     Object library . . . . . . .   *SRCLIB___   Name, *CURLIB, *SRCLIB
     Replace object . . . . . . .   N            Y=Yes, N=No
     Compile in batch . . . . . .   Y            Y=Yes, N=No
     Run in batch . . . . . . . .   N            Y=Yes, N=No
     Save session defaults  . . .   Y            Y=Yes, N=No
     Save/Restore option  . . . .   1            1=Single, 2=All
     Job description  . . . . . .   *USRPRF___   Name, *USRPRF, F4 for list
       Library  . . . . . . . . .   _____    Name, *CURLIB, *LIBL
     Change type and text . . . .   N            Y=Yes, N=No
     Option file  . . . . . . . .   QAUOOPT___   Name
       Library  . . . . . . . . .   QGPL_____   Name, *CURLIB, *LIBL
     Member . . . . . . . . . . .   QAUOOPT___   Name
     Full screen mode . . . . . .   Y            Y=Yes, N=No
     Scan hierarchy . . . . . . .   Y            Y=Yes, N=No
     Search path  . . . . . . . .   *DFT_____   Name, *DFT
     Build scope  . . . . . . . .   1            1=Normal, 2=Limited, 3=Extended


 F3=Exit     F4=Prompt     F5=Refresh     F12=Cancel
```

For brevity, only four input fields will be explained here. You can obtain additional information by pressing the Help key or by referring to the PDM manual.

- Object library: Option 14 in the WRKMBRPDM panel lets you compile a source member. Unless you press the F4 key when you select option 14, PDM creates the compiled object in the library you specify here. You can put a fixed library name (if all your compiled objects go to the same library, which is unlikely), *CURLIB, or *SRCLIB.

    *CURLIB places the compiled object in the current library. Avoid this setting unless you know for sure which library is your current library; you could "lose" a newly created object. Worse, it could end in QGPL if you do not have a current library. You should always use *SRCLIB, which places the compiled object in the same library where your source code is. If you ever need to compile into a different library, press F4 instead of Enter when you select option 14 to compile.

- Compile in batch: Option 14 in the WRKMBRPDM panel (which programmers use all the time) lets you compile a source member. This compile can be run either in batch mode or interactively. If you want to run the compile in batch mode (recommended), enter a Y in this input field; otherwise, enter an N.

- Change type and text: The WRKMBRPDM panel shows the type and the text description of the members contained in the file you are examining. When you select N in this field, WRKMBRPDM protects the type and the text from input, so you cannot change them. If you would rather have the type and text input-capable, select a Y in this field. Remember that N protects type and text from accidental erasure or change.

- Full-screen mode: Normally, all three main panels (WRKxxxPDM) contain a list of available numeric options and a list of function keys. These lists are provided at the cost of reducing the number of libraries, objects or members. If you select Y in this input field, PDM enters the full-screen mode. WRKxxxPDM will omit the numeric option list and the function key list in order to make room for more items. When you gain more experience with PDM, you should consider selecting full-screen mode.

Section 2: SEU

SEU stands for **S**ource **E**ntry **U**tility. SEU is the AS/400's main source code editor. It is so important that all programmers should get acquainted with it. SEU is a full-screen editor. Although not as powerful as most PC-based editors, it is the most powerful editor IBM has ever made available on any midrange machine.

A Sample SEU Session

You can start SEU in two ways: by using the Start SEU (STRSEU) command or by selecting option 2 from PDM. Start SEU to begin editing a new source member in source file MYLIB/QCLSRC. The name of the member will be CLSAMPLE, and the member type is CLP:

```
STRSEU SRCFILE(MYLIB/QCLSRC) SRCMBR(CLSAMPLE) TYPE(CLP)
```

The system presents the following panel:

```
Columns . . . :    1  71          Edit                    MYLIB/QCLSRC
SEU==> _____      CLSAMPLE
        *************** Beginning of data ********************************
',,,,,,
',,,,,,
',,,,,,
',,,,,,
',,,,,,
',,,,,,
',,,,,,
',,,,,,
',,,,,,
',,,,,,
',,,,,,
',,,,,,
',,,,,,
',,,,,,
',,,,,,
',,,,,,
',,,,,,
',,,,,,
',,,,,,
',,,,,,
            ***************** End of data *******************************
 Member CLSAMPLE added to file MYLIB/QCLSRC.                              +
```

Your panel may look different. It may have fewer open lines between the "Beginning of data" and "End of data" markers. Later you will see how you can change yours the same way.

Note that you can enter data in two main areas. The left-hand column (filled with apostrophes) is the line command area. In this area, you can enter special commands to insert, delete, and move lines. The actual data entry area where you enter the actual source code occupies most of the screen, however.

Because member CLSAMPLE is a CL source member, begin by entering a PGM command. In the main entry area, type PGM:

```
Columns . . . :    1  71              Edit                    MYLIB/QCLSRC
SEU==> _____         CLSAMPLE
         *************** Beginning of data ************************************
''''''  PGM
''''''
''''''
''''''
''''''
''''''
''''''
''''''
''''''
''''''
''''''
''''''
''''''
''''''
''''''
''''''
''''''
''''''
         ***************** End of data ****************************************
Member CLSAMPLE added to file MYLIB/QCLSRC.
```

AS/400 Primer

Because the source type is CLP, SEU knows that the source code will consist of commands. Commands can be prompted using the F4 key. SEU lets you prompt for the PGM command by pressing the F4 key (with the cursor still on the same line):

```
                        Program (PGM)
Type choices, press Enter.
Label  . . . . . . . . . . . .   name_____
Parameter CL variable names  . .  &option____   Variable name
             + for more values    _____
Comment  . . . . . . . . . . .   _____
_____
_____
_____




                                                              Bottom
F3=Exit    F4=Prompt    F5=Refresh    F12=Cancel   F13=How to use this display
F24=More keys
```

This is the command prompter for the PGM command. Because you are entering source code, the prompter shows two input fields it never showed before: Label and Comment. Enter "name" in the Label input field, and "&option" in the first input line that follows. Then press Enter:

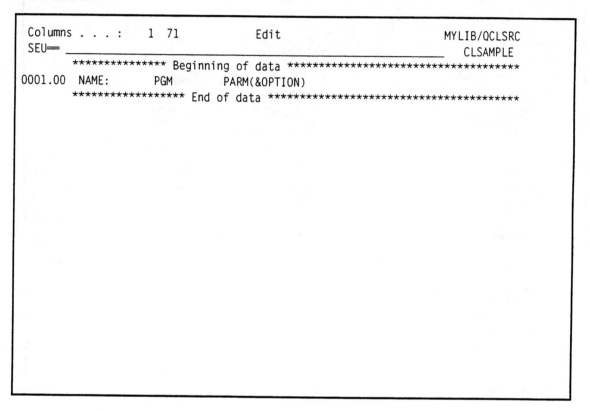

The command prompter formats the PGM command into your source member. The label automatically goes on column 2, followed by a colon. The command name goes on column 14, and the first parameter's keyword (inserted by SEU for you) begins on column 25.

This activity can continue for many more commands and become the source code for a complete program in this member. When you are done entering the statements, press F3 to exit SEU. SEU presents the following panel:

```
                              Exit
 Type choices, press Enter.

   Change/create member  . . . . . . .  Y            Y=Yes, N=No
     Member  . . . . . . . . . . . . .  CLSAMPLE__   Name, F4 for list
     File  . . . . . . . . . . . . . .  QCLSRC____   Name, F4 for list
       Library . . . . . . . . . . . .  MYLIB_____   Name
     Text  . . . . . . . . . . . . . .  Sample CL program_____

   Resequence member . . . . . . . .   Y            Y=Yes, N=No
     Start . . . . . . . . . . . . .   0001.00      0000.01-9999.99
     Increment . . . . . . . . . . .   01.00        00.01-99.99

   Print member  . . . . . . . . . . .  N            Y=Yes, N=No

   Return to editing . . . . . . . . .  N            Y=Yes, N=No

   Go to member list . . . . . . . . .  N            Y=Yes, N=No



 F3=Exit    F4=Prompt    F5=Refresh    F12=Cancel
```

If you do not change anything and press Enter, SEU updates source member CLSAMPLE in MYLIB/QCLSRC. At this point, you have the chance to enter some text description for the source member, or to resequence the statements. Then press Enter.

Coding RPG/400 Source in SEU

RPG/400 is just as easy to code with SEU. SEU has prompt formats for all RPG/400 specification types (plus variations). For example, there is a prompt format for the F-spec, and another for each variety of F-spec (such as KRENAME).

Chapter 22 - IBM Utilities

To edit a new source member called RPGSAMPLE in source file MYLIB/QRPGSRC, run the following command:

```
STRSEU SRCFILE(MYLIB/QRPGSRC) SRCMBR(RPGSAMPLE) TYPE(RPG)
```

```
 Columns . . . :   1  71          Edit                        MYLIB/QRPGSRC
 SEU== _____         RPGSAMPLE
         *************** Beginning of data *************************************
 ,,,,,,,
 ,,,,,,,
 ,,,,,,,
 ,,,,,,,
 ,,,,,,,
 ,,,,,,,
 ,,,,,,,
 ,,,,,,,
 ,,,,,,,
 ,,,,,,,
 ,,,,,,,
 ,,,,,,,
 ,,,,,,,
 ,,,,,,,
 ,,,,,,,
 ,,,,,,,
 ,,,,,,,
 ,,,,,,,
         ****************** End of data ****************************************
 Member RPGSAMPLE added to file MYLIB/QRPGSRC.
```

AS/400 Primer

To start coding the RPG/400 program, enter an F-spec. SEU provides a prompt format for the F-spec. To display, enter the P line command in the line command column, followed by the name of the prompt format (F, for the F-spec), as follows:

```
 Columns . . . :    1   71         Edit              MYLIB/QRPGSRC
 SEU==  _____        RPGSAMPLE
         *************** Beginning of data ************************************
PF
,,,,,,,
,,,,,,,
,,,,,,,
,,,,,,,
,,,,,,,
,,,,,,,
,,,,,,,
,,,,,,,
,,,,,,,
,,,,,,,
,,,,,,,
,,,,,,,
,,,,,,,
,,,,,,,
,,,,,,,
,,,,,,,
,,,,,,,
,,,,,,,
         ***************** End of data ****************************************
```

When you press Enter, SEU presents the F-spec prompt at the bottom of the screen, and also shows the lines currently entered (if any) at the top, as follows:

```
Columns . . . :    1  71           Edit                        MYLIB/QRPGSRC
SEU== _____          RPGSAMPLE
      *************** Beginning of data *************************************
0001.00
      *************** End of data *******************************************




















Pmt  SeqNbr   FName      Type Desig EOF Seq Fmt RcdLen Mode KeyLen RAT
 F   0001.00 _____    _    _    _   _   _   _____  _    __     _
             Org Ov KeyLoc Ext Device  K Exit  Entry   Add  Cond
              _   _  ____   _  _____  _ ____  _____    _    _
```

All you need to do now is fill out the input fields and press Enter. SEU will format the F-spec and log it at the top of the screen.

SEU Line Commands

SEU allows you to execute numerous line commands. They will not all be listed here. You can obtain a list by pressing the Help key with the cursor located at the line command column. Following are the most important line commands:

- Delete. Enter a **D** line command and press Enter; SEU deletes the line that contains the **D** command. You can enter more than one **D** and press Enter and SEU will honor all requests at once.

    To delete a block of consecutive lines, enter the **DD** command on the beginning line, another **DD** command on the ending line and press Enter. You also can enter

AS/400 Primer

the letter **D** followed by a number (such as 10) to delete that number of consecutive lines. The deletions at the line where you enter the **D** command.

- Insert. Enter an **I** line command and press Enter; SEU opens up a blank line for you. You can open up more than one line by entering **I** followed by a number (such as 15 for fifteen new lines).

- Copy. Enter a **C** line command on the line you want to copy. Then enter an **A** command on a line if you want the copy to go after that line, or use the **B** command on a line if you want the copy to go before that line.

  You also can copy a group of consecutive lines by entering **CC** on the first line to be copied and again **CC** on the last line. Then use the **A** or **B** commands to place the copy in the right place.

- Prompt. Enter a **P** command on a line to have SEU invoke the correct prompt format for the line as it is written. For example, if the line contains an E-spec (in a source of type RPG), the **P** command displays the prompt format for the E-specs.

  If the line is blank or if you want to override the prompt you would get by default, you can follow the **P** with the identification code for the prompt format. For example, you can change a blank line into a C-spec by using the **PC** command. If you are not sure about the identification code of the format, use a question mark instead. If you run the **P?** command, SEU will show you a list of available prompt formats.

  The **I** (insert) and **P** (prompt) commands can be combined to insert a new line and invoke the prompter at the same time. For example, you can enter **IPF** to insert a new F-spec.

- Shifting the code. If you are using a free-format language like C or PL/I, you can indent your code. If you insert a test condition in an existing program, you may be turning existing code into a new block that never existed before. Because it is a block, it should be indented. Rather than inserting blank spaces (which may not always work), you can use the **R** command to shift the code one column to the right, or the **L** command to shift it one column to the left.

  Normally, however, you will want to shift the code more than one column. In that case, follow the **R** or **L** command with a number, such as **R3** to shift the code 3 columns to the right. You can also shift a group of consecutive lines with the **RR** or **LL** commands (followed optionally by the number of columns, as in **RR3** or **LL6**).

- Shifting the Window. SEU always shows a piece of the actual code. There may be code farther to the right that will not fit on the screen. In that case, you can shift the window through which you are looking at the code with the **W** command. For example, **W31** shifts the window so that the first column shown on the left is column 31.

- Moving forward or backward. You can always use the Roll keys to page forward or backward. If the distance you have to cover is large, you can use the positioning commands. For example, you can enter a statement number and press Enter. SEU automatically moves the window so that the first line is the statement you requested. Or, you can enter a command such as **+150** to advance 150 statements, or **-270** to go back 270 statements.

Top-Line Commands

SEU has an input-capable line, near the top of the screen labeled "SEU===>" where you can enter special commands. No matter where your cursor is, F10 takes it to the top-line command-entry field. Once you execute a top-line command, F10 takes the cursor back to the place it came from.

Here are some top-line commands:

- Quickly move to top or bottom. The **T** command (or **TOP**) shifts the window so it begins with the first statement in the source member. The **B** command (or **BOTTOM**) shifts the window so it ends with the last statement in the source member.

- Finding a string. If you want to find a character string in the source member, use the **F** command. For example, if you enter **F EXFMT**, SEU searches the source member for the first occurrence of EXFMT.

- Changing strings. Use the **C** command to replace one string with another. For example, to change the first EXFMT into a WRITE, run the **C EXFMT WRITE** command. If you follow it with **ALL**, SEU replaces all occurrences of EXFMT with WRITE.

- Upper/lower case. Use the SET CAPS ON command to force SEU to accept only capital letters. Use SET CAPS OFF to allow both upper and lowercase input.

☞ SEU has more commands. If you need more information, place the cursor in the SEU===> prompt and press the Help key. For more detailed help about a particular command, type the command name (for example, C for the change command) and press the Help key.

AS/400 Primer

Function Keys

Besides the obvious function keys (F3=Exit, F4=Prompt, F5=Refresh and F12=Cancel), SEU supports three that present other panels.

F13 lets you customize your SEU session. For example, you can control how much SEU advances or goes back when you press the Roll keys. Choose the Cursor setting (**C**). With the **C** setting, the Roll keys roll only enough to move the line (where the cursor is placed) on the top line or bottom line, depending on the direction of the roll. The **C** setting gives you complete control over the Roll keys.

Here is the screen that F13 presents:

```
                          Change Defaults
  Type choices, press Enter.

     Object library . . . . . . . . . . .   *SRCLIB    Name, *CURLIB, *SRCLIB
     Replace object . . . . . . . . . . .   Y          Y=Yes, N=No
     Compile in batch . . . . . . . . . .   Y          Y=Yes, N=No
     Run in batch . . . . . . . . . . . .   N          Y=Yes, N=No
     Save session defaults  . . . . . . .   Y          Y=Yes, N=No
     Save/Restore option  . . . . . . . .   1          1=Single, 2=All
     Job description  . . . . . . . . . .   ERNIE      Name, *USRPRF, F4 for list
     Library  . . . . . . . . . . . . . .   ERNIE      Name, *CURLIB, *LIBL
     Change type and text . . . . . . . .   N          Y=Yes, N=No
     Option file  . . . . . . . . . . . .   QAUOOPT    Name
     Library  . . . . . . . . . . . . . .   QGPL       Name, *CURLIB, *LIBL
     Member . . . . . . . . . . . . . . .   QAUOOPT    Name
     Full screen mode . . . . . . . . . .   Y          Y=Yes, N=No
                                                                        More...

  F3=Exit   F4=Prompt   F5=Refresh   F12=Cancel
```

While the **F** and **C** top-line commands let you perform some finding and changing, they do not allow as many options as F14 does.

Here is the screen presented by F14:

```
                        Find/Change Options

 Type choices, press Enter.

   Find  . . . . . . . . . . . . .  _____
   Change  . . . . . . . . . . . .  _____
   From column number  . . . . . .  1__       1-80
   To column number  . . . . . . .  80_       1-80 or blank
   Occurrences to process  . . . .  1         1=Next, 2=All
                                              3=Previous
   Records to search . . . . . . .  1         1=All, 2=Excluded
                                              3=Non-excluded
   Kind of match . . . . . . . . .  2         1=Same case
                                              2=Ignore case
   Allow data shift  . . . . . . .  N         Y=Yes, N=No

   Search for date . . . . . . . .  92/06/21  YY/MM/DD or YYMMDD
     Compare . . . . . . . . . . .  _         1=Less than
                                              2=Equal to
                                              3=Greater than

 F3=Exit    F5=Refresh       F12=Cancel   F13=Change session defaults
 F15=Browse/Copy options     F16=Find     F17=Change
```

The F15 key lets you display and/or copy either another source member, a spool file or an output queue. While you perform this function, the SEU display splits in two halves: upper (current edit session) and lower (the other item). Here is what F15 presents:

```
                    Browse/Copy Options
 Type choices, press Enter.

    Selection  . . . . . . . . . .   1            1=Member
                                                  2=Spool file
                                                  3=Output queue
    Copy all records . . . . . . .   N            Y=Yes, N=No
    Browse/copy member . . . . . .   RPGSAMPLE_   Name, F4 for list
       File  . . . . . . . . . . .      QRPGSRC___   Name, F4 for list
       Library . . . . . . . . . .         MYLIB_____   Name, *CURLIB, *LIBL

    Browse/copy spool file . . . .   RPGSAMPLE_   Name, F4 for list
       Job . . . . . . . . . . . .      RPGSAMPLE_   Name
       User  . . . . . . . . . . .         MALERN____   Name, F4 for list
       Job number  . . . . . . . .          *LAST_   Number, *LAST
       Spool number  . . . . . . .          *LAST    Number, *LAST, *ONLY

    Display output queue . . . . .   QPRINT____   Name, *ALL
       Library . . . . . . . . . .      *LIBL_____   Name, *CURLIB, *LIBL

 F3=Exit      F4=Prompt        F5=Refresh       F12=Cancel
 F13=Change session defaults   F14=Find/Change options
```

F16 repeats the last Find operation, F17 repeats the last Change operation, and F21 opens up a window from which you can enter and execute any system commands.

Section 3: SDA

SDA is an acronym for **S**creen **D**esign **A**id. it is a utility that lets you create panels (screens) or simple menus for your interactive programs. SDA has so much functionality that this section cannot possibly do it justice. Rather than going over each feature in detail, the utility will be presented by designing a very simple display file. SDA can also be used to create menus, but the menu creation features will not be discussed.

Starting Up SDA

You can launch SDA by choosing an option 17 from PDM, if you want to work on an existing display file source member. In all other cases, you need to run the Start SDA (STRSDA) command:

STRSDA

SDA presents its main menu:

```
                    AS/400 Screen Design Aid (SDA)
 Select one of the following:

        1. Design screens
        2. Design menus
        3. Test display files










 Selection or command
 ===> 1_____

 F1=Help    F3=Exit    F4=Prompt    F9=Retrieve    F12=Cancel
                                   (C) COPYRIGHT IBM CORP. 1981, 1991.
```

AS/400 Primer

Select option 1 to design a display file. SDA asks you what source file and source member you want to use:

```
                             Design Screens
 Type choices, press Enter.

    Source file  . . . . . . . .   qddssrc___   Name, F4 for list
      Library  . . . . . . . .    mylib_____   Name, *LIBL, *CURLIB
    Member . . . . . . . . . .    dspsample_   Name, F4 for list










 F3=Exit      F4=Prompt      F12=Cancel
```

The example provided above works with source member DSPSAMPLE in source file MYLIB/QDDSSRC. Press Enter. The following panel appears:

```
                         Add New Record
    File . . . . . . :    QDDSSRC         Member . . . . . . :    DSPSAMPLE
       Library . . . :    MYLIB           Source type  . . . :    DSPF
    Type choices, press Enter.

       New record . . . . . . . . . . . . . . .   PANEL_____   Name

       Type . . . . . . . . . . . . . . . . . .   RECORD       RECORD, USRDFN
                                                               SFL,    SFLMSG
                                                               WINDOW, WDWSFL
                                                               PULDWN, PDNSFL
                                                               MNUBAR







       F3=Exit      F5=Refresh      F12=Cancel
```

This panel tells you that there are no records in the file. There are not yet any defined record formats for the display file you are designing. The display shows the name of the source file and source member you selected, and has automatically appended a source type of DSPF.

AS/400 Primer

Note that one of the options you can select (documented near the top of the panel) is option 1 to add. Enter an option 1 below "Opt" and a record name of PANEL below "Record" as shown below:

```
                  Work with Display Records

 File . . . . . . :   QDDSSRC          Member . . . . . . :   DSPSAMPLE
   Library . . . . :   MYLIB           Source type  . . . :   DSPF

 Type options, press Enter.
   1=Add            2=Edit comments      3=Copy         4=Delete
   7=Rename         8=Select keywords   12=Design image

 Opt  Order   Record       Type      Related Subfile   Date      DDS Error
 1_           PANEL_____
    (No records in file)




                                                                  Bottom
 F3=Exit                  F12=Cancel      F14=File-level keywords
 F15=File-level comments  F17=Subset      F24=More keys
```

Press Enter. This information tells SDA that you want to add a record format named PANEL to the display file. Naturally, SDA needs some additional information, so it asks for it using the following panel:

```
                        Add New Record
   File . . . . . . :   QDDSSRC          Member . . . . . :   DSPSAMPLE
      Library . . . :   MYLIB               Source type . . . :   DSPF

   Type choices, press Enter.
     New record . . . . . . . . . . . . .   PANEL_____   Name
     Type   . . . . . . . . . . . . . . .   RECORD       RECORD, USRDFN
                                                         SFL,    SFLMSG
                                                         WINDOW, WDWSFL
                                                         PULDWN, PDNSFL
                                                         MNUBAR













   F3=Exit     F5=Refresh     F12=Cancel
```

The type of record you want to add is RECORD, so you can leave the default value given by SDA and press Enter. You will use RECORD in the majority of cases. SFL and SFLMSG are also used, but not as often. USRDFN is a very advanced, complicated feature that will not be discussed in this book.

SDA presents the following panel when you press Enter:

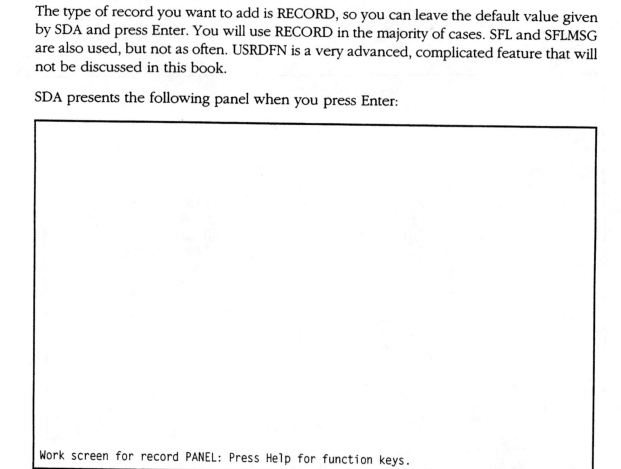

This blank panel (except for the informational message at the bottom, which disappears if you press Enter again) is your work area. You can design the panel here, using special codes, commands and function keys.

For example, to add a title to this panel, type the text shown below. Make sure to enclose the text in single quotes. Do not worry that it is not centered. Press Enter.

```
'This is the panel title'
```

When you press Enter, SDA creates a constant field that contains the text you entered. SDA knows it is a constant field because you enclosed it in single quotes. The quotes can be omitted if you are only adding a single word. If you had omitted the single quotes in the example given above, SDA would have created five constant fields, that each contained one word.

AS/400 Primer

You can center the field automatically by using the **ac** command (automatic centering). Type the a in the space immediately before the field, and the **c** overlapping the first character of the field. Do not worry that the beginning T is missing. SDA will not forget it.

```
acis is the panel title
```

Press Enter. SDA centers the title automatically, as follows:

```
                    This is the panel title
```

Now move two lines down (use the arrow keys or the new line key) and add the constant 'Vendor number' as far to the left as possible. Do not forget to enclose 'Vendor number' in single quotes. Press Enter. SDA adds that constant field to the screen. Now, you can create a data field with the **+b(6)** command. The **+** means that you are adding a field. The **b** means that the field is alphanumeric, both for input and output. The **(6)** indicates that the field will be six positions long.

Here is what the panel should look like:

```
                    This is the panel title
Vendor number +b(6)




```

Press Enter. SDA adds the input/output field and replaces your command with a representation of the actual field. Because the field allows input, SDA underlines it (by default, OS/400 underlines input-capable fields). The screen should look like this:

```
                          This is the panel title
    Vendor number   BBBBBB




















```

Other codes define fields of different types and usages. For alphanumeric fields, **i** defines an input-only field, **o** defines an output-only field, and **b**, as you have seen, defines an input/output field. Numeric fields use a code of **3** for input only, **6** for output only, and **9** for input/output.

Therefore, you can add an input-only numeric field, seven digits long (with one decimal place) by using the **+3(7,1)** command.

The new field has no name so far. Actually, SDA has assigned it a generic name that means nothing, so you should rename the field. The easiest way to rename it is by entering a **?** command immediately before the field, as follows:

```
                    This is the panel title
Vendor number ?BBBBBB



```

Press Enter. SDA prompts you (at the bottom of the work screen) for the field name and length. Type VENDOR (the new name of the field). The length is already given, so you do not have to change it:

```
                        This is the panel title
 Vendor number   BBBBBB










 VENDOR____ Length: 00006 TEXT:
```

AS/400 Primer

Press Enter. The field is now named VENDOR. Now, to change some of its attributes, enter the * command immediately before the field:

```
                    This is the panel title
Vendor number *BBBBBB
```

Press Enter. SDA responds by presenting a panel with many options. You can enter a Y on the line that contains the options you want to edit. For example, let's see what "General keywords" do for the VENDOR field:

```
                         Select Field Keywords

   Field . . . . . :   VENDOR            Usage . . :  B
   Length . . . . :   6                  Row . . . :  3    Column . . . :  17

   Type choices, press Enter.
                                      Y=Yes   For Field Type
       Display attributes  . . . . . . . .  _     All except Hidden
       Colors  . . . . . . . . . . . . .    _     All except Hidden
       Keying options  . . . . . . . . . .  _     Input or Both
       Validity check  . . . . . . . . . .  _     Input or Both, not float
       Input keywords  . . . . . . . . . .  _     Input or Both
       General keywords  . . . . . . . .    Y     All types
       Database reference  . . . . . . .    _     Hidden, Input, Output, Both
       Error messages  . . . . . . . . . .  _     Input, Output, Both
       Message ID (MSGID)  . . . . . . .    _     Output or Both
       TEXT keyword  . . . . . . . . . . _____
   _____




   F3=Exit    F12=Cancel

```

AS/400 Primer

SDA presents another panel that lets you enter general-purpose DDS keywords that will slightly modify the VENDOR field:

```
                      Select General Keywords
  Field . . . . . :  VENDOR           Usage . . :  B
  Length . . . . :  6                 Row . . . :  3      Column . . . :  17
  Type parameters and choices, press Enter.

    Keyword     Text or Value                                    More
    ALIAS       _____
    INDTXT  __  _____
    DFT         _____
    DFTVAL      _____
    CNTFLD      000
                                        Keyword    Y=Yes   Indicators/+
    Default value . . . . . . . . . . . DFTVAL
    Retain field on display . . . . . . PUTRETAIN    _     __ __ __
    Override data . . . . . . . . . . . OVRDTA       _     __ __ __
    Override attributes . . . . . . . . OVRATR       _     __ __ __
    Translate characters  . . . . . . . CHRID        _

    Alter IGC type  . . . . . . . . . . IGCALTTYP    _

    F3=Exit    F12=Cancel
```

From this panel, you could assign VENDOR a default value, for example. This way, the panel would have the VENDOR field already filled in by a value you expect the user to type most of the time.

Working with Fields

From the work panel you can press F4 to obtain a list of all the fields you have defined in the record format. For example, this is what the list of fields would look like at the present time:

```
                          Work with Fields
   Record . . . :    PANEL

 Type information, press Enter.

   Number of fields to roll . . . . . . . . . . . . . . . . . _6

 Type options, change values, press Enter.
   1=Select keywords    4=Delete field

 Option   Order   Field       Type Use  Length  Row/Col  Ref Condition  Overlap
    _      __10   This is th    C          23    01 029
    _      __20   Vendor num    C          13    03 002
    _      __30   VENDOR____    B           6    03 017



                                                                       Bottom
 Add      _____   _____    H    _____   Hidden
 Add      _____   _____    M    _____   Message
 Add      _____   _____    P    _____   Program-to-system

 F3=Exit    F6=Sort by row/column    F12=Cancel
```

There are three fields. At order 10 and 20, there are two constant fields (as identified by a C under "Type"). At order 30, there is a data field (it has a name: VENDOR), and its usage is B (both input and output). SDA gives you the length of the fields and their absolute location within the screen.

From this screen, you can edit any of the existing fields using option 1. You can also rename data fields by typing over the field name (in this case, by typing over the name VENDOR with something else). You can rearrange the fields by changing their order. If the fields are not in correct sequence, F6 sorts the fields by their row/column position.

AS/400 Primer

Finishing Up

Press F12 from the work screen to tell SDA that you are done with that record format. SDA again shows the list of records. Note that this time, record PANEL shows up. The panel even tells you when you maintained it last:

```
                     Work with Display Records
  File . . . . . . :   QDDSSRC           Member . . . . . . :  DSPSAMPLE
     Library . . . :   MYLIB                Source type . . . :  DSPF

  Type options, press Enter.
     1=Add              2=Edit comments      3=Copy           4=Delete
     7=Rename           8=Select keywords   12=Design image

  Opt  Order    Record          Type        Related Subfile   Date        DDS Error
  __   ____
  __     10    PANEL           RECORD                         06/21/92




                                                                       Bottom
  F3=Exit                F12=Cancel       F14=File-level keywords
  F15=File-level comments F17=Subset      F24=More keys
  Record PANEL added to member DSPSAMPLE.
```

Suppose you do not need to add any other record formats to the display file. Press F12 to tell SDA that you are done working with this source member. SDA presents the final panel:

```
                 Save DDS - Create Display File
  Type choices, press Enter.

     Save DDS source  . . . . . . . . . . . .   Y            Y=Yes
       Source file  . . . . . . . . . . . . .   QDDSSRC___   F4 for list
         Library  . . . . . . . . . . . . . .   MYLIB_____   Name, *LIBL ...
       Member . . . . . . . . . . . . . . . .   DSPSAMPLE_   F4 for list
       Text . . . . . . . . . . . . . . . . .                _____

     Create display file  . . . . . . . . . .   Y            Y=Yes
       Prompt for parameters  . . . . . . . .   _            Y=Yes
       Display file . . . . . . . . . . . . .   DSPSAMPLE_   F4 for list
         Library  . . . . . . . . . . . . . .   MYLIB_____   Name, *CURLIB
       Replace existing file  . . . . . . . .   _            Y=Yes
     Submit create job in batch . . . . . . .   Y            Y=Yes
     Specify additional
       save or create options . . . . . . . .   _            Y=Yes




  F3=Exit    F4=Prompt    F12=Cancel
```

Take advantage of the opportunity to add text description to the source member, so it will be easier to identify when you see it in PDM. The "Create display file" determines whether to compile the source member you have edited with SDA. The field always defaults to Y.

If you press Enter, SDA saves the edits you have made in the source member and compiles the display file. You also can press F3 to kill the whole editing session, or F12 to go back to SDA for more work.

FURTHER READING

IBM's *PDM User's Guide and Reference*.

IBM's *SEU User's Guide and Reference*.

IBM's *SDA User's Guide and Reference*.

23

Journaling and Commitment Control

Section 1: Journaling

A journal is a form of a diary. If you keep a journal, you probably record in it all the things that happen to you. The AS/400 is also capable of keeping a journal and recording events in it. For this reason, journaling can be thought of as a permanent record of some of the things that happen in the computer.

Although journaling can be used to record any event, it is usually reserved for the recording of changes in key database files. Unlike journals that people keep, the AS/400 can keep many journals simultaneously.

☞ Once the system records an event in a journal, it is safe from tampering. Even QSECOFR cannot alter it by any means.

Journals And Journal Receivers

Journaling requires two objects at minimum: a journal (*JRN) and a journal receiver (*JRNRCV).

- The journal receiver is the object where the events are recorded. Each event is recorded as a journal receiver entry, which is automatically time-stamped and identified with the name of the user who originated it and the complete qualified name of the job the user was running.

The journal receiver must be created first using the Create Journal Receiver (CRTJRNRCV) command, as follows:

```
CRTJRNRCV JRNRCV(MYLIB/RCV0001) THRESHOLD(10000)
```

This command creates a journal receiver in MYLIB called RCV0001. For reasons that will become apparent, journal receiver names should always end in four digits beginning with 0001. The THRESHOLD parameter is the size, in KB, that, when the journal reaches it, will trigger a notification. A value of 10,000 is 10,000KB (10MB). When the journal receiver grows to that size, the system sends message CPF7099 but keeps recording.

- The journal is a channel through which an event reaches the journal receiver. A journal can have one or two journal receivers attached; if it has one, events are recorded in that journal receiver only. If it has two, the same event is recorded in both receivers as an added precaution.

Once the journal receiver exists, you can then create the journal with the Create Journal (CRTJRN) command:

```
CRTJRN JRN(MYLIB/JOURNAL) JRNRCV(MYLIB/RCV0001) +
       MSGQ(QSYSOPR)
```

With this message you create a journal called JOURNAL in MYLIB, and attach to it the journal receiver you created before. The MSGQ parameter names the message queue to which the system sends message CPF7099 when the journal receiver's size threshold is reached.

Journaling Files

Events more likely to be journaled are changes made in database files. When you journal a physical file, the system records an image of the record as it was before the change, and an image of the record after the change. You can also request to record only the "after" images.

Journaling a physical file can simplify data recovery. If you save a journaled file weekly and save the journal and journal receiver daily (or every other hour), and you lose the

Chapter 23 - Journaling and Commitment Control

file, you can restore the file from last week's backup and use the journal to reapply all the updates your users have made into the file.

Journaling also can work the other way around. If you run a mass-update program that adversely affects a journaled file, you can undo the mass update by removing the changes recorded in the journal. However, you can only undo the changes if you are recording both "before" and "after" images of the database records in your journals.

Here are the details:

- Start journaling with the Start Journal Physical File (STRJRNPF) command. In order to run the STRJRNPF, the physical file must not be in use by anyone. After you run STRJRNPF, the file can be again used as usual:

```
STRJRNPF FILE(ITMMST) JRN(MYLIB/JOURNAL) IMAGES
```

This command requests both "before" and "after" images of the records that are changed. IMAGES(*AFTER) can be used if you would rather record only "after" images.

- Immediately afterwards, save the file with the Save Changed Object (SAVCHGOBJ) command, as follows:

```
SAVCHGOBJ OBJ(ITMMST) LIB(...) DEV(SYSTAP01) +
          OBJTYPE(*FILE) OBJJRN(*YES)
```

When you run this command, the system allows you to apply journaled changes to the file, which is the reason you are journaling the file. The key is the OBJJRN(*YES) parameter.

You can stop journaling a physical file with the End Journal Physical File (ENDJRNPF) command.

Journaling with SNDJRNE

As mentioned earlier in this chapter, you can use journaling to record all kinds of events. Journaling database changes is automatic, but other events must be recorded manually with the Send Journal Entry (SNDJRNE) command. Once recorded, you can view the journal entries with the Display Journal (DSPJRN) command.

The basic format of the SNDJRNE command (which can be included in your CL programs) is as follows:

```
SNDJRNE JRN(MYLIB/JOURNAL) TYPE('SV') +
        ENTDTA('Security violation')
```

This command records a journal entry of type SV (which is a code you can make up). The data is "Security violation" in this case, but it can be anything you want. If you include the SNDJRNE command in your CL programs, you can use CL variables and add their values to the ENTDTA parameter, such as:

```
SNDJRNE JRN(MYLIB/JOURNAL) TYPE('SV') +
        ENTDTA('Security violation by user' *BCAT +
        &USER *BCAT 'at workstation' *BCAT &WS)
```

The only restriction SNDJRNE imposes on you is that the value in the TYPE parameter must be greater than hexadecimal C000. If you make sure that the first character is a letter (which is at least x'C1'), this will not be a problem.

Maintaining Journal Receivers

Journal receivers grow in size as more and more entries are recorded. Periodically, you need to maintain the journal:

- Change journal receivers. You run the Change Journal (CHGJRN) command to detach the journal receivers currently in use and attach new ones. The CHGJRN can take care of the creation of the new journal receivers for you and even give them their names. This feature is why it is best to give journal receivers names ending in four digits. it is simple for CHGJRN to generate a new name by adding 1:

    ```
    CHGJRN JRN(MYLIB/JOURNAL) JRNRCV(*GEN)
    ```

- Save the old journal receiver to tape or diskette (diskette may be impractical because journal receivers can be large objects):

    ```
    SAVOBJ OBJ(RCV0001) LIB(MYLIB) DEV(SYSTAP01) +
           OBJTYPE(*JRNRCV)
    ```

- Delete the old journal receiver from the system:

    ```
    DLTJRNRCV JRNRCV(MYLIB/RCV0001)
    ```

Journaling for Recovery

The most important application of journaling is that it provides a relatively easy and painless path to recover database files, especially those that change too much too quickly.

Chapter 23 - Journaling and Commitment Control

If a file undergoes many updates in a short period of time, a daily backup may not be enough to guarantee recovery.

Journaling, on the other hand, records all the database changes in the physical files that you update through your application programs or utilities such as DFU or SQL. With journaling, you can recover database files in two different ways: forward or backward.

Forward Recovery. Use forward recovery if you need to restore a database file from backup media (tape or diskette), and you want to reapply all the database operations recorded in the journal up to the present point.

Run the Work with Journals (WRKJRN) command.

```
                          Work with Journals

 Type options, press Enter.
   2=Forward recovery        3=Backout recovery    5=Display journal status
   6=Recover damaged journal 7=Recover damaged journal receivers
   9=Associate receivers with journal

 Opt  Journal     Library     Text
  2   JOURNAL     MYLIB




















                                                                     Bottom
 Command
 ===> _____
  F3=Exit    F4=Prompt    F9=Retrieve    F12=Cancel
```

From the panel presented, select option 2 to perform forward recovery. Press Enter. The following panel appears:

```
                      Work with Forward Recovery
   Journal  . . . . . :   JOURNAL         Library  . . . . . :   MYLIB

   Position to  . . . . .  _____
   Library  . . . . . . .  _____

   Type options, press Enter.
     1=Add member to list   2=Apply journaled changes   3=Restore
     4=Remove member from list

   Opt     File            Library          Member        Status
           _____        _____         _____
    _      MYFILE          MYLIB            MYFILE




                                                                  Bottom
   F3=Exit    F12=Cancel
```

Select option 2. The system guides you through a series of steps necessary to restore your database file successfully and apply the journaled operations. These steps include the deletion of dependent logicals, restore from tape, and recreation of the logicals.

Backward Recovery. Journaling can also work in reverse. If you are journaling your Accounting files and run your year-end General Ledger close, your database files go through a massive update process. If you are later informed that the fiscal year should not have been closed yet, journaling can help you undo the year-end close.

Run the WRKJRN command and select option 3 to perform backward recovery. The following panel appears:

```
                     Work with Backout Recovery
Journal . . . . . . :   JOURNAL         Library . . . . . . :   MYLIB

Position to  . . . . .  _____
Library  . . . . . . .  _____

Type options, press Enter.
  1=Add member to list    2=Remove journaled changes
  4=Remove member from list

Opt     File            Library         Member          Status
 _      _____        _____        _____
 _      MYFILE          MYLIB           MYFILE


                                                                Bottom
F3=Exit    F12=Cancel
```

Now select option 2 to remove all the database operation changes you have journaled. You will have to know when to stop undoing operations, of course. You will need to run the DSPJRN command to find the exact journal entry sequence number where you need to stop.

Section 2: Commitment Control

The Concept

Commitment control is a way to ensure that a single transaction, which consists of more than one database update, is executed in its entirety or not at all. For example, suppose your Customer Service clerk is entering new sales orders into your Order Entry and Billing software. Each "transaction" is a sales order, which is usually comprised of a header and line items.

If you do not use commitment control, the system may have an inconsistent database if the clerk's job were to end abnormally after he starts one order, but before he completes the data entry. For example, he may have just completed the header portion. Immediately after your program writes the header to the database, power fails and the system shuts down. Now you have a sales order header in your database that has no line items associated with it. Depending on how the software was designed, your software may not allow you to resume entry or even delete the order.

Under commitment control, on the other hand, all database updates that make up a single transaction are performed at once. Your programs still perform the same write, update or delete operations on the database files, but they are only queued. When the program encounters a commit operation, however, all queued database operations are carried out at once. Therefore, if power fails somewhere in the middle, no database updates would have taken place because the operations were only in the queue.

Prerequisites for Commitment Control

You cannot choose to use commitment control, arbitrarily, on any file or group of files. The system requires you to do the following:

- The files that are going to be operated upon with commitment control must be journaled, and such journaling must be performed in the same journal. Refer to the previous section about journaling, and note in particular, the material about the STRJRNPF command.

- You must run the Start Commitment Control (STRCMTCTL) command before you attempt to use commitment control.

- Your HLL program can then run using commitment control. Files must be identified as committable. In RPG/400, identify the files in the F-specs using a continuation (K) line with an entry of COMIT (with only one M).

- After your HLL program ends, you must run the End Commitment Control (ENDCMTCTL) command.

The COMMIT and ROLLBACK Operations

Although the actual process is much more complicated, the following description is enough for our purposes. Any program that is running under commitment control queues all database change operations (write, update, delete) for all committable files, and locks the changed records. When the program reaches a COMMIT operation, all queued operations are carried out at once, which releases all changed records.

In RPG, the COMMIT operation is spelled COMIT. Each time your program executes the COMMIT operation, the system writes all the database operations that were in the queue, and a boundary entry that marks the COMMIT operation into the journal receiver. As the program continues executing, it runs more database operations which, again, are queued instead of carried out. Next time the program reaches the COMMIT operation, all database operations are carried out at once, recorded in the journal receiver, and the loop continues.

The ROLLBACK operation performs the inverse operation. ROLLBACK (which is spelled ROLBK in RPG) clears the queue of database operations that are accumulating before COMMIT is executed, which releases all affected records.

In the sales order example at the beginning of this section, the data entry clerk may be about to finish entering a new sales order when he realizes that he entered an incorrect customer number on the very first display. By this time, the HLL program he is running has queued quite a few write and update operations, but it has not reached the COMMIT operation yet. You can provide a function key to abort the sales order. The HLL program then executes a ROLLBACK, the queue is cleared, and the database is as it was before the sales order entry began.

FURTHER READING

IBM's *Backup and Recovery Guide*.

24

Understanding the S/36 Environment

When the AS/400 was being designed, one of the key features in the plan was to make it possible for the AS/400 to run S/36 software with as little modification as possible. Because the two machines differ so much in their architecture, however, it was necessary to create a special environment that would mimic the S/36 architecture as closely as possible. The result of this quest is the S/36 Execution Environment, which can be abbreviated as S/36EE or S/36E.

When you enter the S/36E, you can pretend you are using a real S/36 instead of the AS/400. The AS/400 responds to the usual S/36 control commands and procedures, can be programmed as if it were a S/36, and in general can be used as such. There are some differences, however, for the S/36E is not an exact replica of the real S/36.

Section 1: AS/400 Versus S/36

The AS/400 and the S/36 are actually two different worlds. This section explains some of the key differences you need to be aware of, in order to take advantage of the S/36E and administer it successfully.

Libraries and Objects

The concept of object is paramount on the AS/400. Practically everything you can manipulate, including libraries, is an object of some kind. On the AS/400, all objects are contained in libraries. For example, an AS/400 library can contain executable programs, data areas, database files and commands. An S/36 library, on the other hand, cannot contain everything. There are certain objects such as folders and data files that fall outside of libraries.

The difference is important. Data files are unique on the S/36. If you create a file named VENDORS, no other file can have that name (unless you use date-differentiated files, but that is another subject). In contrast, you can create many files, all named VENDORS, on the AS/400 if you put them in different libraries. Combined with the library list support (a concept that is practically nonexistent on the S/36), the AS/400 allows you to create multiple environments. Some libraries may contain production data, others may contain test data. All of them can run the same set of programs because they are accessing equally-named files in different libraries.

Source Code

The AS/400 keeps source code in separate members within a source physical file. For example, the source code for RPG program XYZ would be in member XYZ of source file QRPGSRC, in whatever library you are going to place the compiled program (although this is not required). Its file and source member are a three-step hierarchy: library, source file and source member.

☞ Because the source member is in a source file and since there can be several source files in a library (with arbitrary names), a library can contain any number of identically-named source members. You can take advantage of this feature to keep older versions of source code online. Create another source file and copy the source there before you make modifications.

The S/36 does not allow this type of duplication. Source code is contained in source and procedure library members. It is a two-step hierarchy only: library and member. The source file concept does not exist and, because there can be only one source or procedure name of a given name, the S/36 will not allow duplication of source members.

Chapter 24 - Understanding the S/36 Environment

Names

Always remember that the AS/400 supports 10-character names for everything, while the S/36 poses certain restrictions. Some of the most notable differences are:

- User names can be up to eight characters long on the S/36. The AS/400 allows 10 characters.

- Workstation names (display stations, printers and diskette drives) must be two characters long on the S/36. The AS/400 allows names of any length up to 10 characters.

- Files, libraries and library members can have names of up to eight characters on the S/36. Again, the maximum is 10 on the AS/400.

- User passwords must be 4 characters long on the S/36 (no more, no less). The AS/400 allows any length between 1 and 10 characters.

Jobs

The concept of *interactive job* is different in the two machines. In the AS/400, an interactive job is the entire event between sign-on and sign-off to a display station. Everything the user does between sign-on and sign-off is part of the interactive job. When the user runs a command, that event is called a request.

In the S/36, the span of time between sign-on and sign-off is called a session. Each time the user runs a procedure, a new job starts within the session and is given a different number. When the procedure ends and the user is returned to the menu, the job ends, but the session continues.

S/36E Structure

To make effective use of the S/36E, you will need at least a basic understanding of how it is organized.

The S/36E is supported by the existence of several libraries: QSSP (which contains the S/36 SSP), #LIBRARY (with the user objects you would have placed in #LIBRARY on the S/36), and QS36F (which will contain all your data files). Other than these three libraries, there are the usual #RPGLIB, #SDALIB and #SEULIB.

The AS/400 does more than you think each time you execute the BLDLIBR procedure. First, it runs the CRTLIB command to create the actual library. Then it runs two CRTSRCPF commands to create source files QS36PRC (where you will put all your procedure members) and QS36SRC (where you will put all your source members). Source files for subroutine or load members are not mentioned because these are actual objects (type *PGM or *FILE, for example) contained in the library.

Once the library is ready, you can use the SEU procedure to edit source and procedure members exactly as you did on the S/36. For example:

```
SEU NEWPGM,R,,,MYLIB
```

The S/36E starts SEU for source member NEWPGM (type RPG36) in source file MYLIB/QS36SRC. You do not have to be concerned about what source file is used because the S/36E handles it for you. To you, it would seem that the source member is directly attached to the library (even though it is not); that feature creates a feeling of continuity with the real S/36.

Section 2: Entering the Environment

When you switch from the native environment to the S/36E, the input you type into the command line shifts to all uppercase letters (as it works on the S/36). When you return to the native environment, input appears in lowercase. You can enter the S/36E in three ways.

The STRS36 Command

You can use the Start System/36 (STRS36) command to enter the S/36E. This command has three parameters, all of which are optional:

- MENU. Defaults to *SAME, but you can change it to any menu name. *SAME means that the menu you have on the screen will not be replaced by another menu when you enter the S/36E. Otherwise, the system will display the menu you request as it enters the S/36E.

- CURLIB (Current Library). Also defaults to *SAME, which means that your job's current library does not change. If you use the value *SAME and have no current library, the S/36E uses #LIBRARY as your current library. You can also enter any valid library name.

Chapter 24 - Understanding the S/36 Environment

- PRC (Procedure). Defaults to *NONE, which means that no procedure will start running as you enter the S/36E. You can enter a valid procedure name, which must be located in the library specified in CURLIB.

The STRS36PRC Command

The Start S/36 Procedure (STRS36PRC) command allows you to run a S/36E procedure. You can run this command from the command line or from a CL program, but never from within another S/36E procedure. If you want to run a S/36E procedure from within another procedure, you would use the usual //INCLUDE statement in the OCL.

If you run the STRS36PRC command from the native environment (not in the S/36E), the system enters the S/36E to run the procedure and then exits the S/36E which leaves you in the native environment when the procedure ends.

STRS36PRC has three parameters:

- PRC (Procedure). Enter the name of the procedure here.

- CURLIB (Current Library). Enter the name of the library where the S/36E is to find the procedure you want to run. You can use the default value of *SAME, which will use whatever library happens to be your current library at that time. If you do not have one, #LIBRARY is used.

- PARM (Parameters). Enter a character string that contains all the parameters for the procedure, separated by commas. PARM is optional; if you do not enter anything, the procedure you are about to run receives no parameters.

S/36E at Sign-On

You can set up some user profiles (or all) so that every time your users sign on they enter the S/36E without doing anything special. This option is most convenient when the application programs you use on a daily basis are still programmed in the S/36E.

There are two ways to set up users for automatic S/36E entry:

1. Create or change user profiles with SPCENV(*S36). This parameter establishes the fact that, for that one user, the sign-on special environment is S/36E. Other users can have SPCENV(*NONE) if they need to work in the native environment.

2. Create or change user profiles with SPCENV(*SYSVAL) and make sure that system value OSPCENV has the value *S36. This method is preferred when the majority of users need to be in the S/36E. You can still keep some users in the native environment by specifying SPCENV(*NONE) in their user profiles.

From then on, all affected users will enter the S/36E automatically upon sign-on; they will not have to do anything special.

Section 3: Leaving the Environment

When you are done using the S/36E and want to return to the native environment, you need to tell the system so.

- If you entered the S/36E with the STRS36 command, all you need to do is execute the End System/36 (ENDS36) command. This command effectively ends your stay in the S/36E and takes you back to the native environment. This command has no parameters.

- If you entered the S/36E with the STRS36PRC command, you do not have to do anything to leave the S/36E, because the system takes you back to the native environment automatically when the procedure ends.

- If you entered the S/36E at sign-on by having SPCENV(*36) in your user profile (or through system value QSPCENV), you cannot leave the S/36E to go to the native environment.

☞ You will discover, however, that you do not have to leave the S/36E to execute native commands or use native applications. You can enter native commands while in the S/36E. The system will accept them and execute them correctly. For example, even though the Change User Profile (CHGUSRPRF) command is a native command, you can run it while in the S/36E.

Chapter 24 - Understanding the S/36 Environment

Section 4: Maintaining the Environment

The CHGS36 Command

On the S/36 you would perform many configuration tasks using the CNFIGSSP procedure. When you use the S/36E, however, you need to use the Change System/36 (CHGS36) command.

This command can be run only when there are no users currently using the S/36E because the AS/400 must be able to have exclusive use of it during the execution of the CHGS36 command.

The CHGS36 command presents the following panel:

```
                  Change S/36 Environment Configuration

S/36 Environment . . . . . . . . . . :    #LIBRARY

Type options, press Enter.
  2=Change

Option     Configuration Description
  _        S/36 display IDs
  _        S/36 printer IDs
  _        S/36 tape IDs
  _        S/36 diskette ID
  _        S/36 3270 device emulation values
  _        S/36 environment values
  _        S/36 MRT security and performance




F3=Exit    F12=Cancel
```

From this panel, you can enter an option 2 next to the item you want to maintain and press Enter. The CHGS36 command takes you to a secondary panel from which you can actually perform the maintenance you need to do.

Changing Devices

The first four options in the main panel (shown above) are used to maintain physical devices that are already connected and configured to the AS/400. Because the S/36E has different requirements, these requirements must be specified in the special panels presented by the S/36E.

For example, the S/36E requires all devices to have two-character names, in accordance with the S/36 naming scheme. Because the AS/400 uses device names that can have up to 10 characters, the CHGS36 command lets you give each AS/400 device an S/36-style name.

For example, here is the panel from which you maintain display devices:

```
                      Change S/36 Display IDs

  S/36 Environment . . . . . . . . . . :    #LIBRARY

  Type new/changed values, press Enter.

  AS/400            S/36           S/36 Default
  Display           Display ID     Printer ID
  SYSDSP01          W2             __
  SYSDSP02          W3             __
  EDTDSP02          W5             __
  EDTDSP03          W6             __
  SYSDSP01A         WB             __
  SFWDSP01          WC             __
  SFWDSP01A         WD             __
  SFWDSP01B         WE             __
  EDTDSP03A         WG             __
  EDTDSP01          W4             __
  EDTDSP01S1        W7             __
  EDTDSP01S2        W8             __
                                                              More...
  F3=Exit    F5=Refresh    F6=Sort S/36 display IDs    F10=Set S/36 display IDs
  F12=Cancel
```

As you can see, the AS/400 display device SYSDSP01 has a S/36E equivalent of W2. If a user signs on to SYSDSP01 and starts the S/36E, a substitution expression such as ?WS? would return the value W2. You can change these values if you want. You can also assign a default printer ID for each display station, but this step is optional.

To maintain printers, you use the following panel:

Chapter 24 - Understanding the S/36 Environment

```
                       Change S/36 Printer IDs

 S/36 Environment . . . . . . . . . . . :   #LIBRARY

 Type new/changed values, press Enter.

 AS/400          S/36        Lines       Characters
 Display      Printer ID   Per Inch      Per Inch        Font
 SFWPRT01         P1           _             __           __
 SYSPRT01         P2           _             __           __
 EDTPRT04         P4           _             __           __
 EDTPRT05         P5           _             __           __
 EDTPRT01         P3           _             __           __




                                                               Bottom
 F3=Exit    F5=Refresh    F6=Sort S/36 printer IDs   F10=Set S/36 printer IDs
 F12=Cancel
```

This panel is similar to the previous one, but you are maintaining printer IDs instead of display IDs. In addition, you can specify the default lines per inch, characters per inch and font ID used by each printer.

Changing Environment Values

The most important maintenance option is the one labeled "S/36 environment values" on the main panel. When you select it with an option 2, you get the following panel:

```
                    Change S/36 Environment Values

  S/36 Environment . . . . . . . . . . . . :    #LIBRARY

  Type choices, press Enter.

    S/36:
      Default session library . . . . . . . .    _____
      Default files library . . . . . . . . .    QS36F_____
      Use library list for files  . . . . . .    N           Y=Yes, N=No
      Date differentiated files . . . . . . .    N           Y=Yes, N=No
      Shared opens of files . . . . . . . . .    Y           Y=Yes, N=No
      Record blocking when sharing files  . .    N           Y=Yes, N=No
      Store deleted files in cache  . . . . .    N           Y=Yes, N=No
      Default lines per page  . . . . . . . .    066         1-112
      Default forms . . . . . . . . . . . . .    *STD_____
      Default message action  . . . . . . . .    *HALT_____  *CONTINUE, *IGNORE,
                                                             *HALT, *CANCEL
      Halt options  . . . . . . . . . . . . .    03

                                                                       More...
  F3=Exit    F5=Refresh    F10=Set to default values    F12=Cancel
```

Some entries may be familiar to you already if you have experience with the S/36's CNFIGSSP procedure. Other options are new because they apply to the AS/400's implementation of the S/36E. For example:

- Default files library. The S/36E keeps your data files in a single library. When the AS/400 was first designed, the developers forced you to use a library named QS36F to keep all your files. Now you have an option, but QS36F is still the initial value given to this parameter.

- Use library list for files. You can select to take advantage of the native environment's library list support to locate your files. If you are not comfortable with the concept (or if you do not know much about it), you should stick to what you already know (i.e. having all your data files in one place, so you know where to look).

- Shared opens of files. When you select this option, the S/36E behaves like the S/36 in that once a file is opened by one program, other programs take less time to access

Chapter 24 - Understanding the S/36 Environment

the same file because it is already open. The difference is that the S/36 also shares storage indexes, while the AS/400 in S/36E will not.

- Store deleted files in cache. The AS/400's architecture makes file creation and deletion a time-consuming and resource-intensive process. S/36 software, however, often creates and deletes work files because this process is simple and quick on the S/36. When the S/36E deletes a file, the file is not actually deleted. The file is only made unavailable. If a subsequent operation requests that the file be created again, the file is made available once more, as an empty file.

Section 5: Operations

The whole idea behind the S/36E is to let you control, operate and program the AS/400 as if it were a real S/36. To make the charade more realistic, IBM even allows you to use, on the AS/400, the same control commands you use on a S/36.

For example, you can run the STATUS USERS (D U) or CANCEL PRINT (C P) control commands while in the S/36E. The AS/400 "translates" these commands into standard native commands, however, and presents displays that are not those you are used to seeing on the S/36.

For example, the D W command actually runs the WRKCFGSTS command and presents the WRKCFGSTS panel. The panel has an S/36 flavor, however, because it shows the S/36E device names (W1, W2, etc.) instead of the native, 10-character names.

Unsupported Commands

A few control commands are not supported because they do not make sense in the AS/400 architecture. For example, the ASSIGN (A) command is not supported because none of its functions apply to the AS/400. The unsupported commands are:

ASSIGN (A), CONSOLE, MODE, POWER, PRTY and REPLY (R).

FURTHER READING

IBM's *AS/400 Concepts and Programmer's Guide for the S/36E.*

IBM's *System Reference for the S/36 Environment.*

25

Programming in the S/36 Environment

How you program the AS/400 depends on what environment you are using. If you use the S/36 Execution Environment (S/36EE or S/36E), you have to use different rules and an entirely different mindset than if you were programming in native.

This chapter briefly explains the main concepts you need to know when you program in OCL and the key differences between RPG II in the S/36E and RPG/400 in native. This chapter assumes that you have previous programming experience on a real S/36.

Section 1: OCL

SSP Procedures

The S/36E supports most of the SSP procedures of the true S/36. The exceptions are because of differences in architecture, which make it impractical or downright impossible to support certain functions.

For example, the S/36 needs to run the COMPRESS procedure periodically in order to gather all available disk space (which may be scattered in tiny fragments throughout the disks) in a single spot. Because of the single-level storage architecture of the AS/400, this procedure is completely useless.

The supported procedures run without modification and have identical syntax, so you can execute any of them without worrying that you are actually using an AS/400.

#STRTUP1 and #STRTUP2

You can create a STRTUP1 or STRTUP2 procedure (or both) in #LIBRARY or in the system operator's sign-on library, just like you can on the S/36. The AS/400, however, treats both procedures the same way. #STRTUP1 and #STRTUP2 are executed after other jobs are allowed to run. In other words, both procedures are treated as #STRTUP2.

☞ If you need to run a procedure before anyone signs on or other jobs run, you must do some native programming. The system value QSTRUPPGM contains the qualified name of the start-up program that runs during IPL. All you need to do is change this program to include the Start S/36 Procedure (STRS36PRC) command so it executes your procedure as part of the start-up process. The start-up program is discussed in Chapter 2.

Unsupported and Ignored Procedures

Some SSP procedures are not supported and others are ignored. Non-supported procedures are those that generate an error message if you attempt to run them. If unsupported procedures are included in a user procedure, the user procedure ends with an error message. Ignored procedures are those procedures that, although they are not used in the S/36E, are still allowed in S/36E procedures, but the system does nothing when it encounters ignored procedures.

- Non-supported procedures (* indicates a S/34 procedure): ALERT, ALOCFLDR, ALTERBSC, ALTERCOM, ALTERSDL*, APAR, APPNINFO, ARCHIVE, ASM, ASMLOAD, ASMSAVE, AUTO*, BACKUP*, BALPRINT, BASIC, BASICP, BASICR, BASICS, BASLOAD, BASSAVE, BGUATTR, BGUCHART, BGUDATA, BTUGRAPH, BGULOAD, BGUSAVE, BUILD, CGULOAD, CGUSAVE, CGUXLATE, CNFIGICF, CNFIGSSP, CNFIGX25, COBLOAD, COBOL*, COBOLC, COBOLCG*, COBOLG*, COBOLONL, COBOLP, COBSAVE, COBSDA, COBSEU, COPYDIAG, DEFINEID, DEFINEPN, DEFINLOC, DEFINX21, DEFINX25, DELNRD, DFA, DFULOAD, DFUSAVE, DICTLOAD, DICTSAVE, DISABLE, DLSLOAD, DLSSAVE, DOCCNV, DOCPLOAD, DOCPSAVE, DSULOAD, DSUSAVE, DUMP, EDITNRD, ENABLE, EP-

Chapter 25 - Programming in the S/36 Environment

DOWNL, EPLMRG, ERAP, FORTC, FORTCG, FORTGO, FORTLOAD, FORTONL, FORTP, FORTRANC, FORTSAVE, FORTSDA, FORTSEU, HISTCOPY, HISTCRT*, HISTORY, ICFDEBUG, ICVERIFY, IDDUXLAT, INITDIAG, INIT9332, IPL, IWLOAD, IWPTLOAD, IWPTSAVE, IWSAVE, KEYS, LANLOAD, LANSAVE, LISTNRD, LOAD3601, LRTRLOAD, LRTRSAVE, MAINTX25, MCSCONV, MOVEFLDR, MSGFILE, OFCBPRT, OFCCANCL, OFCCOMM, OFCCONV, OFCDATA, OFCINSTL, OFCLOAD, OFCMAINT, OFCQ, OFCSAVE, OFCSTART, OLINK, OLPDLOAD, OLPDSAVE, OVERRIDE*, PASSTHRU, PATCH, PCEXCH, PCOLOAD, PCOSAVE, POST, PROBLEM, PROFLOAD, PROFSAVE, PTF, QRYLOAD, QRYSAVE, RELOAD*, REQUESTX, RESTEXTN, RESTFLDR, RESTNRD, RETRIEVE, ROLLKEYS, RPGLOAD, RPGONL, RPGP, RPGSAVE, SAVEEXTN, SAVEFLDR, SAVENRD, SDALOAD, SDASAVE, SECDEF, SECEDIT, SECLIST, SECREST, SECSAVE, SERVICE, SERVLOG, SETALERT, SETCOMM, SETDUMP, SEULOAD, SEUSAVE, SHRFLOAD, SHRFSAVE, SMF, SMFDATA, SMFPRINT, SMFSTART, SMFSTOP, SOFTWARE, SPECIFY*, SRTXLOAD, SRTXSAVE, STARTM, STATEST, STOPGRP, STOPM, STRTGRP, SWDLOAD, SWDSAVE, TAPESTAT, TEXTCONV, TEXTLOAD, TEXTREL, TEXTSAVE, TRACE, TRNMGR, WSFLOAD, WSFSAVE, WSULOAD, WSUSAVE, WSUTXCR, WSUTXEX, WSUTXRV, XREST*, XSAVE*.

- Ignored procedures: ALOCLIBR, CACHE, COMPRESS, CONDENSE, IDDURBLD, KEYSORT.

New Procedure (FLIB)

The FLIB procedure allows you to specify which library is to supply the data files for the session. By default, that library is QS36F, but you can change it for the duration of your session with the FLIB procedure. If you want to make the change permanent, you need to run the Change S/36 (CHGS36) command.

FLIB's second parameter allows values LIBL and NOLIBL. With this parameter, you can specify whether you want your session to use the native library list support to locate data files if they do not happen to be in your files library.

Both parameters are optional, but at least one must be specified. If you omit one of the parameters, your session's setting (that would be controlled by the missing parameter) will not change. For example, if you execute:

```
FLIB ,LIBL
```

AS/400 Primer

Because the first parameter is not given, your session's files library remains unchanged. However, because you selected LIBL for the second parameter, your session will start using the library list support.

☞ The changes made by FLIB do not become effective immediately. The changes are deferred until the first-level procedure ends.

Non-Supported and Ignored OCL Statements

- Non-supported OCL statements: COMM, POWER
- Ignored OCL statements: ABEND, IMAGE, REGION, RESERVE

New OCL Statements

- // FILELIB: Similar to the FLIB procedure, but more powerful. It has three keyworded parameters:

    NAME: Where you enter the name of the files library. You can also specify 0 if you want to use the default files library as defined by the CHGS36 command.

    LIBL: Where you indicate if you want to use the library list support. You must enter YES or NO. Only the current files library is searched if NO is specified.

    SESSION: Where you indicate whether the values you are assigning to the NAME and LIBL parameters apply to current values or session values. YES means that they apply to your session; NO means that they apply to the current values.

- // TIMERSET: This OCL statement lets you prepare your system for an automatic, unattended IPL at some future date and/or time, or to prepare the system for automatic IPL after a power failure, or for remote IPL. Although useful, the function of the TIMERSET statement can be programmed better using Operational Assistant's Automatic Power Schedule. See Chapter 2.

    Examples of TIMERSET:

    ```
    // TIMERSET TIMED-YES,DATE-050392,TIME-070000
    ```

    The above statement prepares the system for automatic, unattended IPL on May 3, 1992 at 7:00 a.m.

Chapter 25 - Programming in the S/36 Environment

```
// TIMERSET RESTART-YES
```

This statement indicates that the system should re-IPL after a power failure.

```
// TIMERSET REMOTE-YES
```

This statement indicates that remote IPL should be allowed.

```
// TIMERSET QUERY-YES
```

This statement lists the current settings made with // TIMERSET in the current SYSLIST device.

Mixing OCL and CL in Procedures

S/36E procedures let you mix S/36E OCL and native OS/400 commands within the statements. Native commands can be placed anywhere you can place the name of a procedure or an OCL statement, except between the // RUN and the // END statements.

Each time a procedure encounters a new statement, it tries to execute it as an OCL statement first. If it is not an OCL statement, it tries to execute it as a procedure. If it is not a procedure, it executes it as a native command. This means that you cannot include commands that have the same name as an OCL statement or a procedure, unless you qualify the command to force the OCL interpreter to recognize it as a command.

This qualification can be made with a command label or a library name (or *LIBL). For example, suppose you have a command named FILE (which matches the name of an OCL statement) and you want to run it in a procedure. Here is how you can code it:

```
// X: FILE          (uses a command label, X)
// *LIBL/FILE       (uses a library qualifier, *LIBL)
```

You can also mix OCL constructs within a native command. For example, an OCL statement such as the following is perfectly valid:

```
// CRTLIB LIB(?1?)
```

This statement uses the value of parameter 1 as the value to be passed to the LIB parameter of the native CRTLIB command. Here is another example:

```
// EVALUATE P4='CRTLIB LIB(?5?)'
     // ?4?
```

363

The first statement assigns a command string with an embedded substitution expression that is evaluated first to parameter 4. If parameter 5 has the value MYLIB, P4 obtains the value 'CRTLIB LIB(MYLIB)'. The second statement executes that command.

☞ If the CL command ends in error, the ?MSGID? substitution expression will contain the ID of the *ESCAPE message issued by the CL command. If the CL command ends normally, ?MSGID? is blank. After executing a CL command, your OCL procedure can check ?MSGID? to see if the command executed correctly.

New Substitution Expressions

There are four subsitution expressions that have been created specifically for the S/36E (they are not available on the real S/36). These are:

- ?FLIB?, which returns the name of the current files library.

- ??, which returns the name of the session files library.

- ?MSGID?, which returns a native, seven-character message ID if the native command just executed ended in error. If the command ends normally, ?MSGID? is blank.

- ?DEV'unit'?, which returns the native, 10-character name of the device whose two-character unit is given. For example, ?DEV'W1'? returns the 10-character device name associated with S/36E device W1.

Unsupported IF Expressions

The S/36E does not support the following two IF control expressions:

```
// IF ENABLED-YES (or -NO)
// IF LISTDONE-YES (or -NO)
```

Section 2: RPG II

Most business applications written for the S/36 are written in RPG II. If you migrate one of those applications to the AS/400 under the S/36E, the application program usually works unmodified. Usually, you only need to recompile it.

Chapter 25 - Programming in the S/36 Environment

Still, there are some differences between the version of RPG II you use on a real S/36 and the version you use on the AS/400. The purpose of this section is not to teach you RPG II or even to present the language because you are probably already familiar with it. This section lists the differences between the implementations. You must be aware of these differences to write correct programs on the S/36E.

Compiling Programs

If you compile an RPG II program with the Create S/36E RPG Program (CRTS36RPG) or Create S/36E Auto Report Program (CRTS36RPT) commands, you can use a program name that has up to eight characters. The following parameters of the RPGC procedure are ignored:

- Produce a diagnosed source member (DSM or NODSM)
- Override print option (SOURCE, PSOURCE or NOSOURCE)
- Override debug option (DEBUG or NODEBUG)
- Override size to execute (2 to 64)
- Halt on serious error (HALT or NOHALT)
- Create program that must be link-edited (OBJECT or NOOBJECT)
- Name of subroutine input library
- Size of work files in blocks (1 to 9999)
- Create program with memory-resident overlays (MRO or NOMRO)

Some parameters of the AUTOC procedure are ignored as well. The list is identical to the one shown above, except the first parameter (DSM/NODSM), which does not apply to AUTOC.

Files With Several Record Types

Files that have more than one record type are an everyday occurrence in most S/36 installations. Despite the fact that the AS/400 does not allow different record types in a single physical file, the S/36E can process such files because migrated files in the S/36E are usually "flat." They have no external definition (DDS) that describes the fields in detail.

When you get ready to leave the S/36E and start programming in native, you will wonder how you can emulate the multiple record type file. The process involves the following steps:

- Create a separate physical file for each record type. You will want to describe in full all the fields contained in the record.

- Create a multi-format logical file that sits on top of all the separate physical files. Your RPG programs then can process this logical file as if it were a file that has multiple record types.

For more information on this topic, refer to Chapter 18.

Fields

Differences related to fields include:

- You cannot use the same field name in two or more data structures. For example, data structures DS1 and DS2 cannot both have a subfield named DATA. The S/36 gives you a warning message, but the AS/400 aborts the compile.

- If a data structure contains a subfield that has been defined elsewhere (such as in an I-spec or C-spec), the subfield must agree in data type and length or an error will occur. The S/36 gives you a warning message, but the AS/400 aborts the compile.

- The Dup key presents a problem with numeric fields. Define a character field in the I-specs for the WORKSTN file that completely overlaps the numeric field you want to test. Then compare this field against hex **1C** to detect if the Dup key has been pressed.

- If you use the **Y** edit code in a numeric field that is less than three or more than six digits long and you do not specify an ending position in the O-specs, the S/36 and the AS/400 RPG II will place the edited value in different places.

Unsupported Features

The AS/400 version of RPG II ignores all input in columns 10 to 14 of the H-spec. In the S/36 version, these columns control the object output; they list options and size to execute.

The AS/400 version of RPG II does not support SUBR22.

Chapter 25 - Programming in the S/36 Environment

New Operation Codes

The AS/400 version of RPG II supports all the opcodes used in native RPG/400 to call other programs. Therefore, your RPG II programs can use any or all of the following operation codes:

- CALL. Starts executing the program named in Factor 2. The name can be contained in a character literal or variable.

- PLIST. Marks the beginning of a list of parameters. When Factor 1 has the value *ENTRY, it signals the entry point to a program, when another program calls it.

- PARM. PARM follows either CALL or PLIST. Each PARM operation describes one parameter.

- FREE. If program A calls program B, program A can remove program B from memory with the FREE operation. Next time it calls B, B will have to be reloaded from disk.

- RETRN. Marks a point from which a program returns control to its caller.

Differences in Old Operations

Three operations work slightly differently in both systems: SETLL, EXCPT and READ.

- SETLL. On the AS/400 RPG II, SETLL actually positions the file to a particular record. The system actually performs a database I/O operation, and the system expects SETLL to be followed by an input operation such as READ. If the program attempts to perform an output or update operation, the program ends in error. The S/36 RPG II would have voided the SETLL if the program executed an output or update operation instead of input, and processing would have continued, with the SETLL canceled.

- EXCPT. If EXCPT and a subsequent C-spec operation are both conditioned by an overflow indicator, and EXCPT outputs to the file that uses the overflow indicator, the second operation may not execute if the overflow condition no longer exists. This situation occurs because the AS/400 tests the indicator for each operation, even if the same indicator is used. The S/36 does not; it tests the indicator only once, which may cause both operations to be carried out, even if the overflow condition does not exist by the time the program executes the second operation.

- When you READ a workstation file that has the Roll keys defined, you must code an indicator in columns 56-57. If you do not, the Roll keys generate a keyboard error "Function key is not allowed," even if you define them in the screen format member's key mask. If you use a primary workstation file (using the RPG cycle), you need to use the INFSR file continuation and define an information subroutine.

Differences in Limitations

The AS/400 and the S/36 RPG II have different limitations. For the most part, the limits are higher on the AS/400.

- The number of files in a program. The S/36 RPG II allows a maximum of 20. The AS/400 version allows up to 50.

- Chain, demand and full-procedural files. The S/36 allows 15, but the AS/400 allows 50.

- EXCPT names. The S/36 RPG II allows a maximum of 64 EXCPT names. there is no limit on the AS/400.

- Arrays and tables. The S/36 allows a maximum of 75. The AS/400 raises the limit to 200.

- Data structures. The S/36 allows a maximum of 75. The AS/400 has no limit.

- Internal subroutines. With S/36 RPG II, you can have an unlimited number of BEGSR operations, if you do not exceed the 64KB program size. On the AS/400, you cannot write more than 9999 in the same program, even though programs can be much larger.

- OR lines in I- or O-specs. The S/36 allows a maximum of 20. The AS/400 has no limit.

- Match field and control level field length. The S/36 lets you use a maximum aggregate length of 144. The AS/400 allows 256.

- DEBUG operation. The S/36 lets you use any record length that is valid. The AS/400 does not let you use any record length lower than 80. Also, while CRT is a valid file for the DEBUG operation on the S/36, it is invalid on the AS/400.

- In-line comments. Comments can be written on columns 81-96 on any line in S/36 RPG II. The AS/400 allows only 81-91.

- Program size. The S/36 lets you compile programs that can be as large as 64KB. The AS/400 has no practical limit.

FURTHER READING

IBM's *System Reference for the S/36 Environment*.

IBM's *System/36-Compatible RPG II User's Guide and Reference*.

Part VII:
Troubleshooting

26

Basic Troubleshooting

Never forget that computers are machines. They have no common sense and possess no trace of intelligence. They require help from a human being whenever a problem arises.

Still, OS/400 contains a certain amount of forethought that was carefully programmed by IBM. The system can usually help you solve even severe problems.

Section 1: Severe Trouble

Severe trouble can be arbitrarily defined as the kind of trouble that renders the entire system nonoperational.

Power Failure

You can avoid trouble caused by power failures by purchasing an uninterrupted power supply (UPS) unit and connecting it between the raw utility power supply and the system.

If the power fails and you do not have a UPS unit, or the UPS unit did not work, you cannot do much until power returns. You might place a rush order for a UPS unit or call for repairs of your existing UPS.

AS/400 Primer

☞ When power returns, IPL the system. If the system was busy when the power failed (which it almost certainly was), this IPL will take much longer than usual because the system needs to rebuild the access paths of database files that were open when the power failed.

Once IPL completes, you should ask your users to return to whatever they were doing before the power failure and make sure that the last transaction they entered was recorded. If you do not use commitment control, there is a good chance that data may be lost.

The System Freezes Up

If your system freezes up (i.e., it does not respond to input from any display station), go to the control panel on the CPU. The yellow Data windows should have an 8-character system reference code (SRC), such as B900 3004. The orange System Attention light may also be lit.

IBM's *System Operator's Guide* (SC41-8082) contains problem summary forms in Appendix B. Make a photocopy of the form supplied in the book and return the original to the book. Then fill out the copy you made and describe the problem and indicate which control panel lights are on. Write down the SRC shown in the yellow Data windows. Be sure to jot down the date and the time the system froze.

Appendix A of the System Operators' Guide contains a list of SRCs and what you may be able to do when they appear. Try to follow the instructions listed there. If you cannot follow the instructions, or they do not solve the problem, continue with a manual IPL as follows:

- Turn the key lock switch to Manual.
- Use the Select switch to display function 03.
- Press the Enter button on the control panel.

Your system may now become operational. If it does not, record the new SRCs on another problem summary form and call IBM for hardware support.

Chapter 26 - Basic Troubleshooting

Other Severe Trouble

The *System Operator's Guide* contains detailed instructions about what you can or should do in cases of severe trouble. Pay particular attention to Chapter 14 and Appendix A.

Section 2: Mild Trouble

Arbitrarily defined, mild trouble is the kind of problem that does not render the entire system non-operational.

A Display Station Does Not Work

- **No reaction when powered on.**

    Check the power cable to make sure that it is still connected to the outlet on the wall.

    Check that the outlet has power.

- **Smoke or burning odors.**

    Turn the display station off immediately. There may be a short circuit in its circuitry that can cause a fire.

- **No sign-on display**.

    Check the intensity knob. Sometimes the knob may be turned to the minimum by accident.

    Go to another display station and vary on the failing display station with the Vary Configuration (VRYCFG) command.

    Check that the interactive subsystem is started (typically QINTER) using the Work with Subsystem Jobs (WRKSBSJOB) command.

- The keyboard **does not work.**

    If your keyboard is detachable, make sure that the cable is firmly connected to the body of the display station.

    Check the input-inhibited indicator on the screen. If it is on, the system may be busy processing the last request. If there is a blinking four-digit number on the bottom-left corner of the screen, press the Help key, and the system will explain the problem. Then press the Reset key (also labeled Error Reset key on older display stations).

The user may have entered the Setup, Record or Play mode by pressing the corresponding key. Press the appropriate key again to exit these modes.

A Printer Does Not Work

- **No reaction when powered on.**

    Check the power cable to make sure that it is still connected to the outlet on the wall.

    Check that the outlet has power.

- **Smoke or burning odors.**

    Turn the printer off immediately. There may be a short circuit in its circuitry that can cause a fire.

- Nothing prints.

    The printed output you are expecting may be directed to another printer, or output queue that is not currently attached to the printer.

    Check the printer's message queue for pending inquiry that may explain why the printer is not printing. The messages may reveal printer-related problems such as the need to change forms or that the printer ran out of paper. If you do not know the name of the printer's message queue, use the Display Device Description (DSPDEVD) command and supply the name of the printer.

    If the printer is a laser printer, it may have run completely out of toner and thus could be printing blank pages.

    Check that the printer is varied on with the Work with Configuration Status (WRKCFGSTS) command. If it is varied off, vary it on now.

    Check that the printer writer is started with the Work with Writers (WRKWTR) command. If it is not started, start it now. You may have to reply to a printer message immediately after starting it.

Chapter 26 - Basic Troubleshooting

A Tape Drive Does Not Work

- **No reaction when powered on.**

    Check the power cable to make sure that it is still connected to the outlet on the wall.

    Check that the outlet has power.

    Smoke or burning odors.

    Turn the tape drive off immediately. There may be a short circuit in its circuitry that can cause a fire.

- No reaction to SAVxxx or RSTxxx **commands.**

    Some save and restore commands take a while before your tape drive reacts because the system needs to do some housekeeping chores. Save or restore operations that involve large objects such as libraries will cause the most delay. Give your system time.

    Check that the tape drive is varied on with the WRKCFGSTS command. If it is not varied on, vary it on.

    Check the system operator's message queue (QSYSOPR) for pending inquiry messages that may explain why the tape drive is not working.

    Check that you have mounted a tape into the drive, and that the tape drive is in a ready state.

- **Errors occur during the tape operation.**

    Clean the tape path of your tape drive. The tape path can become dirty and prevent your tape drive from operating.

    Check that the tape you have supplied is properly initialized. If the tape is not initialized, initialize it.

    Try a different tape. Tapes can become damaged or they can wear out after use.

FURTHER READING

IBM's *System Operator's Guide*.

27

Using ECS

Virtually all AS/400s come with Electronic Customer Support (ECS). ECS takes advantage of the extensive communications capabilities built into OS/400 to make it possible for the system administrator or operator to report problems, request PTFs and connect with IBMLink, IBM's information service.

In order to make ECS possible, the IBM technician who installs your system creates line, controller and device descriptions that you can leave unchanged. The installer also enters the initial values for the telephone numbers you or your system can call to get in touch with IBM.

Section 1: Managing ECS

The phone numbers you or your system call to reach IBM may change after installation. For example, you may move your system to a new location that is serviced by another IBM location, or IBM may reorganize its customer support structure.

Changing Your Own Identification

Each time you contact IBM to get a new PTF or report a problem, your computer identifies you automatically. Your computer gives IBM your company name, mailing address, phone number and the name of the person to contact.

If this information changes (your company moves, changes phone numbers or changes name), you need to change this information in your AS/400's records.

First, run the following command:

GO PROBLEM2

and then select option 5:

```
PROBLEM2                    Problem Handling
                                                          System:    MC PGMR
  Select one of the following:

      1. Program temporary fix
      2. Work with alerts
      3. Performance tools
      4. Programming language debug
      5. Work with support contact information
      6. Copy screen image
      7. Work with alert descriptions

     70. Related commands




  Selection or command
  ===> 5_____

  F3=Exit   F4=Prompt   F9=Retrieve   F12=Cancel   F13=Information Assistant
  F16=AS/400 Main menu
  (C) COPYRIGHT IBM CORP. 1980, 1993.
```

Chapter 27 - Using ECS

Select option 2:

```
                 Work with Support Contact Information
                                                        System:   MC PGMR
   Select one of the following:

        1. Work with question and answer (Q & A) database
        2. Work with local service information
        3. Work with IBM product information
        4. Work with technical information exchange (TIE)
        5. Work with upgrade order information
        6. Work with service providers




   Selection or command
   ===> 2_____

   F3=Exit    F4=Prompt    F9=Retrieve    F12=Cancel
   (C) COPYRIGHT IBM CORP. 1980, 1991.
```

AS/400 Primer

Select option 2 to change:

```
                   Work with Local Service Information
                                                      System:    MC PGMR
  Select one of the following:

       1. Display service contact information
       2. Change service contact information












  Selection
       2

  F3=Exit    F12=Cancel
```

Now examine the current values. If you need to change anything, type over the values. If you make a mistake and want to return all input fields to their original value, press F5.

Chapter 27 - Using ECS

If you need an explanation for any of the fields shown, press the Help key. When you are done changing, press Enter. If you change your mind and decide not to change anything, press F12.

```
                    Change Service Contact Information
                                                    System:    MC_PGMR
 Type changes, press Enter.

   Company . . . . . . . . . .  Midrange Computing_____
   Contact . . . . . . . . . .  Richard Shaler_____
   Contact telephone numbers:
     Primary . . . . . . . . .  (619) 931-8615____
     Alternative . . . . . . .  (619) 931-8617____
   Fax telephone numbers:
     Primary . . . . . . . . .
     Alternative . . . . . . .
   Mailing address:
     Street address   . . . . . 5650 El Camino Real_____
                                Suite 225_____
                                _____
     City/State  . . . . . . .  Carlsbad, CA_____
     Country . . . . . . . . .  USA_____
     Zip code  . . . . . . . .  92008_____

                                                          More...
   F3=Exit    F4=Prompt    F5=Refresh    F12=Cancel
```

Voice Phone Numbers for IBMLink

Once in a while, you may run into trouble while using IBMLink. For example, your password may expire, or you may not remember it.

AS/400 Primer

To display or change the phone numbers you use to call an IBM representative in these cases, run the following command:

GO PROBLEM2

and select option 5:

```
PROBLEM2                    Problem Handling
                                                        System:    MC PGMR
Select one of the following:

     1. Program temporary fix
     2. Work with alerts
     3. Performance tools
     4. Programming language debug
     5. Work with support contact information
     6. Copy screen image
     7. Work with alert descriptions

    70. Related commands




Selection or command
===> 5_____

F3=Exit    F4=Prompt    F9=Retrieve    F12=Cancel    F13=User support
F16=AS/400 Main menu
(C) COPYRIGHT IBM CORP. 1980, 1991.
```

Chapter 27 - Using ECS

Select option 3 to display/maintain phone numbers to call if you are having problems with IBMLink:

```
                  Work with Support Contact Information
                                                        System:    MC PGMR
  Select one of the following:

        1. Work with question and answer (Q & A) database
        2. Work with local service information
        3. Work with IBM product information
        4. Work with technical information exchange (TIE)
        5. Work with upgrade order information
        6. Work with service providers







  Selection or command
  ===> 3_____

  F3=Exit    F4=Prompt    F9=Retrieve    F12=Cancel
```

Select option 1 to display, or option 2 to change:

```
                      Work with IBM Product Information
                                                       System:    MC PGMR
 Select one of the following:

      1. Display product contact information
      2. Change product contact information










 Selection
      2

 F3=Exit    F12=Cancel
```

The information is displayed. The phone numbers are in the middle of the screen.

```
                    Change Product Contact Information
                                                        System:   MC PGMR
 Keyboard identifier
   description . . . . . . . :   United States/Canada

 Type changes, press Enter.

   Remote source:
     Name . . . . . . . . .   IBM Link Support_____
     Address . . . . . . .    _____
                              _____
                              _____
                              _____

   Telephone number  . . . .  (800) 543-3912   (800) 727-2222
   3270 printer emulation         Y                Y=Yes, N=No
   Double-byte character set      N                Y=Yes, N=No




 F3=Exit    F5=Refresh    F12=Cancel
 F14=Select keyboard identifier description
```

Voice Phone Numbers for Reporting Problems

Normally you would use ECS to report computer problems (hardware or software) using the AS/400 itself. If you cannot connect through ECS, or if you have a problem, you can display or change the phone numbers to call to reach an IBM representative.

Begin by executing the following command:

GO PROBLEM2

and then select option 5, followed by option 6.

AS/400 Primer

```
                    Work with Support Contact Information
                                                          System:   MC PGMR
 Select one of the following:

       1. Work with question and answer (Q & A) database
       2. Work with local service information
       3. Work with IBM product information
       4. Work with technical information exchange (TIE)
       5. Work with upgrade order information
       6. Work with service providers









 Selection or command
 ===> 6_____

 F3=Exit    F4=Prompt    F9=Retrieve    F12=Cancel
 (C) COPYRIGHT IBM CORP. 1980, 1991.
```

The AS/400 lists all the service providers you have on file. There may be more than one; For example, you may use IBM for hardware and system software, but use a business partner for application software and yet another company for non-IBM hardware.

Chapter 27 - Using ECS

To display IBM's information, select option 5; to change it, select option 2. In either case, place the option number next to the entry labeled *IBMSRV:

```
                      Work with Service Providers
                                                      System:    MC PGMR
 Position to  . . . . .  _____    Control point
   Network ID . . . . .  _____

 Type options, press Enter.
   1=Add   2=Change   3=Copy   4=Remove   5=Display

        Control
 Opt    Point         Network ID    Description
 __     _____      _____      _____
  2     *IBMSRV                     IBM Service Support




                                                                  Bottom
 F3=Exit    F5=Refresh    F12=Cancel    F22=Change IBM service route
 (C) COPYRIGHT IBM CORP. 1980, 1991.
```

AS/400 Primer

The phone numbers are displayed. You can change them by typing over them and pressing Enter.

```
                         Change Service Provider
                                                    System:    MC PGMR
  Control point  . . . . . . . . . . . :   *IBMSRV
  Network ID  . . . . . . . . . . . :
  Description  . . . . . . . . . . :     IBM Service Support

Type changes, press Enter.

  Service support center telephone numbers:
    Hardware service  . . . . . . .  18004267378_____
    Software service  . . . . . . .  18002375511_____




                                                              Bottom
  F3=Exit    F5=Refresh    F12=Cancel
```

Changing IBMLink Connection Number

You can change the number your AS/400 dials when you start an IBMLink session. Begin by running the following command:

CALL QTIPHONE

Chapter 27 - Using ECS

The system presents the prompt for the Change Data Area (CHGDTAARA) command. On the last line ("new value") it shows the current telephone number your system is calling to reach IBMLink. This number is the primary telephone number.

```
                        Change Data Area (CHGDTAARA)

 Type choices, press Enter.

 Data area specification:
   Data area  . . . . . . . . . .   QTITELE___      Name, *LDA, *GDA
     Library  . . . . . . . . .     QUSRSYS___     Name, *LIBL, *CURLIB
   Substring specifications:
   Substring starting position .    1___            1-2000, *ALL
   Substring length . . . . . . .   32__            1-2000
 New value  . . . . . . . . . . .   'SST:18005554567'_____




                                                                      Bottom
 F3=Exit    F4=Prompt    F5=Refresh    F12=Cancel   F13=How to use this display
 F13=More keys
```

You can change the number by typing over it. When you press Enter, the system presents the secondary telephone number in a similar display:

```
                    Change Data Area (CHGDTAARA)

 Type choices, press Enter.

 Data area specification:
   Data area  . . . . . . . . . .   QTITELE___      Name, *LDA, *GDA
     Library  . . . . . . . . .     QUSRSYS___      Name, *LIBL, *CURLIB
   Substring specifications:
   Substring starting position .    51__            1-2000, *ALL
   Substring length . . . . . . .   32__            1-2000
 New value  . . . . . . . . . . .   'SST:18005554567'_____




                                                                      Bottom
 F3=Exit    F4=Prompt    F5=Refresh    F12=Cancel    F13=How to use this display
 F13=More keys
```

Again, you can change the number by typing over it. When you press Enter, the system lets you change two more numbers and then displays all four values using the Display Data Area (DSPDTAARA) command.

Chapter 27 - Using ECS

Changing Problem Reporting Connection Number

You can change the number your AS/400 dials when you report a hardware or software problem (with the Analyze Problem [ANZPRB] command). Begin by running the following command:

```
CALL QESPHONE
```

The system presents the prompt for the CHGDTAARA command. On the last line ("new value"), it shows the current telephone number your system is calling to reach hardware or software service. This number is the primary telephone number.

```
                         Change Data Area (CHGDTAARA)

 Type choices, press Enter.

 Data area specification:
   Data area  . . . . . . . . . .   QESTELE___      Name, *LDA, *GDA
     Library  . . . . . . . . . .   QUSRSYS___      Name, *LIBL, *CURLIB
   Substring specifications:
   Substring starting position  .   1___            1-2000, *ALL
   Substring length . . . . . . .   32__            1-2000
 New value  . . . . . . . . . . .   'SST:18005554567'_____




                                                                        Bottom
 F3=Exit    F4=Prompt    F5=Refresh    F12=Cancel    F13=How to use this display
 F13=More keys
```

You can change the number by typing over it. When you press Enter, the system presents the secondary telephone number in a similar display:

```
                       Change Data Area (CHGDTAARA)

 Type choices, press Enter.

 Data area specification:
   Data area  . . . . . . . . . .   QESTELE___      Name, *LDA, *GDA
     Library  . . . . . . . . .     QUSRSYS___      Name, *LIBL, *CURLIB
   Substring specifications:
   Substring starting position  .   51__            1-2000, *ALL
   Substring length . . . . . . .   32__            1-2000
 New value  . . . . . . . . . . .   'SST:18005554567'_____








                                                                      Bottom
 F3=Exit   F4=Prompt   F5=Refresh   F12=Cancel   F13=How to use this display
 F13=More keys
```

Again, you can change the number by typing over it. When you press Enter, the system lets you change two more numbers and then displays all four values using the DSPDTAARA command.

Section 2: Uses of ECS

To Call IBM

ECS can be used to contact IBM in three different ways. Each one requires a different command:

Chapter 27 - Using ECS

- ANZPRB. Use the Analyze Problem (ANZPRB) command to report hardware or software problems you encounter with your AS/400. The ANZPRB command is described in Chapter 28.

- SNDPTFORD. Use the Send PTF Order (SNDPTFORD) command to place an order for PTFs. You can order either individually or in cumulative packages. SNDPTFORD can also be used to obtain information about PTFs. The SNDPTFORD command is described in Chapter 29.

- WRKPRDINF. Use the Work with Product Information (WRKPRDINF) command to start an IBMLink session. IBMLink is an optional, chargeable service you may or may not use. With IBMLink you can ask questions about any aspect of the AS/400 and receive answers from IBM personnel. IBMLink also enables you to find out if any problems have been reported with products or to obtain pricing for IBM products.

Other Uses

ECS uses an ordinary modem and telecommunications setup. You can use the ECS equipment and setup to connect with other computer systems as well. Although IBM may not have intended it, it is possible and perfectly legal.

For example, you can use the ECS line for temporary communications with a remote workstation controller that has one or more attached devices (display stations and printers).

You also can use the ECS setup to contact bulletin board services (BBSs) that cater to IBM midrange professionals. Additional setup is required because you are usually connecting to a microcomputer.

FURTHER READING

IBM's *Electronic Customer Support User's Guide*.

28

Reporting Problems

You are likely to come across problems during the operation or programming of your AS/400. Older systems require that you pick up the phone, call IBM and describe the problem to them. On the AS/400, all you have to do is run the Analyze Problem (ANZPRB) command and use ECS.

Section 1: The ANZPRB Command

The ANZPRB command is how you begin reporting a problem you have encountered. Rather than give a theoretical explanation on how this command works, a walk-through approach will be used.

For the sake of illustration, imagine that you executed the Work with Output Queues (WRKOUTQ) command to list the spool files contained in output queue QPRINT. After you examine the first page, you press Roll Up and WRKOUTQ ends abnormally with a function check message; (CPF9999) on the bottom line of your screen. No other indication is given as to what went wrong.

In this problem situation, you suspect there is a bug in the WRKOUTQ command, and you use ANZPRB to report it to IBM. You type:

AS/400 Primer

ANZPRB

and press F4. The system prompts you for the ANZPRB command, as follows:

```
                        Analyze Problem (ANZPRB)

 Type choices, press Enter.

 Analysis type . . . . . . . . .   *MENU__       *REMOTE, *LOCAL, *MENU












                                                                    Bottom
 F3=Exit   F4=Prompt   F5=Refresh   F12=Cancel   F13=How to use this display
 F24=More keys
```

Chapter 28 - Reporting Problems

The system asks if you are going to analyze a problem in a local or a remote system, or if you would rather be shown a menu that lists the options. You leave the default value (*MENU), and press Enter.

```
                      Select Type of System
                                                System:    MC PGMR
 Select one of the following:

   System with the problem is
      1. This AS/400 or attached devices
      2. Another AS/400
      3. Another type of system, not an AS/400













 Selection or command
 ===> 1_____

 F3=Exit    F4=Prompt    F9=Retrieve    F12=Cancel
```

AS/400 Primer

Because the error occurred on your own system, you select option 1 and press Enter. You could have skipped this panel by answering *LOCAL on the command prompter, but the time savings are minimal.

```
                    Analyze a New Problem
                                              System:    MC PGMR
 Select one of the following:

   Analyze a Problem
       1. Job or program problem (application or system)
       2. System performance problem
       3. Hardware problem
       4. Communications hardware problem

   Describe a Problem
       5. Problem occurred during IPL of this AS/400
       6. Job or program problem (application or system)




 Selection or command
 ===> 6_____

 F3=Exit    F4=Prompt    F9=Retrieve    F12=Cancel
```

Chapter 28 - Reporting Problems

You really do not want to analyze the problem, just report it. To report it, you need to describe it first; therefore, you have to choose either option 5 or 6. Because the problem did not occur during IPL, option 6 is the only viable alternative. You type a 6 and press Enter.

```
                         Select Product
                                                  System:   MC PGMR
   Position to . . . . . . .  _____     Product

   Type option, press Enter.
     1=Select


                    Product
   Opt   Product    Option    Description
    _    5738AF1    *BASE     Advanced Function Printing Utilities/400
    _    5738CB1    *BASE     SAA COBOL/400
    _    5738CX1    *BASE     SAA C/400
    _    5738DCT    *BASE     Language Dictionaries/400
    _    5738OS1    *BASE     OSI Communications Subsystem/400
    _    5738PC1    *BASE     PC Support/400
    _    5738PL1    *BASE     AS/400 PL/I
    _    5738PT1    *BASE
    _    5738PW1    *BASE     AS/400 Application Development Tools
    _    5738QU1    *BASE     Query/400
    _    5738RG1    *BASE     SAA RPG/400
                                                                More...
   F5=Refresh    F11=Display releases    F12=Cancel

   (C) COPYRIGHT IBM CORP. 1980, 1993.
```

AS/400 Primer

Now you have to select, the product that does not work as it should from this panel. This panel will obviously change from system to system, depending on what program products are installed. You need to select OS/400 because the failing command, WRKOUTQ, is part of the OS/400 operating system. OS/400 is not listed on this panel, so press Roll Up to display the next page:

```
                          Select Product
                                                    System:   MC PGMR
  Position to . . . . . . .  _____  Product

  Type option, press Enter.
    1=Select


                  Product
  Opt   Product   Option   Description
   1    5738SS1   *BASE    Operating System/400
   _    5738ST1   *BASE    SAA Structured Query Language/400
   _    5738TC1   *BASE    TCP/IP Connectivity Utilities/400
   _    5738WP1   *BASE    SAA OfficeVision/400
   _    5738999   *BASE    AS/400 Licensed Internal Code




                                                              Bottom
  F5=Refresh    F11=Display releases    F12=Cancel
```

Chapter 28 - Reporting Problems

OS/400 is on the first line. You can select it by typing in a 1 and pressing Enter.

```
                      Select Product Option
                                                  System:   MC PGMR
        Position to . . . . . . .  _____    Product

        Type option, press Enter.
          1=Select

                        Product
        Opt   Product   Option   Description
         1    5738SS1   *BASE    Operating System/400
         _    5738SS1   1        OS/400 - Extended Base Support
         _    5738SS1   2        OS/400 - Online Information
         _    5738SS1   3        OS/400 - Online Education
         _    5738SS1   4        OS/400 - S/36 and S/38 Migration
         _    5738SS1   5        OS/400 - System/36 Environment
         _    5738SS1   6        OS/400 - System/38 Environment
         _    5738SS1   7        OS/400 - Example Tools Library
         _    5738SS1   8        OS/400 - AFP Compatibility Fonts
         _    5738SS1   9        OS/400 - *PRV CL Compiler Support
         _    5738SS1   10       OS/400 - 9406 Problem Analysis
                                                           More...
        F5=Refresh    F11=Display releases    F12=Cancel

        (C) COPYRIGHT IBM CORP. 1980, 1992.
```

AS/400 Primer

This panel lets you select which part of OS/400 is at fault. Select the first option, base operating system because it is the most appropriate choice. Type in a 1 and press Enter.

```
                      Select Product Function
                                                    System:    MC PGMR
 Product . . . . . . . . . . . . :  Operating System/400
 Option  . . . . . . . . . . . . :  Operating System/400


 Type option, press Enter.
   1=Select


            Product
 Opt        function
  1         CL (Control Language)
  _         Procedures Language 400/REXX
  _         Intelligent printer data stream (IPDS)
  _         Communications
  _         Interactive Data Definition Utility (IDDU)
  _         AS/400 Sort
  _         AS/400 Data File Utility (DFU)
  _         System/36 Data File Utility (DFU)
  _         Other


                                                              Bottom
 F3=Exit    F12=Cancel
```

Chapter 28 - Reporting Problems

Because WRKOUTQ is a CL command, selecting the top choice seems logical.

```
                      Select Product Function
                                                    System:   MC PGMR
 Product . . . . . . . . . . . . :   Operating System/400
 Option  . . . . . . . . . . . . :   Operating System/400
 Previous selection  . . . . . . :   CL (Control Language)

 Type option, press Enter.
   1=Select


         Product
 Opt     function
  _      Compilation
  1      Run time








                                                              Bottom
 F3=Exit    F12=Cancel
```

AS/400 Primer

This panel asks you if the error occurred when you were compiling a CL program or when you were running it. Although you weren't running any program (WRKOUTQ failed while executed manually), "run time" is the closest of the two choices to what really happened.

```
                    Specify Message Information
                                              System:    MC PGMR
Do the following, then return here.
 o  Press F14 to view the messages associated with your job.
 o  Press the function key to display detailed messages.
 o  Find the first escape message in the list of messages after the
    failing command by doing the following for each message:
       -  Put the cursor on the message.
       -  Press the Help key.
       -  Check the Message type field for " ESCAPE."
                                                              More...
Type choices, press Enter. If there are no messages related to the problem,
  just press Enter.

          Message  . . . . . . .  CPF9999      ID
          Code . . . . . . . . .  _____     Code
          From program . . . . .  _____     Name
          To program . . . . . .  _____     Name




     F3=Exit    F12=Cancel    F24=More keys
```

Chapter 28 - Reporting Problems

Now you can indicate what message you received (if any). If you did not receive a message, you would just press Enter. You received CPF9999, so you type it in the "message field." Because you do not know the rest of the information (or forgot to record it), you leave it blank.

```
                       Enter Problem Description
                                                    System:    MC PGMR
 Type description, press Enter.

   Problem description . . .   WRKOUTQ command ended abnormally_____












 F3=Exit    F5=Refresh    F12=Cancel
```

☞ On this panel, you can briefly describe the problem you experienced. The input field will have a bland, default problem description that is too generic to be of help to the person who takes care of your case. It is better if you type in something meaningful. This information is also logged into your own system, so being specific will help you later.

405

AS/400 Primer

In this case, you can type "WRKOUTQ command ended abnormally" and press Enter. You do not have to explain everything here. You will get another chance later.

```
                          Save Problem Data
                                                System:    MC PGMR
 A PTF for the problem was not found on the local system. If you have
 APAR data to be saved, you may want to save this data now. This data
 may be requested if you report the problem and a PTF cannot be found.



 Type choice, press Enter.

 Save APAR data . . . . . . . .    n    Y=Yes, N=No







 F3=Exit    F12=Cancel
```

Chapter 28 - Reporting Problems

This panel applies only if the system cannot find a PTF that addresses the problem you are reporting already on the system. Answering Y (yes) lets you collect data that IBM can use to create an APAR. For the purpose of this illustration, skip this step and answer N (no).

```
                        Report Problem
                                               System:    MC PGMR
  The problem has been logged.


  Select one of the following:

       1. Prepare service request












  Selection
      _

  F3=Exit    F13=Add notes    F12=Cancel
```

AS/400 Primer

☞ When you reach this display, *stop!* Note that F13 allows you to add notes to the problem you are reporting. Press F13 instead of Enter.

```
                            Enter Notes
                                                    System:    MC PGMR
 Problem ID . . . . . . . :   9218039950
 Current status . . . . . :   READY
 Problem  . . . . . . . . :   WRKOUTQ command ended abnormally


 Type notes, press Enter.
 I ran a WRKOUTQ OUTQ(QPRINT). When I pressed Roll Up to see the second
 page, WRKOUTQ ended abnormally, returning me to the menu. The bottom
 line of the menu showed CPF9999 (function check)._____
 _____
 _____
 _____
 _____
 _____
 _____
 _____



                                                                 Bottom
 F3=Exit      F6=Insert line   F12=Cancel   F14=Delete line   F17=Top
 F18=Bottom   F20=Right
```

You can now describe in detail what happened. Be as specific as possible because doing so shortens the research time IBM needs to solve your problem.ANZPRB

Chapter 28 - Reporting Problems

If you need more space, position the cursor at the last line and press F6. You can also press F14 to delete single lines. When you are done, press F3 or F12.

```
                          Enter Notes
.....................................................................  m:    MC PGMR
:                                                                   :
:                         Exit Notes                                 :
:                                                                   :
:  Type choice, press enter:                                         :
:                                                                   :
:  Option  . . . .  1      1=Save notes and exit                     :
:                          2=Exit without saving notes               :
:                          3=Resume entering notes                   :
:                                                                   : second
:  F12=Cancel                                                        : ttom
:                                                                   :
:...................................................................:  _____
                                                                        _____
   _____
   _____
   _____
   _____
   _____
   _____
   _____
                                                                    Bottom
 F3=Exit      F6=Insert line    F12=Cancel    F14=Delete line    F17=Top
 F18=Bottom   F20=Right
```

AS/400 Primer

Select option 1 (it may be there by default) and press Enter. This option saves the notes you have entered.

```
                        Report Problem
                                              System:    MC PGMR
 The problem has been logged.


 Select one of the following:

      1. Prepare service request









 Selection
      1

 F3=Exit    F13=Add notes    F12=Cancel
```

Chapter 28 - Reporting Problems

Select option 1 (you cannot select anything else) and press Enter.

```
                       Verify Contact Information
                                                  System:    MC_PGMR
 Type changes, press Enter.

     Company . . . . . . . . . .  Midrange Computing_____
     Contact . . . . . . . . .    Richard Shaler_____
     Contact telephone numbers:
       Primary . . . . . . . .    (619) 931-8615_____
       Alternative . . . . . .    (619) 931-8617_____
     Fax telephone numbers:
       Primary . . . . . . . .
       Alternative . . . . . .
     Mailing address:
       Street address  . . . . .  5650 El Camino Real_____
                                  Suite 225_____
                                  _____
       City/State  . . . . . .    Carlsbad, CA_____
       Country . . . . . . . .    USA_____
       Zip code  . . . . . . .    92008_____




                                                              More...

 F3=Exit    F4=Prompt    F5=Refresh    F12=Cancel
```

AS/400 Primer

This panel already will be filled with your company's data. You can override the data if you have to. Pay particular attention to the contact name (yours) and the primary telephone number. IBM will need this information to call you back. When you are done, press Enter.

```
                    Select Problem Severity
                                             System:    MC PGMR
 Problem ID . . . . . . . . . :  9218039950
 Current status . . . . . . . :  READY
 Problem  . . . . . . . . . . :  WRKOUTQ command ended abnormally




 Select one of the following:

     1. High    - Requires immediate solution
     2. Medium  - Restricts function
     3. Low     - Limits function
     4. None    - Operates with full function




 Selection
      2

 F3=Exit    F12=Cancel
```

Now you must indicate the severity of the problem you are reporting. It is tempting to give it a High grade, but it is better to be honest. Not being able to use the WRKOUTQ command is annoying, but there are other ways to get the information you need (WRKSPLF, for instance).

Chapter 28 - Reporting Problems

For this example, therefore, enter a Medium grade (option 2) and press Enter.

```
                         Select Service Provider
                                                    System:   MC PGMR
 Position to . . . . . . .  _____   Control point
   Network ID . . . . . .   _____

 Type option, press Enter.
   1=Select

         Control
 Opt     Point        Network ID    Description
  1      *IBMSRV                    IBM Service Support




                                                                Bottom
 F5=Refresh    F12=Cancel
 (C) COPYRIGHT IBM CORP. 1980, 1991.
```

413

AS/400 Primer

Now you must select whom you want to call for help. You may have more than one service provider. For example, you may use IBM for hardware and system software, use a business partner for your application software, and use a third provider for the miscellaneous non-IBM hardware you purchased. *IBMSRV is IBM's Service Support. Select the provider of your choice (or the one that applies to the situation) and press Enter.

```
                         Select Reporting Option
                                                   System:    MC PGMR
 Problem ID . . . . . . . . . :   9218039950
 Current status . . . . . . . :   READY
 Problem  . . . . . . . . . . :   WRKOUTQ command ended abnormally



 Select one of the following:

      1. Send service request now
      2. Do not send service request
      3. Report service request by voice




 Selection
       1

 F3=Exit    F12=Cancel
```

Finally, be sure to select option 1 and press Enter. Option 1 transmits the problem description through ECS. You have finished reporting the problem.

Chapter 28 - Reporting Problems

Section 2: Working with Problem Logs

The WRKPRB Command

The AS/400 keeps track of all problems you encounter (both hardware and software) in a problem log. It even generates problem logs of its own. You can obtain a list of these problem logs with the Work with Problems (WRKPRB) command.

The WRKPRB command has a number of parameters to let you select which problem logs you want displayed. If you do not enter any parameter values, WRKPRB presents all problem logs by default:

```
                        Work with Problems
                                                    System:    MC PGMR
  Position to . . . . . .  _____       Problem ID

  Type options, press Enter.
    2=Change    4=Delete    5=Display details   6=Print details
    8=Work with problem    9=Work with alerts   12=Enter notes

  Opt  Problem ID  Status       Problem Description
   __  9218039950  READY        WRKOUTQ command ended abnormally
   __  9217848512  OPENED       Media error found on volume  on device .
   __  9217847610  OPENED       Media error found on volume  on device .
   __  9217847514  OPENED       Media error found on volume  on device .
   __  9217846732  OPENED       Media error found on volume  on device .
   __  9217641478  OPENED       Device  is not ready.




                                                                Bottom
  F3=Exit     F5=Refresh   F6=Print list      F11=Display dates and times
  F12=Cancel  F16=Report prepared problems    F24=More keys
```

Note that the first problem is the problem you logged in the walk-through exercise you went through in the previous section. The other problem logs shown in the figure were generated by the system, presumably, during save/restore operations that failed.

415

From this panel, you can edit problem logs by entering option numbers and pressing the Enter key. For example, using option 12 would let you enter or change the notes associated with a particular problem.

Deleting Old Problem Logs

As problem logs accumulate, you will notice that they begin to use up disk space. Therefore, you should keep an eye on problem logs so they do not proliferate.

You can delete problem logs individually by selecting option 4 from the panel shown below:

```
                         Work with Problems
                                                    System:    MC PGMR
 Position to . . . . . . .  _____
                                      Problem ID

 Type options, press Enter.
    2=Change    4=Delete    5=Display details    6=Print details
    8=Work with problem     9=Work with alerts   12=Enter notes

 Opt   Problem ID   Status        Problem Description
  __   9218039950   READY         WRKOUTQ command ended abnormally
  __   9217848512   OPENED        Media error found on volume  on device .
  __   9217847610   OPENED        Media error found on volume  on device .
  __   9217847514   OPENED        Media error found on volume  on device .
  __   9217846732   OPENED        Media error found on volume  on device .
  __   9217641478   OPENED        Device  is not ready.




                                                               Bottom
 F3=Exit       F5=Refresh     F6=Print list     F11=Display dates and times
 F12=Cancel    F16=Report prepared problems     F24=More keys
```

You may want to run the Delete Problem (DLTPRB) command instead, as follows:

`DLTPRB PRBID(*ALL) STATUS(*VERIFIED *CLOSED) DAYS(7)`

This command deletes all problem logs that are at least seven days old and have a status of *VERIFIED or *CLOSED (resolved problems).

Chapter 28 - Reporting Problems

☞ You also can use Operational Assistant. Select option 1 from the CLEANUP menu.

Whether you use the WRKPRB panel or the DLTPRB command, you may run into a snag that prevents you from deleting certain problem logs. There is a system value (QPRBHLDITV) that determines how long a problem log must be held on the system before deletion is possible. You can always change this system value to a lower value (even zero) if you want absolute control over which problem logs are deleted.

FURTHER READING

IBM's *System Operator's Guide*.

29

PTF Management

Section 1: Overview

What Is a PTF?

PTF stands for **P**rogram **T**emporary **F**ix. When IBM becomes aware of a bug in its software (either a bug discovered by IBM or reported to IBM by someone like you), IBM first creates an APAR (Authorized Program Analysis Report) to study the problem and, if warranted, creates a PTF that eradicates the bug.

The reason its called "temporary" is because IBM takes note of the problem and makes sure that the next release or modification of the software does not have the same bug.

Reporting a Problem

☞ If you have a problem with your system that looks like a genuine bug, you should report it to IBM immediately. Do not assume that someone else has reported it before you and that IBM already has a PTF to correct it.

AS/400 Primer

You could be the first person to discover the bug, and it could be you who opens the APAR that ultimately generates the PTF. You can report a problem either by calling IBM Software Service or through ECS. ECS is described in Chapter 27.

Individual and Cume PTFs

As time passes, PTFs increase in numbers. For example, if a new release of the operating system is made available on January 1, there may be only 10 PTFs by February 1, but by March 1 there may be 20 more.

Each PTF corrects one problem and one problem only. They are called *individual* PTFs. IBM also puts together *cumulative* ("cume") PTFs, which are packages that contain most of the individual PTFs that have been issued since the beginning of the current release of the software. As time passes, IBM adds more individual PTFs, which necessitates a new cumulative PTF.

☞ By far, the easiest way to manage PTFs is through the cume PTF packages. However, not all PTFs are made available through cume PTF packages. Although it should not happen, it does, and you need to keep up with the current PTFs as they are released.

HIPER PTFs

Some PTFs are so important and so necessary that IBM labels them HIPER. HIPER stands for **Hi**gh Impact, **Per**vasive. This type of PTF is for the kind of bug that can bring your computer down, adversely affect its performance, or produce unpredictable results.

☞ HIPER PTFs are usually in a classification by themselves and should receive top priority in your strategy to load them into your system. Never dismiss or overlook a HIPER PTF. Some HIPER PTFs will not apply to your system, however; only you can be the judge.

For example, there may be a HIPER PTF to correct a problem with the COBOL compiler. If you do not have COBOL installed on your system or you do not use it, you do not need to worry about this PTF, no matter how important it may be in other AS/400 installations.

Cover Letters

All PTFs have a cover letter, which is a document that explains the contents of the PTF you have ordered, what the PTF fixes, and other information. You should read the cover letter even if you think you know everything about the PTF.

When you request PTFs by ECS, the cover letter is placed in file QAPZCOVER (library QGPL), in a member named with a P followed by the PTF number. You can display the cover letter with the Display Physical File Member (DSPPFM) command. You can also print it with the Copy File (CPYF) command which specifies TOFILE(QSYSPRT).

Section 2: Requesting PTFs

The SNDPTFORD Command

You can pick up the phone and call your IBM office to request a PTF. However, the easiest and most convenient way to order PTFs is through ECS using the Send PTF Order (SNDPTFORD) command.

```
SNDPTFORD PTF((SF99211) (SF98211)) PTFPART(*ALL) +
          DELIVERY(*ANY) ORDER(*REQUIRED) REORDER(*NO)
```

With this command, you order two PTFs: SF99211 and SF98211. PTFPART(*ALL) means that you want to receive both the cover letter and the actual PTF code. You could also request PTFPART(*CVRLTR). In this case you receive only the cover letter.

DELIVERY(*ANY) indicates that if the PTF is small enough, it should be transmitted to you through the ECS line. This transmission avoids the need to load the PTF into your system. If the PTF is too large (for example, a cume PTF package), IBM will (at its option) send you a tape, which you normally receive within 48 hours, and which frequently will arrive in only 24 hours. If you specify DELIVERY(*LINKONLY), the PTF is sent through the ECS line.

ORDER(*REQUIRED) means that, if the PTF you are ordering has another PTF as a prerequisite, the other PTF should be sent to you as well. For example, if you are ordering PTF B but IBM has decided that in order to install B you need PTF A, use ORDER(*REQUIRED) to get both. The opposite value is ORDER(*PTFID), which gets you only the PTF you ordered, even if it has a prerequisite. Use *PTFID if you know what the prerequisites are, and you know that you already have them.

With REORDER(*NO), you indicate that you are placing your original order for this PTF. Your system will check whether you already have the PTF loaded and/or applied. If you do, the SNDPTFORD command ends in error because the system is trying to help you avoid a duplicate order. REORDER(*YES) comes in handy when you have loaded and/or applied the PTF, but you lost the cover letter. You can reorder the cover letter only using PTFPART(*CVRLTR) and indicate REORDER(*YES).

Determine the PTF Number

No matter how you go about requesting PTFs, you must have the PTF number to place the order. If a friend or a fellow AS/400 administrator tells you about a PTF you think you need, be sure to obtain the PTF number from that person.

IBM has created some "reserved" PTF numbers that you can use to your advantage. In the list that follows, **v** is the OS/400 version number, **r** is the release number, and **m** is the modification level. Therefore, for V2R1M0, **vrm** is replaced by **210**.

Reserved PTF Number	Description
MF98vrm	Cume HIPER PTF package for reported hardware problems. The M in the PTF number stands for machine, and the F for fix.
SF97vrm	Software PTF summary listing. It tells you the number of the latest cume PTF package, when it became available, and when you can expect the next cume package. The S in the PTF number is for software, the F for fix.
SF98vrm	Cume HIPER PTF package for reported software problems.
SF99vrm	Cume PTF package for other software problems (not HIPER).
SHnnnnn	Individual PTF for MAPICS or CMAS. Each n represents a numeral of a five-digit sequence number.

Section 3: Installing PTFs

All PTF installation activities must be done with the system set to IPL area **B**, as shown on the control panel of the CPU. If your control panel shows an A, you must change it to a B before you go any further.

Chapter 29 - PTF Management

To change it, do the following:

- Request to end all subsystems:

  ENDSBS SBS(*ALL) OPTION(*IMMED)

- Wait for all subsystems to end.

- IPL the system as follows:

  PWRDWNSYS OPTION(*IMMED) RESTART(*YES) IPLSRC(B)

When IPL completes, your system will be set to IPL area B.

Cumulative PTF Packages

☛ Before you do anything else, be sure to read the PTF cover letter and the instructions that come with the shipping information letter. You must follow the instructions exactly. Do not skip any steps.

Most times, cume PTF packages require that you IPL your system one or more times. For this reason, you need to have the system all to yourself (in a "restricted state" or "dedicated," as it is usually called).

After you IPL the system for the last time (as directed by the installation instructions you received), you should verify that the PTF installation was successful. To do that, run the GO LICPGM command to display the Licensed Programs Menu. Select option 50 and press Enter twice.

The system presents a series of messages that inform you whether the PTF was installed successfully or not. Look for the word "failed" anywhere in the messages, such as "Loading of PTFs failed," "Marking of PTFs for delayed application failed," or even "Applying PTFs failed."

Individual PTFs

☛ Read all cover letters for the PTFs you are going to install. If the cover letters or installation instructions have any special instructions, be sure to follow them exactly.

Sign on as QSECOFR and get your system into a restricted state by ending all subsystems. See Chapter 2 for more information. Follow the directions to shut down the system, but do not run the PWRDWNSYS command.

Start backing up OS/400 to tape using the SAVSYS command. If you have backed it up after the last time you installed PTFs, you do not have to do it again.

Use the GO PTF command to go to the PTF menu and then select option 8 to install a PTF. Then type *SERVICE or the name of your tape drive, depending on how you received the PTF: *SERVICE for ECS, or a tape drive name if you received a tape from IBM. Then press Enter.

The system will give you instructions on the screen. You must follow these instructions exactly. When done, the system checks that all prerequisite PTFs are loaded. If they are, the system applies the PTFs and IPLs itself.

When IPL is complete, be sure to check the cover letters for any further activities you may have to perform after the installation.

Section 4: Managing PTFs

Displaying PTFs

After loading and/or applying PTFs, you can display them. The Display PTF (DSPPTF) command, in its simplest form, gives you a list of all PTFs currently on your system and their status:

```
DSPPTF
```

Chapter 29 - PTF Management

```
                        Display PTF Status
                                                  System:    MC_PGMR
 Product ID  . . . . . . :   5763999
 IPL source  . . . . . . :   #MACH#B
 Release . . . . . . . . :   V3R1M0


 Type options, press Enter.
   5=Display PTF details    6=Print cover letter    8=Display cover letter

        PTF                                 IPL
 Opt    ID       Status                     action
  _     TL95016  Temporarily applied        None
  _     TL94350  Superseded                 None
  _     TL94340  Superseded                 None
  _     TL94329  Superseded                 None
  _     TL94318  Superseded                 None
  _     TL94308  Superseded                 None
  _     TL94297  Superseded                 None
  _     MF08441  Temporarily applied        None
  _     MF08438  Permanently applied        None
                                                             More...
 F3=Exit    F11=Display alternate view    F12=Cancel
```

The status shown can be applied temporarily, applied permanently, loaded, or superseded. From the panel presented, you can select option 5 to display the contents of an individual PTF. This additional information is brief (and sometimes confusing), but it can be helpful.

The DSPPTF command accepts several parameters to narrow down the list of PTFs it is to display. For example, you can enter the licensed program number (such as 5738SS1 for OS/400 or 5738RG1 for RPG/400) in the LICPGM parameter. You can also request that the list go to the printer or to an outfile with the OUTPUT parameter.

Applying PTFs Permanently

PTFs are applied temporarily by default. The system keeps two versions of the system objects affected by PTFs. The old one is in IPL area A and the new one is in area B. Because the system has the two versions, you can go back to a status prior to the application of a particular PTF.

When you apply a PTF permanently, however, the system replaces the original object with the new one. You cannot go back. If you apply a PTF temporarily and then decide to apply it permanently, the objects that were in IPL area B are copied to area A, and the space in area B is freed. Applying PTFs permanently gives you additional disk space.

Before applying PTFs permanently, you can remove them with the Remove PTF (RMVPTF) command that is discussed below. Make sure that the PTFs you have applied temporarily are, in fact, working before you apply them permanently. Sometimes IBM issues PTFs that do more damage than good. These PTFs are reported in the HIPER PTF packages as "PTFs in error."

If you think you are ready to apply PTFs permanently, you can use the DSPPTF to find out what PTFs have an "applied temporarily" status. These PTFs are the ones you need to apply permanently (either all or some, as you decide). Armed with this information, you can run the Apply PTF (APYPTF) command, as follows:

```
APYPTF LICPGM(...) SELECT(...) APY(*PERM) DELAYED(*YES) +
       IPLAPY(*YES *APYPERM)
```

In the LICPGM, enter the licensed program number fixed by the PTFs you are going to apply permanently. For example, use 5738SS1 for OS/400.

The SELECT parameter can have a list of up to 50 PTF numbers you want to apply, or you can enter *ALL if you prefer to apply all PTFs for the licensed program number indicated in the LICPGM parameter.

DELAYED(*YES) IPLAPY(*YES *APYPERM) means that the application of the PTFs will be delayed until the next unattended IPL. At that time, the system will apply all selected PTFs permanently.

Removing PTFs

The Remove PTF (RMVPTF) command allows you to remove PTFs that have been loaded but not applied, or have been applied temporarily. For an example:

```
RMVPTF LICPGM(5738SS1) SELECT(SF12345) RMV(*PERM) +
       DELAYED(*YES) IPLRMV(*YES)
```

This command removes PTF number SF12345 from licensed program 5738SS1 (OS/400). Removal is permanent and will be performed during the next unattended IPL.

FURTHER READING

IBM's *System Operator's Guide*.

Part VIII: Appendix

ILE Concepts

Prior to V2R3, the AS/400 was a collection of different environments and implementations for the various programming languages. This lack of integration made it difficult to write an application that consisted of several programs written in different languages. Yet, you should use the right tool for the job. Because each programming language has its advantages and disadvantages, they can be regarded as different tools. You should be sure to use the right one for the task at hand.

For example, it would be disastrous to write an application that requires high mathematical computations in a language like RPG that has only the four basic operations plus square root. Although you can (if you are clever and do not mind the performance hit) code an RPG program that calculates the trajectory of the next unmanned probe to Jupiter, this sort of program would be better coded in a language such as C that offers the trigonometric and logarithmic functions required for the job.

The example above is an exaggeration. No one would use an AS/400 for astronomical computations. However, the example illustrates the point: no matter how knowledgeable and comfortable you are with one programming language, you are probably hurting yourself if you try to do everything in that one language. This need to improve multi-language applications brought about ILE.

What is ILE?

ILE is an Integrated Language Environment. It hides the differences between languages because the language-specific compiler is not used to create the executable *PGM object. First, you must create module (*MODULE) objects with the CRTxxxMOD command (such as CRTRPGMOD if the module's source code is written in RPG). Once you have all the modules created, you bind them all together into a *PGM object with the Create Program (CRTPGM) command.

Note that the *PGM object does not exist in the language-specific stage of the generation process because the creation of the *PGM object requires the existence of *MODULE objects. As far as the CRTPGM command is concerned, therefore, it makes no difference what language you have used to create the component modules because all these modules already exist in machine language.

Calling Programs and Modules

Before ILE, all you could call from one program was another program (a *PGM object). The program could be identified with a literal or a variable, but that made absolutely no difference until the program was executed. The compiled calling program was practically the same, whether you used a literal or a variable.

Under ILE there are additional considerations you should note. You can use another method for calling a program or module: the call by copy. In RPG terms, it is the CALLB op code. When you code a CALLB 'ABC' line in your RPG module and compile it, the module will include all executable code in module 'ABC' which results in a duplication of the executable code. Although the new module will be larger, it will execute much faster because all the necessary code is right there. The module does not have to retrieve another object from DASD, load it into main storage, and run it. The module executes probably as quickly as an internal subroutine.

The downside is that the executable code is now in two places: the original 'ABC' module and the new module you just compiled, which has the CALLB instruction. This duplication wastes DASD space and creates a problem when module 'ABC' has to be maintained. Knowing that program maintenance is an everyday affair, you will have to recompile every module where module 'ABC' is called by copy and then recreate all the *PGM objects where the just-recompiled modules are used.

ILE Concepts

Service Programs

A service program (*SRVPGM) object is similar to a *PGM object, except that you can call any of its modules with a CALLB without copying the executable code. Service programs are the best of both worlds. You get the high performance of the CALLB operation without the penalty of the duplication of executable code. The disadvantage of using service programs is that, if program X uses service programs A,B and C, the first activation of X must locate, load and activate A, B and C as well, which results in a great number of machine instructions.

Still, service programs are great for utility-type procedures that may be used by many other application programs. Functions such as string manipulation (capitalization, find-and-replace, pattern scanning and so on) can be coded in service programs and accessed from many programs.

ILE Languages

IBM has not made an ILE version of every programming language in existence prior to V2R3. In fact, only C/400 benefits from ILE at first. COBOL and RPG follow in 1994. At press time it is not certain whether there will be an ILE CL. All other languages (BASIC, PL/I, Pascal, FORTRAN) have been left out.

Business as Usual

If you have a hard time understanding ILE, do not worry. You can take your time because you can keep doing business as usual. The CRTxxxPGM commands that create *PGM objects directly out of language-specific source code are still there. You do not have to start coding every new application in ILE, nor do you have to convert your existing applications to ILE. If it's not broken, don't fix it.

FURTHER READING

IBM's *Integrated Language Environment Concepts*, for V2R3.

Glossary

Authority Permission to access an object or to perform a certain function. System security is based on granting and revoking authorities. See also *private authority*, *public authority*, and *special authority*.

Backup Process of saving files and other important objects from the computer's DASD units to other media (usually tapes and diskettes).

Batch Job Type of job that runs "in the background" without user intervention. Batch jobs are usually started with the Submit Job (SBMJOB) command.

Central Processing Unit Main component of a computer system, which houses the "brain" of the machine. Also known as CPU.

CL See *Control Language*.

CL/free Free-format version of CL developed by Picante Software of Eugene, Oregon.

Command Order you give the system to perform a particular task. Commands have unique names and can be typed and executed from a display station or included in CL programs for sequential processing. See also *menu*.

Command Prompter Flexible prompt display automatically created for all commands, which allows the user to enter parameter values without having to memorize the command syntax.

Commitment Control Technique used to guarantee that separate but related database changes take place all together or not at all. This technique guarantees consistent databases.

Computer Room In a building, the area reserved for the computer CPU and supporting devices, such as the system console, system printer, tape drives, etc.

Console. See *system console*.

Control Language Programming language available on all AS/400s used primarily for controlling the system and performing system-related tasks. Usually known as CL. CL programs consist of commands.

Controlling Subsystem When someone signs on to the system console, that interactive job runs in the controlling subsystem. Only the controlling subsystem is active during restricted states ("dedicated mode"). The controlling subsystem is named in system value QCTLSBSD.

CPU See *central processing unit*.

Data Description Specifications Also called DDS. Programming language used to describe files.

DDS. See *Data Description Specifications*.

Dedicated Mode See *restricted state*.

Device Description Object (type *DEVD) which describes a physical or virtual device that is attached to the system. Display stations and printers, for example.

ECS See *electronic customer support*.

Electronic Customer Support Also called ECS. Facility included in OS/400 that lets the system operator or administrator contact IBM (or another service provider) through the AS/400. This facility simplifies the reporting of problems and the ordering of PTFs.

Glossary

Help OS/400 facility that displays information (either generic or context-sensitive) about any topic related to the AS/400 computer. Also the key that starts the help facility (usually called the Help key).

Initial Program Load Also called IPL. Process of starting up the computer, usually by powering it up and starting the operating system.

Interactive Job Type of job that runs "in the foreground," always communicating with a user through a display station. Interactive jobs are started by signing on to a display station.

IPL See *initial program load*.

Job Unit of work that takes place in a subsystem. See also *batch job* and *interactive job*.

Job Description Object (type *JOBD) which provides the initial settings (or attributes) for a job to be started.

Job Log Record of events that have taken place during a job. The job log can be displayed anytime during the existence of the job and can be printed at the end of the job.

Journaling Technique that keeps track of system events, particularly database file changes, in order to facilitate recovery.

Library Object (type *LIB) which is used as a container for all other object types.

Library List List of library names, used to locate objects in the system without referencing any library name where they may reside.

Logical File Type of file that never contains any data. A logical file can only contain pointers to records in a physical file, in order to describe a different access path.

Maintenance Agreement Contract between you and a company that pledges to repair your system's hardware. Maintenance agreements can also include provisions for PTFs, software upgrades and preventive maintenance.

Menu Object (type *MENU) that presents a panel listing several options, which the user can select by typing a number and pressing Enter. Menus simplify computer usage. See also *command*.

Message Queue Object (type *MSGQ) where messages accumulate until they are dealt with and erased.

Message A form of communication between two users, a user and a program running on the system, or two programs.

Operational Assistant Facility provided by OS/400 that simplifies the operation and administration of the AS/400 system. Usually abbreviated OA.

Output Queue Object (type *OUTQ) where spooled reports accumulate waiting for their turn to be printed.

Password Private, secret code the user types after the user profile name when signing on to positively identify himself or herself.

PDM See *Program Development Manager*.

Physical File Type of file that can actually contain data for permanent storage. Contrast with logical file.

Printer Writer System-generated program that transmits spool files from an output queue to a printer device, where it is ultimately printed.

Private Authority Authority given specifically and directly to a particular user. Contrast with *public authority*.

Program Object (type *PGM) that actually performs some kind of work. Programs are first coded in a source member, using a particular language (such as CL or RPG), and then compiled to create the *PGM object.

Program Development Manager Also called PDM. Licensed utility designed by IBM to provide an easy interface between the programmer and the system.

Program Temporary Fix Also called PTF. Patch to be applied to your software to remove a problem.

PTF. See *Program Temporary Fix*.

Public Authority Authority enjoyed by a user when the user has not been given any private authority to an object. Contrast with *private authority*.

Glossary

QHST. See *system log*.

QSYSOPR IBM-supplied user profile for the system operator. Also the name of a message queue where the system logs many problems.

Recovery Process of retrieving lost information from backup media, or to become operational after a system disaster or failure.

Report Program Generator Also called RPG. High-level language used for many types of business data processing applications. RPG is the de facto programming language on the AS/400.

Restricted State State in which the system only runs the controlling subsystem and allows no jobs to run except the interactive job from the system console. Also known as dedicated mode.

RPG See *Report Program Generator*.

RPG/free Free-format version of RPG developed by Picante Software of Eugene, Oregon.

Screen Design Aid Also called SDA. Licensed utility designed by IBM to facilitate the creation of display files and menus.

SDA See *Screen Design Aid*.

SEU See *Source Entry Utility*.

Source Entry Utility Also called SEU. Licensed utility designed by IBM to serve as the main source code editor.

Special Authority Authority to perform certain system-related tasks, such as backing up the system and controlling security.

Spool File Report to be printed, which has been generated by a program and placed into an output queue.

Start-Up Program Unique program in the entire system that is automatically executed during IPL. You can specify which program to run during IPL by naming it in system value QSTRUPPGM.

Subsystem Complex entity where work takes place in the form of jobs.

System Console Unique display station, locally attached to the system, with which the system communicates exclusively during attended IPLs. The system console's name is in system value QCONSOLE.

System Log Record of events that happen throughout the system. Also known as QHST.

System Operator Person who is in charge of overseeing the use and functioning of the system, and is responsible of keeping it up and running. The system operator is usually the person who schedules power up and power down and performs system troubleshooting.

System Value System configuration item that can only be displayed or changed, but never deleted.

System/36 Environment Facility of OS/400 that allows you to operate and program the AS/400 as if it were a System/36, with a minimum of discrepancies. Usually abbreviated S/36E.

Troubleshooting The process of finding the cause of and solution to a problem.

Uninterrupted Power Supply Piece of hardware that provides emergency electrical power for the computer in case of blackouts. It usually regulates the incoming utility power to remove surges, spikes and other irregularities. Also known as UPS.

Upgrade Move your software or hardware forward after improvements have been made by the manufacturer. For software, this implies new releases of the software (with new features or fixed problems). For hardware, it usually implies newer models or higher capacity.

UPS See *uninterrupted power supply*.

User Profile Object (type *USRPRF) that describes a computer user and serves to identify the user. The user profile name is what the user types at the sign-on display in order to sign on.

Index

*

#LIBRARY, 196, 208, 349, 360
#RPGLIB, 196
#SDALIB, 196
#STRTUP1, 360
#STRTUP2, 360
%SST, 258
*ADD, 138
*ALL, 139
*AND, 260
*AUTL, 203
*BCAT, 258
*CAT, 258
*CHANGE, 139
*CMD, 203
*CTLD, 203
*DEVD, 204
*DLT, 139
*DOC, 204
*DTAARA, 204
*DTAQ, 204
*ESCAPE Messages, 262
*EXCLUDE, 139
*FILE, 204
*FLR, 205
*JOBCTL, 141, 161
*JOBD, 205
*JOBQ, 205
*JRN, 206, 337
*JRNRCV, 206, 337
*LIB, 206

*LIBCRTAUT, 128
*LIND, 206
*MENU, 206
*MODULE, 207
*MSGF, 206
*MSGQ, 207
*NOT, 260
*OBJEXIST, 138
*OBJMGT, 138
*OBJOPR, 138
*OR, 260
*OUTQ, 207
*PGM, 207
*PNLGRP, 207
*READ, 138
*S36, 208
*SAVSYS, 140
*SBSD, 207
*SPLCTL, 161
*SRVPGM, 208
*SYSVAL, 123
*TCAT, 258
*UPD, 139
*USE, 139
*USRPRF, 208
// END, 363
// FILELIB, 362
// INCLUDE, 351
// RUN, 363
// TIMERSET, 362
/COPY, 229
01-99, 272
1P, 273

?DEV'unit'?, 364
?FLIB?, 364
?MSGID?, 364

A

Access paths, 217, 235, 372
ADDAUTLE, 148
ADDJOBQE, 45
ADDLFM, 218
ADDLIBLE, 211
ADDPFM, 216
Address, 235
ADDWSE, 44
Administrator, 184
Air Conditioning, 6
Alphanumeric, 231
Alternate Console, 26
ALTQSYS, 112
ANDxx, 276
ANZPRB, 391, 393, 395
    Describing the Problem, 408
    Sample Session, 395, 414
APAR, 419, 420
Application Software, 9
APYPTF, 189, 426
Architecture, 191, 203
Arrays, 270
AS/400 Main Menu, 107
ASCII, 62, 64
Assign, 258
ASSIST, 78
Assistance Level, 136

Index

AT(*ENTER), 44
AT(*SIGNON), 44
Attention Key, 143
Attention Key Handling Programs, 136, 146
Authorities, 128, 137
Authorization Lists, 147
Automatic Backup Schedule, 77, 80
Automatic Cleanup, 81
Automatic Configuration, 12, 149
Automatic Power Schedule, 77, 87
    Description, 22
    Setup, 22
Auxiliary Storage, 84

B

Backing Up, 64, 424
Backup, 69
    Automatic, 80
    Configuration, 69
    Device Descriptions, 68
    Differential, 67
    Documents, 68
    File Members, 66
    Folders, 68
    Incremental, 67
    Libraries, 65
    Objects, 66
    QSYS, 68
    Run, 88
    Saving Changed Objects, 67
    Setup, 91
    System, 67
    System Values, 69
    User Profiles, 68
    Why It is Necessary, 61
Backup List, 66
Backward Recovery, 342
Batch Jobs, 19, 42, 154
BBS, 271, 393
BEGSR, 278
BLDINDEX, 216
BLDLIBR, 350
Book Manager, 178
Break Message, 20
Bug, 183, 419
Built-in Battery, 6
Bulletin Board, 271, 393
Burning Odors, 373, 374, 375

C

C P, 358
C-spec, 271
Cabling, 7
CABxx, 279
Calculation, 271
CALL, 278, 367
Cardboard, 8
Carpets, 7
CD ROM, 178
Central Processing Unit, 15
CHAIN, 275
Charting Paper, 8
CHGCLNUP, 81

441

CHGCMDDFT, 112
CHGCURLIB, 209
CHGDEVDSP, 165, 166
CHGDEVxxx, 151
CHGDTAARA, 264, 389, 391
CHGJOB, 36
CHGJOBD, 36, 155
CHGJOBQE, 45
CHGJRN, 340
CHGLIBL, 210
CHGMSGQ, 60, 101
CHGOUTQ, 156, 161
CHGPF, 216, 223
CHGPRTF, 166
CHGPWD, 80, 131
CHGPWRSCD, 88
CHGS36, 353, 361
CHGSBSD, 43
CHGSPLFA, 50, 54
CHGSYSLBL, 211
CHGSYSVAL, 11, 12, 17, 19, 69, 72, 125, 265
CHGUSRPRF, 11, 136, 141, 145, 147, 156, 352
CHGVAR, 256, 258
CHGWTR, 58
CHGxxxF, 223, 224
CICS, 103
CL, 255, 267
    CALL, 261
    Command Parameters, 255
    Commands, 255
    Data Areas, 264

DCLF, 266
DO and ENDDO, 259
ENDPGM, 262
Error Handling, 262, 264
Executing Other Programs, 261
Execution Control, 259, 262
Files, 266, 267
Giving Variables Values, 258
GOTO, 261
IF and ELSE, 259
MONMSG, 263, 264
Parts of a Program, 256
Retrieve Job Attributes, 265
Retrieve User Profile, 266
Retrieving Data, 264, 266
RETURN, 262
System Values, 265
Variables, 257
When Not To Use, 256
When To Use, 256
CL/free, 259
Cleanup
    Automatic, 81
CLOF, 287
CLRDKT, 64
CLRPFM, 216
CLRSAVF, 74
CNFIGSSP, 208, 353
Coding Sheets, 270
Color, 244
Column Heading, 233
COMIT, 344, 345
Command

Index

    Lengthening Parameters, 115
    List Parameters, 115
    Naming System, 103
Command Prompter, 113, 117, 155
    Changing Parameters, 115
    Description, 113
    Function Keys, 116
    Help, 116
    Parameters, 114
    Using, 114
Commands, 103, 117
    Changing Defaults, 111
    Customizing, 111
    Finding the Proper One, 105
    Guessing Names, 104
    List by Menus, 107
    Modifiers, 104, 109
    Verb, 103
    Verbs, 108
COMMIT, 345
Commitment Control, 343, 345, 372
    COMMIT, 345
    Definition, 343
    Prerequisites, 344
    ROLLBACK, 345
Committable, 344, 345
Communications, 7, 377
    Configuring, 82
COMP, 279
Company Name, 378
Compiles, 43
COMPRESS, 359
Compressing Objects, 175

Computer Room
    Description, 5
    Flooring, 7
    Layout, 8
    Requirements, 6
Concatenation, 258
Conditioning Indicators, 275
Configuration, 12, 89, 162
    Backup, 69
    Restoring, 72
Control, 270
Control Language, 255
Control Level, 273, 274
Control Panel, 15, 372, 422
Cover Letter, 421, 423
CPF, 255
CPF9999, 395, 405
CPROBJ, 175
CPU, 15, 25, 30, 372, 422
CPYF, 216, 217, 421
CPYSRCF, 217
CRTAUTL, 148
CRTCLPGM, 19
CRTDEVDSP, 164
CRTDEVPRT, 56, 159, 162
CRTDEVxxx, 151
CRTDSPF, 221
CRTDTAARA, 264
CRTDUPOBJ, 43, 113, 165, 290
CRTJOBD, 155, 156
CRTJRN, 338
CRTJRNRCV, 338
CRTLF, 218, 236, 241, 283, 284

CRTLIB,   112, 128, 193, 197, 350
CRTOUTQ,   156, 161
CRTPF,   215, 217, 232
CRTPRTF,   222
CRTS36RPG,   365
CRTS36RPT,   365
CRTSAVF,   73
CRTSBSD,   43
CRTSRCPF,   217, 350
CRTUSRPRF,   11, 124, 136, 141, 144, 147
CRTxxxF,   223
CSSF,   103
CUA,   249
CUA Standards For Displays,   249

D

D U,   358
D W,   358
Damaged Objects,   172
DASD,   171, 191
Data,   214
Data Processing,   5
Data Structures,   270, 366
Database Operations,   269
Daylight Savings Time,   127
DCL,   256, 258
DCLF,   257, 266
DDS,   214, 218, 221, 223, 229, 253, 273, 284, 288, 365
   A-Specs,   230
   Another Key,   236
   Defining by Reference,   231, 234
   Definition,   229
   Display File,   246
   Display Files,   244, 249
   Field Names,   231
   Format Selector Programs,   243
   How To Code,   230, 232
   Join Logical Files,   238, 240
   Keywords,   232
   Multi-Format Logical Files,   241, 244
   Physical Files,   232, 235
   Printer Files,   250
   Selecting and Omitting Records,   237
   Simple Logical Files,   235, 238
   Syntax,   230
DDS Display Files,   245
   Constants,   246
   CUA standards,   249
   Design Standards,   249
   Error Messages,   248
   Function Keys,   245
   Record Formats,   245
   Using In A Program,   247
   Variables,   246
DDS Printer Files,   253
   Design Considerations,   250
   Using In a Program,   253
Dedicated Service Tools,   25
Default Values,   111
Dehumidifier,   6
DELET,   276
Deleted Records,   216
Departments,   160

Index

DESCEND, 282
Destroyed Objects, 172
Device Descriptions, 10, 12, 148, 153, 175
   Backup, 68
   Changing, 150
   Configuring, 150
   Creating, 150
   Definition, 148
   Deleting, 150
   Displaying, 150
   Listing, 152
   Maintaining, 150
   Naming, 149
   Setup, 11
Device Files, 221
Devices, 83
Disaster, 72
Disaster Recovery Plan, 65, 73
Disk Drives, 184
Disk Space, 84
Diskette Drive, 63
Diskettes, 73
   Active Files, 64
   Erasing, 64
   Initialization Format, 63
   Initializing, 63
Display File, 273
Display Stations, 12, 22, 41, 44, 82, 184
   Time-Out, 129
   Unattended, 129
DLTDEVD, 151

DLTDTAARA, 264
DLTF, 194, 216, 284
DLTJOBD, 155
DLTJRNRCV, 340
DLTLIB, 175, 193, 199
DLTLICPGM, 199
DLTOUTQ, 156
DLTOVR, 225, 226, 287
DLTPRB, 416
DLTSBSD, 43
DLTSPLF, 55
DLTUSRPRF, 141, 145, 194
DO, 277
Do Until, 277
Do While, 277
Documents, 172, 196
   Backup, 68
   Restoring, 71
DOUxx, 277
DOWxx, 277
Draw the Walls, 8
DSCJOB, 80
DSPAUTL, 148
DSPAUTLOBJ, 148
DSPAUTUSR, 147
DSPDEVD, 151, 374
DSPDTAARA, 264, 390, 392
DSPFD, 214
DSPFFD, 214, 288
   DSPJOB, 32
     DSPJOBD, 155
     DSPJOBLOG, 34, 35
     DSPJRN, 339

445

DSPLIB, 198, 202
DSPLOG, 36
DSPMSG, 26, 27, 59, 92, 98, 163
DSPOBJD, 152
DSPPFM, 195, 216, 421
DSPPTF, 424, 426
DSPPWRSCD, 88
DSPSBSD, 188
DSPSPLF, 51
DSPSYSSTS, 86, 173
DSPSYSVAL, 16, 19, 125, 265
DSPTAP, 185
DSPUSRPRF, 145, 147
DSPWSUSR, 94
DST, 25
Dup Key, 366

E

E-spec, 270
Earthquake, 72
EBCDIC, 62, 64
ECS, 6, 93, 377, 395, 420, 421, 424
   Changing Your Own Identification, 378
   IBMLink Connection Phone Number, 388
   IBMLink Voice Phone Numbers, 381
   Managing, 377, 392
   Reporting Problems Connection Number, 391
   Reporting Problems Phone

Numbers, 385
   Uses Of, 392
   Using, 377, 393
Edit Code, 234
EDTAUTL, 148
EDTLIBL, 210
EDTOBJAUT, 161
Electromagnet, 63
Electronic Customer Support, 6, 377
ELSE, 276
Employees, 161
ENDCLNUP, 82
ENDCMTCTL, 344
ENDCPYSCN, 93
ENDDO, 277
ENDIF, 276
Ending Jobs Immediately, 21
ENDJRNPF, 339
ENDPGM, 257
ENDRMTSPT, 93
ENDS36, 352
ENDSBS, 11, 21, 40, 42, 188, 423
ENDSL, 278
ENDSR, 278
ENDWTR, 57
ERRMSG, 248
ERRMSGID, 248
Error Messages
   Displaying, 248
Error Reset Key, 374
Error Situations, 262
ERRSFL, 248
EXCPT, 276, 367

Index

EXSR, 278
Extension, 270
External Definition, 267, 271
External File Definition, 288

F

F-spec, 270
Factor 1, 275
Factor 2, 275
Field Name, 366
Fields, 214, 229, 270
    Excluding From Record, 219
File, 270
File Key
    Defining Another, 236
File Members
    Backup, 66
    Restoring, 71
    Working With, 300
File Names, 349
File Overrides, 167, 224, 228
    Accumulating, 225
    Commands, 225
    Definition, 224
    How To Use Them, 226
    Problems You May Encounter, 226
    Scope, 225
File Sharing, 223
    Disadvantages, 224
    How to Code, 223
Files, 213, 228, 229, 272, 348
    Adding/Removing Simple Logical

Members, 218
    Classification, 213
    Database, 215
    Display, 221
    Display and Printer, 221
    Externally Described, 229
    Join Logical, 219, 220
    Members, 215
    Physical, 214, 217
    Printer, 222
    Program Described, 229
    Record Formats, 214
    Record Structure in Join Logicals, 219
    Sharing, 223, 224
    Simple, 217
    Simple Logical, 218, 219
    Source, 217
    Using Simple Logical, 218
Fire, 65, 72
    Prevention, 8
Fixed-Length Record, 271
FLIB procedure, 361
Flood, 65, 72
Floods, 7
FMTDTA, 287, 290
    Disadvantages, 288
    Example, 288
Folders, 172, 196
    Backup, 68
    Restoring, 71
Form Type, 53, 58, 222
FORMAT, 234

Format Name, 243
Format Selector Programs, 243
Forward Recovery, 341
FREE, 367
Free Format, 271
FROMLIBR, 74
Full-Procedural, 271
Function Key, 222
Function Keys, 272

G

Garbage, 81
Getting Up And Running, 5
Glossary, 433
GOTO, 279
Group Profiles, 146
GRTOBJAUT, 148, 161

H

H-spec, 270
H1-H9, 272
Halon, 8
Hardware, 184
Header, 270
Help, 29
Help Key, 29, 35, 52, 59, 116, 117, 195, 311, 313, 374, 381
Help Support, 93, 117, 122, 195
High-Level Language, 269
Highlighting, 222
HIPER PTFs, 420

History File, 36
History Logs, 174
HLDOUTQ, 49
HLDSPLF, 56
HLDWTR, 58
Housekeeping, 171
Humidity, 6

I

I-spec, 270
IBM Technician, 9
IBMLink, 377, 381, 388, 393
IDDU, 230
IFxx, 276
ILE, 429
    Calling Programs and Modules, 430
    Languages, 431
    Service Programs, 431
ILE Concepts, 429
IMAGES(*AFTER), 339
IMAGES(*BOTH), 339
INDARA, 245
Indicators, 272
Information, 214
Information Assistant, 85
Information Systems, 5
Initial Menu, 145
Initial Program, 145
INLLIBL, 210
Input, 270
Input Inhibited Indicator, 373
Inquiry Messages, 374, 375

Index

Installation, 5
   Display Stations, 10
   Hardware, 9
   IBM's Part, 9
   OS/400, 9
   Printers, 10
   Software, 9
   Your Part, 10
Interactive Job, 349
INZDKT, 63
INZTAP, 62
IPL, 15, 22, 24, 43, 45, 189, 360, 372, 422, 423, 425
   Attended, 16
   Manual, 372
   Unattended, 15, 171
IPL Options, 16
IPLs, 25
ITER, 277
Iterate, 277

J

Job, 167
   Change, 32
   Display, 32
   End, 32
Job Accounting, 36
Job Attributes, 153
Job Description, 36, 167
Job Descriptions, 153, 155
   Changing, 155
   Creating, 155
   Definition, 153
   Deleting, 155
   Displaying, 155
   Maintaining, 155
   Naming, 154
   Why Use Them, 154
Job Log
   Print Control, 36
Job Logs, 33, 34, 175
Job Queue Entries, 43, 45
Job Queues, 42, 45, 153, 195
Jobs, 79
   Active, 30
Join Fields, 239
Journaling, 337, 343, 344
   After Images, 338
   Before Images, 338
   Database Files, 338
   Journal Receivers, 337
   Journals, 337
   Maintaining Journal Receivers, 340
   Manual Entries, 339
   Recovery, 340

K

KA-KN, 272
Key, 218
Key Fields, 231, 282
Key Lock, 16
Keyboard, 373
KEYFLD, 284

Keywords, 256
KP-KY, 272

L

L-spec, 270
L0-L9, 273
L1-L9, 274
Labels, 272
Laser Printer, 374
Last Record, 273
LEAVE, 277
Libraries, 192, 294, 348
   Creating, 197
   Deleting, 199
   Displaying, 198
   IBM, 193, 196
   Product, 196
   QDOC, 196
   QGPL, 195
   QHLPSYS, 195
   QSPL, 195
   QSYS, 194
   QTEMP, 201, 203
   QUSRSYS, 194
   Restoring, 70
   Saving, 65
   Special Environments, 196
   User, 197, 201
   Working with, 197
   Working With Objects, 199
Library List, 154, 160, 208, 212
   Changing, 210
   Current Library, 209
   Definition, 208
   Product Library, 209
   Structure, 209
   System Portion, 209, 210
   User Portion, 210
   Using, 211
Library Names, 349
LIBRLIBR, 103
Licensed Program Products, 196
Limited Capabilities, 11, 145
Line Counter, 270
LMTCPB, 11
Locate Objects, 208
LODPTF, 189
Logical, 217
LR, 273, 274

M

Magnetic Fields, 8
MAINT(*DLY), 283
MAINT(*IMMED), 283
MAINT(*REBLD), 283
Maintenance, 6
   Agreements, 170
   IPLing Regularly, 171
   Mechanical, 169, 170
   Preventive, 169
   Reclaiming Storage, 171, 176
   Selecting A Vendor, 170
Manuals, 85, 177, 182
   Administration, 181

Index

CD ROM, 178
Computerized, 178
Identification Code, 177
Operations, 181
Printed, 177
Programming, 179
Masking Tape, 8
Mass-Update Programs, 269
Matching Record, 273
Member Names, 349
Members, 216, 294
Combining, 219
Memory, 191
Memory Allocations, 43
Memory Pools, 43
Menu, 78
  ASSIST, 79
  BACKUP, 80
  Backup Tasks, 80
  CLEANUP, 81, 175, 417
  Cleanup Tasks, 81
  CMDPWR, 22
  CMNCFG, 82
  Commands by Subject, 110
  Commands By Verb, 108
  Configuring Communications, 82
  Device Status, 83
  DEVICESTS, 83
  DISKTASKS, 84
  Documentation and Problem Handling, 93
  INFO, 85
  LICPGM, 193, 199, 423
  MAJOR, 107
  Major Command Groups, 107
  MANAGESYS, 86
  Operational Assistant Main, 79
  POWER, 87
  Power Commands, 22
  Power On and Off Tasks, 87
  PROBLEM2, 378, 382, 385
  PTF, 424
  RUNBCKUP, 88
  SETUP, 89
  SETUPBCKUP, 91
  SUPPORT, 118
  System Management, 86
  TECHHELP, 92
  Technical Support Tasks, 92
  User Support & Education, 118
  USERHELP, 93
  VERB, 108
Menus, 316
Message, 95
  Displaying, 98
  Inquiry, 97
Message ID, 263
Message Queue, 26, 37, 58, 96, 97, 98, 100, 146, 151, 374
Messages, 26, 79, 98, 262
  Answering QSYSOPR, 28
  Break, 99, 102
  Break-Handling Program, 101
  Description, 95
  Displaying, 99
  Erasing, 99

Getting Help, 29
Help Key, 29
Inquiry, 27
Printer, 58
Removing, 99
Sending, 95, 97
Microcode, 193
Modem, 93
MONMSG, 257, 263
MR, 273

N

Named Constants, 270
New Release, 183, 190
   Applying PTFs Permanently, 189
   Backing Up, 187
   Checking Tapes Received, 185
   Estimating Down Time, 186
   Finishing Up, 190
   Getting a Dedicated System, 188
   Initializing Tapes, 186
   Inventory Of Tapes, 185
   Load Cume PTF Package, 189
   Obtaining Latest Cume PTF Package, 185
   Performing The Upgrade, 187, 190
   Placing Your Order, 184
   Preparing For The Upgrade, 184, 186
   Printing Subsystem Descriptions, 188
   Saving Configuration, 187
   Saving System Values, 187
   Scheduling Downtime, 186
   The Actual Upgrade, 189
   Verifying, 190
   Why Upgrade?, 183

O

O-spec, 271
OA-OG, 273
Object Locks, 33
Object Type, 192, 203
Objects, 192, 203, 208, 294, 348
   Authorization list, 203
   Command, 203
   Controller Description, 203
   Data Area, 204
   Data Queue, 204
   Device Description, 204
   Document, 204
   File, 204
   Folder, 205
   Job Description, 205
   Job Queue, 205
   Journal, 206
   Journal Receiver, 206
   Library, 206
   Line Description, 206
   Menu, 206
   Message File, 206
   Message queue, 207
   Module, 207
   Output Queue, 207
   Panel group, 207

Index

Program, 207
Restoring, 71
S/36 Machine Description, 208
Saving, 66
Service Program, 208
Subsystem Description, 207
User Profile, 208
OCL, 196
ODP, 223
OfficeVision, 172, 196, 204, 205
Opcodes, 274, 275, 367
Open Data Path, 223, 284
Open Files, 33
Operating System, 183, 194
Operation, 271, 274
Operation Extender, 275
Operational Assistant, 22, 37, 66, 77, 93, 135, 175, 417
Menus, 78
Starting Up, 78
OPNQRYF, 230, 284, 287
Definition, 284
QRYSLT In CL Programs, 286
Selecting and Omitting Records, 285
Sorting, 284
Using, 287
ORxx, 276
OS/400, 194, 377
OTHER, 278
Out of Paper, 58
Output, 271
Output Queues, 47, 49, 56, 146, 151, 153, 155, 157, 159, 162, 222, 374
Assigning To Users, 156
Changing, 156
Creating, 156
Definition, 155
Deleting, 156
Description, 47
Displaying, 48
Holding, 49
Maintaining, 156
Naming, 156
Releasing, 49
Security Concerns, 161, 162
Some Ideas, 159
Where To Place Them, 160
OV, 273
Overflow, 270
Overflow Indicators, 273
OVRDBF, 225, 287
OVRDSPF, 225
OVRPRTF, 167, 225, 270
OVRxxxF, 224, 225

P

Packed Decimal, 231
Packing Lists, 9
Panels, 316
Paper Jam, 58
Parameter, 278
PARM, 256, 278, 367
Passwords, 11, 80, 128, 349, 381
Management, 130
PC, 178, 204

PC Support, 196, 204, 205
PDM, 196, 197, 199, 293, 303, 317
    Changing Defaults, 302
    Customizing, 302
    Main Menu, 294
    Starting Up, 294
    Working With Libraries, 295
    Working With Members, 300
    Working With Objects, 297
Performance, 41, 42, 223, 287
Person To Contact, 378
PGM, 256
Picante Software, 259, 271
Planning Physical Space, 5
PLIST, 367
Pointers, 235, 282
Power Down
    Announcing, 20
Power Failures, 6, 371
Power Supply, 6
Power Surges, 6
Powerdown
    Description, 19
Powering Down, 19, 22, 87
Powering Up, 15, 19, 87
Print Key, 136, 155, 165, 246
Printer Device, 146
Printer File, 167, 273
Printer Writers, 56, 58, 374
    Changing, 58
    Description, 56
    Ending, 57
    Holding, 58

Releasing, 58
Starting, 57
Printers, 12, 22, 56, 82, 151, 162, 184
    Assigning to a User, 164
    Automatic On-Line, 162
    Message Queue, 163
Printing, 159
    Routing, 166, 167
    Workstations, 164, 166
Priority, 33
Problem
    Analyzing, 92
    Solving, 92
Problem Logs, 174, 415
    Deleting Old Ones, 416
    Working With, 415
Problem Summary Forms, 372
Problems, 83, 395, 415
    Documenting, 93
    Reporting, 93
    Solving, 93
Processing Unit, 6
Program
    Start-Up, 16
Program Stack, 33
Programmers, 160, 184, 293
PRTDEVADR, 83, 152
PTF, 92, 185
PTFs, 175, 193, 393, 419, 426
    Applying Permanently, 425
    Cover Letters, 421, 423
    Cumulative (cume) Packages, 420
    Definition, 419

Index

Displaying, 424
HIPER, 420
If You Suspect a Bug, 419
Individual, 420
Installing, 422, 424
Installing Cume PTFs, 423
Installing Individual PTFs, 423
Installing IPL Area, 422
Managing, 424, 426
PTF Number, 422
Removing, 426
Requesting, 421, 422
Public Authority, 162
Punched Cards, 270
PWRDWNSYS, 11, 21, 22, 88, 189, 423

Q

QABNORMSW, 133
QAPZCOVER, 421
QASTLVL, 135
QATNPGM, 124, 136
QAUTOCFG, 12, 134, 150, 162
QBASE, 13, 39, 40, 41, 45
QBATCH, 31, 42, 44
QCONSOLE, 134
QCRTAUT, 128
QCTL, 40, 41, 45
QCTLSBSD, 40, 45, 135
QCURSYM, 127
QDATE, 126
QDATFMT, 126
QDATSEP, 126
QDAY, 126
QDDSSRC, 230
QDECFMT, 127
QDEVNAMING, 134
QDFTOWN, 172
QDOC, 68, 172, 196, 204, 205
QDSCJOBITV, 130, 134
QDSPSGNINF, 131
QESPHONE, 391
QGPL, 195, 209, 421
QHLPSYS, 195
QHOUR, 126
QHST, 36, 172, 174
QINACTITV, 129
QINACTMSGQ, 129
QINTER, 31, 41, 42, 43, 373
QIPLDATTIM, 88, 135
QIPLSTS, 133
QLMTDEVSSN, 131
QLMTSECOFR, 132
QMAXSGNACN, 132
QMAXSIGN, 132
QMINUTE, 126
QMODEL, 133
QMONTH, 126
QPDA, 196
QPGMR, 43
QPRBHLDITV, 417
QPRINT, 48, 155, 159, 165, 395
QPRTDEV, 134, 167
QPRTKEYFMT, 136
QPWDEXPITV, 130

455

QPWDLMTAJC, 130
QPWDLMTCHR, 131
QPWDLMTREP, 131
QPWDMAXLEN, 130
QPWDMINLEN, 130
QPWDPOSDIF, 131
QPWDRQDDGT, 131
QPWDRQDDIF, 131
QPWDVLDPGM, 131
QPWRDWNLMT, 135
QRCL, 172, 175
QRCLAUTL, 172
QRCLnnnn.DOC, 172
QRCLnnnn.FLR, 172
QRPG, 196
QRPG38, 196
QRPLOBJ, 175
QRYSLT, 285
QS36ENV, 208
QS36F, 196, 349
QS36PRC, 350
QS36SRC, 350
QSECOFR, 13, 129, 148, 337, 423
QSECOND, 126
QSECURITY, 11, 72, 127, 143, 171
QSPCENV, 136, 352
QSPL, 57, 58, 195
QSRLNBR, 133
QSSP, 196, 349
QSTRPRTWTR, 133
QSTRUPPGM, 16, 19, 45, 135, 360
QSYS, 68, 112, 132, 144, 165, 190, 192, 194, 209

QSYS38, 196
QSYSLIBL, 132, 210
QSYSOPR, 13, 26, 28, 29, 58, 92, 97, 99, 137, 152, 163, 185, 375
QSYSPRT, 165
QTEMP, 193, 290
QTIME, 126, 265
QTIMSEP, 126
QTIPHONE, 388
Query Management, 230
Query/400, 230
QUSRLIBL, 133, 210
QUSRSYS, 194
QYEAR, 126

R

Racks, 6
Radar Station, 8
Radio, 8
Radiofrequency, 8
Raised Floor, 7
RCLDLO, 172
RCLSPLSTG, 174
RCLSTG, 171, 193
RCVF, 267
READ, 275, 367
READ/DOS, 178
READE, 275
READP, 275
Record Formats, 215, 220, 221, 232, 241, 250
Record Selection, 219

Index

Record Types, 365
Records, 229, 231, 270, 272, 281
Recovery, 338
REDPE, 275
REF, 234
REFDATE, 67
REFFLD, 234
REFTIME, 67
Reply, 27
Report Programs, 269
Reporting Problems, 377, 395, 417
Requesting PTFs, 377
Reset Key, 374
RESTORE, 75
Restoring, 69, 72
    Configuration, 72
    Documents, 71
    File Members, 71
    Folders, 71
    Libraries, 70
    Objects, 71
    System Values, 72
Result Field, 275
Resulting Indicators, 275
RETRN, 367
RF, 8
RGZPFM, 175, 216
RLSOUTQ, 49
RLSSPLF, 56
RLSWTR, 58, 256
RLU, 223, 250
RMVAUTLE, 148
RMVJOBQE, 45

RMVLIBLE, 211
RMVM, 216, 218
RMVPTF, 426
RMVWSE, 44
RNMM, 216
RNMOBJ, 12
ROLBK, 345
ROLLBACK, 345
Routing Entries, 43
RPG, 269, 279
    C-Spec Syntax, 274
    C-Specs, 274, 279
    Cycle, 273
    File I/O Operations, 275
    Fixed Format, 271
    Free Format, 271
    Identifiers, 272
    Indicators, 272
    Logical Variables, 272
    Names, 272
    Specifications, 270
    Structured Operations, 276
    Unstructured Operations, 279
    Variables, 272
RPG Cycle, 273
RPG II, 364
RPG/400, 196, 231
RPG/free, 271
RPGC Procedure, 365
RSTCFG, 190
RSTDLO, 71, 196
RSTLIB, 70, 74, 194, 196
RSTOBJ, 71, 194

RSTS36LIBM, 75
RSTxxx, 375
RTVCLSRC, 19
RTVDTAARA, 265
RTVJOBA, 265
RTVSYSVAL, 265
RTVUSRPRF, 266
RVKOBJAUT, 161

S

S/36E, 347, 358
    Comparing Systems, 347, 350
    Configuring, 357
    Device Names, 354
    Entering, 350
    Leaving, 352
    Maintenance, 353, 358
    Operations, 358
S/36E Programming, 359, 368
    Mixing OCL and CL, 363
    OCL, 359, 364
    RPG, 368
    RPG II, 364
Sabotage, 72, 137
SAVCHGOBJ, 67, 194, 339
SAVDLO, 68, 187, 196
SAVE, 74
Save Commands, 64, 74
Save File, 73
Save Files, 73, 74
    Creating, 73
    Description, 73
    Using, 73
Saving, 64, 69
    Automatic, 80
SAVLIB, 65, 74, 89, 187, 194, 196
SAVOBJ, 66, 194, 340
SAVS36F, 75
SAVS36LIBM, 75
SAVSAVFDTA, 74
SAVSYS, 67, 74, 89, 187, 194, 424
SAVxxx, 375
SBMJOB, 45, 154, 202
Screens, 316
SDA, 222, 244, 250, 316, 335
    Adding a Constant Field, 322
    Adding an Alphanumeric Field, 325
    Adding Other Fields, 327
    Automatic Centering, 323
    Changing Field Attributes, 330
    Compiling, 335
    Fields, 333
    Finishing Up, 334
    Main Menu, 317
    Sample Session, 317
    Starting Up, 317
    Work Area, 322
    Working with Fields, 333
    Working with Records, 319
Search Index, 119
Sector Size, 63
SECURE(*YES), 226
Security, 10, 137
    Authorities, 137
    Idle Display Stations, 129

Index

Initial Setup, 10
Levels, 142, 143
Private Authorities, 139
Public Authorities, 140
Special Authorities, 140
Security Level, 143
Security Levels, 11, 127, 142
Security Risk, 129
SELEC, 278
Selecting and Omitting Records, 237
Sensitive Information, 137
Sequence, 281
Specifying, 282
Service Providers, 386, 414
Session, 349
SETLL, 367
Setup, 89
SEU, 230, 244, 303, 314, 315, 316
Browsing Another Member, 315
Changing Strings, 313, 314
Coding RPG, 308
Copying from Another Member, 316
Copying Lines, 312
Customizing Session, 314
Deleting Lines, 311
Displaying an Output Queue, 316
End Session, 307
Finding Strings, 313, 314
Function Keys, 314
Inserting Lines, 312
Line Commands, 311
Lowercase, 313
Moving Forward or Backward, 313
Moving To Top or Bottom, 313
Opening a Command Entry Window, 316
Prompt Format, 312
Prompting CL Commands, 305
Prompting RPG Specifications, 309
Repeating the Last Change, 316
Repeating the Last Find, 316
Sample Session, 303
Shifting Code, 312
Shifting Window, 312
Top-Line Commands, 313
Uppercase, 313
SEU procedure, 350
SHARE(*YES), 223, 287
Short Circuit, 373, 374, 375
Sign-Off, 349
Sign-On, 349
Sign-On Control, 131
Sign-On Display, 41, 373
Single-Level Storage, 191
SLTCMD, 105, 266
Smoke, 373, 374, 375
SNDBRKACT, 100
SNDBRKMSG, 20, 21, 79, 100
SNDF, 267
SNDJRNE, 339
SNDMSG, 37, 60, 79, 96, 100
SNDPTFORD, 393, 421
SNDRCVF, 267
Sort Specifications, 288
Sorting, 281, 290
Disadvantages of FMTDTA, 288

Example Using FMTDTA, 288
FMTDTA, 287, 290
How to Sort OPNQRYF, 284
Including and Omitting Records from Logical Files, 283
Logical Files, 282, 284
OPNQRYF, 287
OPNQRYF Definition, 284
Performance of Logical Files, 283
QRYSLT In CL Programs, 286
Selecting and Omitting Records Using OPNQRYF, 285
Using Logical Files, 283
Using OPNQRYF, 287
Source Code, 217, 300, 348
Source Code Editor, 303
SPCENV(*NONE), 351
SPCENV(*S36), 351, 352
SPCENV(*SYSVAL), 352
Special Authority, 145
Specification ID, 270
Spikes, 6
Spool File Members, 174
Spool Files, 79, 222, 395
   Changing, 53
   Controlling, 50
   Deleting, 55
   Displaying, 51
   Holding, 56
   Redirecting, 50
   Releasing, 56
   Restarting, 56
Sprinklers, 7

SQL/400, 230
SRC, 372
SSP Procedures, 359
SST, 141
Start-Up Program, 16, 18, 43, 135, 360
   Changing, 45
Static Electricity, 7
STG(*FREE), 65
STRCLNUP, 82
STRCMTCTL, 344
STRCPYSCN, 92
STREDU, 86
STRJRNPF, 339, 344
STRPDM, 294
STRPRTWTR, 57, 58, 256
STRRMTSPT, 93
STRS36, 350, 352
STRS36PRC, 351, 352, 360
STRSBS, 45
STRSCHIDX, 85
STRSDA, 317
STRSEU, 19, 303
Subfiles, 222, 269
SUBR22, 366
Substring, 258
Subsystem
   Controlling, 41, 45
   Creation, 43
   Interactive, 41
Subsystem Descriptions, 13, 43, 195
   Setup, 13

Index

Subsystems, 10, 13, 39, 42, 44, 45, 188
  Description, 39
  Ending, 19
  Maintaining Your Own, 42
  Multiple, 40, 41
Support, 183
Switchboard, 6
System
  Backup, 67
  Checking Activity, 30
  Control, 25
  Management, 86
System Activity, 25
System Attention light, 372
System Console, 6, 16, 21, 25, 41, 134, 149, 172
System Failure, 72
System Help, 117, 122
System Log, 36
System Operator, 16, 26, 97, 184
System Operators, 161
System Printer, 6
System Reference Code, 372
System Service Tools, 141
System Value
  Editing, 127
System Values, 123, 136, 167, 193
  Backup, 69
  Changing, 125
  Currency Symbol, 127
  Decimal Format, 127
  Default Public Authority, 128
  Definition, 123
  Device-Related, 133
  Displaying, 125
  Idle Display Stations, 129
  Interactive Job Settings, 135
  Library List, 132, 133
  Library List System Portion, 132
  Listing, 124
  Original Default Value, 124
  Password Management, 130
  Power Up & Power Down, 135
  Referencing, 123
  Restoring, 72
  Security, 127
  Security Level, 127
  Sign-On Control, 131
  System Control, 133, 136
  System Date, 126
  System Time, 126
System/36 Environment, 347, 358
  Comparing Systems, 347, 350
  Configuring, 357
  Device Names, 354
  Entering, 350
  Leaving, 352
  Maintenance, 353, 358
  Operations, 358
System/36 Environment Programming, 359, 368
  Mixing OCL and CL, 363

461

OCL, 359, 364
RPG II, 364, 368

T

Tables, 270
TAG, 279
Tape Device, 62
Tape Drives, 6, 184
Tapes, 73
    Active Files, 62
    Density, 62
    Erasing, 63
    Initializing, 62
    Rewind, 62
    Rewinding, 65
    Unload, 62
    Unloading, 65
Target Release, 65
Technician, 169
Telephone, 6
Television, 8
TFRJOB, 44
Thermostat, 6
Time Slice, 33
TOLIBR, 75
Toner, 374
Transaction, 343
Trouble
    Display Station Does not Work, 373
    Mild, 373, 375
    No Printout Generated, 374
    Power Failure, 371

Printer Does not Work, 374
    Severe, 371, 373
    System Freezes Up, 372
    Tape Drive Does not Work, 375
Troubleshooting, 371, 375
Twinax, 7
Twisted Pair, 7

U

Uncrating Instructions, 9
Underline, 222, 244
Uninterrupted Power Supply, 6, 371
UNIQUE, 233
Unsupported Procedures, 360
UPDAT, 276
Upgrade to a New Release, 113
UPS, 6, 371
User Class, 145
User ID, 11
User Messages, 95, 102
User Names, 349
User Profiles, 10, 12, 96, 143, 146, 167, 175, 208
    Backup, 68
    Changing, 144
    Creating, 144
    Definition, 143
    Deleting, 144
    Displaying, 144
    Maintaining, 144
    Name, 11
    Naming, 144

Index

Setup, 12
UserProfiles, 128
Utilities, 184
Utility Power Supply, 371

V

Variables, 272
Vary On, 14
Views, 217, 282
VOL(*MOUNTED), 62
Volume ID, 62, 63, 64
VRYCFG, 373

W

Walking Space, 6
WHxx, 278
Work Management, 40
Workstation Controller, 26, 83, 151, 152
Workstation Controller is the System Console, 25
Workstation Controllers, 82
Workstation Entries, 43, 44
Workstation Names, 349
Workstations, 167
   Output Queue, 165
   Printer Device, 165
   Printer File, 165
WRITE, 276
WRKACTJOB, 20, 30, 31
WRKCFGSTS, 14, 152, 374, 375
WRKDEVD, 83, 151, 153
WRKFLR, 84
WRKJOBD, 155
WRKJRN, 341, 343
WRKLIB, 84, 197
WRKLIBPDM, 197, 294, 295
WRKMBRPDM, 294, 300
WRKMSG, 79, 87
WRKOBJ, 199
WRKOBJOWN, 84
WRKOBJPDM, 199, 294, 297
WRKOUTQ, 48, 51, 54, 55, 56, 156, 395, 412
WRKOUTQD, 156
WRKPRB, 92, 174, 415, 417
WRKPRDINF, 393
WRKPTF, 92
WRKSBSD, 188
WRKSBSJOB, 31, 40, 373
WRKSLPF, 79
WRKSPLF, 50, 51, 54, 55, 56, 87, 412
WRKSYSSTS, 173, 193
WRKSYSVAL, 17, 19, 40, 69, 72, 112, 124, 125, 265
WRKUSRJOB, 20, 32, 51, 79, 87, 100
WRKUSRPRF, 90, 145
WRKWTR, 374

Z

Zoned Decimal, 231